lonely planet

Midwest USA

Great Lakes to Great Plains

Great Lakes
p49

Great Plains
p138

Lauren Keith, Ann Babe, Amy C Balfour, Katy Spratte Joyce, Michael Mackie, Karla Zimmerman

FROM LEFT: RUDY BALASKO/SHUTTERSTOCK, RACHEL P. PHOTOGRAPHY/SHUTTERSTOCK, NAYADADARA/SHUTTERSTOCK

Chicago skyline (p54)

CONTENTS

Plan Your Trip

The Guide

Duluth (p130), Minnesota

Mountain goat, Custer State Park (p209), South Dakota

Toolkit

Storybook

Tallgrass Prairie National Preserve (p160), Kansas

THE MIDWEST

THE JOURNEY BEGINS HERE

When I was a kid, my Oklahoma-born, Dust Bowl–fleeing grandpa bought me a book called *If You're Not from the Prairie*. The book is an illustrated poem in which every stanza starts with the title phrase and then describes some of the landscape's defining features: the endless sky, the yawning flatness, the seas of waving grasses and the bitter cold. It's a beautiful poem that's so protective of place, but as a kid trying to be cool in Middle America, it fell, well, flat. At that time in my life, it was hard to feel proud of the place I came from, derided as culture-less flyover country. I spent much of my adult life living 5000 miles away from home, but I've now moved back, and the dynamism of the modern Midwest amazes me. Maybe we both just needed some time to grow and find our feet – and remember our prairie roots.

Lauren Keith

@noplacelike_it

Lauren is a guidebook author who grew up in Kansas and moved back to the Great Plains after living overseas for more than a decade. She's often found somewhere between the Midwest and the Middle East.

My favorite experience is walking in Kansas' **Tallgrass Prairie National Preserve** (p160). The wind, meadowlarks and bison root me right back at home no matter how long I've been away.

WHO GOES WHERE

Our writers choose the places which, for them, define the Midwest.

CAVAN-IMAGES/SHUTTERSTOCK

Chicago (p54) is my favorite place. That's why I've lived here for 35 years! The skyline amazes me. Every time I take the L toward downtown, it's like the buildings pop up and expand storybook-style. I love Lake Michigan spilling over the horizon, baseball at Wrigley Field, the beer gardens, Millennium Park's free outdoor concerts and water-squirting public art. Still not bored after all this time!

Karla Zimmerman

@karlazimmerman

Karla writes about travel. She researched Illinois, Wisconsin and Minnesota for the Great Lakes chapter.

BO SHEN/GETTY IMAGES

Clocking in at more than 31,000 sq miles, Lake Superior is so vast it could be mistaken for an ocean, and its rocky, rugged shoreline is a watercolor dream. One glimpse of the towering rainbow sandstones at **Pictured Rocks National Lakeshore** (p108), and it'll be easy to see how it got its name.

Ann Babe

annbabe.com

Ann Babe writes about travel, culture and belonging. She researched Michigan, Ohio and Indiana for the Great Lakes chapter.

RANDY RUNTSCH/SHUTTERSTOCK

Driving the **Peter Norbeck Scenic Byway** (p208) in the Black Hills of South Dakota is a blast. The Iron Mountain Rd section loop the loops through the pines while the 14-mile Needles Hwy leg twists past otherworldly granite spires. And oooh, those sketchy one-way tunnels. You'll be sucking in your stomach as you drive through the Needle's Eye – it's just 8ft wide!

Amy C Balfour

@AmyCBalfour

Amy is a writer covering travel, food and adventure. She researched Iowa, North Dakota and South Dakota for the Great Plains chapter.

CONTRIBUTING WRITERS

Michael Mackie

@m2esq

Michael wrote the essay on State Fair culture (p240). He hosts Get Lost!, *a Midwest-based TV travel show.*

Katy Spratte Joyce

@katysjoyce

Born in the Midwest, Katy's passionate about covering her home region.

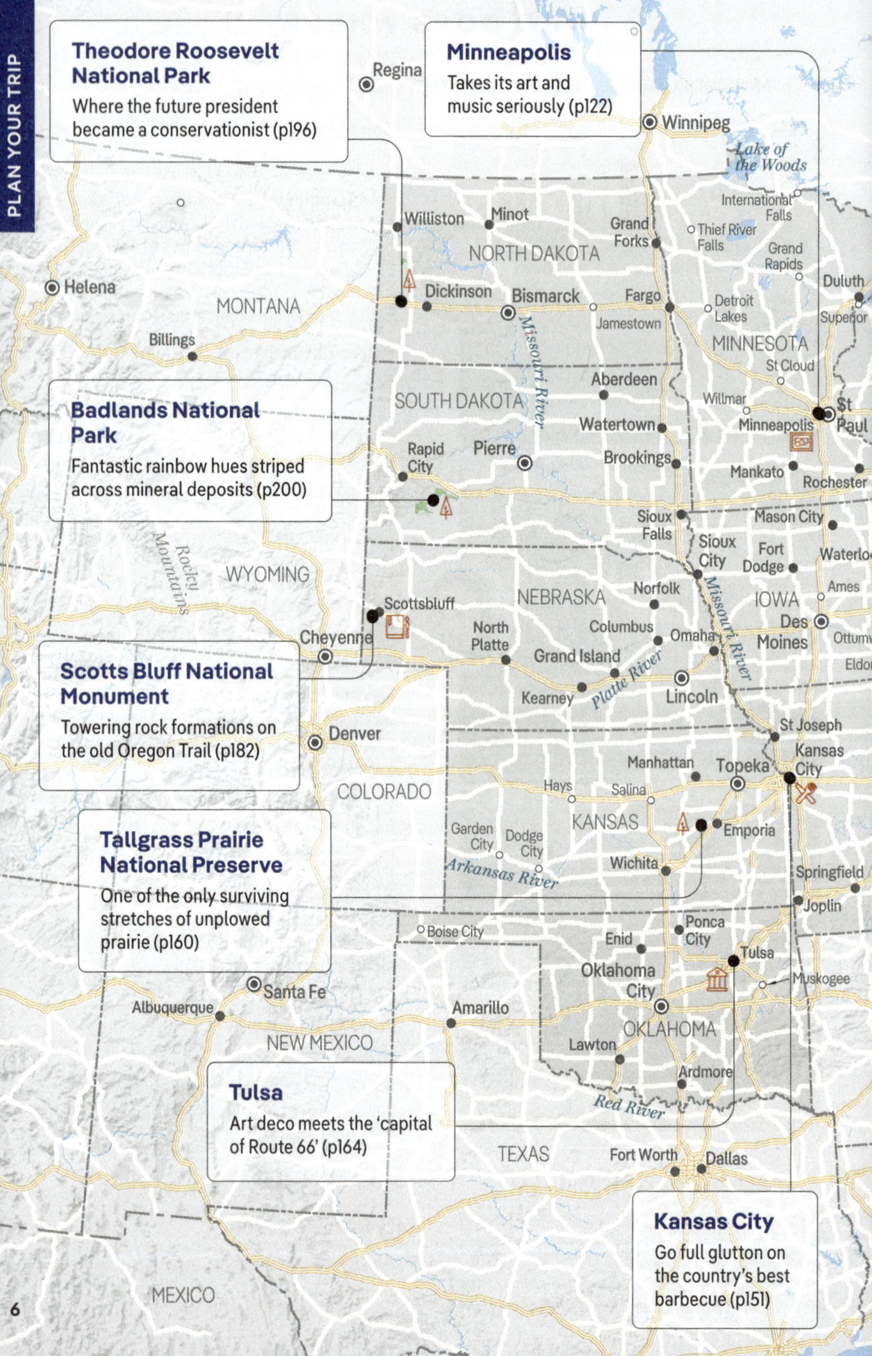
Theodore Roosevelt National Park
Where the future president became a conservationist (p196)
Minneapolis
Takes its art and music seriously (p122)
Badlands National Park
Fantastic rainbow hues striped across mineral deposits (p200)
Scotts Bluff National Monument
Towering rock formations on the old Oregon Trail (p182)
Tallgrass Prairie National Preserve
One of the only surviving stretches of unplowed prairie (p160)
Tulsa
Art deco meets the 'capital of Route 66' (p164)
Kansas City
Go full glutton on the country's best barbecue (p151)
Regina
Winnipeg
Lake of the Woods
International Falls
Thief River Falls
Grand Forks
Grand Rapids
Duluth
Superior
Williston
Minot
NORTH DAKOTA
Dickinson
Bismarck
Jamestown
Fargo
Detroit Lakes
MINNESOTA
St Cloud
Helena
MONTANA
Billings
Missouri River
Aberdeen
SOUTH DAKOTA
Willmar
Minneapolis
St Paul
Watertown
Rapid City
Pierre
Brookings
Mankato
Rochester
Sioux Falls
Mason City
Sioux City
Fort Dodge
Waterloo
Rocky Mountains
WYOMING
NEBRASKA
Norfolk
IOWA
Ames
Scottsbluff
Columbus
Omaha
Des Moines
Cheyenne
North Platte
Grand Island
Platte River
Lincoln
Kearney
Denver
St Joseph
Kansas City
Manhattan
Topeka
COLORADO
Hays
Salina
KANSAS
Garden City
Dodge City
Emporia
Arkansas River
Wichita
Springfield
Joplin
Boise City
Ponca City
Enid
Tulsa
Muskogee
Oklahoma City
Santa Fe
Albuquerque
Amarillo
NEW MEXICO
OKLAHOMA
Lawton
Ardmore
Red River
TEXAS
Fort Worth
Dallas
MEXICO

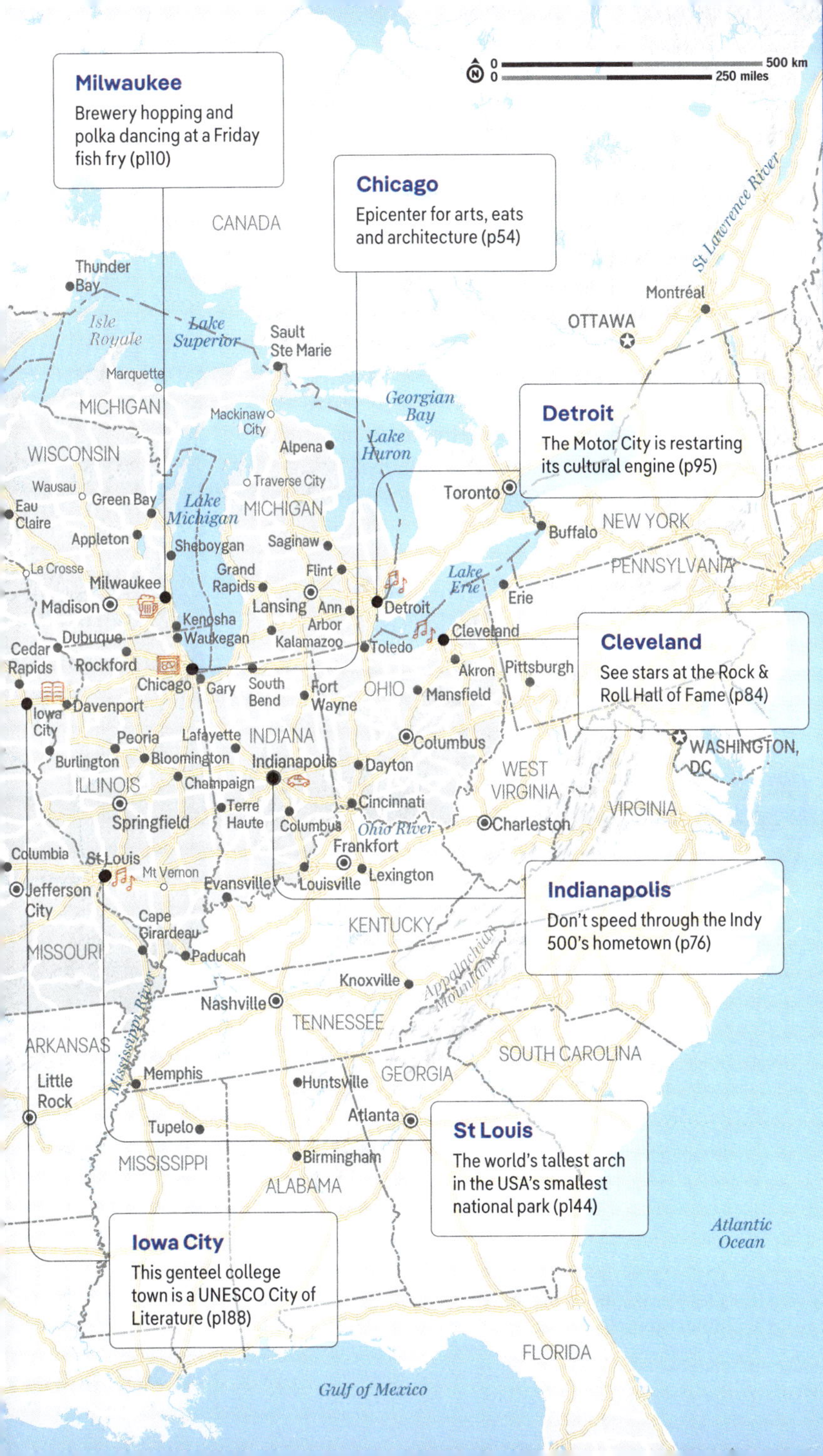
0 500 km
0 250 miles
Milwaukee
Brewery hopping and polka dancing at a Friday fish fry (p110)
Chicago
Epicenter for arts, eats and architecture (p54)
Detroit
The Motor City is restarting its cultural engine (p95)
Cleveland
See stars at the Rock & Roll Hall of Fame (p84)
Indianapolis
Don't speed through the Indy 500's hometown (p76)
St Louis
The world's tallest arch in the USA's smallest national park (p144)
Iowa City
This genteel college town is a UNESCO City of Literature (p188)
CANADA
St Lawrence River
Montréal
OTTAWA
Thunder Bay
Isle Royale
Lake Superior
Sault Ste Marie
Marquette
MICHIGAN
Mackinaw City
Georgian Bay
Lake Huron
Alpena
WISCONSIN
Traverse City
Wausau
Eau Claire
Green Bay
Lake Michigan
MICHIGAN
Toronto
Buffalo
NEW YORK
Appleton
Sheboygan
Saginaw
La Crosse
Grand Rapids
Flint
PENNSYLVANIA
Lake Erie
Milwaukee
Erie
Madison
Lansing
Ann Arbor
Detroit
Kenosha
Waukegan
Kalamazoo
Cleveland
Dubuque
Cedar Rapids
Toledo
Rockford
Akron
Pittsburgh
Chicago
Gary
South Bend
Fort Wayne
OHIO
Mansfield
Davenport
Iowa City
INDIANA
Columbus
WASHINGTON, DC
Peoria
Lafayette
Burlington
Bloomington
Indianapolis
Dayton
WEST VIRGINIA
ILLINOIS
Champaign
Springfield
Terre Haute
Columbus
Cincinnati
Charleston
VIRGINIA
Ohio River
Frankfort
Columbia
St Louis
Mt Vernon
Jefferson City
Evansville
Louisville
Lexington
Cape Girardeau
KENTUCKY
MISSOURI
Paducah
Appalachian Mountains
Knoxville
Nashville
TENNESSEE
ARKANSAS
Mississippi River
SOUTH CAROLINA
Memphis
Little Rock
Huntsville
GEORGIA
Atlanta
Tupelo
MISSISSIPPI
Birmingham
ALABAMA
Atlantic Ocean
FLORIDA
Gulf of Mexico

COMEBACK CITIES

Chicago often takes top billing for travelers to the Midwest, but other cities across the region are stepping up to steal some of the limelight and show off their own big personalities. Money is being poured into projects to revitalize downtowns, upgrade infrastructure and transform abandoned formerly industrial areas into hip hangouts. These initiatives are making the Midwest one of the country's most dynamic regions to visit.

FROM LEFT: APN PHOTOGRAPHY/SHUTTERSTOCK; W_LEMAY, CC BY-SA 2.0, VIA WIKIMEDIA COMMONS ©; NAYADADARA/SHUTTERSTOCK

Streetcars

It's easier than ever for Midwest travelers to ditch their cars. New and expanded streetcar lines have come to Kansas City (pictured; p151) and Detroit (p95) and soon to Omaha (p176).

Historic Stays

Old buildings are being converted into impressive hotels, including **The National** (a 1930s bank; pictured; p212) in Oklahoma City and **21c Museum Hotel** (a former YMCA; p212) in St Louis.

Presto Change-O

Check out transformed warehouse districts in Omaha (Old Market; p176), Milwaukee (Third Ward; p114) and Kansas City (West Bottoms). St Louis' City Museum (p144) put a 10-story slide in an old shoe warehouse.

Tulsa (p164)

BEST CITY EXPERIENCES

Seek out edgy street art, learn about Motown music and tour former factories in can-do ❶ **Detroit** (p95).

Dirty your fingers on barbecue in ❷ **Kansas City** (p151) and get a cultural hit in its museums, galleries and sports stadiums.

Stand among a forest of stunning art deco skyscrapers downtown and fuel up on food hall grub on Route 66 in ❸ **Tulsa** (p164).

Walk the RiverFront in ❹ **Omaha** (p176) and cross the bridge into Iowa before toddling over the cobblestones in the Old Market.

Check out museums devoted to neon and the Underground Railroad and then drink at the myriad breweries in ❺ **Cincinnati** (p87).

ART ATTACK

Searching for the heart of the Heartland? Find the key to the Midwest's past and present in its incredible art museums, which are chock-full of representations of the region created by born-and-bred as well as adopted residents. Many galleries are in venerable old buildings that provide a stately, refined atmosphere for visitors perusing the pieces, but they have been updated to feature modern and contemporary works, including more from Native and female creators.

FROM LEFT: JOE TAYLOR CINEMA/SHUTTERSTOCK, LAUREN KEITH/LONELY PLANET, DOMENICO LACAVA/SHUTTERSTOCK

American Regionalism

Regionalism was a Depression-era movement that depicted small-town America. Iowan Grant Wood (p186), Missourian Thomas Hart Benton and Kansan John Steuart Curry were the three giants of the scene.

State Capitols

State capitol buildings are amazing places to see gorgeous and often over-the-top art, usually built by local creators or with state-sourced materials.

Open Sesame

Many cultural spots across the Midwest are closed on Mondays or Tuesdays – or both – so check museum websites before you go.

Art Institute of Chicago (p55)

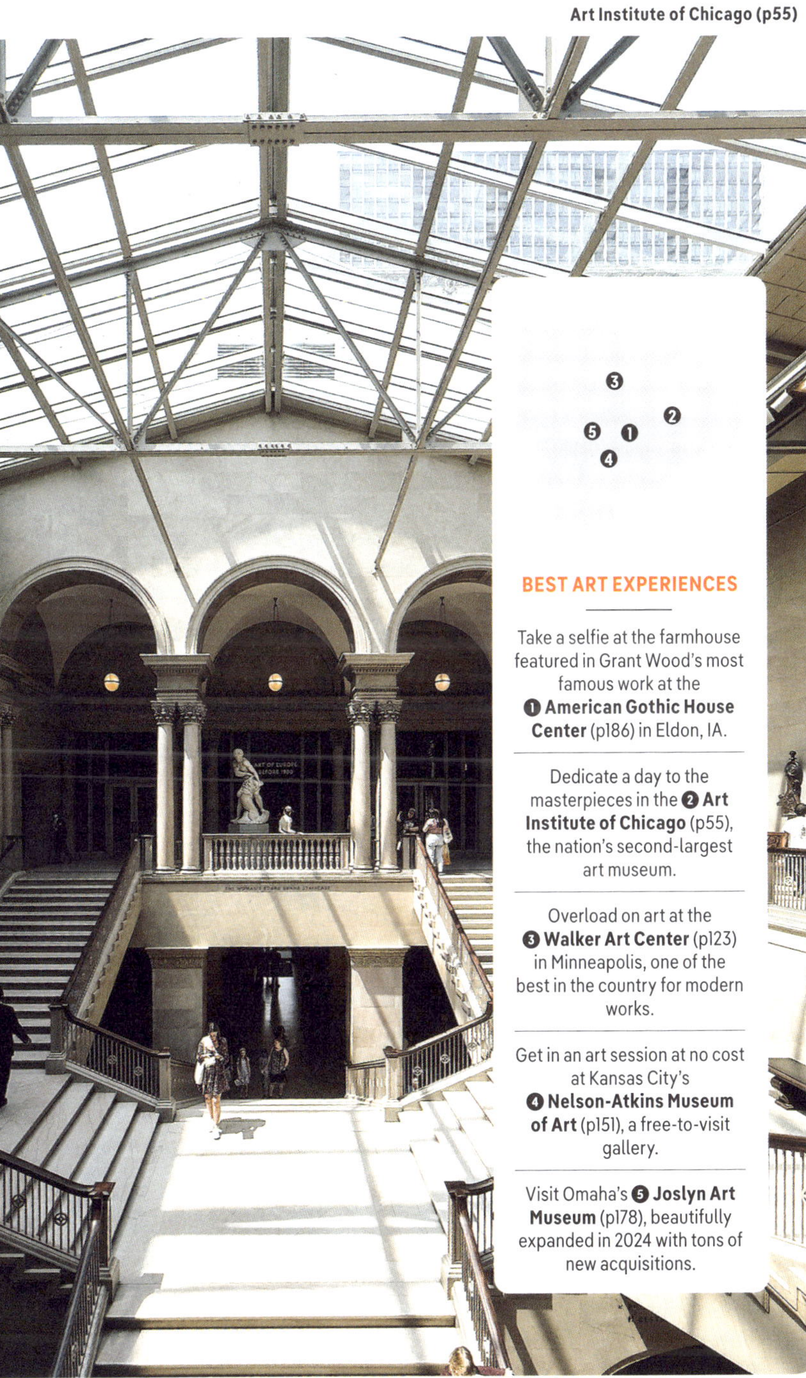

BEST ART EXPERIENCES

Take a selfie at the farmhouse featured in Grant Wood's most famous work at the ❶ **American Gothic House Center** (p186) in Eldon, IA.

Dedicate a day to the masterpieces in the ❷ **Art Institute of Chicago** (p55), the nation's second-largest art museum.

Overload on art at the ❸ **Walker Art Center** (p123) in Minneapolis, one of the best in the country for modern works.

Get in an art session at no cost at Kansas City's ❹ **Nelson-Atkins Museum of Art** (p151), a free-to-visit gallery.

Visit Omaha's ❺ **Joslyn Art Museum** (p178), beautifully expanded in 2024 with tons of new acquisitions.

MATT GUSH/SHUTTERSTOCK

Greenwood Rising (p166), Tulsa

BLACK HISTORY

The Midwest has often been at the center of the tug-of-war between opposing sides culturally and geographically, including during the country-dividing question over slavery in the 19th century. Black people fleeing violence and oppression in the South settled in the region, building thriving communities despite conflicting laws and attitudes.

Skate Culture

In Detroit, Black roller-skating culture grew in popularity with Motown music and remains a beloved pastime. Detroit's first Black-owned skating rink, RollerCade (p100), is still open.

George Floyd Square

In 2020, a white police officer killed George Floyd, a 46-year-old Black man, in Minneapolis. The site (p125) is now a place of reflection where visitors come to pay their respects.

BEST BLACK HISTORY EXPERIENCES

Explore ❶ **18th and Vine** (p153), Kansas City's vibrant Black neighborhood, home to museums and Missouri's first Black-owned brewery.

Understand the significance of the Supreme Court's ❷ **Brown v Board of Education** (p159) decision at a formerly segregated elementary school in Topeka, KS.

Walk through ❸ **America's Black Holocaust Museum** (p114) in Milwaukee, WI, founded by a lynching survivor.

See what remains of ❹ **Nicodemus** (p160), the first all-Black town west of the Mississippi, founded by formerly enslaved people in western Kansas.

Learn the history of Tulsa's Black Wall Street, destroyed in some of the country's worst race riots, at ❺ **Greenwood Rising** (p166).

NATIVE STORIES

The Native American cultures of the Great Plains came to epitomize 'Indians' in the popular American imagination, in part because they put up the longest fight against the USA's westward expansion. Native Americans today make up about 2% of the US population, and Oklahoma, once unwanted 'Indian Territory', is rich in sites that interpret Native American life.

❸ ❷

❹

❶❺

BEST NATIVE AMERICAN HISTORY EXPERIENCES

Meet the 39 tribes of Oklahoma at OKC's ❶ **First Americans Museum** (p224), perhaps the best Native American cultural institution in the country.

Hike the trails around Iowa's ❷ **Effigy Mounds National Monument** (p143), made up of more than 200 animal-shaped burial mounds in the bluffs above the Mississippi River.

Visit important cultural and historic locations, including the Wounded Knee Massacre site, on the ❸ **Pine Ridge Indian Reservation** (p201) in South Dakota.

Clap eyes on the 44ft-tall ❹ **Keeper of the Plains** (p162), an iconic sculpture in Wichita, KS, that's illuminated nightly by a ring of fire.

Sip a drink at OKC's ❺ **Skydance Brewing Co** (p173), which combines Native American culture and stories with excellent craft beer.

Cahokia City

Among North America's most significant prehistoric cultures were the Mound Builders. In Illinois, Cahokia (pictured; p73) was once a metropolis of 20,000 people, the largest in pre-Columbian North America.

Festivals & Powwows

Native American heritage festivals take place across the Midwest, including the Red Earth Festival (pictured; p169) in Oklahoma City and powwows at Haskell Indian Nations University in Lawrence, KS.

Trail of Tears

In the 1830s, tens of thousands of Native Americans were forced to march from the southeastern US to Indian Territory, now commemorated with a national historic trail (p170; *nps.gov/trte*).

SPORTS MAD

What really brings Americans together, sometimes slathered in blue body paint or with foam-rubber cheese wedges on their heads, is sports. Rooting for your chosen sports team transcends a person's status as liberal or conservative, atheist or evangelical, married or single, and provides a social glue that binds people together in an increasingly fragmented country.

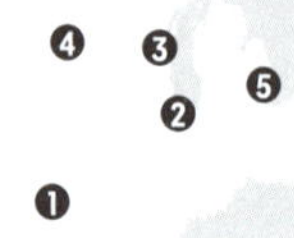

BEST SPORTS EXPERIENCES

Watch the KC Current play the beautiful game at ❶ **CPKC Stadium** (p151), the first arena in the world purpose-built for a professional women's sports team.

Take yourself out to the ballgame at Chicago's ❷ **Wrigley Field** (p61), which still has original features, such as the hand-turned scoreboard.

Dive into the history of the Green Bay Packers – the NFL's smallest-market team but one of its most successful – at ❸ **Lambeau Field** (p120) in Wisconsin.

Learn to sling a 42lb granite stone at ❹ **St Paul Curling Club** (p129) in Minnesota, the country's largest club.

Root for the home team in downtown ❺ **Detroit** (p98), the only US city with all its major league men's sports teams in the same neighborhood.

FROM LEFT: MATT FOWLER KC/SHUTTERSTOCK, JEFF BUKOWSKI/SHUTTERSTOCK

Soccer Capital of America

Kansas City (p151) is the smallest metropolitan area – and the only place in the Midwest – to host some of the 2026 World Cup matches.

Tailgating

Pre-game activities include tailgate parties in stadium parking lots, where fans drink beer and grill at the back of their cars and pickup trucks.

Women's Sports

Some Midwest sports bars show only women's games, including A Bar of Their Own in Minneapolis, Whiskey Girl Tavern in Chicago and The Dub in Kansas City.

THOMAS BARRAT/SHUTTERSTOCK

Rookery (p59), Chicago

FOLLOWING FRANK LLOYD WRIGHT

Wisconsin-born Frank Lloyd Wright is arguably America's most famous and prolific architect. His designs became known as the Prairie School, the first uniquely American architecture style. In a career spanning more than 70 years, he designed some 1100 buildings – more than 530 of which were constructed.

Organic Architecture

Wright's buildings sought to mirror their place in the plains, emphasizing the horizontal with long, low roof lines and rows of windows that connect to the outdoors.

Price Tower

Wright's only realized skyscraper is the 19-story Price Tower in Bartlesville, Oklahoma, which is set to reopen as a hotel in 2027.

BEST FLW ARCHITECTURE EXPERIENCES

Admire Wright's remodel of the ❶ **Rookery** (p59) in Chicago, with a light-filled atrium and 'floating' staircases.

Step into the ❷ **Frank Lloyd Wright Home & Studio** (p69) in Oak Park, IL, a town with more FLW-designed buildings than anywhere else in the world.

Visit ❸ **Taliesin** (p116) in Spring Green, WI, where the architect lived off and on for five decades.

Stay overnight at the Wright-designed ❹ **Historic Park Inn Hotel** (p193) in Mason City, IA.

Tour ❺ **Frank Lloyd Wright's Allen House** (p162) in Wichita, KS, finished in 1918 and still home to original furniture and fittings.

OFFBEAT ATTRACTIONS

We're here for the weird, and the backroads and small towns of the Midwest deliver it in spades. Sure, you could zoom from A to B on the interstate, but then you'd miss all the balls of twine, extremely niche museums curated by dedicated residents, and places that tack on more superlatives than you thought possible. Pull over and check out the biggest, longest, deepest, wackiest and undeniably best oddball attractions across the region.

Route 66

The Mother Road has fostered a strong tradition of kooky roadside attractions, and it's a treasure trove. Don't miss the American Giants Museum (pictured; p72) in Atlanta, IL.

Carhenge

A faithful reproduction of England's Stonehenge made from 39 smashed-up automobiles? You have to see it to believe it in Alliance, NE (p181).

City Museum

The coolest museum in St Louis – and maybe the Midwest – has the most boring-sounding name, but the rooftop Ferris wheel hints at its hilarity (p144).

World's Largest Cuckoo Clock (p87), Sugarcreek, Ohio

BEST OFFBEAT EXPERIENCES

Reenact the woodchipper scene from the movie *Fargo* at its namesake town's ❶ **visitor center** (p195).

Drop by the ❷ **World's Largest Collection of the World's Smallest Versions of the World's Largest Things** (p163), which embodies the bonkers spirit of Lucas, KS.

Pass by miles of billboards and then pull into ❸ **Wall Drug** (p204) in South Dakota for 5¢ coffee and other distractions.

Head to Sugarcreek, the 'Little Switzerland of Ohio', to see the ❹ **World's Largest Cuckoo Clock** (p87), ahem, clocking in at 23ft.

Squeeze yourself into Wisconsin's ❺ **House on the Rock** (p116), stuffed with folk art and a glass-walled 'infinity room'.

COLLEGE TOWNS

You don't have to be a student to go back to school in the Midwest's cool college towns. University students make up a significant percentage of the population of these towns, which punch well above their weight when it comes to food, drink and cultural attractions. The open-air campuses, many with gorgeous historic architecture, are free to wander around, making college towns destinations in their own right as well as good spots to break up a long drive.

FROM LEFT: JAMIE LAMOR THOMPSON/SHUTTERSTOCK, SUZANNE TUCKER/SHUTTERSTOCK, NICHOLAS J KLEIN/SHUTTERSTOCK

Home Team

Feel the full spirit of college towns when the university teams have a game on, but beware of sky-high accommodation prices if you're planning to stay.

Bookworms

The University of Iowa (pictured; p188) in Iowa City is famed for its writing program. Read Jane Smiley's *Moo* for a sharp parody of the town and school.

Notre Dame

Notre Dame (p80) in Indiana is touted as one of the country's most beautiful higher-education campuses. Take a free walking tour to see it for yourself.

Stupa, Bloomington (p80), Indiana

BEST COLLEGE TOWN EXPERIENCES

All are invited for a beer and a brat at the student union at the University of Wisconsin in ❶ **Madison** (p114).

Cheer on the Jayhawks at Allen Fieldhouse in ❷ **Lawrence** (p159), KS, which holds the Guinness World Record for the loudest college basketball arena.

Find Tibetan stupas and restaurants in ❸ **Bloomington** (p80), where the Dalai Lama's brother taught at Indiana University.

Lounge around coffee shops in downtown ❹ **Ann Arbor** (p101), home to the University of Michigan.

Try to snag a seat at Memorial Stadium in ❺ **Lincoln** (p179), NE – all 85,000 of them often sell out for the Cornhuskers' football games.

REGIONS & CITIES

Find the places that tick all your boxes.

Great Plains
p138

Great Plains

SURPRISING CITIES AND PRISTINE PRAIRIE

Despite its lack of name recognition, the oft-overlooked Great Plains has wide-ranging appeal. You'll find a mix of vibrant cities and charming small towns, memorable settings for road trips (Route 66, the Great River Road), rich Native heritage, and the otherworldly landscapes of the Badlands and the Black Hills.

Great Lakes

OVERLOOKED BEAUTY IN THE USA'S HEARTLAND

The Windy City reigns over this region with its glittering skyline, electric arts scene and deep-dish Midwestern pride. Five mighty lakes link everything else – their coasts covered in golden dunes, moose-tracked forests, and cities like Milwaukee and Detroit, mid-renaissance revival. Everything from quirky roadside attractions to pristine canoe paths through the wilderness awaits.

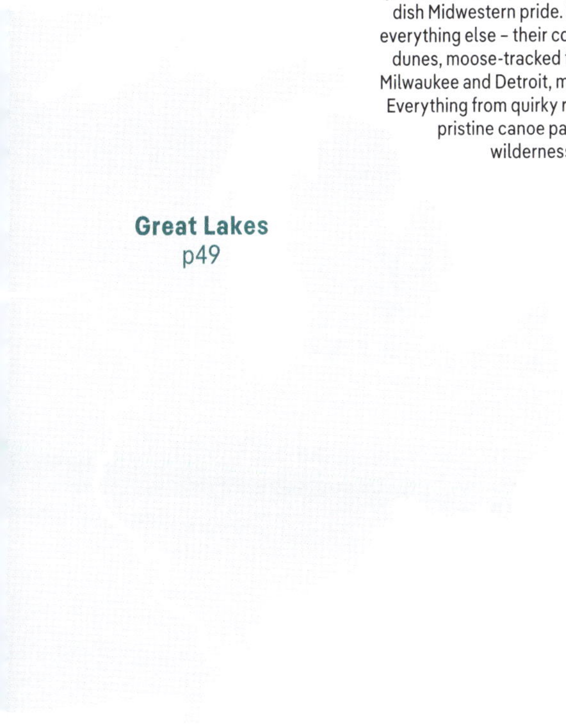

Great Lakes
p49

LAUREN KEITH/LONELY PLANET

ITINERARIES

Union Station (p153), Kansas City

Midwest City Hopping by Train

Allow: 7 days **Distance:** 960 miles

The Midwest isn't the easiest place to travel without a car, but you can leave the driving to someone else and still see some of its best cities by Amtrak train. This 'road trip' by rail heads to the region's cultural highlights, showcasing the diversity of its urban personalities.

MINNEAPOLIS 2 DAYS

Walk in the footsteps of Minneapolis' most famous former resident, rock star musician **Prince** (p123), and then continue the creative streak at the **Walker Art Center** (p123), one of the nation's top spots for modern art. Don't miss the famous *Spoonbridge & Cherry* next door at the **Minneapolis Sculpture Garden** (p125). Stroll along the Mississippi River downtown, stopping for photos on the **Endless Bridge** (p127). After dark, rock out to live music at **First Avenue & 7th St Entry** (p127) or catch a show at the **Guthrie Theater** (pictured; p127). *7½ hr*

2

CHICAGO 3 DAYS

The Midwest's 'capital', Chicago is a behemoth of art and architecture. The Windy City is the birthplace of the skyscraper, best seen aboard a cruise on the **Chicago Architecture Center's First Lady** (p57), which glides through glass 'canyons' along the Chicago River. See the sights around **Millennium Park** (pictured; p56) and then check out what's hanging on the walls of the **Art Institute of Chicago** (p55). When hunger strikes, slide into a booth to devour **deep dish pizza** (p54) and then burn some calories by laughing your ass off at an **improv comedy club** (p61). *5hr*

FROM LEFT: JEFF BUKOWSKI/SHUTTERSTOCK, CHUCK ECKERT/GETTY IMAGES

0 200 km
0 100 miles
START
St Cloud
Willmar
Minneapolis
1
St Paul
Eau Claire
WISCONSIN
Wausau
Green Bay
Traverse City
MICHIGAN
Appleton
Lake Winnebago
Sheboygan
MINNESOTA
Brookings
Mankato
Rochester
Mauston
La Crosse
7½hr
Lake Michigan
Grand Rapids
Madison
Milwaukee
Racine
Kenosha
Kalamazoo
Waukegan
Sioux Falls
Mason City
Mississippi River
Dubuque
Rockford
Fort Dodge
Waterloo
Sioux City
Cedar Rapids
Chicago
2
South Bend
Gary
IOWA
Ames
Joliet
Missouri River
Iowa City
Davenport
INDIANA
Des Moines
Ottumwa
Omaha
Peoria
Lafayette
Burlington
Bloomington
ILLINOIS
5hr
Indianapolis
Lincoln
Champaign
NEBRASKA
MISSOURI
Springfield
Terre Haute
St Joseph
Manhattan
Topeka
Kansas City
4
Columbia
St Louis
3
Sedalia
Mount Vernon
Evansville
KANSAS
END
6hr
Jefferson City
Emporia
Ozark Mountains
Ohio River
KENTUCKY

3

ST LOUIS 1 DAY

On the sunset side of the Mississippi River, St Louis was considered the door to the West, embodied by the soaring **Gateway Arch** (pictured; p150), the tallest in the world and now an urban national park. Ride the 1960s capsule cars to the top for city-spanning views and then loosen your limbs at **City Museum** (p144), an all-ages playground inside an old shoe warehouse. Sample unique St Louis foods, such as pizza with Provel cheese at **Imo's** (p148) or toasted ravioli at **Charlie Gitto's** (p148). STL is the home of **Budweiser** (p148), but its **craft beer breweries** (p149) are no slouches. *6hr*

4

KANSAS CITY 1 DAY

Get sauced at Kansas City's **barbecue joints** (p151) or just learn a little history (and dive into a ball pit of 'beans') at the newly-opened **Museum of BBQ** (p153). Resume your schooling at the **National WWI Museum** (p151), the country's congressionally designated museum dedicated to the Great War, and then head to the historic Black neighborhood of 18th and Vine (pictured) to check out the **Negro Leagues Baseball Museum** (p153) and Missouri's first Black-owned **brewery** (p153). Enjoy a nightcap of Kansas City jazz at the **Blue Room** (p153) or an old fashioned garnished with Prohibition history at **J Rieger** (p153).

FROM LEFT: STLJB/SHUTTERSTOCK, PHOTOTRIPPINGAMERICA/SHUTTERSTOCK

WILDNERDPIX/SHUTTERSTOCK

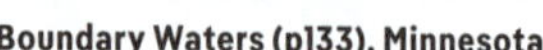

Boundary Waters (p133), Minnesota

ITINERARIES

Lake Country

Allow: 7 days **Distance:** 835 miles

Get ready to splash around the Great Lakes, America's 'third coast'. Bounce between cultured cities and quaint vacation towns on the Lake Michigan shoreline and then detour to the urban waters of Minneapolis before reaching Lake Superior. From here, trade your car for a canoe to explore the wild Boundary Waters.

1 CHICAGO 2 DAYS

Chicago might be the biggest city in the Midwest, but Lake Michigan laps at its doorstep. Hit up one of its 22 free **public beaches** (p66) or cycle the 18-mile Lakefront Trail at the water's edge. Other good outdoorsy spots include **Lincoln Park** (p61) – Chicago's largest green space at 1200 acres – and **The 606** (pictured; p64), a repurposed train track for cyclists and pedestrians that runs past factories and residents' backyards. 1½hr

2 MILWAUKEE 1 DAY

Start your journey north with a short jaunt to traipse along Milwaukee's **RiverWalk** (p113) and scope out architect Santiago Calatrava's **Milwaukee Art Museum** (pictured; p113). At night, visit one of two dozen-plus **beer halls** (p111) and finish strong by eating a classic Wisconsin **fish fry** (p113). 2¼hr

Detour: *Between Chicago and Milwaukee, stop in Racine to see the Prairie School architecture of Wisconsin-born Frank Lloyd Wright. Spend 2hr.* 45min

3 DOOR COUNTY 1 DAY

Door County, Wisconsin's limestone 'thumb', sticks out 75 miles into Lake Michigan, and this summer vacation destination is all rural charm and natural beauty. Kayak around the cliffs of **Cave Point** (pictured; p118), trek the tranquil shoreline of **Newport State Park** (p118) and finish with a fish boil at the **Old Post Office Restaurant** (p119) as the sun slides into the lake. 4¾hr

FROM LEFT: ANTWON MCMULLEN/SHUTTERSTOCK, ABHISHEK CHANDRA/500PX, KENNETH KEIFER/SHUTTERSTOCK

CANADA
International Falls
Thunder Bay
Isle Royale
0 200 km
0 100 miles
END
6 Grand Marais
2hr
Silver Bay
Houghton
Sault Ste Marie
Grand Rapids
Duluth
5
Ashland
Marquette
MINNESOTA
Superior
MICHIGAN
Mackinaw City
2¼hr
Iron Mountain
Escanaba
WISCONSIN
Rhinelander
St Cloud
Menominee
Traverse City
4¾hr
Wausau
Sturgeon Bay
Willmar
St Paul
Green Bay
3 Door County
Minneapolis 4
Shawano
Menomonie
Eau Claire
Appleton
Manitowoc
Oshkosh
MICHIGAN
2¼hr
Sheboygan
Mankato
Rochester
Fond du Lac
Muskegon
Grand Rapids
La Crosse
Port Washington
Milwaukee 2
Madison
45min
Racine
Mason City
Kenosha
Kalamazoo
Waukegan
Benton Harbor
Fort Dodge
Dubuque
Rockford
1½hr
Waterloo
Chicago 1
South Bend
IOWA
Ames
Cedar Rapids
Gary
Michigan City
Davenport
ILLINOIS
Des Moines
Iowa City
La Salle
START
INDIANA

4
MINNEAPOLIS 1 DAY

Drive into the 'Land of 10,000 Lakes' and see a good selection of them in Minnesota's largest city. Walk, kayak or cycle around **Bde Maka Ska** (p127) or chill out at its beach. Admire the roaring power of **Minnehaha Falls** (pictured; p127), a 53ft-tall waterfall a 15-minute drive from downtown, set in a stunning limestone gorge among nearly 200 acres of woodlands with riverside trails. *2¼hr*

5
DULUTH 1 DAY

From Duluth, Hwy 61 meanders alongside the shoreline of Lake Superior, through cliffs and tall trees to the Canadian border. State parks worth stretching your legs in, line the way. The five cascades, a scenic gorge and easy trails draw carloads of visitors to **Gooseberry Falls State Park** (pictured; p131). Hwy 61 is 150 miles long and drivable in three hours, but most travelers spend much longer. *2hr*

6
GRAND MARAIS 1 DAY

Base yourself in artistically inclined Grand Marais (p132). After getting a load of the galleries in town, check out nature's handiwork by driving along the **Gunflint Trail** (pictured; p133) or renting a canoe and paddling into the **Boundary Waters** (p133). This ancient superhighway, once an important navigational route for Indigenous travelers, is now the second-largest wilderness east of the Rockies.

FROM LEFT: CHRIS LABASCO/SHUTTERSTOCK, LINDA MCKUSICK/SHUTTERSTOCK, TAMMI MILD/GETTY IMAGES

BARRY WINIKER/GETTY IMAGES

Endless Bridge (p127), Minneapolis

ITINERARIES

Great River Road

Allow: 7 days **Distance:** 800 miles

This epic 2340-mile roadway edges the Mississippi River from its headwaters in northern Minnesota's pine forests south to New Orleans. The scenery along North America's second-longest river is astonishing. Limestone cliffs, forests, meadows and farmland are part of the backdrop, along with smokestacks, riverboat casinos and urban sprawl.

1 MINNEAPOLIS 1 DAY

Minneapolis owes its existence to the Mississippi, which cuts through downtown. Enter the blue Guthrie Theater to see the view from the **Endless Bridge** (p127), a far-out cantilevered walkway. Water-powered sawmills along the river fueled a timber boom in the mid-1800s. Wheat from the prairies also needed to be processed, so flour mills were big business, and their abandoned remains are still visible in **Mill Ruins Park** (pictured; p127). 2¼hr

2 PEPIN ½ DAY

The Mississippi River forms Wisconsin's southwestern border, and the state's sections of the Great River Road (pictured) are among the most beautiful. *Little House on the Prairie* author Laura Ingalls Wilder was born in Pepin, which has a **museum** (p117) on the land once homesteaded by Ma and Pa Ingalls. Foodies shouldn't miss book-stuffed **Harbor View Cafe** (p117), a stalwart of the Slow Food scene. 2½hr

3 EFFIGY MOUNDS & PIKES PEAK ½ DAY

Enter Iowa, where the Great River Road hugs the Mississippi along the state's eastern edge. Move south to **Effigy Mounds National Monument** (pictured; p143) and hike on trails that lead to hundreds of Native burial mounds in the bluffs above the river. Historic McGregor is the gateway to **Pikes Peak State Park** (p190), a reserve at the confluence of the Wisconsin and Mississippi Rivers. 1¼hr

FROM LEFT: MELISSAMN/SHUTTERSTOCK, JOHN BRUESKE/SHUTTERSTOCK, ZACK FRANK/SHUTTERSTOCK

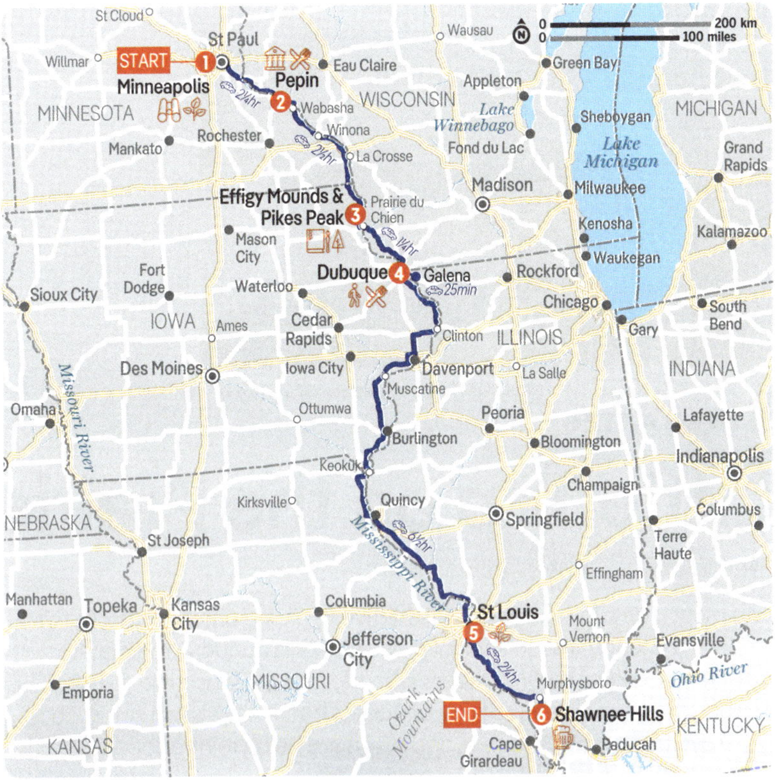

START
1 St Paul
Minneapolis
2¼hr
2 Pepin
2½hr
3 Effigy Mounds & Pikes Peak
1¼hr
4 Dubuque
Galena
25min
6½hr
5 St Louis
2¼hr
END
6 Shawnee Hills

0 200 km
0 100 miles

4

DUBUQUE 2 DAYS

Undergoing an urban renaissance, Dubuque (p185) sits between the Mississippi River and seven steep limestone hills. Walk on the 9-mile path along the riverfront and visit the regenerated Millwork District (pictured), whose former wood-working factories now house mural-covered restaurants and bars. 6½hr

Detour: *Galena was once the wealthiest city in Illinois and was briefly home to the 18th president, Ulysses S Grant. Spend 4hrs. 25min*

5

ST LOUIS 2 DAYS

Fur trapper Pierre Laclède put down stakes at the junction of the Mississippi and Missouri Rivers in 1764. The hustle picked up greatly when prospectors discovered gold in California in 1848 and St Louis became the jumping-off point for get-rich-quick dreamers. **Gateway Arch National Park** (pictured; p150) is the emblem of that history, and the world's tallest arch soars high above the Mississippi in downtown STL. 2¼hr

6

SHAWNEE HILLS 1 DAY

Southern Illinois looks wildly different from the rest of the state. Slightly inland from the river, the Shawnee Hills appear to be mini mountains. Hike among the dramatic sandstone formations in **Shawnee National Forest** (pictured; p73) and then reward your efforts with a beer at weekend-only **Scratch Brewing** (p73), a destination brewery that uses bark and berries foraged from its farm in wild ales and sours.

FROM LEFT: PIXEL PERFECT PIX/SHUTTERSTOCK, JON REHG/SHUTTERSTOCK, YUZIS/SHUTTERSTOCK

ZACK FRANK/SHUTTERSTOCK

Theodore Roosevelt National Park (p196)

ITINERARIES

Little Trip on the Prairie

Allow: 7 days **Distance:** 1170 miles

The most iconic landscape of the Midwest, prairie once covered a third of North America. These seas of grass are vastly underappreciated, both today and by early pioneers who plowed the land, unknowingly altering these ecosystems forever. Today, tracts have been set aside to preserve this precious terrain, and bison are being reintroduced.

1 THEODORE ROOSEVELT NATIONAL PARK 1 DAY

Wildlife abounds in this 110-sq-mile national park (p196) in North Dakota. Drive the 36-mile Scenic Loop to see bison, elk (pictured) and pronghorn in the grasses framed by elegant rock formations. Short hikes lead to stunning viewpoints and past prairie dog towns. If you're short on time, stop by the Painted Canyon Visitor Center to get the best of the park in a quick hit.

5hr

2 CUSTER STATE PARK 1 DAY

The only reason that South Dakota's 111-sq-mile Custer State Park (p209) isn't a national park is that the state nabbed it first. It boasts one of the world's largest bison herds. You might also spot elk, pronghorns, mountain goats, bighorn sheep, coyotes, prairie dogs, mountain lions and bobcats along the 18-mile Wildlife Loop, which passes over stone bridges and untouched meadows. *1¾hr*

3 BADLANDS NATIONAL PARK 2 DAYS

There's nothing bad about South Dakota's Badlands National Park (p200). Set off on the Badlands Loop Rd to marvel over its otherworldly landscape of rocky spikes and rainbow hues. It's surrounded by the Buffalo Gap National Grassland. Together they protect one of the country's largest stands of prairie grasslands, on which a 1000-strong herd of bison roams. *7½hr*

FROM LEFT: ALICIA MARVIN/SHUTTERSTOCK, PAUL TESSIER/SHUTTERSTOCK, IAN SAFRANSCHI/SHUTTERSTOCK

4

HOMESTEAD NATIONAL HISTORICAL PARK ⏱ 1 DAY

The Homestead Act of 1862 altered the region by allowing public land (which was Native land before the Indian Removal Act of 1830) to be privately owned. The first piece of prairie claimed through the Act is now encompassed by Nebraska's Homestead National Historical Park (p180). The land was claimed 10 minutes after midnight on the day the Act went into effect. 🚗 *3hr*

5

TALLGRASS PRAIRIE NATIONAL PRESERVE ⏱ 1 DAY

The tallgrass prairie (p160) in the Flint Hills of Kansas survived by a fluke of nature: the rocky soil was too difficult to plow. The 11,000-acre preserve's trails blend history with the outdoors, leading through a pasture that's home to 90-some bison, reintroduced after a 150-year absence, and a one-room stone schoolhouse that was open from 1882 to 1930. 🚗 *2¾hr*

6

JOSEPH H WILLIAMS TALLGRASS PRAIRIE PRESERVE ⏱ 1 DAY

Hollywood spotlit the Osage Nation with 2023's *Killers of the Flower Moon*, and the Oklahoma town of Pawhuska was the hub of its production. That film focused on oil, but the Joseph H Williams Tallgrass Prairie Preserve (p169) outside town reflects the beauty of this landscape before the boom. This bison-dotted preserve is the world's largest protected area of its kind.

FROM LEFT: EWY MEDIA/SHUTTERSTOCK, RICARDO REITMEYER/SHUTTERSTOCK, TROY A. THOMAS/SHUTTERSTOCK

WHEN TO GO

In summer, hit up the Midwest's lakefront beaches and wild rivers. Spring brings blossoms and a post-winter reawakening, while fall inspires leaf-peeping.

Summer is the peak season for travel, with tons of festivals, days by the lake or pool, baseball games and beer gardens. However, the temperatures in July and August can be roasting, often exacerbated by high humidity. Things start to wind down in September and October when kids head back to school, but the weather remains pleasant, and plenty of big events keep the party going. Color-changing trees dot the landscapes, but soon enough, the bitter wind and cold begin to bite. You have to bundle up, but visiting the Midwest in winter is doable. Cities twinkle with holiday cheer, and prices drop, but beware of blizzards and ice storms closing down roads for days. Warmth creeps back in April and May, and outdoor action begins anew.

Saving Strategies

January to March is cheapest for hotels, but there's a catch: lots of businesses in small towns and rural areas close for winter.

I LIVE HERE

FLUTTERS OF SPRINGTIME

Ted Nelson is a Chicago-based outdoor adventure travel blogger and photographer. *@travelingted*

In spring, millions of birds fly over Chicago. I enjoy seeking out and photographing warblers, orioles and tanagers in places like Montrose Point Bird Sanctuary. As the weather warms, Chicago is also a surprising hub for canoeing, kayaking and SUP on the rivers and Lake Michigan. Paddling is a great way to view birds along the shoreline and, if kayaking downtown, a beautiful spot to view the Chicago skyline.

Split Rock Lighthouse, Minnesota (p122)

COOLER BY THE LAKE

In spring, summer and early fall, it can be 10°F to 15°F colder by the Great Lakes than it is a few miles inland because the water's large mass stays chilled and creates cool breezes that lower lakefront temperatures.

Weather through the Year: Chicago

JANUARY	FEBRUARY	MARCH	APRIL	MAY	JUNE
Avg. daytime max: **32°F**	Avg. daytime max: **36°F**	Avg. daytime max: **47°F**	Avg. daytime max: **59°F**	Avg. daytime max: **71°F**	Avg. daytime max: **80°F**
Days of precipitation: 2	Days of precipitation: 2	Days of precipitation: 2	Days of precipitation: 4	Days of precipitation: 4	Days of precipitation: 4

WINDY CITY?

Chicago's nickname refers to verbose politicians, not its climate. The city actually is not that gusty compared to others. Chicago's average wind speed is 10.5mph, while Omaha's is 12.8mph and Oklahoma City's is 12.4mph, to name just a few that out-bluster the Windy City.

Biggest Fests in the Midwest

For **St Patrick's Day**, a local plumbers' union dyes the Chicago River shamrock green – using a non-toxic, plant-based powder – just in time for a parade celebrating all things Irish in the Windy City (p52). **March**

Drawing in more than a million visitors, the **Iowa State Fair** is so much more than butter sculptures and country music. Try all sorts of food on a stick and coo over farm animals (p190). **August**

Dubbed 'the world's largest music festival', Milwaukee's nine-day **Summerfest** puts hundreds of rock, blues, country and alternative bands on stage (p113). **June and July**

The country's biggest Oktoberfest celebration, **Oktoberfest Zinzinnati** brings out the beer, bratwurst and Bavarians in all of us. Nearly half a million people descend on downtown Cincinnati (p88). **September**

Wacky & Wonderful Festivals

The best way to beat the heat in Kansas? Head to Humboldt, population 1816, for **Water Wars**, an all-town, family-friendly water fight. No one goes home dry (p159). **August**

Prairie du Sac, WI, hosts the annual **Cow Chip Throw**, in which 800 competitors fling dried manure patties; the record is 248ft (p116). **August or September**

For **Cleveland Kurentovanje**, the city's large Slovenian population gathers at this cultural festival that takes place the weekend before the start of Lent. A parade led by Kurenti, fuzzy mythical monsters that wear bells to chase away winter, is the highlight (p88). **February or March**

Watch competitive fence painting, frog jumping and a lookalike competition at the **National Tom Sawyer Days** in Hannibal, MO, the childhood hometown of Mark Twain (p155). **July**

I LIVE HERE

PRAIRIE FIRE

Heather Brown is a park ranger at the Tallgrass Prairie National Preserve in Kansas. *facebook.com/NPS.TallgrassPrairie*

Prescribed burns in spring turn the prairie black, exposing limestone outcroppings and surface rocks. It looks like the moon's surface, only to turn into a beautiful green carpet with just a little moisture. Nighttime burns in the Flint Hills bring a serene yet wild feel as the night is broken up by the sound of crackling and the scent of fire as the flames lick at the grasses.

Burns in the Flint Hills (p160), Kansas

EXTREME TEMPERATURES

Because of its geographical position between the cold of Canada and the warm, moist air from the Gulf of Mexico, the region is subject to extreme temperatures and huge fluctuations. North Dakota has hit both -60°F and 121°F.

JULY	AUGUST	SEPTEMBER	OCTOBER	NOVEMBER	DECEMBER
Avg. daytime max: **85°F**	Avg. daytime max: **83°F**	Avg. daytime max: **76°F**	Avg. daytime max: **63°F**	Avg. daytime max: **48°F**	Avg. daytime max: **37°F**
Days of precipitation: 4	Days of precipitation: 4	Days of precipitation: 3	Days of precipitation: 3	Days of precipitation: 2	Days of precipitation: 2

FROM LEFT: MIKE OSINSKI/SHUTTERSTOCK, FEATUREFLASH PHOTO AGENCY/SHUTTERSTOCK

Summertime, Detroit (p95)

GET PREPARED FOR THE MIDWEST

Useful things to load in your bag, your ears and your brain.

Clothes

Layers Summers in the Midwest can be downright steamy. Or not! A storm can blow in and drop the temperature fast, so be prepared for multiple seasons in a day, no matter the time of year. Spring and fall are temperamental, and the temperature can fluctuate by 30°F or more in a single day. Frigid summertime air-conditioning can make a light sweater worthwhile indoors. Winter can whip up heavy snow and wind, so pack your warmest coat, hat and gloves when visiting from November through March.

Keep it casual In general, comfort is valued over high fashion. You're fine to wear jeans and T-shirts to most restaurants and bars.

Shoes Wear comfortable shoes or sandals for exploring cities. In winter, make sure your footwear is warm and waterproof.

Manners

Greetings A smile and a nod go a long way. Shake hands on more formal occasions.

Smoking Lighting up indoors is illegal in most places, though there are exceptions.

Cannabis Laws vary by state, with some allowing recreational use and others not allowing anything. Road trippers beware: federal law prohibits carrying cannabis across state lines, even if it's legal in both states.

READ

The Devil in the White City (Erik Larson; 2003) Historical nonfiction novel about a serial killer during the 1893 Chicago World's Fair.

The Night Watchman (Louise Erdrich; 2020) An evening guard at a North Dakota factory fights for Native rights in Washington, DC.

The Topeka School (Ben Lerner; 2019) A family drama featuring a Class of '97 high school senior and his psychoanalyst parents.

Native Son (Richard Wright; 1940) A young Black man is jailed after accidentally killing a white woman in 1930s Chicago.

Words

Here's a little local lingo used around the Midwest.

As all get out Very or extremely: 'It's hot as all get out.'
Chicago Handshake An Old Style beer and a shot of Malört liqueur served together.
Cornhole A bar or yard game in which bean bags are tossed at an inclined board with a hole in it.
CTA The abbreviation for Chicago Transit Authority, the organization responsible for the trains and buses.
Dibs The technically illegal practice of using lawn chairs, milk crates or other junk to reserve the on-street parking space you shoveled out after a snowstorm.
Fixin' to About to do something.
Gonna sneak past ya Said politely when walking around someone who is in your way.
Jeet Shortened spoken form of 'did you eat?'.
Nader A tornado.
Ope An exclamation when you accidentally bump into someone, similar to oops or sorry.
Pop The Midwest's name for a sugary, fizzy drink. East Coasters call it soda, and Southerners call it Coke, regardless of the brand.
The L Short for 'elevated', referring to Chicago's train system – even when it's underground.
Y'all Plural 'you' (you all), used to address a group of people.
You betcha 'You're welcome' or an enthusiastic yes.

WATCH

The Bear (Christopher Storer; 2022–present) Luscious shots of Chicago show up in this TV series about a fictional chef.

Field of Dreams (Phil Alden Robinson; 1989) Kevin Costner is an Iowa farmer who builds a baseball diamond.

Fargo (filmmakers and cast pictured; Coen Brothers; 1996) Black comedy about a financially desperate car salesman's crime gone wrong.

Three Billboards Outside Ebbing, Missouri (Martin McDonagh; 2017) A grieving mother uses billboards to publicly challenge local police.

Twister (Jan de Bont; 1996) A stormchaser is determined to improve tornado warning systems after losing her father.

LISTEN

This American Life Weekly radio show (available as a podcast) started in Chicago with stories ranging from humorous to thought-provoking.

The Rise and Fall of a Midwest Princess (Chappell Roan; 2023) Breakthrough pop album from a Missouri-born queer artist known for her camp outfits.

Purple Rain (Prince; 1984) The Minneapolis native hit superstardom with this album, also a movie soundtrack, which sold more than 13 million copies.

Bird: The Complete Charlie Parker on Verve (Charlie Parker; 1990) Decades after his death, this saxophonist remains the auditory ambassador of Kansas City jazz.

Isle Royale National Park (p107), Michigan

TRIP PLANNER

THE MIDWEST'S NATIONAL PARKS

National parks in this part of the country are some of the least known in the USA, but the breadth of activities they offer is like a cross-section of the American experience. They serve as a reminder of why national parks are still celebrated as America's best idea.

Pick Your Park

INDIANA

Indiana Dunes National Park

Day trippable from Chicago, Indiana Dunes (p79) became the USA's 61st national park in 2019, stretching along 15 miles of the Lake Michigan shoreline.

MICHIGAN

Isle Royale National Park

Free of vehicles and roads, Isle Royale National Park (p107) is the place to go for peace and quiet. Its appeal is summed up in one remarkable statistic: Isle Royale gets fewer visitors in a year than Yellowstone National Park gets in a day.

MINNESOTA

Voyageurs National Park

Voyageurs National Park (p134), which marks the border between the USA and Canada, is almost 40% water and accessible by hiking or motorboat only – the waters are mostly too wide and too rough for canoeing.

MISSOURI

Gateway Arch National Park

This urban space, the smallest in the national park system, might seem like a far cry from the likes of Yellowstone or Yosemite. Gateway Arch (p150) rises from the heart of St Louis, and it's proof of the adaptability of the national park idea.

PARKS APPS & PODCASTS

National Park Service *(nps.gov)* The NPS app features maps, self-guided tours, accessibility information and updates on park conditions.

AllTrails *(alltrails.com)* Lists of trails with user reviews, current conditions and real-time tracking while hiking. It's worth paying for AllTrails+ to download maps offline and get wrong-turn alerts.

Recreation.gov Reserve campsites, permits and day-use passes for national parks and other federal areas.

National Park After Dark *(npadpodcast.com)* Two friends investigate the dark underbelly of America's natural treasures, with fascinating histories, tragic events and firsthand anecdotes.

GuideAlong *(guidealong.com)* Self-guided audio tours that are ideal for road-trippers.

NORTH DAKOTA

Theodore Roosevelt National Park

Future president Theodore Roosevelt retreated from New York to this remote spot in his early 20s after losing both his wife and mother in a matter of hours. His time there inspired him to become an avid conservationist, and he set aside a quantity of land larger than Texas, the now Theodore Roosevelt National Park (p196).

OHIO

Cuyahoga Valley National Park

The Cuyahoga River (p86) snakes through a forested valley, earning its Native name of 'crooked river'. Its evocative moniker hints at the mystical beauty that the park engenders on a cool morning when mists thread the woods.

SOUTH DAKOTA

Badlands National Park

The otherworldly landscape of Badlands National Park (p200) is a spectacle of sheer walls and fantastic rainbow hues. Looking over the bizarre formations is like seeing an ocean boiled dry.

Wind Cave National Park

Wind Cave National Park (p202) contains 167 miles of mapped passages and 60- to 100-million-year-old calcite formations that look like honeycomb.

CHERI ALGUIRE/SHUTTERSTOCK

Wind Cave National Park (p202), South Dakota

PROTECTED PLACES BEYOND THE PARKS

The jurisdiction of the National Park Service also includes national monuments, preserves, lakeshores, rivers and historical parks.

- **Lincoln Home National Historic Site, IL** (p69) Preserves a four-block neighborhood around Abraham Lincoln's house.
- **Effigy Mounds National Monument, IA** (p143) Native burial mounds sit in the bluffs above the Mississippi River.
- **Tallgrass Prairie National Preserve, KS** (p160) Seas of grass are the most emblematic landscape of the Midwest, but only a fraction remains today, mostly in Kansas' Flint Hills.
- **Pictured Rocks National Lakeshore, MI** (p108) A riotous rainbow of color in its cliffs and caves, where blue and green minerals have striped the red and yellow sandstone.
- **Ozark National Scenic Riverways, MO** (p155) Float or paddle two wild rivers in the first national park established to protect a waterway.
- **Scotts Bluff National Monument, NE** (p182) Rising 800ft above the plains, this rock formation was an important landmark on the Oregon Trail.
- **Dayton Aviation Heritage National Historical Park, OH** (p92) See where the Wright brothers developed their ideas about flight.
- **Minuteman Missile National Historic Site, SD** (p204) During the Cold War, the Great Plains housed 1000 intercontinental ballistic missiles, now retired.
- **Apostle Islands National Lakeshore, WI** (p120) Kayak or take a boat trip around the rugged rock islands floating in Lake Superior.

RANDY RUNTSCH/SHUTTERSTOCK

Iron Mountain Rd (p208), South Dakota

TRIP PLANNER

ROAD TRIPPING THE MIDWEST

Fall for the Midwest from the driver's seat. Wide-open spaces are sewn together by designated scenic byways and backroads, in a collage of tiny towns, historic sites, welcoming cities and natural wonders. Whether you've got two days or 10, there's a route worth roaming.

Choose Your Trip

ROUTE 66

Starting in Chicago on its 2248-mile journey west to Los Angeles, Route 66 is the country's classic road trip, passing through the Midwest states of Illinois, Missouri, Kansas and Oklahoma. Though it was officially decommissioned in 1985 and replaced by interstates on many stretches, following its original tracks leads you to kooky roadside attractions, old-timey gas stations, Norman Rockwell–ish soda fountains and vinyl-clad mom-and-pop diners.

GREAT RIVER ROAD

The Great River Road traces the Mississippi through Minnesota, Wisconsin, Iowa, Illinois, Missouri and states further south along federal, state and county routes. Start in Minnesota's pinewood forests, end beneath Louisiana's moss-mired oaks and discover America's beating heart in between in Brainerd, MN, as seen in the Coen Brothers' movie *Fargo*; Spring Green, WI, where architect Frank Lloyd Wright cut his teeth; and historic Dubuque, IA, with narrow streets lined with Victorian-era houses.

MINNESOTA'S HIGHWAY 61

Hwy 61 (p131) connects Louisiana and Canada, but the prettiest section rolls through Minnesota, also called the North Shore All-American Scenic Drive. Play Bob Dylan's 1965 album *Highway 61 Revisited*

ROAD TRIP CHECKLIST

Join an automobile association Some international automobile associations have reciprocal agreements with their US counterparts, so check whether you can bring a member card from home. Associations such as AAA provide 24-hour emergency roadside assistance and discounts on lodging and attractions.

Pack repair tools Make sure your vehicle has a spare tire and toolkit, including jack, jumper cables, ice scraper, tire pressure gauge and emergency equipment, such as flashers.

Have maps handy Bring paper maps or download offline maps before venturing into remote areas.

Carry your driver's license and proof of insurance Never get behind the wheel without them.

while soaking up the sights. Duluth, Dylan's birthplace, is the world's most inland port city, where grassy sand dunes stretch into Lake Superior. A rocky coastline follows, passing eight state parks before reaching the Canadian border. Chase waterfalls, spot lighthouses, dine on freshwater fish and sun yourself on public beaches.

PETER NORBECK SCENIC BYWAY

A roller-coaster ride through stunning scenery, Peter Norbeck Scenic Byway (p208) is an oval-shaped route made of four roads that link beautiful destinations in South Dakota's Black Hills. Iron Mountain Rd (Hwy 16A) is the favorite of the four, with wooden bridges, virtual loop the loops and narrow tunnels that frame Mt Rushmore.

MICHIGAN'S M-22

This state highway (p105) is Michigan's most scenic, hugging the shore of Lake Michigan for more than 100 miles. It passes Sleeping Bear Dunes National Lakeshore, a worthy diversion with Caribbean-blue waters and tons of beaches and secluded islands, as well as tiny fishing towns, where you can still watch the catch of the day being cleaned and smoked among the shanties.

Sign for Route 66 (p161), Kansas

TLF IMAGES/SHUTTERSTOCK

GAS STATION SNACKS

Gas stations are for fueling up – not just your vehicle but yourself too. Eating at a gas station might seem like it should be a last-ditch effort for sustenance, but many Midwest road-trippers have snacks they swear by.

- **Buc-ee's** If there's such a thing as a cult gas station chain, this beaver-mascoted, Texas-started spot is it. Beaver Nuggets (puffed corn with a caramel coating) are a favorite. Limited Midwest presence, but one opened in Springfield, MO, in 2023, and more are set for Kansas City and Wisconsin.
- **Casey's** Beloved for its breakfast pizzas made with scrambled eggs, bacon, cheese and sausage gravy sauce; found in all Midwest states.
- **Kwik Trip** Known for its baked goodies made in-house, including dunkers (doughnuts made for dunking in coffee) and glazers (glazed doughnuts); locations in Michigan, Minnesota and Wisconsin, as well as Iowa, Illinois and South Dakota under the name Kwik Star.
- **Maverik** Expanding east from Utah, with made-to-order burritos and street tacos, plus house-made cookies. Locations in Kansas, Michigan, Missouri, Nebraska, Oklahoma and South Dakota.
- **QuikTrip** Ranking the best foods from its roller grills – steak and cheese taquitos, egg rolls, buffalo chicken bites – is a Midwest pastime. Open in Illinois, Indiana, Iowa, Kansas, Missouri, Nebraska, Ohio and Oklahoma; also known as QT and not to be confused with Kwik Trip.

BRENT HOFACKER/SHUTTERSTOCK

Wisconsin cheese curds

THE FOOD SCENE

The Midwest's range of restaurants, from the mom and pop to the Michelin starred, will satisfy all types of eaters.

You won't leave the Midwest hungry. This region is tops for serving meat-heavy, carb-loaded American comfort foods, such as pot roast, steak and chicken dinners. Add walleye, perch and other freshwater fish in towns near the Great Lakes. Chicago stands tall as the Midwest's best place to pile a plate, though other major cities aren't far behind and have their own unique foods and traditions. Many of the most popular foods arrived with immigrants, once from Central and Eastern Europe, then Mexico, and more recently from Somalia, India and the Middle East. Native cuisine, made with ingredients truly local to the land – bison, chokecherries, black walnuts – is making a comeback.

As the breadbasket of America, some Midwest states dedicate 60% to 90% of their land to farming. Kansas grows the most wheat, while Iowa sprouts the most corn. Nebraska has the second-largest number of beef cattle in the country, and Iowa raises nearly a third of the nation's hogs. All of this ends up on plates here and across the USA.

Best Midwest Dishes

BISCUITS AND GRAVY
Biscuits topped with sausage or mushroom gravy for breakfast.

BURNT ENDS
The charred point end of beef brisket, a must-order in Kansas City.

CHEESE CURDS
Small fresh pieces of curdled milk that squeak when you bite into them.

CHICAGO DOG
Beef weenie with a garden of toppings; don't you dare add ketchup.

Wisconsin Cheese

Wisconsin is cheesy and proud of it. The state pumps out 3.5 billion pounds of cheddar, Gouda and other cheesy goodness – a quarter of America's hunks – from its cow-speckled farmland per year. Swiss, German and Scandinavian immigrants settled in Wisconsin in the 1800s and put their old-country cheesemaking skills to work, and the state has been America's Dairyland ever since. Green County is said to have the nation's greatest concentration of cheesemakers. As you're road-tripping through, you can stop at local dairy farms and shops and learn your artisanal from farmstead, Gruyere from Gouda, curd from whey. **Ellsworth Cooperative Creamery** (p117) in western Wisconsin is the state's largest cheese curd producer, and it's a Wisconsin rite of passage to bite into a curd and hear it squeak.

The Bear Effect

If you've come to Chicago just for deep dish, you're doing it wrong. The Windy City's food scene is receiving more recognition but remains criminally underrated. Hole-in-the-wall eateries sit alongside fine-dining restaurants adorned with Michelin stars. Shining a spotlight on the scene is *The Bear*, a TV show that follows a high-flying chef who leaves his job in Michelin-starred restaurants to return to his hometown of Chicago and run his family's Italian beef shop. The show has received huge praise, and the Emmys and Golden Globes have come pouring in. As of 2025, four seasons have been released, and the show has been renewed for a fifth. Restaurant cameos to look out for include **Pequod's** (p54) and **Kasama** (p60).

PALPLANER/SHUTTERSTOCK

Detroit-style pizza

Time-Honored Traditions

Some Midwestern food and restaurants lean heavily on the nostalgia. Started in the 1930s post-Prohibition, supper clubs are a type of time-warp restaurant common in the upper Midwest, with surf 'n' turf menus and extensive cocktail lists. Wisconsin loves a Friday fish fry, a communal meal of beer-battered cod while listening to polka music, often at a brewery. Route 66 is still lined with old-school, mom-and-pop diners that fuel up road-trippers with big portions of burgers, fries and shakes.

Specialties

Pizza

Introduced to the US by Italian immigrants in the late 19th century, this affordable treat takes more forms than you might think.

Deep dish Chicago's most famous concoction: a thick pie with tons of tomato sauce and cheese; the cousin of a casserole or quiche.

Tavern-style The antidote to deep dish that also originated in Chicago: thin-crust pizza cut into squares.

Detroit-style Rectangular pies with airy crusts and crispy cheese that's caramelized at the corners.

St Louis–style Cracker-thin crust topped with Provel, a mix of cheddar, Swiss and provolone cheese.

CONCRETE
Frozen custard blended with fruit or candy; so thick that it's served upside down.

FISH FRY
Wisconsin's tradition: deep-fried fish served with fries, coleslaw and tartar sauce.

PIZZA
Chicago deep dish, tavern-style or made with St Louis' unique cheese blend.

PORK TENDERLOIN
An Indiana-invented sandwich with buttermilk-soaked pork that's breaded and fried.

STEAK
Prime cuts of beef sourced from local ranches and served with lots of sides.

Burgers & Sandwiches

Loosemeat sandwich Instead of being packed together in a patty, the ground beef is crumbly. Started in 1926 in Iowa at Maid-Rite, which still has franchised locations around the region. Nu Way Cafe in Wichita, KS, also has its own version.

Runza Nebraska's most iconic food, sold at the statewide chain of the same name: a rectangle of yeast-dough bread filled with ground beef and onions. Called bierocks in Kansas.

Horseshoe Find it in Springfield, IL, and almost nowhere else: an open-faced stack that consists of thickly sliced toasted bread topped with meat, French fries and a Welsh rarebit cheese sauce.

Europe Inspired

Toasted ravioli A St Louis specialty; it's said these breaded and deep-fried pockets of meat were invented when a chef accidentally dropped a ravioli in hot oil instead of water.

Italian beef Thin-sliced roast beef sandwich sopped in gravy and spicy pickled vegetables; best in Chicago.

Cincinnati chili

Cincinnati chili Greek immigrants first added cinnamon, clove, nutmeg and allspice to the popular meat stew and then poured it over spaghetti.

Sauces

Ranch dressing Found across the USA, but the Midwest wants it as a dipping sauce for *everything:* pizza, mozzarella sticks, sandwiches and fries.

Sweet Treats

Gooey butter cake This dense, uber-sweet cake made with flour, butter, sugar and eggs hails from St Louis.

Sugar cream pie Indiana's unofficial state pie, filled with cream, sugar and cornstarch.

MEALS OF A LIFETIME

Owamni (p124) Experience true North American Indigenous food made with Native ingredients in Minneapolis.

Kasama (p60) Line up for Filipino breakfast sandwiches and sweets by day; splurge on the 13-course fine-dining tasting menu by night in Chicago.

Joe's Kansas City Bar-B-Que (p153) Some of KC's best burnt ends are served in a gas station.

The Committee Chophouse (p178) Romantic, low-lit steakhouse in Omaha with a summertime 'steak flight' sourced from Nebraska ranches.

Northwestern Steakhouse (p192) This Mason City, IA, spot is renowned across the state for its Greek-style broiled steaks. Order the spaghetti as your side.

THE YEAR IN FOOD

SPRING

When daytime temperatures reach at least 40°F but nights are still freezing, sugar maples in Illinois and other forested areas start to drip sap (pictured) for syrup. By mid-April, farmers markets are setting up.

SUMMER

The scent of burgers announces outdoor barbecue season. Shucks of fresh corn (pictured) are sold on the side of the road, and u-pick farms are full of families scavenging for berries.

AUTUMN

Apples hang heavy, waiting to be picked for cider. Kids run through corn mazes and patches of pumpkins (pictured), which get picked off the vine to be carved up for jack-o'-lanterns and pies.

WINTER

Warm up with bowls of chili (pictured; often paired with a cinnamon roll – trust us, it's amazing) or a hotdish, an upper Midwest casserole – the version with tater tots is a favorite.

TOP: SOPHIE_MARIE/SHUTTERSTOCK; FROM LEFT: LOPOLO/SHUTTERSTOCK, DANITA DELIMONT/SHUTTERSTOCK, DOLORES M. HARVEY/SHUTTERSTOCK, BRENT HOFACKER/SHUTTERSTOCK

BRENT HOFACKER/SHUTTERSTOCK

Loosemeat sandwich

FROM LEFT: MELISSAMN/SHUTTERSTOCK, ADELIA KROUPA/SHUTTERSTOCK

Apostle Islands National Lakeshore (p120), Wisconsin

THE OUTDOORS

What the Midwest might lack in mountains and ocean coastlines, it more than makes up for in whispering grasslands and sublime lakeshores.

No matter your weakness – hiking, kayaking, cycling or simply jumping in an innertube and letting the river do the work – you'll find incredible places to commune with the great outdoors in the Midwest. National parks are natural magnets – and they remain far less busy than their counterparts elsewhere in the country – but look beyond them to find stunning state parks and other protected preserves. The five Great Lakes, a vast landlocked sea, are prime places for adventure.

Paddling & Floating

Paddlers will find their bliss in the Midwest, particularly around the Great Lakes. Lake Superior is a kayaking hot spot, from gliding through arches and sea caves in Wisconsin's **Apostle Islands National Lakeshore** (p120) to paddling by the wildly colored cliffs of Michigan's **Pictured Rocks National Lakeshore** (p108). Canoeing is downright legendary here, too, including 1200 miles of wet and wild routes in Minnesota's **Boundary Waters** (p133).

Missouri's **Ozark National Scenic Riverways** (p155) was the first national park in the country established to protect a waterway, and floating or paddling in the Current and Jacks Fork Rivers is an unmissable experience. The scenery is rural and rugged, and the rivers are untamed and fed by enormous neon-blue springs. Nebraska's **Niobrara National Scenic River** (p183) is a

Top State Parks

CUSTER, SD
Watch Great Plains wildlife, including bison and prairie dogs, and road trip along memorable routes (p209).

JOHNSON'S SHUT-INS, MO
Take a scenic swim in this spot where the Black River rushes through rocky gorges (p155).

STARVED ROCK, IL
Trek 13 miles of trails to waterfalls that pour from glacier-formed sandstone canyons (p69).

FAMILY ADVENTURES

Gathering Place (p168) Romp around the 5-acre adventure playground at the Gathering Place in Tulsa, OK, voted one of the country's best parks.

Wisconsin Dells (p116) Choose a water park – or 20 – and splash it up in the Wisconsin Dells.

Cedar Point Amusement Park (p90) Ride some of the planet's wildest roller coasters and then play at the mile-long beachfront and water park at this Ohio amusement park.

Maquoketa Caves State Park (p186) Crouch and wiggle through underground nooks at this state park in Iowa.

Palisades State Park (p203) Kayak below soaring ancient quartzite formations along Split Rock Creek at South Dakota's Palisades State Park.

Fort Mackinac (p106) Plug your ears as soldiers in 19th-century garb fire muskets and cannons at Fort Mackinac, on a car-free island in Michigan.

similarly protected river route that glides past limestone bluffs, forests and spring-fed waterfalls.

Hiking & Walking

Trails cater to all levels of outdoor expertise, and you don't necessarily have to venture far from the city. Urban wanderers can explore riverside walks, such as Omaha's **RiverFront** (p176) and **The 606** (p64) in Chicago, an elevated former train track that strolls on high past hip restaurants and locals' backyards. Short trails and half-day hikes wind through **Badlands National Park** (p143), **Theodore Roosevelt National Park** (p196), and many other parks and preserves.

RAGBRAI (p194), Iowa

Epic long-distance routes include the 300-mile **Superior Hiking Trail** (p132), which tracks along its namesake lake between Duluth, MN, and the Canadian border; Missouri's 430-mile **Ozark Trail** (p155), which follows wild rivers far from civilization; and the **Greenstone Ridge Trail** (p107), Isle Royale National Park's longest hike at 42 miles; it runs the full length of the island.

Cycling

Iowa is a fantastic state for cycling, with tons of designated bike paths that link cities and suburbs with rural areas. Trails invite riders of all ages and abilities to cycle through welcoming towns and past public art. Central Iowa's **High Trestle Trail** (p191) is a highlight, ending its 25-mile journey at an LED-lit steel frame bridge just north of Des Moines. Cyclists around the world know **RAGBRAI** (p194), a weeklong 470-mile bike ride across the state every July. Wisconsin is another good spot for travelers on two wheels. The **400 State Trail** (p115) takes in a river valley dotted with farms and connects with the Elroy-Sparta State Trail to add on 33 miles.

Look up cycling routes on Rails to Trails (*railstotrails.org*), which has converted more than 41,000 miles of disused train lines across the country into car-free walking and cycling paths. The country's longest is the 239-mile Katy Trail in Missouri.

HOCKING HILLS, OH
Discover a leaf-peeper's dream in fall or set off on short hikes to scenic caves and waterfalls (p92).

FORT ROBINSON, NE
Dig into history at this former frontier fort and stay overnight in former officers' quarters (p182).

NEWPORT, WI
Walk and bird-watch by day and stargaze by night at this officially designated Dark Sky Park (p118).

JUDGE CR MAGNEY, MN
Hike to Devil's Kettle, a famous 50ft waterfall whose flow partially disappears underground (p131).

ACTION AREAS

Where to find the Midwest's best outdoor activities.

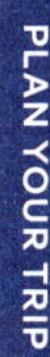

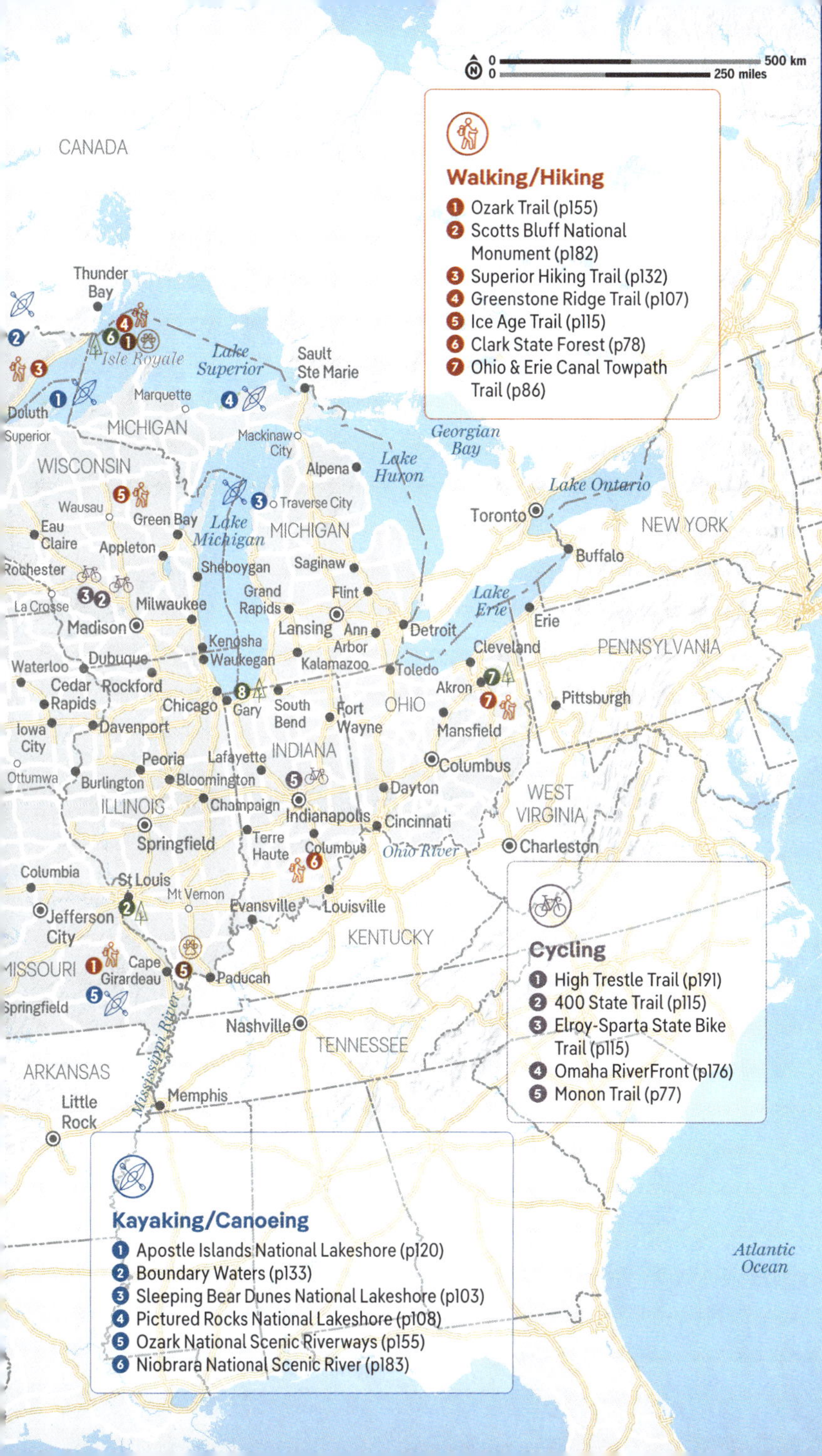
0 500 km
0 250 miles
Walking/Hiking
1 Ozark Trail (p155)
2 Scotts Bluff National Monument (p182)
3 Superior Hiking Trail (p132)
4 Greenstone Ridge Trail (p107)
5 Ice Age Trail (p115)
6 Clark State Forest (p78)
7 Ohio & Erie Canal Towpath Trail (p86)
Cycling
1 High Trestle Trail (p191)
2 400 State Trail (p115)
3 Elroy-Sparta State Bike Trail (p115)
4 Omaha RiverFront (p176)
5 Monon Trail (p77)
Kayaking/Canoeing
1 Apostle Islands National Lakeshore (p120)
2 Boundary Waters (p133)
3 Sleeping Bear Dunes National Lakeshore (p103)
4 Pictured Rocks National Lakeshore (p108)
5 Ozark National Scenic Riverways (p155)
6 Niobrara National Scenic River (p183)
CANADA
Thunder Bay
Isle Royale
Lake Superior
Sault Ste Marie
Duluth
Superior
Marquette
MICHIGAN
Mackinaw City
Georgian Bay
Lake Huron
Alpena
WISCONSIN
Wausau
Green Bay
Traverse City
Lake Michigan
MICHIGAN
Lake Ontario
Toronto
NEW YORK
Buffalo
Eau Claire
Appleton
Sheboygan
Saginaw
Flint
Rochester
La Crosse
Milwaukee
Grand Rapids
Lansing
Ann Arbor
Detroit
Lake Erie
Erie
Madison
Kenosha
Waukegan
Kalamazoo
Toledo
Cleveland
PENNSYLVANIA
Waterloo
Dubuque
Cedar Rapids
Rockford
Chicago
Gary
South Bend
Fort Wayne
OHIO
Akron
Pittsburgh
Mansfield
Iowa City
Davenport
Ottumwa
Burlington
Peoria
Lafayette
INDIANA
Columbus
Bloomington
Dayton
WEST VIRGINIA
ILLINOIS
Champaign
Indianapolis
Cincinnati
Springfield
Terre Haute
Columbus
Ohio River
Charleston
Columbia
St Louis
Mt Vernon
Evansville
Louisville
Jefferson City
KENTUCKY
MISSOURI
Cape Girardeau
Paducah
Springfield
Mississippi River
Nashville
TENNESSEE
ARKANSAS
Memphis
Little Rock
Atlantic Ocean

MIDWEST USA

THE GUIDE

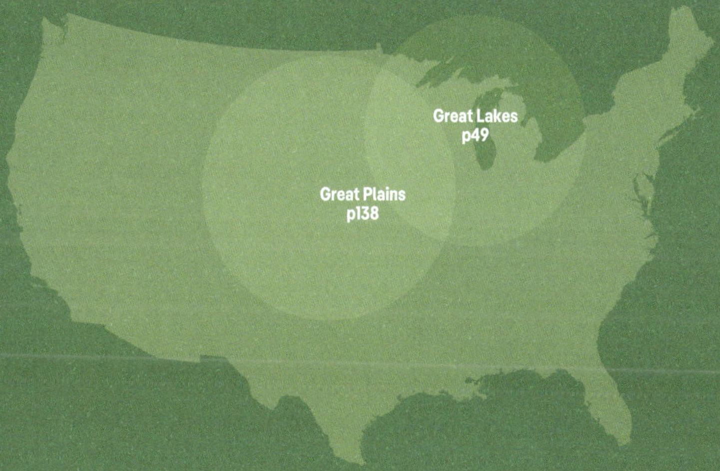

Chapters in this section are organised by hubs and their surrounding areas. We see the hub as your base in the destination, where you'll find unique experiences, local insights, insider tips and expert recommendations. It's also your gateway to the surrounding area, where you'll see what and how much you can do from there.

Custer State Park (p209), South Dakota

MARYGAVANPHOTOS/SHUTTERSTOCK

BO SHEN/GETTY IMAGES

For places to stay in Great Lakes, see p136

Above: Pictured Rocks National Lakeshore (p108); Right: Chicago (p54)

THE MAIN AREAS

CHICAGO
Art, architecture and chowhounds' playground.
p54

ILLINOIS
Land of Lincoln, Wright and Route 66.
p67

INDIANA
Race cars and towering sands.
p74

OHIO
From big cities to Amish villages.
p83

Written and curated by
Karla Zimmerman and Ann Babe

Great Lakes

OVERLOOKED BEAUTY IN THE USA'S HEARTLAND

Unspoiled, uncrowded national parks mix it up with cool cultured cities and pie-baking small towns.

Here we are: the middle of the country. No mountains. No oceans. Flyover territory, right?

Don't be fooled by all the corn. Behind it lurks surfing beaches and Tibetan temples, car-free islands and the green-draped night lights of the aurora borealis. The Great Lakes takes its knocks for being middle-of-nowhere boring, so consider the moose-filled wilderness areas and Hemingway, Dylan and Vonnegut sites to be its little secret.

Roll call for the region's cities starts with Chicago, which unfurls what is arguably the country's mightiest skyline. Milwaukee keeps the beer-and-Harley flame burning, while Minneapolis shines a hip beacon out over the fields. And Detroit rocks, plain and simple.

The Great Lakes themselves are huge, like inland seas, with beaches, dunes, resort towns and lighthouse-dotted scenery. Dairy farms and fruit orchards blanket the region, meaning fresh pie and ice cream aplenty. And when the scenery does flatten out? There's always a goofball roadside attraction, such as the Spam Museum or the world's biggest ball of twine, to revive imaginations.

Most visitors come in summer when the weather is fine for hiking, biking, canoeing and kayaking in the local lakes and forests. Snowmobiling and cross-country skiing take over in the butt-freezing winter (as do eating and drinking in warm taverns). Whatever the season, a true slice of America awaits in the heartland.

DMITRY ZINOVYEV/SHUTTERSTOCK

Minnesota, p122

Hiking, paddling and other outdoor adventures abound, from the moose-teeming northern wilderness to urban areas like Minneapolis and Duluth.

Wisconsin, p110

Beyond the beery cities lies a vast expanse of shimmering islands, lakefront beaches, forested trails and good-time bashes to help celebrate it all.

Illinois, p67

An ancient city, moss-draped swamp and architecture hotbed emerge from the farmland, along with presidential sites and Route 66 corn dogs and kitsch.

CAR

You'll need your own wheels to travel with ease. There's no other way to get to smaller towns and far-flung parks. Even between major cities, trains and buses are scant. And within cities (except Chicago) public transportation is patchy.

TRAIN

Amtrak trains run in the region, but with fairly limited service. Chicago is the hub. Trains go to Milwaukee (seven daily), Minneapolis (two daily), Detroit (three daily), Cleveland (one daily) and Indianapolis (three per week).

FERRY

Two car ferries can save time when driving around Lake Michigan. The *Lake Express* goes between Milwaukee, WI, and Muskegon, MI, in 2½ hours. The SS *Badger* goes between Manitowoc, WI, and Ludington, MI, in four hours.

Find Your Way

The region is vast, around 1000 miles across from east to west. We've picked the places that capture the Great Lakes' down-to-earth culture and quietly sublime landscapes and presented them here state by state.

Michigan, p94

With four of the five Great Lakes kissing its shores, Michigan has beaches and sand dunes galore, plus the history-rich city of Detroit.

Chicago, p54

The heart of the Great Lakes beats in this cloud-scraping metropolis, a cultural stew of art, nightlife and star restaurants with laid-back style.

Ohio, p83

Vibrant cities mix it up with horse-and-buggy Amish communities, moonshine-making hill towns, party islands and a mist-threaded national park.

Indiana, p74

A trek over sand dunes and a hike through the 'Little Smoky Mountains' are among the unexpected pleasures in this state known for car culture.

Plan Your Time

Factor long distances into your planning. For instance, driving from Cleveland to Minneapolis (east to west across the region) is an 11-hour journey on the Interstate. Rural highways add even more to travel times.

ANTHONY GEORGE VISUALS/SHUTTERSTOCK

Garden of the Gods (p73)

Great Lakes Weekend

You can swoop in for a few days and explore one of the cool Great Lakes cities. Chicago is the obvious choice to walk around (and ride the clackety L trains) and take in the **art** (p55), **architecture** (p57), **blues clubs** (p61) and very large **pizza** (p54). Tack on trips to **Wrigley Field** (p61) and an **improv comedy club** (p61), too. Detroit is another great candidate, where you can check out the **public art** (p95), art-deco **architecture** (p98), jazz and **Motown sounds** (p97) and **car-making history** (p99) with a foray to nearby Dearborn. Minneapolis also gives a solid feel for the region. Spend a couple of days enjoying its **rock clubs** (p127), **art museums** (p123) and **lake fun** (p127), along with jaunts to historic Twin City, **St Paul** (p128) and **Prince's pad** (p128) in the suburbs.

Seasonal Highlights

Whenever you visit, the Great Lakes region is having a party somewhere. Music festivals, food fairs, cultural bashes and snow carnivals fill the calendar.

JANUARY

It's cold and snowy, but that doesn't stop locals from donning parkas and heading out to snowmobile, cross-country ski, curl and party at outdoor events, such as the **St Paul Winter Carnival** (p127).

MARCH

St Patrick's Day celebrations make merry in Cleveland, Detroit, Milwaukee and especially Chicago (p54), which famously dyes its river green. Bundle up, because it's usually still cold outside for these shenanigans.

MAY

As the weather warms, wildflowers start to bloom. Indiana Dunes bursts with lupines, mayapples and many more, while Holland explodes in color at its **Tulip Time** (p104) festival.

Four Days to Travel Around

With four days, you can add some outdoor action. Chicago is close to beachy, bird-filled **Indiana Dunes National Park** (p79) and to the **Lake Michigan Shore Wine Trail** (p105) vineyards in southwestern Michigan. Detroit is within range of the soaring sands and blue waters at **Sleeping Bear Dunes National Lakeshore** (p103). Minneapolis is not too far from the wolf-howling wilderness of the **Boundary Waters** (p133) and to the waterfall-laden parks along **Hwy 61** (p131). Cleveland is a stone's throw from time-warped communities in Ohio's **Amish Country** (p91), where horse-drawn buggies rule the roads, and from the misty woods of **Cuyahoga Valley National Park** (p86).

A Weeklong Stay

A week lets you dig deeper into the area. You can combine a couple of cities and their surrounding sights, or strike out for further-flung regions. Michigan's Upper Peninsula takes you into the sparsely populated northern forest where mountain bikers hang out in **Marquette** (p109), and kayakers paddle at **Pictured Rocks National Lakeshore** (p108). A trip in the south along the Ohio River can include **Cincinnati's Brewing Heritage Trail** (p87), southern Indiana's caves and **scenic river towns** (p81) and southern Illinois' rugged **Shawnee Hills** (p73). To really get away from it all, remote **Voyageurs National Park** (p134) and **Isle Royale National Park** (p107) are among the least-visited wilderness areas in the country, where stars, moose, peace and quiet thrive.

JUNE

By mid-month the region is in full swing. It's finally warm, beer gardens hop, beaches splash, and parties such **Summerfest** (p113) rock most weekends.

JULY

The Great Lakes slowly get warm enough to swim in without teeth chattering. Blueberries and peaches are ready to pick, while the **National Cherry Festival** (p104) celebrates Michigan's favorite fruit.

SEPTEMBER

Peak season winds down in the region. But the coolness in the air also means Oktoberfest celebrations are on tap in cities like Columbus and Milwaukee. Cincinnati's **Oktoberfest** (p88) is the nation's biggest.

OCTOBER

Road trips to see fall colors are a big to-do. Hot spots include Door County, Hwy 61, Brown County and the Shawnee Hills. Bountiful harvests mean fresh apples, pumpkins and corn at markets.

Chicago

VISIONARY ARCHITECTURE | LAKEFRONT ALLURE | MUSIC SCENE

GETTING AROUND

The L (a system of elevated and subway trains) is the best way to travel around Chicago. Its eight color-coded lines are easy to use and get you to most sights and neighborhoods. An unlimited-ride day pass costs $5. Buy it at any L station or via the Ventra app *(ventrachicago.com)*, which also is useful for showing train times. Driving can be tough due to heavy traffic and scarce (and expensive) parking.

TOP TIP

Advance bookings are wise, especially during weekends. Most restaurants take reservations via their websites using Tock, OpenTable or Resy. For museums, buying tickets online in advance can often provide cost savings over same-day purchases.

Chicago is the star of the Great Lakes, a big, teeming, tall-skyscraper buzz of energy. While it is the USA's third-largest city, home to 2.7 million people, its low-key cultured awesomeness tends to fly under the radar. It doesn't brag about its star art collections or reasonably priced food scene that rivals the coasts in Michelin stars. It doesn't gloat over its trendsetting architecture and blow-the-roof-off bands on stages nightly. Its sand-and-surf beaches pop up with typical Midwestern modesty. Which is why so many visitors find the city a surprise – an urbane, multicultural metropolis for all.

The top sights are downtown, around the area known as the Loop. But you'll want to head out into further-flung neighborhoods for the best eating and drinking. Great districts to scope include Wicker Park, Pilsen, Logan Square and Andersonville – all jam-packed with inventive storefront restaurants – and the West Loop, where the buzziest dining venues huddle.

Get a Hefty Slice

MAP P60

Try deep-dish pizza

Chicago's foremost food is deep-dish pizza, a hulking mass of crust that rises two inches above the plate and cradles a molten pile of toppings. Try it at **Lou Malnati's** *(loumalnatis.com)*, which lays claim to inventing the cheesy behemoth. **Giordano's** *(giordanos.com)* makes 'stuffed' pizza: a bigger, doughier version of deep dish. A third version is pan pizza, similar to deep dish, but the crust is baked differently and has a ring of crisp, caramelized cheese. **Pequod's Pizza** *(pequodspizza.com)* makes a mighty one.

One piece is practically a meal wherever you go. Expect to wait 40 minutes or so for the hefty pies to cook.

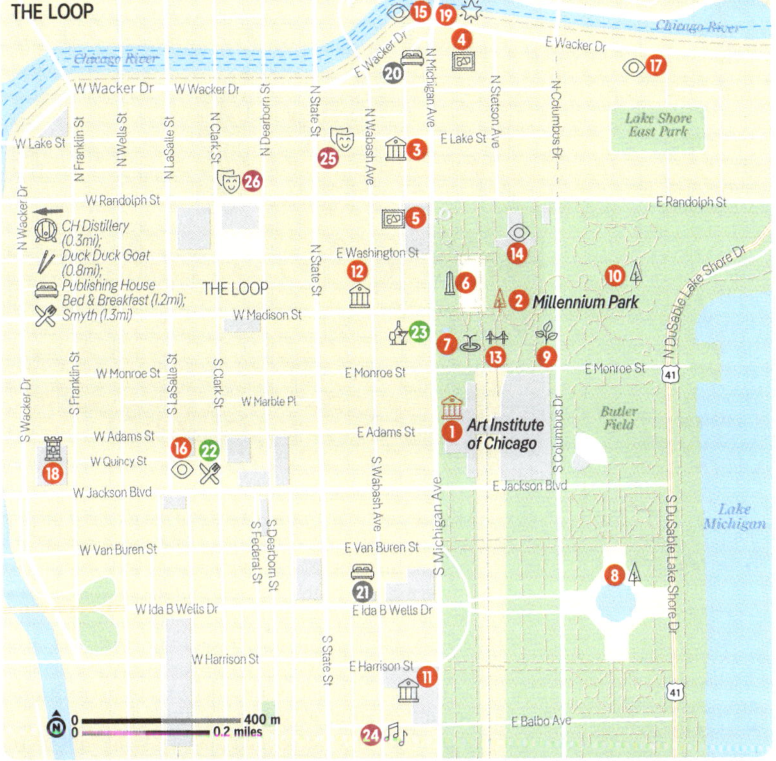

HIGHLIGHTS
1 Art Institute of Chicago
2 Millennium Park

SIGHTS
3 American Writers Museum
4 Chicago Architecture Center
5 Chicago Cultural Center
6 Cloud Gate
7 Crown Fountain
8 Grant Park
9 Lurie Garden
10 Maggie Daley Park
11 Museum of Contemporary Photography
12 Museum of Illusions
13 Nichols Bridgeway
14 Pritzker Pavilion
15 Riverwalk
16 Rookery
17 St Regis Chicago
18 Willis Tower

ACTIVITIES
19 Chicago Architecture Center First Lady River Cruise

SLEEPING
20 Hampton Inn Chicago Downtown/N Loop
21 HI-Chicago

EATING
22 Native Foods

DRINKING & NIGHTLIFE
23 Cindy's

ENTERTAINMENT
24 Buddy Guy's Legends
25 Chicago Theatre
26 Goodman Theatre

Explore the Art Institute's Masterpieces MAP P55

Impressionist paintings star

Allocate at least a few hours to wander through the **Art Institute of Chicago** *(artic.edu; adult/child $32/free)*, the USA's second-largest art museum. The main action happens on the 2nd floor. Stand in awe like Ferris Bueller in front of Georges Seurat's *A Sunday Afternoon on the Island of La Grande Jatte* (Gallery 240). In the adjoining rooms see color-swirled

BEST FAR-FLUNG & OVERLOOKED MUSEUMS

Griffin Museum of Science & Industry: Check out the submarine, coal mine and other mind-blowers at the Western Hemisphere's largest science museum.

Museum of Contemporary Art: The Art Institute's brash, rebellious challenger has a collection that always pushes boundaries.

Museum of Illusions: See your head on a platter and walk on walls at this kid-friendly, date-night favorite.

American Writers Museum: Bibliophiles will have a grand time at the word waterfall, typewriters, book lounge and other hands-on exhibits.

Insect Asylum: Wonderfully offbeat collection of vintage taxidermy and insect aquariums, plus yoga classes surrounded by snakes.

THOMAS BARRAT/SHUTTERSTOCK

canvases by Monet, Renoir and Van Gogh. It takes a while to get through the impressionist and postimpressionist paintings – there are more here than anywhere outside of France. Nearby, Edward Hopper's lonely, neon-lit diner in *Nighthawks* (Gallery 262) and Grant Wood's stern-faced couple in *American Gothic* (Gallery 263) hang in side-by-side galleries.

To take a break from crowds, stroll downstairs to the Thorne Miniature Rooms (Lower Level, Gallery 11) to peer into 68 teeny-tiny, dollhouse-like interiors.

Then head to the light-drenched Modern Wing and up to the 3rd floor to gape at the blue, elongated figure of Pablo Picasso's *The Old Guitarist* (Gallery 391). From here the pedestrian-only **Nichols Bridgeway** arches over into Millennium Park, a fine add-on experience before or after your Art Institute jaunt.

Art by Day, Music by Night

MAP P55

Play in Millennium Park

Located downtown next to the Art Institute, **Millennium Park** *(millenniumpark.org; admission free)* has abundant free and arty sights. The mega draw is **Cloud Gate** – aka the Bean – Anish Kapoor's 110-ton, mirror-smooth sculpture. Go ahead: walk right up to it, feel it, ponder the skyline

EATING IN CHICAGO: LEGENDARY BITES

MAPS P58, P60

Mr Beef: No-frills spot that cooks the spicy, drippy Italian beef sandwich made famous in the TV show *The Bear*. *10am-4pm Mon-Sat* $

Al's #1 Italian Beef: Another longstanding Italian beef purveyor, where queues can be shorter than Mr Beef. *10:30am-midnight Mon-Sat, to 8pm Sun* $

Wieners Circle: Chicago-style hot dogs (with onions, tomatoes, pickle, relish) in a raucous late-night ambience. *11am-2am Sun-Thu, to 4am Fri & Sat* $

Billy Goat Tavern: Mythic subterranean joint for 'cheezborgers,' immortalized in a *Saturday Night Live* skit. *hours vary* $

Lurie Garden

reflection and snap a picture. Then mosey onward to Jaume Plensa's **Crown Fountain**. Its two glass-block towers have video images of Chicagoans spouting water, gargoyle-style. On hot days, it's like a water park when everyone jumps in to cool down. Kids, especially, love it.

For a peaceful patch away from the crowd, seek out the **Lurie Garden**, abloom with prairie flowers. A little river runs through it, where folks kick off their shoes and dangle their feet.

Stay until evening and you might see a Nigerian juju band or a dream pop trio at **Pritzker Pavilion**, the swooping silver band shell designed by architect Frank Gehry. Free concerts take place most nights in summer. For all shows, but especially those by the Grant Park Orchestra, folks bring blankets, food, wine and beer. It's a summer ritual, as the sun dips, corks pop and gorgeous music fills the twilight air. Allow extra time to get in for evening events, as all visitors must go through a security/bag check.

MORE GREAT PARKS

Lincoln Park: Join locals on the running paths, athletic fields and beaches in Chicago's largest green space.

Grant Park: Grassy downtown sprawl dotted by spectacular Buckingham Fountain, which performs an hourly water show.

Northerly Island: Stroll or cycle around this prairie-like refuge, with great skyline views, floating alongside the Museum Campus.

Alfred Caldwell Lily Pool: Enchanting oasis of water lilies and dragonflies that feels like you've stumbled into Monet's Giverny garden.

Montrose Point Bird Sanctuary: Beachside woods known as the Magic Hedge for the 300 bird species that fly through here.

Soak up Chicago's Architecture

MAP P55

Hop on a boat tour, then roam the Riverwalk

Follow the crowds to the docks beneath Michigan Ave, at the north end of the Loop, and climb aboard the **Chicago Architecture Center's First Lady** *(architecture.org; from $56)*. Yes, it's touristy, but it's also marvelous. Grab a seat on deck and look up as you glide under stunning skyscrapers. Docents' design lessons carry on the breeze, so you'll know your beaux arts from international style by journey's end. The boat cruises along the Chicago River for 90 minutes.

Afterward, building buffs can add to their knowledge by ascending to street level and browsing inside the **Chicago Architecture Center**, where

GET YOUR KICKS ON ROUTE 66

A sign across the street from the Art Institute announces the beginning of **Route 66** (p72), which makes a fun road trip through Illinois.

LINCOLN PARK & OLD TOWN

SIGHTS
1 Alfred Caldwell Lily Pool
2 Lincoln Park
3 Lincoln Park Zoo
4 North Avenue Beach
5 Peggy Notebaert Nature Museum

EATING
6 Galit
7 Wieners Circle

DRINKING & NIGHTLIFE
8 Old Town Ale House

ENTERTAINMENT
9 iO Theater
10 Kingston Mines
11 Second City
12 Steppenwolf Theatre

EATING IN CHICAGO: OUR PICKS

MAPS P55, P62, P65

mfk: Spanish dishes and sunny cocktails in a teeny, romantic space that feels like the seaside in Spain. *5-9:30pm Mon-Sat, 4-8:30pm Sun* $$$

Tortello: Bowls of supreme comfort at this cute storefront: fresh pasta made before your eyes. *4:30-9pm Mon, from 11:30am Tue-Thu, from 8am Fri-Sun* $$

Duck Duck Goat: Chinese-inspired dim sum, mains and cocktails from star chef Stephanie Izard. *4:30-10pm Mon-Thu, to 11pm Fri & Sat, 11am-3pm Sat & Sun* $$

Loaf Lounge: Small, sunny bakery-cafe where locals clamor for breakfast sandwiches and the choc cake made famous in *The Bear*. *8am-4pm Wed-Mon* $

exhibits provide a quick primer on local structures and visionaries. Excellent walking tours that explore by theme (art deco, women architects) also depart from here.

Or stay by the water and amble along the 1.25-mile long **Riverwalk** *(chicagoriverwalk.us)*, chock-full of alfresco bars and restaurants from which you can gaze out and admire Chicago's built environment.

Get High in the Sky

MAP P55

Views from the top observatories

For superlative-seekers, **Willis Tower** *(theskydeck.com; adult/child from $32/24)* is it: Chicago's tallest (and the USA's second-tallest) skyscraper, rising 1450ft into the heavens. On the 103rd-floor Skydeck, glass-floored ledges jut out in midair, giving a knee-buckling perspective straight down. Before ascending, you'll make your way through fun interactive exhibits about Chicago, so snap a photo with the giant deep-dish pizza and stand on the replica Second City stage. Timed tickets are available online.

You'll find **360 Chicago** *(360chicago.com; adult/child from $30/20)* on the 94th floor of 875 N Michigan Ave (formerly known as the John Hancock Center). Set next to Lake Michigan, it provides unfettered panoramic vistas. The hair-raiser here is TILT *($9)*, a set of floor-to-ceiling windows that you stand in as they move and tip out over the ground. Nighttime views are particularly impressive, especially during the fireworks shows at nearby Navy Pier.

Navy Pier's Crowd-Pleasers

MAP P60

Ferris wheel, fireworks and views

Amble out on half-mile-long **Navy Pier** *(navypier.org; free)* and a carnival's worth of amusements vie for your attention, from the cloud-brushing **Centennial Wheel** *(adult/child $20/18)* to the horse-bobbing carousel *($6)*, ice-cream shops and margarita-slinging beer gardens. Then again, you can always just promenade along the dock's perimeter and enjoy the cool breezes and stellar skyline views. Crowds amass in summer for the fireworks show on Wednesday and Saturday nights.

Polk Bros Park, by the pier's entrance, has performance lawns for free concerts and movies. Competing tour boats depart from the pier's southern side. Set sail on **Windy** *(lakeshoresail.com; adult/child $49/34)*, a tall-masted

BEST ARCHITECTURE ICONS

Marina City: The twin corncob towers were completed in 1968 and look like something from a space-age *Jetsons* cartoon.

Tribune Tower: The neo-Gothic cloud-poker is inlaid with stones from the Taj Mahal, Great Pyramid, Parthenon and more.

Wrigley Building: Its shimmering white terracotta, French Renaissance details and famous clockface are the stuff of postcards.

St Regis Chicago: Look up at the city's third-tallest tower to see the 'blow-through floor' that reduces sway in the blue-glass skyscraper.

Rookery: Looks hulking and fortresslike outside, but it's light and airy inside, thanks to Frank Lloyd Wright's atrium overhaul.

DRINKING IN CHICAGO: OUR PICKS

MAPS P55, P58, P65

Old Town Ale House: Unpretentious neighborhood favorite for jovial late nights near the the Second City comedy club. *3pm-4am*

Cindy's: Best rooftop in town. Set on the 13th floor of the Chicago Athletic Association Hotel, it unfurls awesome park and lake vistas. *hours vary*

Goose Island Taproom: Chicago's first craft brewer (now Anheuser-Busch owned) retains its indie spirit here. *noon-8pm Wed, Thu & Sun, to 10pm Fri & Sat*

CH Distillery: Polished facility that makes vodka, aquavit, amaro and Malört (Chicago's local liquor that's famous for tasting awful). *hours vary*

- **SIGHTS**
  - 1 360 Chicago
  - 2 Centennial Wheel
  - 3 Chicago Children's Museum
  - 4 Marina City
  - 5 Museum of Contemporary Art
  - 6 Navy Pier
  - 7 Oak Street Beach
  - 8 Polk Bros Park
  - 9 theMart
  - 10 Tribune Tower
  - 11 Wrigley Building
- **ACTIVITIES**
  - 12 Windy
- **SLEEPING**
  - 13 Acme Hotel
- **EATING**
  - 14 Al's #1 Italian Beef
  - 15 Billy Goat Tavern
  - 16 Giordano's
  - 17 Lou Malnati's
  - 18 Mr Beef
- **DRINKING & NIGHTLIFE**
  - 19 Library at Gilt Bar
  - 20 Three Dots & A Dash
- **SHOPPING**
  - 21 Harry Potter Shop
- **TRANSPORT**
  - 22 Shoreline Water Taxi to Museum Campus

schooner, or hop on the **Shoreline Water Taxi** *(shorelinesightseeing.com; adult/child $16/10)* to the Museum Campus.

Feel the Blues

MAPS P55, P58

Drop by an authentic club

The electric blues is Chicago's claim to music fame. When Muddy Waters and friends plugged their guitars into amplifiers here in the 1940s, sound reached new decibel levels. Chicago became the hub for the groundbreaking genre.

EATING IN CHICAGO: MICHELIN-STARRED

MAPS P55, P58, P65, P66

Smyth: Homey spot with three well-earned stars for creative, perfectly executed seafood, seasonal produce and sweets. *5-9pm Tue-Sat* **$$$**

Galit: Lively Middle Eastern restaurant winning raves for its cocktails and tasting menu made for sharing. *5-9pm Tue-Thu, to 9:30pm Fri & Sat* **$$$**

Moody Tongue: Brewery with beers such as Shaved Black Truffle Lager that pair perfectly with New American plates. *5-10pm Wed-Sat* **$$**

Kasama: Walk-in Filipino bakery by day; 13-course, modern Filipino tasting menu by night. *bakery 9am-3pm Wed-Sun, dinner Thu-Sun* **$$$**

The nation's best players trade licks at **Buddy Guy's Legends** *(buddyguy.com; $15-25)*, just south of downtown. The memorabilia-filled room is relatively small, putting you close to the string-benders on stage. Free, all-ages acoustic shows take place at dinner time.

In Lincoln Park, **Kingston Mines** *(kingstonmines.com)* is similarly priced and a bit larger, with two stages where blues bands wail into the wee hours. More crackling grooves fill the air at **Rosa's Lounge** *(rosaslounge.com)*, a real-deal little club with top local players and serious fans who dance the night away. It's further flung in Logan Square.

Improv Night Out

MAPS P58, P65

Laugh-out-loud comedy

Improv comedy began in Chicago, and the city remains a hub for the genre. Seeing a show is raucous fun, as performers create sketches based on suggestions (often alcohol fueled) that the audience shouts out. Polished ensembles riff on politics and pop culture nightly at **Second City** *(secondcity.com; from $41)*, the most famous venue. **iO Theater** *(ioimprov.com; from $30)* is another established spot, where the Improvised Shakespeare Company ad-libs wacky plays in Elizabethan verse. **Den Theatre** *(thedentheatre.com; tickets from $20)* is a relative newcomer, with fringy, offbeat shows. iO and Den typically have more availability. Book all tickets in advance.

Catch a Game at Wrigley Field

MAP P62

The Cubs' historic ballpark

About 5 miles north of downtown, **Wrigley Field** *(cubs.com; around $60)* pops up smack in the middle of a residential neighborhood – aka Wrigleyville – surrounded on all sides by houses, rollicking bars and even a fire station. The ballpark charms with its lived-in environs, as well as its 1914 old-school features, like the hand-turned scoreboard, ivy-covered outfield walls and distinctive neon entrance sign. Seeing a game here, amid diehard Cubs fans, is a blast.

Gates open 1½ hours before the game's start time. It's good to arrive an hour or so early to browse around inside. Check out the Walk of Fame behind the bleachers in right field to learn about Cubs greats through the ages. Watch players take batting practice. Grab a hot dog and Old Style beer: the quintessential Wrigley foods.

Outside, the grassy plaza just north of the main entrance is **Gallagher Way**. On nongame days it's open to the public

BEST EXPERIENCES FOR KIDS

Lincoln Park Zoo: Watch chimpanzees swing, lions roar and penguins waddle, then feed chickens at the on-site farm, all for free.

Peggy Notebaert Nature Museum: Underrated spot to immerse in gentle thrills, such as the butterfly haven, frog marsh and wilderness walk.

Harry Potter Shop: Buy a wand or belly up to the Butterbeer Bar in this theatrical store that steeps you in the wizard's world.

Chicago Children's Museum: Excavate dinosaur bones, climb a ropey schooner and make art, then enjoy the carnival rides on surrounding Navy Pier.

Maggie Daley Park: Take your pick among the free playgrounds, including an enchanted forest to wander through, and a ship to pretend-sail.

DRINKING IN CHICAGO: BEST COCKTAILS

MAPS P60, P63

Three Dots & a Dash: Fun tiki bar with rum flights and its own speakeasy, the Bamboo Room. *4pm-midnight Sun-Wed, to 1am Thu & Fri, 2pm-1am Sat*

Matchbox: Teeny corner bar in West Town pouring martinis, gimlets, pisco sours and other classic drinks since 1945. *3pm-2am*

Library at Gilt Bar: World-class libations with velvet booths, vintage art and speakeasy vibes. *4-10:30pm Sun-Thu, to 11pm Fri & Sat*

Nobody's Darling: Inclusive, off-the-beaten-path bar stirring cocktails so delicious they were named Beard Award finalists. *hours vary*

BEST ROCK & JAZZ CLUBS

Green Mill: Timeless jazz institution with velvet-cushioned booths where gangster Al Capone used to hang out.

Metro: Chicago's premier loud-rock club and a tastemaker for more than 40 years. Bands on the way up thrash first.

Salt Shed: Cool indoor/outdoor venue carved from the old Morton Salt factory, where edgy, genre-spanning artists play.

Hideout: Feels like a retro basement, but with alt-country and indie-pop bands twanging on the small stage under twinkling lights.

Empty Bottle: Scruffy standby that reigns supreme for nightly shows, ranging from indie rock to punk to psych-pop. Cheap beer!

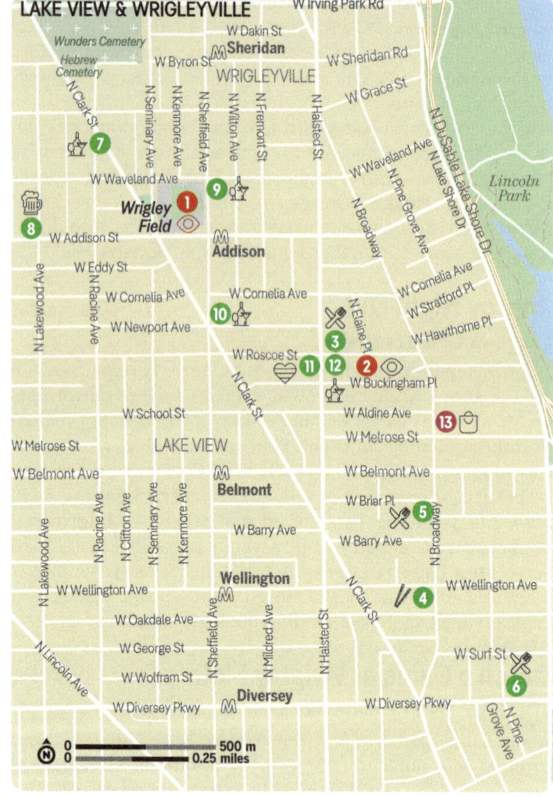

HIGHLIGHTS
1 Wrigley Field

SIGHTS
2 Northalsted

EATING
3 Chicago Diner
4 Crisp
5 Fancy Plants Cafe
6 mfk

DRINKING & NIGHTLIFE
7 GMan Tavern
8 Guthrie's Tavern
9 Murphy's Bleachers
10 Nisei Lounge
11 Roscoe's Tavern
12 Sidetrack

ENTERTAINMENT
see 7 Metro

SHOPPING
13 Unabridged Bookstore

DRINKING IN CHICAGO: TOP WRIGLEYVILLE WATERING HOLES

MAP P62

Nisei Lounge: Festive dive bar to try the Chicago Handshake (an Old Style beer and shot of Malört). *5pm-1:30am Mon-Thu, from 11:30am Fri-Sun*

Guthrie's Tavern: Neighborhood hangout with a glassed-in back porch, patio chairs and board games. *3pm-2am Mon-Fri, from 11am Sat & Sun*

Murphy's Bleachers: Lively, classic saloon steps from the entrance to Wrigley Field's bleacher seats. *11am-2am Mon-Thu, from 9:30am Fri-Sun*

GMan Tavern: Features cool vinyl tunes, eclectic beer and live music beloved by the rock-and-roll crowd. *3pm-2am Mon-Fri, from noon Sat & Sun*

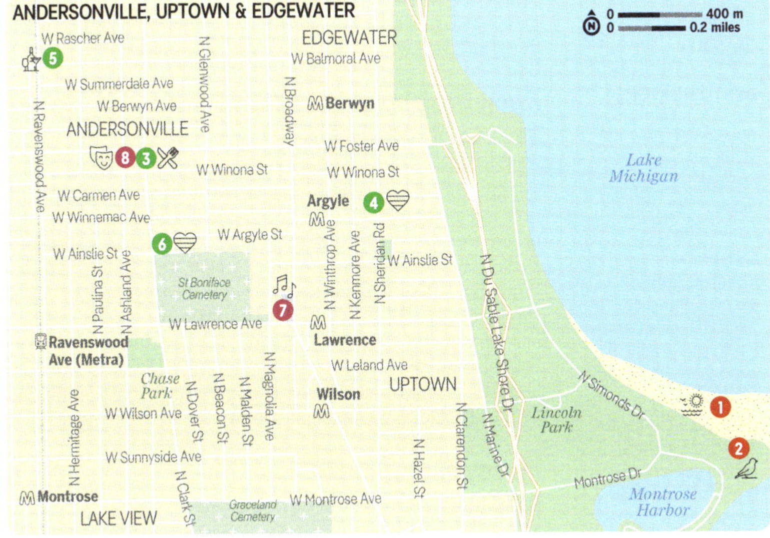

and hosts free movie nights and concerts. On game days it's a beer garden for ticket holders, and kids can run around or cool off in the splash pad.

Buy tickets at the Cubs' website or from online ticket broker StubHub *(stubhub.com)*. Upper Reserved Infield seats are usually pretty cheap. The bleachers are fun. Ninety-minute stadium tours *($30)* are also available most days in season.

SIGHTS
1 Montrose Beach
2 Montrose Point Bird Sanctuary

EATING
3 Hopleaf

DRINKING & NIGHTLIFE
4 Big Chicks
5 Nobody's Darling
6 SoFo Tap

ENTERTAINMENT
7 Green Mill
8 Neo-Futurist Theater

Northalsted Pride

MAP P62

Hot spots in Chicago's LGBTIQ+ hub

Northalsted – sometimes referred to as Boystown, its original name – lies along several blocks of N Halsted and Broadway streets, a short distance east of Wrigley Field. Rainbow crosswalks stripe the intersections, and rainbow pylons rise from the sidewalks. The pylons are part of the Legacy Walk, a mile-long outdoor museum that tells the stories of global LGBTIQ+ icons.

Halsted St holds several thumping bars, as well as thrift and fetish shops to add sass to one's wardrobe. On Broadway, **Unabridged Bookstore** *(unabridgedbookstore.com)* is a community linchpin that stocks everything from gay parenting to queer spirituality titles.

DRINKING IN CHICAGO: BEST LGBTIQ+ BARS

MAPS P62, P63

Sidetrack: Community stalwart with thumping dance music for gay and straight crowds alike. *3pm-2am Mon-Fri, 1pm-3am Sat, noon-2am Sun*

Roscoe's Tavern: Casual bar in front, dance club in back and sun-splashed patio outdoors. *4pm-2am Sun-Thu, from noon Sat & Sun*

Big Chicks: Weekend DJs, a fun dance floor and art displays draw both men and women; cash only. *4pm-2am Mon-Fri, from 9am Sat & Sun*

SoFo Tap: Known for its dog-friendly patio, dartboards, karaoke and bear nights. *5pm-2am Mon-Thu, from 3pm Fri, from noon Sat & Sun*

BEST THEATERS

Check with Hot Tix *(hottix.org)* for discounted theater tickets to shows around the city.

Steppenwolf Theatre: Award-winning drama club of John Malkovich, Tracy Letts, Laurie Metcalf and other Hollywood stars.

Goodman Theatre: A crucible for new and classic dramas that often head to Broadway.

Chicago Theatre: Century-old stunner with an enormous glittering marquee that's an official city landmark and great for photos.

Chopin Theatre: This 1918 venue is full of vintage charm, hosting oddball, thought-provoking plays, concerts and literary events.

Neo-Futurist Theater: The hyper troupe makes a manic attempt to perform 30 original plays in 60 minutes.

To see the area at its peak, visit at night. The neighborhood mellows during the day when it's mostly about shopping (weekdays) and brunch (weekends).

Rock the Shops in Wicker Park

MAP P65

Stock up on stylish wares

A short distance northwest of downtown, the Wicker Park neighborhood brims with record shops, bookstores and vintage marts perfect for an afternoon trawl. Flick through bins of sad-core, post-rock and indie-tronica at **Reckless Records** *(reckless.com)*. Pick up a fringe jacket and Bionic Woman lunchbox at **Kokorokoko** *(kokorokokovintage.com)*. Browse the used tomes filling three floors at **Myopic Books** *(myopicbookstore.com)*. Loads of bars and dining venues pop up in between. Milwaukee Ave is the main vein, flanked by Blue Line L stations at Damen and Division. Wednesday through Saturday afternoon is the sweet spot when most shops are open.

Mosey Along the 606

MAP P65

Neighborhood trail above street level

The **606** *(the606.org)* is an urban-cool elevated path along a repurposed train track now dotted with trees, benches and artworks. Bike or stroll past factories, clattering L trains and locals' backyard affairs. It's great for a morning or afternoon escape.

The trail unfurls for 2.7 miles parallel to Bloomingdale Ave, with its eastern end on Ashland Ave (in Wicker Park), and its western end on Ridgeway Ave (in Humboldt Park). Access points pop up every quarter mile, so it's easy to get on or off the path. Bars and restaurants beckon at ground level.

Blue Line L stations at Western and Damen are within a quick walk. For those wanting to cycle, Divvy bikeshare stations are on Ashland Ave by the trail's eastern end and Milwaukee Ave near **Small Cheval** *(smallcheval.com)*, a festive little shack serving up burgers, fries, milkshakes and beers.

Museum Campus Marvels

MAP P66

Dinosaurs, sharks and asteroids await

Three top-draw museums line up in a row on a lakefront stretch just south of downtown. The mammoth **Field Museum** *(fieldmuseum.org; adult/child $30/23)* houses everything but the kitchen sink. The collection's rock star is Sue, the largest Tyrannosaurus rex yet discovered, who menaces

EATING IN CHICAGO: VEGETARIAN & VEGAN

MAPS P55, P62, P65

Native Foods: Cheery venue for vegan burgers, tacos, hot chicken and meatball sandwiches. *10:30am-8pm Mon-Sat, 11am-7pm Sun* $

Fancy Plants Cafe: Cute vegan spot for a carrot lox bagel, seitan sausage sandwich or smoked lentil lasagna. *8am-4pm* $

Handlebar: Bike-messenger hangout with veg and fish dishes, plus a great back patio for beers. *10am-midnight Mon-Fri, from 9am Sat & Sun* $$

Chicago Diner: Vegetarian comfort food stalwart with vintage red tables and booths. *11am-10pm Mon-Fri, from 10am Sat & Sun* $$

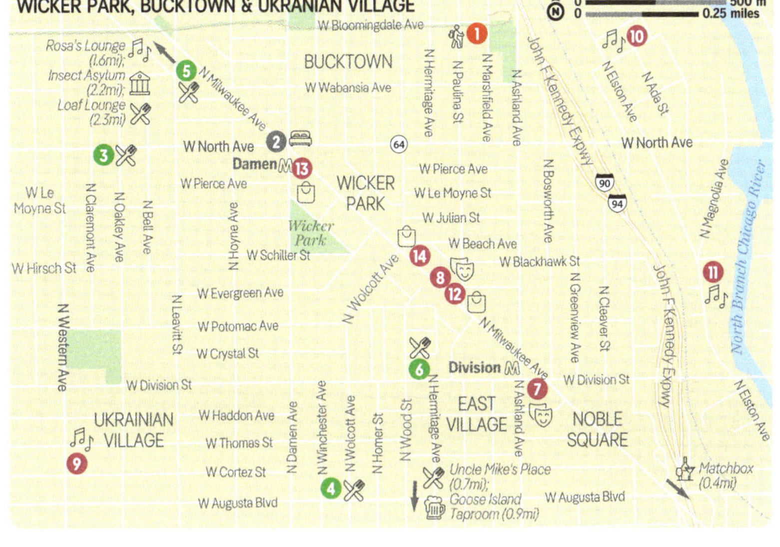

the 2nd floor with her toothy companions. Mummies, gemstones and taxidermy lions are also among the stash of 40 million artifacts.

Next door, the **Shedd Aquarium** *(sheddaquarium.org; adult/child from $39/29)* packs in families that come to gawp at the 32,000 aquatic creatures that live here, including sharks – separated from you by just 5in of Plexiglas – stingrays and rescued sea otters. Building renovations through to 2027 mean some galleries might be closed when you visit.

Space enthusiasts will get a big bang out of the **Adler Planetarium** *(adlerplanetarium.org; adult/child $25/13)* with its collection of sundials and the *Gemini 12* space capsule. To see all three museums in a day, start with Shedd, followed by Field and then Adler.

Cycle the Lakefront

Wind-in-your-hair ride

Lake Michigan edges the city from north to south. It's huge, a freshwater 'sea'; its frothy waves rippling over the horizon with no end in sight. The 18-mile Lakefront Trail is a beautiful route along the water, rolling by beaches, parks and harbors. It's split into separate lanes for walkers and cyclists. Pedaling the path is a blast, a great way to blend into the local scene.

BEST FREEBIES

Chicago Cultural Center: Pop in to see terrific art exhibitions, foreign films and the world's largest Tiffany glass dome.

Chicago Greeter: Have a local take you on a two- to four-hour walking tour; book at least two weeks in advance. *chicago greeter.com*

Art on the Mart: An ever-changing light show projected on a huge building by the Riverwalk each night.

Museum of Contemporary Photography: Small but top-tier venue for works by Henri Cartier-Bresson, Sally Mann, Ai Weiwei and others.

National Museum of Mexican Art: Politically charged paintings and folk art in Pilsen.

BEST BEACHES

Chicago has 22 free public beaches along 26 miles of Lake Michigan waterfront.

12th Street Beach: Small crescent next to the Museum Campus that somehow hides in plain sight and remains serene.

Montrose Beach: Kayak, bird-watch and lounge at the bar while sailboats glide by the dune-backed shore.

North Avenue Beach: Chicago's favorite party beach, with a bar, cafe, volleyball courts, and bicycle and kayak rentals.

Oak Street Beach: Sandy beach downtown for swimming and sunbathing in the shadow of skyscrapers.

Margaret T Burroughs Beach: Play all day at this fab strand with a boat harbor, fishing dock and watercraft rentals.

SIGHTS	5 National Museum of Mexican Art	**EATING**
1 12th Street Beach	6 Northerly Island	8 5 Rabanitos
2 Adler Planetarium	**ACTIVITIES**	**DRINKING & NIGHTLIFE**
3 Field Museum	7 Shedd Aquarium	9 Moody Tongue
4 Margaret T Burroughs Beach		

Get a bike from Divvy *(divvybikes.com; day pass $18)*. Be prepared for crowds on summer weekends, especially heading north, where there are more beaches.

EATING IN CHICAGO: AROUND THE WORLD

MAPS P62, P63, P65, P66

Crisp: Loud music, bright colors and picnic-style tables set the scene for Korean fried chicken and mixed vegetable bowls. *11:30am-9pm Tue-Sun* $

Uncle Mike's Place: Join construction workers, artsy youth and senior citizens chowing rice porridge and Spam at this fab Filipino breakfast diner. *6am-2pm* $$

5 Rabanitos: Unusual spice combinations and addictive salsa and mole make the dishes shine. *11am-9pm Mon-Fri, 9am-10pm Sat, 9am-9pm Sun* $$

Hopleaf: Cozy tavern for Belgian-style mussels, *frites* (fries) and beers from the 68 taps. *noon-11pm Sun-Thu, to midnight Fri & Sat* $$

Illinois

HISTORIC SITES | RURAL LANDSCAPES | WRIGHT DESIGNS

Outside of mighty Chicago, urbanity falls away fast and Illinois opens into a wide horizon of corn and soybean fields. Flat farmland covers three-quarters of the state, with the only real exception coming in the hilly northwest and knobby, bluff-strewn far south.

Road-tripping in Illinois turns up scattered shrines to local hero Abe Lincoln. Then there's Oak Park, the town with the most Frank Lloyd Wright-designed buildings of anywhere in the world. Historic Route 66 slices across the state, leaving a trail of corn dogs, pies and roadside oddities in its wake. Galena in the northwestern region delights with rolling hills and grazing horses near the Mississippi River (which forms most of Illinois' western boundary). Southern Illinois changes up the scene completely, with thick forests, wild rock formations and a cypress swamp for outdoor adventures.

Places

TOP TIP

People tend to forget that Illinois is an agricultural powerhouse. Farm stands are common along the roads in rural areas. Keep an eye out for peaches and apples in southern Illinois, apples in western Illinois, and pumpkins and sweet corn in northern and central Illinois.

Oak Park

See Wright buildings galore

The western Chicago suburb of Oak Park is a repository of famed architect Frank Lloyd Wright's early solo work. Wright lived here for two decades, from 1889 to 1909, and was only 22 years old when he built his Oak Park home, the first house he ever designed. Soon he was drawing up plans for several neighbors. Twenty-five Wright-devised buildings

GETTING AROUND

The main Interstates are I-90 and I-94 that head north to Wisconsin (tolls), I-55 that links Chicago to St Louis following historic Route 66 (no tolls), I-80 that goes east-west passing Chicago to the south (some tolls), and I-57 that runs from Chicago to southern Illinois (no tolls). Amtrak runs a handy train between downtown Chicago and downtown Springfield five times a day. Those trains roll onward to St Louis.

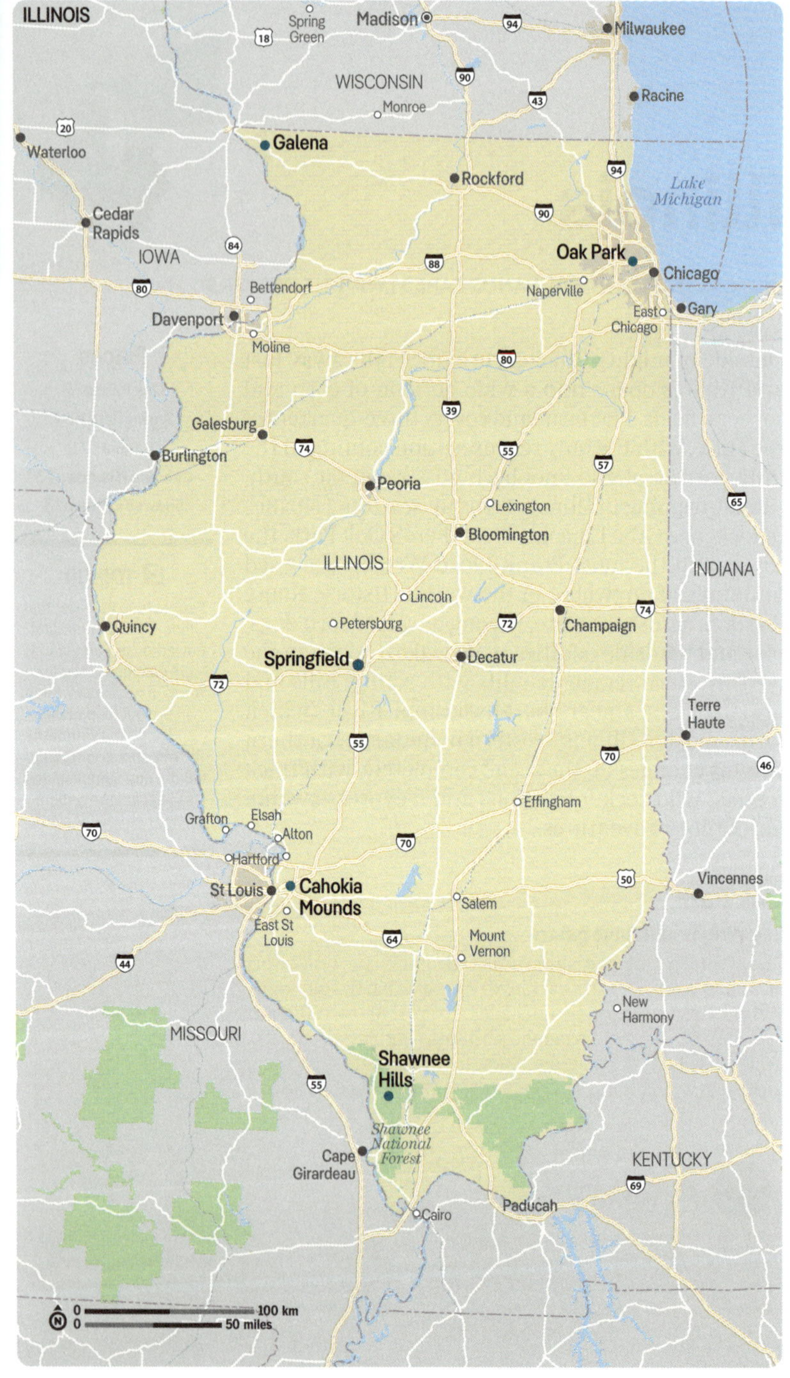
ILLINOIS
Spring Green
Madison
Milwaukee
WISCONSIN
Monroe
Racine
Waterloo
Galena
Rockford
Lake Michigan
Cedar Rapids
IOWA
Oak Park
Chicago
Bettendorf
Naperville
Davenport
East Chicago
Gary
Moline
Galesburg
Burlington
Peoria
Lexington
Bloomington
ILLINOIS
INDIANA
Lincoln
Quincy
Petersburg
Champaign
Springfield
Decatur
Terre Haute
Effingham
Grafton
Elsah
Alton
Hartford
St Louis
Cahokia Mounds
Vincennes
Salem
East St Louis
Mount Vernon
New Harmony
MISSOURI
Shawnee Hills
Shawnee National Forest
Cape Girardeau
KENTUCKY
Cairo
Paducah
0 100 km
0 50 miles

eventually popped up here, the largest concentration anywhere in the world.

The **Frank Lloyd Wright Home & Studio** *(flwright.org/tour/home-and-studio; tours $24)* is the main sight, accessible by guided tour only. It's best to book tickets online in advance. While walk-ups are welcome, slots tend to fill up. The hour-long walk-through reveals a fascinating place filled with original Wright-designed furniture and geometric details that made his Prairie-style architecture distinctive. Look for personal additions, such as the fireplace carved with his family motto: 'Truth is life.'

A half-mile away, Wright's 1908 **Unity Temple** *(flwright.org/explore/unity-temple; tours $18-20)* defies traditional ecclesiastical architecture. Like many of his buildings, the church's entrance is slightly hidden, leading visitors on what he called a 'path of discovery.' Inside, the sanctuary feels much warmer, splashed with sunshine-yellow walls and actual rays streaming in through the skylights.

Monday through Saturday mornings are the best time to visit and take in both sights. If driving, street parking is easy to find. Metra and L trains also have stations nearby.

Where Hemingway grew up

Frank Lloyd Wright wasn't the only influential artist in Oak Park at the turn of the century. Writer Ernest Hemingway grew up in the suburb. He was born in the 2nd-floor bedroom of a sprawling Queen Anne home on Oak Park Ave – a few blocks away from Wright's studio – in 1899. The house has been restored to look as it did then, with old family photos and frilly Victorian decor. Visits to the **Hemingway Birthplace** *(hemingwaybirthplace.com; adult/child $20/free)* are by hour-long guided tour only, offered Thursday through Saturday afternoons, as well as Saturday mornings.

In 1906, the family moved nearby to 600 N Kenilworth Ave. **Hemingway's Boyhood Home** is still a private residence, so you can't go inside, but a plaque marks the location.

Springfield

Follow in Abe Lincoln's footsteps

Illinois' small state capital has a serious obsession with Abraham Lincoln, who spent 24 years here as a young lawyer. A four-block neighborhood of old homes, gravel streets and wooden boardwalks near downtown has been preserved as the **Lincoln Home National Historic Site** *(nps.gov/liho;*

BEST ILLINOIS STATE PARKS

Starved Rock: Hike among 18 waterfall-filled canyons, each slicing through tree-covered, sandstone bluffs (north-central Illinois).

Mississippi Palisades: Hikers and rock-climbers love it, thanks to its Mississippi River–front real estate and dramatic limestone cliffs (northwest Illinois).

Matthiessen: Smaller and less crowded than nearby Starved Rock, but with similar scenery and sunflower fields (north-central Illinois).

White Pines Forest: Getaway to smell the pines, count the stars and stay in rustic log cabins (north-central Illinois).

Giant City: Popular for hiking and climbing amid the striking rock formations and towering trees (southern Illinois).

EATING & DRINKING IN OAK PARK: OUR PICKS

Spilt Milk: Excellent bakery for picking up a quiche, sandwich, scone or slice of creamy, flaky-crust pie. *8am-5pm Mon-Sat, to 2pm Sun* $

Hemmingway's Bistro: A few buildings south of Ernest's birthplace, this elegant spot serves French favorites. *11am-8:30pm* $$$

Citrine Cafe: Devour Mediterranean-influenced pastas, pizzas and seafood dishes, dreamed up by the Serbia-born owner. *hours vary* $$$

Kinslahger Brewing Company: Gorgeous taproom in a retro 1920s building where crisp lagers rule the taps. *4-10pm Wed-Fri, from 2pm Sat & Sun*

WRIGHT SIGHTS WALKABOUT

Gape at some of the 25 buildings Frank Lloyd Wright designed early in his career while living in Oak Park.

START	END	LENGTH
Frank Lloyd Wright Home & Studio	Unity Temple	0.75 miles; 45 minutes

Start at 1 **Frank Lloyd Wright Home & Studio** (p69), the only house you can go inside. (The others are privately owned and not accessible.) Head south on Forest Ave, where Wright-designed residences line both sides of the street. One of the most unusual is 2 **Nathan G Moore House** at 333 Forest Ave. In 1895, attorney Nathan Moore requested a home in Tudor Revival style, which Wright begrudgingly accepted as his first independent commission because he needed the money. Across the street at 318 Forest Ave, the 1902 3 **Arthur Heurtley House** looks much more classically Wright: a low roof, long horizontal lines and leaded glass windows.

Turn east on Elizabeth Ct to find 4 **Laura Gale House** (6 Elizabeth Ct) tucked away among mature trees. It seems modest, but Wright said the residence's cantilevered balconies were the 'progenitor of Fallingwater' in Pennsylvania, perhaps his most famous construction.

Backtrack to Forest Ave. Wright considered 5 **Frank W Thomas House** at 210 Forest Ave the first of his Prairie-style homes. Outside the gate of 6 **Austin Gardens**, a bust of Wright is carved from a boulder.

Continue south on Forest Ave until the intersection with Lake St and turn east. At the corner of Lake and Kenilworth is the hulking concrete block of Wright's 7 **Unity Temple** (p69).

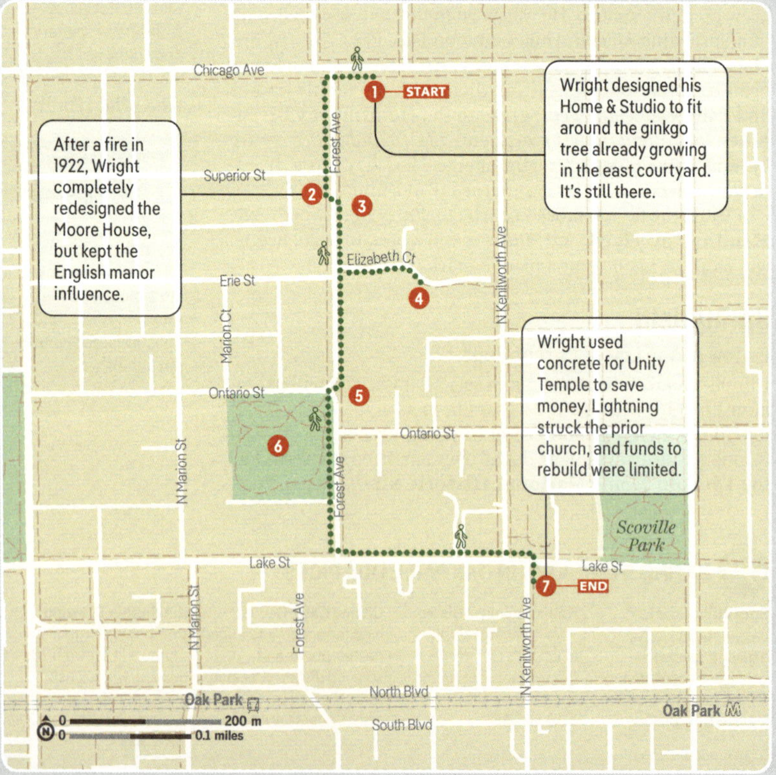

Chicago Ave
START
Wright designed his Home & Studio to fit around the ginkgo tree already growing in the east courtyard. It's still there.
After a fire in 1922, Wright completely redesigned the Moore House, but kept the English manor influence.
Superior St
Forest Ave
Elizabeth Ct
Erie St
Marion Ct
N Kenilworth Ave
Ontario St
Wright used concrete for Unity Temple to save money. Lightning struck the prior church, and funds to rebuild were limited.
N Marion St
Scoville Park
Lake St
END
North Blvd
Oak Park
South Blvd
0 200 m
0 0.1 miles

free). Begin at the park visitor center to get a ticket to enter Lincoln's 12-room abode on a 30-minute ranger-led tour. The house is the only one Lincoln ever owned, and 80% is original, looking as it did when Abe and wife Mary lived here from 1844 until they moved to the White House in 1861.

The modern **Abraham Lincoln Presidential Library & Museum** *(presidentlincoln.illinois.gov; adult/child $15/6)* contains the most complete Lincoln collection in the world. Real-deal artifacts, such as Abe's shaving mirror and presidential seal join whizbang exhibits and Disneyesque holograms that keep the kids agog.

Lincoln's immortal line 'A house divided against itself cannot stand...' was delivered in the **Old State Capitol** *(dnrhistoric.illinois.gov; free)* in the days before the Civil War. Detailed tours outline his early political life, including the dramatic Lincoln–Douglas debates in 1858.

After his assassination, Lincoln's body was returned to Springfield, where it lies today. **Lincoln's Tomb** *(dnrhistoric.illinois.gov; free)* sits in Oak Ridge Cemetery, 2 miles north of downtown. Mary and three of their four sons are buried here, too.

The sites – except the tomb – are in Springfield's center, so park once and walk. All are open daily, except the old capitol (closed Sunday and Monday).

Galena

Evocative mid-1800s boomtown

Tucked in Illinois' northwest corner near the Mississippi River, tiny Galena spreads across wooded hillsides amid rolling, barn-dotted farmland. The town was named after the lead sulfide found here, and was the location of the first mineral rush in the US in the 1820s. At its peak, Galena was the lead-mining capital of the world and had nearly as many residents as Chicago. It was the wealthiest city in Illinois, still reflected in the redbrick mansions in Greek Revival, Gothic Revival and Queen Anne styles that line the streets.

Galena was also home for a short time to Ulysses S Grant, the 18th US president and commanding general of the Union Army during the Civil War. Grant moved to Galena in 1860 to work in his father's leather goods store. When he came back to town following the Civil War, Galena residents gifted him with a two-story brick Italianate-style **home** *(granthome.org; adult/child $5/3),* fully furnished. However, he left for Washington, DC, shortly after and rarely returned. Today, the

WHAT IS A HORSESHOE SANDWICH?

It's on restaurant menus across Springfield but rarely seen anywhere else: the horseshoe sandwich. Loosen your belt before devouring this calorific concoction: an open-faced stack that consists of thickly sliced toasted bread topped with meat, French fries and a Welsh rarebit cheese sauce. It was first served at Springfield's Leland Hotel in 1928.

Hamburger is now the most common meat option for a horseshoe, but originally it was bone-in ham. Some places offer multiple meat options, including Angus beef, chicken breast, corned beef, buffalo chicken, ground lamb, pulled pork, brisket and even a veggie burger. Fortunately, many menus also offer it as a 'ponyshoe' (a smaller size).

EATING & DRINKING IN SPRINGFIELD: OUR PICKS

Luminary Kitchen & Provisions: Its weekly-changing, seasonal menus of New American plates are a treat. *4-9pm Wed-Sat, 10am-2pm Sun* **$$$**

D'Arcy's Pint: Many say this Irish pub makes the best horseshoe sandwich, along with burgers and shepherd's pie. *11am-9pm Tue-Sat* **$$**

Obed & Isaac's: Set in a 150-year-old mansion, this brewery offers sunny rooms for drinking and is also known for its horseshoes. *11am-10pm*

Wakery: Welcoming, artsy space that pours coffee by day and nonalcoholic cocktails, beers and wines by night. *7-11am & 4-10pm Mon-Fri*

ROUTE 66 RAMBLE

Take a drive into yesteryear on the Mother Road past neon-lit diners and oddball roadside attractions.

START	END	LENGTH
Begin Historic Route 66 sign (Chicago)	Cozy Dog Drive In (Springfield)	220 miles; 6 hours

The nostalgic highway rolls for 2400 miles from Chicago to Los Angeles. No time for it? Drive the section between Chicago and Springfield to sample it in a day.

Snap a photo with the 1 **Begin Historic Route 66 Sign** at the northwestern corner of Adams St and Michigan Ave in downtown Chicago. Head a mile southwest and fuel up for the journey at 2 **Lou Mitchell's**, a classic diner.

Motor west to Ogden Ave (aka Old Route 66) and onward through Chicago's western suburbs. Much of Route 66 has been superseded by I-55, so you'll get funneled onto the Interstate eventually. In Bolingbrook take Joilet Rd/IL-53, which parallels I-55. Now you're back on Old Route 66 to mosey into Wilmington to see the 3 **Gemini Giant** – a 28ft fiberglass astronaut that stands guard along the road.

Continue to Pontiac to check out the free, tchotchke-filled museum at the 4 **Route 66 Association of Illinois**. Proceed on the Interstate or Old Route 66 beside it until tiny Atlanta, where 5 **Tall Paul** – a sky-high statue of lumberjack Paul Bunyan – clutches a hot dog. The town's 6 **American Giants Museum** has even more hulking fiberglass creations. Stay the course to Springfield and finish at 7 **Cozy Dog Drive In**, where the corn dog was born.

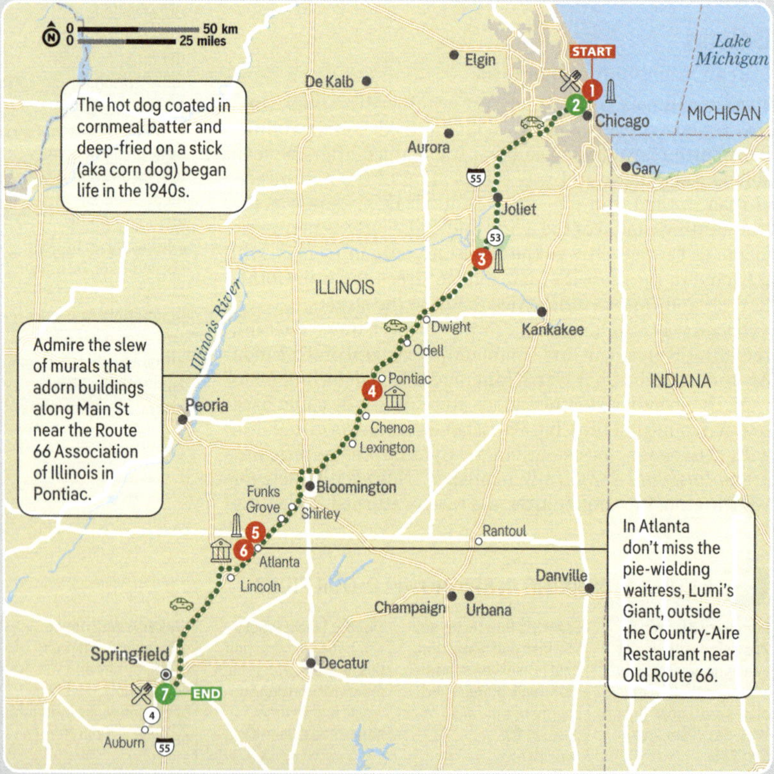

The hot dog coated in cornmeal batter and deep-fried on a stick (aka corn dog) began life in the 1940s.

Admire the slew of murals that adorn buildings along Main St near the Route 66 Association of Illinois in Pontiac.

In Atlanta don't miss the pie-wielding waitress, Lumi's Giant, outside the Country-Aire Restaurant near Old Route 66.

house retains about 90% of its original furnishings, including Grant's favorite green chair, which made it to the White House and back, and Julia Grant's 15lb Bible dating from 1865.

Cahokia Mounds

Ancient city near the Mississippi River

A stone's throw from St Louis, MO, **Cahokia Mounds State Historic Site** *(cahokiamounds.org; free)* is where the largest ancient city in North America once stood. At its peak, c 1100, some 20,000 people lived here – more than London during the same era. It's worth an hour or two of self-guided rambles around the lonely grounds.

About 70 earthen mounds survive, including the massive, 100ft-tall Monk's Mound, which you can climb and see the Gateway Arch and St Louis skyline on a clear day. 'Woodhenge,' a circle of poles used for highly accurate solar observations and date keeping, also impresses.

Shawnee Hills

Where eerie swamp meets vineyards

In the southern part of Illinois, near the border with Kentucky, the forested Shawnee Hills juts up, looking a lot like mini mountains. The rugged area makes for a great weekend break for nature lovers, especially in fall when the trees explode in color.

Start in **Shawnee National Forest** *(fs.usda.gov/shawnee; free)* and its dramatic sandstone rock formations known as **Garden of the Gods** for short trails to big views. About 65 miles southwest, the scenery shifts unexpectedly to Southern-style swampland, complete with moss-draped trees and croaking bullfrogs at **Cypress Creek National Wildlife Refuge** *(fws.gov/refuge/cypress-creek; free)*. **Cache Bayou Outfitters** *(cachebayououtfitters.com; tours adult/child $45/18)* takes you into it by canoe or kayak.

Another surprise in the area: multiple wineries. Sample the wares on the 40-mile **Shawnee Hills Wine Trail** *(shawneewinetrail.com)*. **Blue Sky Vineyard** *(blueskyvineyard.com)* is a sweet stop for a cabernet-style red while listening to live music on the patio.

Finally, if beer is your thing, **Scratch Brewing** *(scratchbeer.com)* hides amid horse-grazing pastures at Shawnee forest's western edge. Bark, berries and herbs foraged from the farm are thrown into the wild ales and sours. The bohemian microbrewery is open Friday through Sunday only.

STAGECOACH TRAIL

For a scenic detour, hop on the 26-mile Stagecoach Trail as an alternative to US 20 for the stretch of the route between Lena and Galena. The twisty road runs through the small communities of Nora, Warren, Apple River and Scales Mound, tempting a longer trip with vineyards and farm-fresh cheese along the way.

The Stagecoach Trail has been a road since the 1830s, and a stagecoach company once operated two daily services that carried passengers, post and parcels between Chicago and Galena. The railroads made the Stagecoach Trail obsolete within two decades. Cars later made the train line obsolete – passenger service ended in 1981. Today the former train station is the **Galena Country Visitor Center**, which has a free parking lot.

EATING & DRINKING IN GALENA: OUR PICKS

Fritz & Frites: This romantic little bistro serves a compact menu of German and French classics. *4-8pm Sun, Wed & Thu, to 9pm Fri & Sat* $$

Otto's Place: Breakfast classics and lunchtime sandwiches served in a historic building with pressed-tin ceilings. *8am-2pm Fri-Sun, to 1pm Mon & Thu* $

Fried Green Tomatoes: Try the lasagna or the espresso-encrusted steak in the building once owned by Grant's father. *hours vary* $$$

Galena Taphouse: Pours beers made within 200 miles of Galena and serves Asian-influenced dishes. *11:30am-10pm Sun-Thu, to midnight Fri & Sat*

Indiana

RACING SPECTACLE | RIVER RIDES | SOARING SANDS

Places

TOP TIP

Go stargazing at Kemil Park at the Indiana Dunes! It's the one part of the park that's open 24 hours, and it's designated an International Dark Sky Community and outfitted with telescopes.

The state revs up around the Indy 500 race, and cars are cherished in Auburn and South Bend. Otherwise, it's often about the slower-paced pleasures in corn-stubbled Indiana: cycling through its center, pie-eating in Amish Country, meditating in Bloomington's Tibetan temples and admiring big architecture in small Columbus. The northwest has moody sand dunes to climb, while the south has caves to explore and rivers to canoe. A quirky labyrinth, bluegrass music shrine and famed, lipstick-kissed gravestone also make appearances across the state.

For the record, folks have called Indianans 'Hoosiers' since the 1830s, but the word's origin is unknown. One theory is that early settlers knocking on a door were met with 'Who's here?' which soon became 'Hoosier.' It's certainly something to discuss with locals, perhaps at a local cafeteria.

Fun fact: Indiana is called 'the mother of vice presidents' for the six veeps it has spawned.

GETTING AROUND

Indianapolis International Airport is the state's largest airport by far, though, depending on where you're going, Louisville, KY, is also an option. There are a couple of smaller airports, including in South Bend. Amtrak stops in Indianapolis en route to Chicago and New York City. Going by Megabus or Greyhound is faster. Driving is fastest; Hwy 46 connects Bloomington, Nashville and Columbus. I-65 and I-69 are the main regional interstates. Within Indianapolis, **IndyGo** *(indygo.net)* runs the local buses – with two BRT lines so far: Red from Broad Ripple to University of Indianapolis, and Purple from downtown to Lawrence – and **Pacers Bikeshare** *(pacersbikeshare.org)* has bike stations along the Cultural Trail downtown.

INDIANA
Waukegan
Lake Michigan
Marshall
MICHIGAN
Elgin
Chicago
Aurora
Gary
Indiana Dunes National Lakeshore
South Bend
Joliet
Auburn
Kankakee
Fort Wayne
Fairmount
ILLINOIS
Lafayette
INDIANA
OHIO
Muncie
Danville
Champaign
Indianapolis
Richmond
Terre Haute
Brown County
Columbus
Bloomington
Charles C. Deam Wilderness
Covington
Madison
Ohio River
Scottsburg
Vincennes
Hoosier National Forest
Milltown
Huntingburg
Louisville
Frankfort
Ohio River
Dale
Evansville
Ohio River Scenic Byway
KENTUCKY
Henderson
Owensboro
Elizabethtown
0
100 km
0
50 miles

INDIANA'S BEST FESTIVALS

Parke County Covered Bridge Festival: Known for its 31 covered bridges, which are celebrated for 10 days each year starting the second Friday of October.

Bill Monroe's Bluegrass Festival: In Morgantown, a bluegrass festival every June named after the finger-picking hero.

Abbey Road on the River: Over Memorial Day weekend at Jefferson's Big Four Pedestrian & Cycling Bridge, the world's largest Beatles and '60s music festival.

Little 500: Bloomington biking bonanza in April, where cyclists ride one-speeds for 200 laps around a quarter-mile track.

Johnny Appleseed Festival: In honor of the pioneering nurseryman, an apple-themed festival in September in Fort Wayne.

BRUCE ALAN BENNETT/SHUTTERSTOCK

Indianapolis Motor Speedway Museum

Indianapolis

The greatest spectacle in racing

Indy's super-sight is the **Indianapolis Motor Speedway** *(indianapolismotorspeedway.com)*, about 6 miles northwest of downtown and home of the 'Greatest Spectacle in Racing,' the Indy 500. Stop in at the **Indianapolis Motor Speedway Museum** *(imsmuseum.org; adult/youth/child $25/18/free)*, which features some 75 racing cars (including former winners) and championship trophies. Limited availability golf-cart tours *(adult/youth $55/35)* of the grounds and track are available from April to October (OK, you're not exactly burning rubber in a golf cart, but it's still fun to pretend while you take a lap!). A short walk from the Speedway, the **Dallara Experience Hub** *(dallara experiencehub.com; $15-30)* is where you can peek at how the speedsters are made, and try a 10-minute driving simulator.

The big race itself is held on the Sunday of Memorial Day weekend and attended by 350,000 crazed fans. If you'll be in town, Grandstand tickets can be hard to come by, so plan ahead. Try general admission, or the prerace trials and practices, for easier access and cheaper prices.

The nation's premier kids' museum

If you're traveling with kiddos, the **Children's Museum of Indianapolis** *(childrensmuseum.org; adult/youth $32/27)* is

EATING IN INDY: OUR PICKS

Milktooth: Breakfast lovers of the world unite for dishes like sweet sourdough waffles and savory Dutch baby pancakes. *10am-3pm Fri-Mon* $$

St Elmo's: Indy's oldest (1902), best steakhouse. Legendary shrimp cocktail, perfectly grilled beef. *4-10pm Mon-Thu, to 11pm Fri, 3-11pm Sat, 4-9pm Sun* $$$

Tinker Street: Fork into seasonal dishes at this New American favorite. Vegetarian and gluten-free options are plentiful. *5-9pm Mon-Thu, to 10pm Fri & Sat, to 8pm Sun* $$$

Bluebeard: Named after the Kurt Vonnegut book, James Beard–nominated fine-dining spot with daily changing menu. *11am-10pm Mon-Thu, to 11pm Fri & Sat, 5-10pm Sun* $$$

a must. It's the world's largest kids' museum, sprawled over five floors holding incredible exhibitions on dinosaurs, space stations and so much more. Indoors, it's centered around a stunning 43ft sculpture by Dale Chihuly that teaches tykes to blow glass (virtually!); and outdoors, the 7.5-acre Sports Legends Experience is the playground of your dreams.

An outing to Newfields

The 152-acre **Newfields** campus houses the **Indianapolis Museum of Art** *(discovernewfields.org; adult/youth/child $20/13/free)*, home to a terrific collection of European art (especially Turner and postimpressionists), African tribal art, South Pacific art, Chinese works, Robert Indiana's original pop-art *Love* sculpture and the largest gallery dedicated to contemporary and modern design in the US.

The campus also includes the **Virginia B Fairbanks Art & Nature Park**, with striking modern sculptures set amid 100 acres of woodlands. The park has its own entrance and is free, and open daily from sunrise to sunset – perfect for an art fix without the admission price. Adjacent to the Madeline F Elder Greenhouse, a seasonal **beer garden** offers a rotating tap list, including an exclusively brewed saison from Sun King Brewery.

Cycle from the Monon Trail to the Indy Cultural Trail

A 26-mile former rail track turned walking and cycling path, the **Monon Trail** *(bikethemonon.com)* plies through some of Indianapolis' coolest districts, stretching from Sheridan in central Indiana, through the North Indy suburb of Carmel, to hip Broad Ripple and eventually to downtown. Rent a set of wheels (outfitters listed on the Monon Trail site), then head to an access point – major ones with parking, restrooms and other infrastructure are located at, among others, 75th St, 96th St and Carmel Central Park (11th St).

At 10th and Lewis Sts, link up with the **Cultural Trail**, an 8-mile urban bike trail that goes through six downtown cultural districts, including Mass Ave, Mile Square and several public art projects. Along the route, several museums are worth a stop. The **Indiana War Memorial** *(indianawarmemorials.org; free)* is a 210ft-tall mausoleum-evoking limestone tribute honoring Hoosier veterans of WWI, while the **Eiteljorg Museum** *(eiteljorg.org; adult/youth $20/12)* features Native American basketry, pots and masks, as well as a Western painting collection with works by Frederic Remington and Georgia O'Keeffe. Eiteljorg is located within the

INDIANA'S CAFETERIA SCENE

Cafeterias are an Indiana tradition, where diners grab a tray, slide it along a metal railing, and load it up with plates of hot and cold dishes. Fried chicken, meatloaf, mac 'n' cheese, freshly baked rolls and sugar cream pie are all beloved staples. One of Indiana's first cafeterias opened in 1900, with many more arriving on the scene in the decades that followed, like Gray Brothers Cafeteria in 1944 and MCL Cafeteria in 1950. Since then, many of Indiana's time-honored neighborhood cafeterias have disappeared – but Gray Brothers and MCL still remain.

DRINKING IN INDY: OUR PICKS

Sun King Brewery: Indy's young and hip swill pints, flights and growlers, and spill onto the patio in summer. *11am-9pm Mon & Tue, to 10pm Wed-Sat, to 8pm Sun*

Slippery Noodle Inn: Indiana's oldest bar (1850), with stints as various venues; now a blues club. *11am-1am Mon-Fri, noon-2am Sat, 4pm-midnight Sun*

Centerpoint Brewing Company: True-to-style beers in a former race-car-engine factory and mail-sorting facility. *3-9pm Mon-Wed, to 10pm Thu, noon-10pm Fri & Sat, noon-8pm Sun*

Metazoa Brewing Co: Pet-friendliest brewery: on-site dog park, donates 5% of profits to animal/wildlife organizations. *1-10pm Mon-Wed, from 11am Thu-Sat, 11am-9pm Sun*

MORE OF INDIANA'S TOP STATE PARKS & FORESTS

Falls of the Ohio State Park: This park has only rapids, no falls, but is of interest for its 390-million-year-old fossil beds.

Clifty Falls State Park: Large, wooded space in Madison with excellent hiking, waterfall views, creeks, canyons and campgrounds.

Turkey Run State Park: Known for its hiking, particularly the ladders of Trail 3, along with horseback riding, swimming and camping.

Mounds State Park: Featuring 10 prehistoric earthworks, largest is the Great Mound, built around 160 BCE by the Adena and Hopewell peoples.

Clark State Forest: Indiana's oldest state forest, which includes part of Indiana's longest hiking trail, the Knobstone Trail.

White River State Park *(whiteriverstatepark.org)*, the urban green space that encompasses seven city attractions, including the Indianapolis Zoo, Indiana State Museum and NCAA Hall of Champions.

Finally, the **Kurt Vonnegut Museum & Library** *(kurt vonnegutlibrary.org; $12/8)* pays homage to the famous author born and raised in Indy, who was an anti-censorship and peace activist. The museum, free the first Monday of the month, exhibits artifacts from his life.

Auburn

Check out classic cars

Classic-car connoisseurs should stop in Auburn, about 50 miles southeast of Amish Country, where the Cord Company produced the USA's favorite autos in the 1920s and '30s. Two remarkable car museums, the **Auburn Cord Duesenberg Automobile Museum** *(automobilemuseum.org; adult/student $15/10)* and the **National Auto & Truck Museum** *(natmus.org; adult/child $12/7)*, are conveniently lined up next door to one another for your car-viewing pleasure. The former has a 120-strong inventory of early roadsters – including Babe Ruth's Auburn 8-88 Roadster and Frank Lloyd Wright's orange Cord L-29 – in a beautiful art-deco setting that was once part of the original Auburn Automotive Company. The latter has a bit of everything, from toy cars to gas pumps to vintage rigs. You can also purchase a 'campus pass' for combined admission *($25/15)*.

South Bend

From horse-drawn carriages to motor vehicles

South Bend's automotive legacy stems from its homegrown carmaker Studebaker (later the Studebaker-Packard Corporation), which started off by manufacturing horse-drawn wagons and carriages in the 1850s, before transitioning to motor vehicles to put out its first electric car in 1902 and first gas-powered car in 1904. The **Studebaker National Museum** *(studebaker museum.org; adult/student/child $11/7/free)* is where you can get a sense of the industry's evolution through the ages, as you meander through three floors of shiny vehicles that range from vintage carriages to a gorgeous 1956 Packard.

EATING IN NORTHERN INDIANA: OUR PICKS

Rise'n Roll: Now a northern Indiana chain, it started here in Middlebury; all because of the sought-after cinnamon-caramel donuts. *7am-4pm Mon-Sat* $

Village Inn Restaurant: Sublime pies in Amish Country, baked in the wee hours of the morning. Burgers, meat loaf and other mains. *5am-8pm Mon-Fri, to 11am Sat* $

Octave Grill: In Chesterton, burgers made with grass-fed beef, paired with a wonderful selection of rotating craft beers. *3-9pm Mon & Thu-Sat, to 8pm Sun* $

Rocco's: A South Bend institution, ladling marinara sauce since 1951. After football games, lines of Notre Dame alums run out the door. *4:30-10:30pm Tue-Sat* $

TOP EXPERIENCE

Indiana Dunes National Park

In addition to being the state's most visited site, attracting 3.5 million visitors per year, sunny beaches, rustling grasses and woodsy campgrounds are the Indiana Dunes' claim to fame. The area is hugely popular on summer days with sunbathers from Chicago and towns throughout Northern Indiana. Beyond its beaches, the area is noted for sweet hiking trails that meander up the dunes and through the woodlands.

National Park Trails

The Dunes, which became the USA's 61st national park in 2019, stretch along 15 miles of Lake Michigan shoreline (swimming allowed). A short walk away from the beaches are several hiking paths; the best are the Bailly-Chellberg Trail (2.5 miles) that winds by a still-operating 1870s farm; and the Heron Rookery Trail (2 miles), where blue herons flock (though there's no actual rookery).

Plants & Wildlife

Oddly, all this natural bounty lies smack-dab next to smoke-belching factories, yet it still boasts remarkable features: it has 1100 native species of plants; dunes formed after melted glaciers, which top out at 192ft; and 370 species of birds. Birding and fishing are popular, as is beachcombing (beach glass collecting allowed, fossil and pebble collecting prohibited).

State Park & Three Dune Challenge

The **state park** is a 2100-acre, shoreside pocket within the national park; it's located at the end of Hwy 49, near Chesterton. Don't miss the **3 Dune Challenge**, a 1.5-mile, 552ft vertical climb to the park's three highest dunes: Mt Jackson (176ft), Mt Holden (184ft) and Mt Tom (192ft). It starts on Trail 8, by the **Indiana Dunes State Park Nature Center**.

TOP TIPS

- America the Beautiful Pass holders are covered to enter the national park area, but not the state park area, of the Indiana Dunes.
- For the state park, entrance is free on weekdays, November to mid-April.
- Kemil Beach is one section of the park that's open 24 hours, for stargazing.

PRACTICALITIES

- indianadunes.com
- national park 6am-11pm, state park 7am-11pm
- 7-day pass per car $12-25

TIBETAN CULTURE IN BLOOMINGTON

The 14th Dalai Lama's brother Thubten Jigme Norbu came here from Eastern Tibet, teaching at Indiana University in the 1960s; Tibetan temples, monasteries and culture followed in his footsteps. In 1979, Thubten Jigme Norbu founded the colorful, prayer-flag-covered Tibetan Mongolian Buddhist Cultural Center to introduce the people of Indiana to Tibetan culture and to support Tibetan exile communities. The center, in southern Bloomington, is a draw for its traditional stupas, gift shop, open meditation sessions and various workshops and retreats. Across the city, in northern Bloomington, the Gaden Khachoe Shing Monastery is another place of peace. And downtown, Tibetan fare features at restaurants like Little Tibet.

Tour the University of Notre Dame

Founded in 1842, the **University of Notre Dame** *(nd.edu)* is often touted as one of the USA's prettiest higher education campuses. To get a good look at it, a free walking tour is recommended (it departs from the **Eck Visitors Center**; times vary and tours are limited to the first 25 people who sign up in person). But if you're short on time, at least pop into the stunning Basilica of the Sacred Heart (a neo-Gothic cathedral awash in stained-glass windows and murals painted by Vatican artist Luigi Gregori); the Golden Dome (the university's main admin building – often considered the nation's leading collegiate landmark – with a gorgeous rotunda topped with a 4400lb statue of Mary); and the Grotto of Our Lady of Lourdes (a recreation of the original in France). All three are next to each other on the north side of God Quad.

Fairmount

Hunt down James Dean's hometown

Pocket-sized Fairmount is but a few streets surrounded by farmland, but it's on the international map as the hometown of 1950s actor James Dean, one of the original icons of cool (he was born 10.5 miles north in Marion but raised by his relatives in Fairmount). Fans can follow Dean's footsteps, from birth to death.

Start at the **James Dean Museum** *(thejamesdeanmuseum.com; adult/child $10/free),* where you can see the world's largest collection of his personal belongings, ranging from his baby crib and high-school car, to his 1955 Triumph TR5 Trophy 500cc and 1947 Czech 125cc motorcycles, and more. (You'll also notice tributes to Garfield creator Jim Davis, Fairmount's other famous figure.) Other spots include the **James Dean Birth Site Memorial**, a 6ft-tall black granite monument erected in 2015 to honor the spot where the House of Seven Gables once stood; the farmhouse where Jimmy grew up; and his often lipstick-kissed **gravestone** in Park Cemetery. There's also a privately owned **James Dean Gallery** *(jamesdeangallery.com; free)* with several rooms of memorabilia in an old Victorian home downtown. Every September, Fairmount celebrates the **James Dean Festival** – thousands of fans pour in for three days of music, classic cars, a James Dean lookalike contest and other events honoring the Hollywood legend.

DRINKING IN NORTHERN INDIANA: OUR PICKS

3 Floyds Brewing: In Munster, Zombie Dust, a flowery pale ale; and Dark Lord, a legendary Russian imperial stout, have a cult following. *noon-7pm Tue-Sat*

18th Street Brewery: Warehouse in Hammond for saisons, sours and IPAs. Also in Gary. *noon-9pm Mon-Thu, 11am-10pm Fri & Sat, 11am-6pm Sun*

Mad Anthony's Auburn Tap Room: Taproom in a historic downtown building with big windows and exposed-brick walls. *11am-10pm, to 11pm Fri & Sat*

Crooked Ewe Brewery: Find a wealth of hops-heavy IPAs at this riverside brewpub in South Bend. Elevated bar fare, including vegan options. *noon-9pm, to 10pm Fri & Sat*

Brown County State Park

Brown County

Indiana's largest state park

A few miles southeast of Nashville, **Brown County State Park** *(browncountystatepark.net; $9/day)* is Indiana's largest state park, known as the Little Smoky Mountains for its steep wooded hills and fog-cloaked ravines. Trails stripe the 15,700-acre stand of oak, hickory and birch trees, and give hikers, mountain bikers and horseback riders access to the area's green hill country. The mile-long **Ogle Hollow Nature Preserve Trail** is a good place to see the rare yellowwood tree and its fragrant blossoms. And **Bean Blossom Overlook** is one of the best spots to take in the color-shifting treetops across Brown County.

Ohio River Scenic Byway

A river town, a cave and Lincoln's boyhood home

The Ohio River marks the state's southern border – and Ohio's and Indiana's, too – with the Ohio River Scenic Byway winding its way through nearly 1000 miles of lush and hilly landscape along the churning waterway. Indiana's 303-mile portion *(ohio riverbyway.com)* of the 943-mile route comprises Hwys 56,

ARCHITECTURAL HERITAGE IN COLUMBUS

When you think of the USA's great architectural cities – Chicago, New York, Washington, DC – Columbus, IN, doesn't quite leap to mind, but it's a remarkable gallery of design. Since the 1940s, Columbus and its leading corporation, Fortune 500 engineering company Cummins, have commissioned some of the world's best architects, including Eero Saarinen, Richard Meier and IM Pei, to create both public and private buildings. More than 70 notable structures and public art pieces span a wide area. Some of the most famous are **First Christian Church**, a brick-and-limestone Modernist masterpiece; and **Miller House & Garden**, the mid-century-modern residence of Cummins president J Irwin Miller – both designed by Saarinen.

EATING & DRINKING IN SOUTHERN INDIANA: OUR PICKS

Samira: Tasty Afghan food in downtown Bloomington: excellent kebabs, vegetarian dishes and lunch buffet. *5-9pm Mon-Sat, plus 11am-2pm Thu & Fri* $$

Henry Social Club: New American fine dining and the best bar in Columbus for a boutique cocktail, set in an open-concept kitchen. *5-9pm Tue-Sat* $$$

Exchange Pub + Kitchen: In New Albany, upmarket pub with an industrial-chic ambience. Burgers do not disappoint. *11am-10pm, to 11pm Fri & Sat, to 9pm Sun* $$$

Wood Shop: In Bloomington, this is the experimental sister site of more mainstream Upland Brewing Co next door – it's the all-sours brewery where funk flows. *5-9pm Fri & Sat*

INDIANA'S HARMONIST & UTOPIAN HISTORY

In southwest Indiana, the Wabash River forms the border with Illinois. Beside it, south of I-64, captivating New Harmony is the site of two early communal-living experiments. In the 1814, the Harmony Society, a German Christian sect led by George Rapp, developed a sophisticated, self-sufficient, model community here while awaiting the Second Coming. In 1825, the Welsh utopian Robert Owen acquired the town, renaming it New Harmony. By 1827, it had failed and dissolved. Today, New Harmony retains an air of contemplation, if not otherworldliness, which can be felt at the town's information center, the Atheneum; the Roofless Church; and the Labyrinth, a recreation of the Harmonists' original hedge-maze design.

ZACK FRANK/SHUTTERSTOCK

Lincoln Boyhood National Memorial

156, 62 and 66, and makes for a scenic drive, with stops at a beautifully preserved mid-19th-century river town, a cave with astonishing underground formations and Abraham Lincoln's boyhood home.

Of all the charms along this stretch, few outdo the convivial and cozy vibe of small town **Madison** *(visitmadison.org)*. Home to the largest contiguous National Historic Landmark District in the US, Madison is a hub of Federal, Greek Revival and Italianate-style architecture along its postcard-perfect Main St. Grab a burger at **Hinkle's** *(hinkleburger.com)*, an old-school diner in action since 1933; and a beer at **Mad Paddle Brewstillery** *(madpaddle.com)*, a couple of blocks south.

Heading west, **Milltown** is where you can access the beautiful **Blue River**, a tributary of the Ohio River that's perfect for a paddle. **Cave Country Canoes** *(cavecountrycanoes.com)* puts on half-, full- or two-day trips (prices vary depending on the group size). About 4 miles west, a plunge into **Marengo Cave** *(marengocave.com; adult/child 40min tour $23/14, 60min tour $26/16, combination tour $32/2)* is highly recommended. The privately owned landmark offers tours walking past stalagmites and other ancient formations.

Then, off I-64 and 4 miles south of **Dale**, the **Lincoln Boyhood National Memorial** *(nps.gov/libo; free)* is where young Abe, who grew up to become the 16th US president, lived from age seven to 21. The memorial also includes admission to a working pioneer farm, open in the summer, that's modeled after the Lincoln farm but is not the original. A 1-mile trail loop from the memorial takes in the highlights.

Ohio

CITY CHARM | ERIE ISLANDS | AMISH COUNTRY

The nation's seventh most populous state has big cities Cleveland, Cincinnati and Columbus that lead its urban charge, rolling out a spread of kicky dining options, IPA-loving breweries and one-of-a-kind museums. Northern Cleveland exudes a feisty, rock-and-roll vibe, while southern Cincinnati feels more languorous and European. Columbus – the largest of the three, with a population of over 900,000 – is the polished tech and art hub that rises up in the middle, home to Ohio State University. Meanwhile, Ohio's rural side is way off the grid, from the horse-and-buggy-filled roads of its enormous Amish community to the moonshine makers in its southeastern hills. It makes for an intriguing mash-up, with just a short drive between wildly different lifestyles. In between, the roadways lead to the world's fastest roller coasters, rocking party islands, beatnik towns, pie shops and a mist-draped national park.

Places

TOP TIP

Camp overnight in Hocking Hills State Park! It's Ohio's favorite park for good reason, and there are abundant campsites available, with spectacular scenery all around.

GETTING AROUND

Cleveland Hopkins International Airport is Ohio's busiest airport – linked to downtown by the Red Line train – followed by Columbus, Cincinnati and Dayton. John Glenn Columbus International Airport is 10 miles east of downtown, while Cincinnati/Northern Kentucky International Airport is in Kentucky. Cleveland, Cincinnati and Sandusky are on Amtrak train routes; Columbus is not. Regardless, Megabus and Greyhound are cheaper and faster. Driving is best. For Cuyahoga Valley, the national park is just off I-77. Amish Country lies between Cleveland (80 miles north) and Columbus (100 miles southwest), with I-71 and I-77 flanking the area. US 33 leads to Logan, and US 23 to Chillicothe and the Hopewell mounds. Within Cleveland, the **RTA** *(riderta.com)* runs buses and trains. Within Cincinnati, there are **Metro** *(go-metro.com)* buses, a **streetcar** *(cincinnatibellconnector.com)* and **Red Bike** *(cincyredbike.org)* stations.

Cleveland

From the Beatles to the Rolling Stones

Cleveland's top attraction, the **Rock and Roll Hall of Fame & Museum** *(rockhall.com; adult/youth/child $39.50/29.50/free)*, is like an overstuffed attic bursting with groovy finds: Jimi Hendrix's Stratocaster, Prince's Cloud #2 Blue Angel Guitar, Keith Moon's platform shoes, John Lennon's Sgt Pepper suit and a 1966 piece of hate mail to the Rolling Stones from a cursive-writing Fijian. It's more than memorabilia, though. Multimedia exhibits trace the history and social context of rock music and the performers who created it.

EATING IN CLEVELAND: OUR PICKS

Citizen Pie: Wood-fired Neapolitan-style pizzas, with a mighty smoked pepperoni. Second location in Ohio City. *noon-9pm Tue-Sat, to 8pm Sun* $

Mitchell's Ice Cream: Mitchell's revamped an old movie theater. Watch through big glass windows as staff blend the rich flavors. One of 10 locales. *11am-10:30pm* $

Abundance Culinary: Four types of dumplings, along with rice, noodles and mains, plus Sichuan-inspired cocktails. *8am-10pm Tue-Thu, to 11pm Fri & Sat* $$

Zhug: Upmarket Mediterranean mezze (braised lamb, smoked calamari and roasted vegetables) in casual environs. *4-10pm Mon-Thu, to 11pm Fri & Sat* $$$

Why is the museum in Cleveland? Because this is the hometown of Alan Freed, the disc jockey who popularized the term 'rock and roll' in the early 1950s, and because the city lobbied hard and paid big. Be prepared for crowds.

Explore the arts and entertainment

Cleveland's fine and performing arts are sure to keep you entertained day and night. Begin at the **Cleveland Museum of Art** *(clevelandart.org; free; closed Mondays)*, a mammoth collection of European paintings; African, Asian and American art; and special paid exhibitions – all set around a dazzling, light-drenched atrium. Head to the 2nd floor for works from Impressionists, Picasso and surrealists. Interactive touchscreens are stationed throughout, providing fun ways to learn more; download the free ArtLens app for additional content. Free guided tours depart at 1pm and 1:30pm each day; they're limited to 15 participants, so advance tickets are recommended.

Nighttime is show time at the city's **Playhouse Square** *(playhousesquare.org)*, the nation's second-largest theater district. Several stages comprise the elegant performing arts center, which hosts theater, opera, ballet and beyond. Take note of the massive sparkler dangling above: that's North America's largest outdoor chandelier, 44ft tall and shining with 4200 faux crystals.

A walk on the West Side

The West Side is home to some of Cleveland's hippest neighborhoods. Start your day at the **West Side Market** *(westsidemarket.org)*, a European-style market overflowing with greengrocers and their produce, as well as purveyors of Hungarian sausage, Italian cannoli and Polish pierogi. The surrounding **Ohio City** is an ultra walkable little enclave known for its historic buildings, vibrant street art, cute boutique shops, delicious dining scene and several breweries, including the tried-and-true **Great Lakes Brewing Company** *(greatlakesbrewing.com)*, cozy **Bookhouse Brewing** *(bookhouse.beer)* and Eastern European newcomer **Hansa Brewery** *(hansabrewery.com)*. Also here, in a pocket called Hingetown, is **Transformer Station** *(clevelandart.org; free; open Thursday to Sunday)*, a Cleveland Museum of Art–affiliated gallery that showcases emerging artists, new media and live music at a repurposed industrial substation.

Nearby, the west bank of the Flats is home to the **Greater Cleveland Aquarium** *(greaterclevelandaquarium.com;*

LAY OF 'THE LAND'

Nicknamed 'The Land,' Cleveland is bisected by the Cuyahoga River, which divides the West and East sides. The city's center is at **Public Square**, with most major attractions downtown on the lakefront. Nearby, the Warehouse District and the Flats are abuzz with a youthful vibe. Eastward are Asiatown, University Circle, Little Italy, Coventry Village and Collinwood. Westward are hip Ohio City and Tremont, straddling I-90; the western bank of the Flats; and Gordon Square Arts District, a fun pocket along Detroit Ave between W 56th and W 69th Sts. Cleveland's public transit system, the RTA, is a handy network of buses, a three-line train service and a trolley that runs between Public Square and the Wolstein Center.

DRINKING IN CLEVELAND: OUR PICKS

Noble Beast Brewing Co: A homey place for German-style ales and pub fare. *11:30am-11pm Tue-Thu, to midnight Fri & Sat to 10pm Sun*

Millard Fillmore Presidential Library: Tell your pals you're going to a presidential library. It's actually a dive bar in Collinwood. *4pm-2:30am Mon-Fri, from noon Sat & Sun*

Jerman's Cafe: One of Cleveland's oldest bars, opened in 1908 by a Slovenian immigrant. Just a few beers on tap. *noon-1am Mon & Tue, to 2am Wed-Sat, 1pm-midnight Sun*

Great Lakes Brewing Company: Second-biggest craft-beer maker in the state wins prizes for its brewed suds. *11:30am-10pm Mon-Thu, to 11pm Fri & Sat, 11am-5pm Sun*

TOP EXPERIENCE

Cuyahoga Valley National Park

The Cuyahoga River worms over a forested valley, earning its Native American name of 'crooked river' (or possibly 'place of the jawbone'). Either name is evocative, and hints at the mystical beauty that Ohio's only national park engenders on a cool morning, when the mists thread the woods and all you hear is the honk of Canadian geese and the fwup-fwup-whoosh of a great blue heron flapping over its hunting grounds.

Brandywine Falls

KARENFOLEYPHOTOGRAPHY/SHUTTERSTOCK

TOP TIPS

- Parking lots at the Ledges and Brandywine Falls fill up quickly. Opt for mornings, evenings and weekdays.
- The Boston Mills Visitor Center is a good starting point.
- If you cycle, hike or run along the towpath trail in one direction, ride the train back for just $5.

The Ledges

This overlook is probably the most photographed place in the park, with an unobstructed vista looking west over the valley to eternity. There's a loop trail nearby, a little over 2 miles in length, that's a nice leg stretcher.

Brandywine Falls

Long considered one of the park's best attractions, this pretty spill of ice-cold water sits in a wooden idyll, and is accessed via a 1.5-mile round-trip hike that features some light elevation gain (160ft).

Ohio & Erie Canal Towpath Trail

The park's main trail follows the old Ohio & Erie Canal, which once served as one of the primary historical arteries into the American west. Boats pulled by mules ran adjacent to this path, now an ideal thoroughfare for hikers and cyclists, intersecting with many of the park's other trails.

Cuyahoga Valley Scenic Railroad

An old-school iron carriage *(cvsr.org; adult/child from $25/20)* chugs along a pleasant course from Akron to Independence, going through the heart of the park, with a depot midway at Peninsula. The most expensive seats have glass-topped domes, and special themed rides are offered, too. A full round trip takes around 3½ hours.

PRACTICALITIES

- nps.gov/cuva
- 24hr
- free

adult/child $20/14), a fun and interactive experience for the littles in tow, while **Tremont** and its bevy of trendy bars are a treat for the bigs. In summer, white-sand **Edgewater Park Beach** comes alive with sunbathers, swimmers and concession stands. Finish at nearby **Gordon Square Arts District** *(gordonsquare.org)* for dinner at **Blue Habanero** *(bluehabanerocleveland.com)*, a show at the **Cleveland Public Theatre** *(cptonline.org)* or live music (and a loaded hot dog!) at **Happy Dog** *(happydogcleveland.com)*.

Cincinnati

Get acquainted with Over-the-Rhine

At downtown's northern edge, the historic **Over-the-Rhine** (OTR) neighborhood is home to an impressive collection of 19th-century Italianate and Queen Anne buildings that have morphed into trendy dining venues, bars and shops. Begin at **Findlay Market** *(findlaymarket.org)*, the wrought-iron-framed structure in continuous operation since the 1850s; and mosey around the more than 50 stalls, where you can find meat, cheese, pastries, produce, flowers and more. For a truly local experience, cross the street to **Eckerlin Meats** *(eckerlinmeats.com)* and try some homemade *guetta*, a pan-fried patty made of ground meat and steel-cut oats, often served for breakfast in a sandwich or omelet. It's a unique food you won't find anywhere else besides Cincinnati and Northern Kentucky.

From there, it's on to **Cincinnati's Brewing Heritage Trail** *(brewingheritagetrail.org)*. Findlay marks one of two trailheads – the other being at Grant Park – for this fun three-quarter-mile route that takes you past classic brewhouses and historic saloons in the neighborhood. Markers along the way tell how Cincy was one of the nation's leading beer producers in the late 1800s. Download the free app for a self-guided tour or book a guided tour.

Go museum-hopping

Cincinnati has several museums of note close to downtown, not far from the riverfront, that make for a full day of history and arts. Starting in the West End, begin at the **Cincinnati Museum Center** *(cincymuseum.org; adult/child $19.50/12.50)*, a complex that includes the **Museum of Natural History & Science** (with a cave inside!), a children's museum and a history museum. The complex occupies the 1933 Union Terminal, an art-deco jewel still used by Amtrak; its interior features fantastic murals made of local Rookwood tiles.

OHIO'S QUIRKY SIGHTS

World's Largest Rubber Stamp (Cleveland): At Willard Park, Claes Oldenburg's 70,000lb 'Free' stamp sculpture is a photo-op favorite.

American Sign Museum (Cincinnati): An awesome cache of flashing, lightbulb-studded beacons in an old parachute factory.

World's Largest Cuckoo Clock (Sugarcreek): A 23ft-tall clock lets loose every half-hour, when a mechanical Bavarian couple dances a polka.

Christmas Story House (Cleveland): The original house of the 1983 film *A Christmas Story* sits in Tremont, complete with a leg lamp.

Paul A Johnson Pencil Sharpener Museum (Logan): One man's trove of 3400 pencil sharpeners, reportedly the USA's largest.

EATING IN CINCINNATI: OUR PICKS

Eagle OTR: Serving modern soul food, including fried chicken with spicy honey, white cheddar grits and spoon bread. *11am-10pm Sun, to 11pm Mon-Thu, to midnight Fri & Sat* $

Bee's Barbecue OTR: Tasty brisket, ribs, pulled pork and other offerings in casual environs with welcoming staff. *11am-11pm Tue-Thu, to midnight Fri & Sat, to 9pm Sun* $$

Bridges: Build your own Nepali rice bowl with meat/vegan toppings at this homey spot in Northside. Other locations: downtown, Elmwood. *11am-9pm Mon-Thu, to 10pm Fri & Sat* $$

Sotto: Italian fine dining tucked in a downtown basement. Reservations are a must. *11am-2pm & 4-10pm Mon-Thu, to 11pm Fri, 4-11pm Sat, 4-9pm Sun* $$$

OHIO'S BEST FESTIVALS

Cleveland Kurentovanje: The city's large Slovenian population gathers at this multiday spring festival, where a parade is led by Kurenti, the mythical monsters who chase away winter.

Bockfest Cincinnati: Each March, traditional Bock beers flow at venues across Over-the-Rhine.

Oktoberfest Zinzinnati: Beer, bratwursts and mania. It's the US' largest Oktoberfest celebration, with well over half a million revelers convening at Sawyer Point.

IngenuityFest: In Cleveland, a three-day fall festival full of art, technology and creative experiences.

Blink: Large-scale light projections and interactive art feature at this four-day event in Cincinnati in the fall.

Over in downtown Cincy, the **National Underground Railroad Freedom Center** *(freedomcenter.org; $16.50/11.50)* details the city's history as a prominent stop on the Underground Railroad and a hub for abolitionist activities. The center displays artifacts along the historical road from slavery to freedom, and also covers modern struggles for civil rights. A few blocks north is the **Contemporary Arts Center** *(contemporaryartscenter.org; adult/child $12/free)*, displaying modern art in an avant-garde building designed by Zaha Hadid.

Eastward, round out the day at the **Cincinnati Art Museum** *(cincinnatiartmuseum.org; free)*, where its impressive collection spans 6000 years, with an emphasis on ancient Middle Eastern and European art.

Cross the Ohio River by foot

The mighty Ohio River is the border between Ohio and Kentucky, with a couple of notable bridges connecting Cincinnati to its southern neighbors. For those interested in a little jaunt into Kentucky, it's simple and straightforward to go via one bridge, then return via the other, while also enjoying the lovely green space that flanks the river on each side. Begin by walking around the well-tended **Smale Riverfront Park**, then take the **John A Roebling Suspension Bridge** *(roeblingbridge.org)* across to Covington, KY. A forerunner of John Roebling's famous Brooklyn Bridge in New York, the elegant 1867 spanner features Romanesque arches and draped cables that are highly photogenic. From Covington, it's an easy 30-minute walk through General James Taylor Park to Newport, where you can take the pedestrian-only **Purple People Bridge** *(purplepeoplebridge.com)* back to Cincy. You'll be deposited at **Sawyer Point**, a nifty park dotted by whimsical monuments and flying pigs.

Columbus

Stroll through a German village

Wandering through this remarkably large, restored all-brick **German Village** *(germanvillage.com)*, a half-mile south of downtown, feels like you've entered the 19th century. The historic village, first platted in 1814, is complete with cobbled streets, beer halls, cute boutique shops, arts-filled parks, and Italianate and Queen Anne architecture. The **German Village Society** has archives and maps.

Bibliophiles should stop in at the **Book Loft** *(bookloft.com)*, a sprawling bookshop occupying a block of pre-Civil War

DRINKING IN CINCINNATI: OUR PICKS

Uncle Leo's: Friendly bartenders will serve you a 'spaghett' – Miller High Life with, usually, Aperol. *4-11pm Mon-Wed, to 1am Thu, to 2am Fri, noon-2am Sat, noon-11pm Sun*

Rhinegeist Brewery: One of Ohio's biggest breweries. Try Truth IPA or 20 other brews on tap. Picnic tables and a rooftop. *3-10pm Mon-Thu, noon-1am Fri & Sat, noon-9pm Sun*

Longfellow: Cozy and candlelit cocktail bar in a vintage building with creaking hardwood floors and exposed brick walls. *4pm-2am Wed-Fri, from 2pm Sat & Sun*

Low Spark: Easygoing spot; cocktails served at a bar set around an illuminated fish tank. *4pm-midnight Mon-Wed, to 2:30am Thu & Fri, noon-2:30am Sat, noon-10pm Sun*

CHRISTIAN HINKLE/SHUTTERSTOCK

John A Roebling Suspension Bridge

buildings, where you're guaranteed to get lost in the labyrinth of 32 rooms stacked to the rafters with bestsellers, children's books, manga, memoirs and more. After, head over to **Schmidt's** *(schmidthaus.com)* to shovel in Old Country staples like sausage and schnitzel, but save room for the whopping half-pound cream puffs.

Peep at Ohio's biggest planetarium

COSI *(cosi.org, adult/child from $30/25),* an acronym for the Center of Science and Industry, ranks high in the pantheon of children's museums around the country, with 300-plus hands-on exhibits that include a dinosaur gallery (with a mechanical T. rex), space gallery (with a replica space station to explore) and high-wire unicycle ride. Ohio's largest planetarium, a native prairie, live science shows and a 3D theater round out the whopping spread. Check the calendar for special events, too, like COSI Farm Days and COSI After Dark.

Sandusky

Get topsy turvy and go round and round

In summer the good-time resort region of Erie Lakeshore is one of the busiest places in Ohio. Boaters come to party, daredevils come to ride roller coasters, and outdoorsy types

TOP ART SPOTS IN COLUMBUS

Otherworld: Futuristic, fantastical art museum: 32,000 sq ft of immersive mixed-reality installations.

Short North Arts District: Hosts a gallery hop the first Saturday of each month, featuring exhibitions, live performances and vendors.

Columbus Museum of Art: Highlights include Edward Hopper's *Morning Sun* and several works by Henri Matisse and Pablo Picasso.

Franklinton Fridays: Area galleries, studios and bars put on an art crawl on the second Friday of each month, with food and entertainment.

Wexner Center for the Arts: Ohio State University's contemporary arts center has cutting-edge art exhibits, films and performances.

EATING & DRINKING IN COLUMBUS: OUR PICKS

DK Diner: Classic diner experience in Grandview: omelets, corned beef hash, and biscuits and gravy. *6am-3pm Mon & Tue, to 9pm Wed-Fri, 7am-9pm Sat, 7am-3pm Sun* $

Hoyo's Kitchen: *Hoyo* is 'mother' in Somali, and the siblings running this venue use Mom's recipes. It's in North Market Downtown. *11am-7pm Tue-Sat, to 5pm Sun* $$

Service Bar: It's in Middle West Spirits Distillery, so signature cocktails are made with bourbon fresh from the tanks. Also serves food. *5-10pm Wed & Thu, from 4pm Fri & Sat*

Land-Grant Brewing Co: Couple of dozen taps, and flights. Rotating food-truck line up. *3-10pm Mon-Wed, 11am-10pm Thu, 11am-midnight Fri & Sat, 11am-8pm Sun*

CANTON: BIRTHPLACE OF THE NFL

You may be wondering why the **Pro Football Hall of Fame** is located in Canton, Ohio. It's because Canton is where the American Professional Football Association, which later became the National Football League (NFL), was founded on September 17, 1920. Back then, Canton had its own team, the very successful Canton Bulldogs, who played in the Ohio League, winning titles in 1916, 1917 and 1919, before joining the national league and becoming a 1922 and 1923 champion there too – the NFL's first two-time champion. The Bulldogs' players included the legendary Jim Thorpe. All that and the people of Canton campaigned mightily for it.

Cedar Point

come to cycle and kayak. The season lasts from mid-May to mid-September – and then just about everything shuts down.

For kids (and adults) who love a thrill, a stop at **Cedar Point** *(cedarpoint.com; from $70)* is a must. As one of the world's top amusement parks, it's known for its 18 adrenaline-pumping roller coasters, with such stomach-droppers as Steel Vengeance, which provides 27 seconds of weightlessness, the most 'airtime' of any coaster on the planet.

Nearby, the whimsical **Merry-Go-Round Museum** *(merrygoroundmuseum.org; adult/youth/child $10/6/free)* features a fully refurbished, vintage Allan Herschell carousel headlined by lead horse, the c 1915 Stargazer. Children will delight in taking a spin atop antique ponies, or maybe a lion, an elephant, a pig or an ostrich – and even a less traditional sea monster. In addition to enjoying the museum's centerpiece, you can also go on a tour to learn about merry-go-round history and culture, and watch artisans at work as they restore period pieces.

Kelleys Island

Gargantuan glacial grooves

For a tamer experience, Kelleys Island offers pretty 19th-century buildings, pleasant beaches and scenic landscapes.

EATING & DRINKING ON THE ERIE LAKESHORE: OUR PICKS

Topsy Turvey's Bar & Grill: Wharf-side venue with Lake Erie perch, homemade chili, and Cuban and other sandwiches. *11am-8pm Mon-Fri, from 9am Sat & Sun* $$

Village Pump: Old-school Kelleys Island tavern. Tuck into fried perch, walleye bites and lobster chowder. Brandy Alexander is the house cocktail. *11am-9pm* $$

Forge: In an old blacksmith shop in Put-In-Bay. Stoke your taste buds with crepes and more. *9am-10pm Mon, Thu & Fri, from 8am Sat & Sun, 5-10pm Wed* $$

Beer Barrel Saloon: A Put-In-Bay pub with plenty of space for imbibing – its bar is 406ft long, billed as the world's longest. *noon-11pm*

Get there by ferry *(kelleysislandferry.com; round-trip adult/youth/child $24/16/free)*, which departs from Marblehead (about 30 minutes one way). Once deposited on the island's south shore, take a moment to appreciate the petroglyphs of **Inscription Rock**, not far from the ferry terminal. Native Americans who used the island as a hunting ground carved symbols into this boulder sometime between 1200 and 1600. It's not known exactly who made them, but historians believe they're the work of either the Late Prehistoric Period Sandusky culture, or the Erie, Cat, Neutral or other Indigenous peoples living in the region when Europeans arrived.

On the island's north shore, another wonder awaits: glacial grooves raked through the limestone. Created some 18,000 years ago, they're the largest and most easily accessible glacial grooves in the world, with gouges some 400ft long, 35ft wide and up to 10ft deep. If you're looking to camp overnight, **Kelleys Island State Park** features a popular ground with over 100 tent and RV sites, 6 miles of hiking trails with birds flitting by and a secluded, sandy beach.

Ohio Amish Country

Spend time in the USA's second-largest Amish community

A sojourn in the region provides pleasures of a slow kind. **Kidron**, on Rte 52, makes a good starting point, and if it's a Thursday, there's no better place than **Kidron Auction** *(kidronauction.com)*. Follow the buggy lineup down the road to the livestock barn. Hay and straw get auctioned at 10:15am, followed by cows at noon, pigs at 1pm, and sheep and goats after that. Next up is **Lehman's** *(lehmans.com)*, the Amish community's main purveyor of modern-looking products that use no electricity, housed in a 32,000-sq-ft barn.

About 25 minutes south, at **Yoder's Amish Home** *(yodersamishhome.com; adult/child $15/10)*, tour a local home, one-room schoolhouse and barn, before taking a buggy ride through a field. Over near Berlin, stop in at **Heini's Cheese Chalet** *(bunkerhillcheese.com)* to grab abundant samples of its 100% natural, unpasteurized cheeses, then stock up on all the Gouda, bleu, cheddar and other varieties you could want. Across the street, **Kauffman's Country Bakery** *(kauffmanscountrybakery.com)* has the fresh bread to pair with it. Pick up a couple of loaves, and maybe a cinnamon pretzel doughnut or mint fudge brownie while you're at it.

Further southwest at **Hershberger's Farm & Bakery**, gorge on dozens of kinds of pie, homemade ice-cream cones and

MORE ABOUT THE AMISH

Rural Wayne and Holmes counties are home to the USA's second-largest Amish community. Visiting here is like entering a preindustrial time warp. Descendants of conservative Dutch-Swiss religious factions who migrated to the USA during the 18th century, the Amish continue to follow the Ordnung (way of life), in varying degrees. Many adhere to rules prohibiting the use of electricity, telephones and motorized vehicles. They wear traditional clothing, farm the land with plow and mule, and go to church in horse-drawn buggies. Others are not so strict. Keep in mind the Amish typically view photographs as taboo, so don't take photos of people without permission.

EATING & DRINKING IN AMISH COUNTRY: OUR PICKS

Mrs Yoder's Kitchen: In Mt Hope, enjoy homey Amish fare in simple environs. Order mains à la carte, or fill up a plate at the buffet. *11am-7pm Mon-Sat* $

Boyd & Wurthmann Restaurant: In Berlin, sample pancakes, pies and Amish specialties such as country-fried steak. Cash only. *5:30am-3:30pm Mon-Thu, to 7:30pm Fri & Sat* $

Park Street Pizza: It seems all of Sugarcreek is here at night. Wood-fired pies with farm-grown ingredients. *3-9pm Tue-Thu, from 11am Fri & Sat, 11am-8pm Sun* $

Wooly Pig Farm Brewery: Part of a 90-acre Fresno farm. Sit outside or in the tasting room for German-style beers. *1-9pm Wed & Thu, to 10pm Fri, noon-10pm Sat, noon-7pm Sun*

MORE OF OHIO'S TOP STATE PARKS & FORESTS

Malabar Farm State Park: This park in Lucas has a lot going on: hiking and horse trails, tractor-drawn farm tours and more.

John Bryan State Park: The highlight at this Yellow Springs park is Clifton Gorge, cut by the pretty Little Miami River.

Hueston Woods State Park: In College corner, golfing, horseback riding, fishing, camping, a nature center and a covered bridge.

Mohican-Memorial State Forest: Between Cleveland and Columbus, more than 4000 acres of forest with over 50 miles of hiking and cycling trails.

South Bass Island State Park: Set atop white cliffs on the island's southwest side, featuring a fishing pier, small rocky beach and watercraft rentals.

seasonal produce from the market inside. Pet the farmyard animals *($8)* and take pony rides *($5)* and draft horse rides *($6)* outside.

Logan

Ohio's most beloved park

Twelve miles southwest of Logan is Ohio's most popular park, **Hocking Hills** *(ohiodnr.gov; free)*. Splendid to explore in any season, it's especially lovely in autumn. Thirty miles of hiking trails meander through the forest past waterfalls and gorges. Two of the park's most famed spots are **Ash Cave** and **Old Man's Cave**, where several short paths (less than a half-mile) deliver scenic payoffs beset with cascades. Nearby **Cedar Falls** has a half-mile trail edged by steep rock walls that leads to a peaceful waterfall and pool. You can also rent a boat and paddle the Hocking River. The visitor center has maps and exhibits of the area's unique geology. There are also cabins and campsites for spending the night.

Also inside Hocking Hills is the **John Glenn Astronomy Park** *(jgap.info; free)*, where visitors have the awe-inspiring opportunity to gaze up at some of the country's darkest skies. The park features 12 telescopes – including one of Ohio's largest – that allow earthlings obsessed with the universe to peer at stars, planets, the moon, nebulae, galaxies and comets, with astronomers and other star experts nearby to interpret what you're seeing. Programs, which are free but should be reserved in advance, take place on Friday and Saturday nights, weather permitting, from March through November. Check the park's Facebook page for the most up-to-date information.

In addition to the small, retractable-roof observatory, there is the adjacent Solar Plaza that has been designed to capture the sun's rays during solstices and equinoxes – a tradition practiced at Stonehenge, England; Chaco Canyon, New Mexico; and elsewhere for centuries.

Dayton

On the aviation trail

Dayton leans hard on its 'Birthplace of Aviation' tagline, and the Wright sights definitely deliver. Begin your day of aircraft admiration on the West Side at the **Dayton Aviation Heritage National Historical Park** *(nps.gov/daav; free)*, where the visitor center, **Wright Cycle Company shop** and

EATING & DRINKING IN SOUTHEASTERN OHIO: OUR PICKS

Union Street Diner: Fueling Athenians for decades; everything from omelets and hash browns to chicken-fried steak, pies and milkshakes. *8am-2pm* $

Little Fish Brewing Co: Taproom and beer garden in Athens. Saisons and sours are the specialty. *noon-10pm Tue-Thu, to 11pm Fri, 11am-11pm Sat, 11am-10pm Mon*

Brewery 33: In Logan, sip craft beer, agave cocktails, cider or mead. Dogs bring their humans for the outdoor seating. *noon-9pm Mon-Thu, to 10pm Fri & Sat, to 8pm Sun*

Hocking Hills Moonshine: A stop at this Logan distillery won't disappoint. Friendly staff will give you a tour with very affordable samples, too. *11am-8pm Mon-Sat*

ARTHURGPHOTOGRAPHY/SHUTTERSTOCK

Ash Cave, Hocking Hills

original site of the Wright Brothers' home are all within a one-block radius, between W 3rd and 4th Sts, and S Williams and Shannon Sts. The visitor center screens a film about the Wright Brothers in the original location of their second print shop, while the cycle company presents exhibits in the original building of their fourth bike shop – yes, Orville and Wilbur were busy men.

A couple of miles south in **Carillon Historical Park**, the **Wright Brothers National Museum** is where you'll see the 1905 Wright Flyer III biplane and a replica of the Wright workshop. And about 10 miles northeast is the **Huffman Prairie Flying Field**, looking much as it did in 1904. Walk the 1-mile trail that loops around, pausing at the history-explaining placards. Indoors to out, it's a surprisingly moving experience to see the cluttered workshop where Orville and Wilbur conjured their ideas and the lonely field where they tested their plane.

Then there's the **National Museum of the US Air Force** *(nationalmuseum.af.mil; free)*, a mind-blowing expanse with miles of planes, rockets and more. Located at Wright-Patterson Air Force Base, the staggering complex of hangars holds just about every aircraft you can think of from through the ages – from a Wright Brothers 1909 Flyer to a Sopwith Camel (WWI biplane). Be sure to visit Building 4 for spacecraft and presidential planes (including the first Air Force One).

The aircraft-themed attractions don't stop there. Finish off your day with a cold one at **Warped Wing Brewing Company** *(warpedwing.com)*, which takes its name from the Wright brothers' breakthrough concept of wing-warping.

OHIO'S ADENA & HOPEWELL HERITAGE

Long before the Europeans came, the Ohio River Valley was the Native home in the Early and Middle Woodland periods (200 BCE to 500 CE) of the, respectively, Adena and Hopewell peoples, whose legacies can still be seen in the huge geometric earthworks and burial mounds they left behind. Of all the mounds that dot Southeastern Ohio, Serpent Mound in Peebles, 50 miles southwest of Chillicothe, is perhaps the most captivating. The giant, uncoiling snake stretches over a quarter of a mile and is the largest effigy mound in the world. South of Columbus, about 3 miles north of Chillicothe, variously shaped ceremonial mounds spread over 13-acre Mound City, a mysterious town of the dead. It's part of the **Hopewell Culture National Historical Park**.

Michigan

BEACH TOWNS | WINE COUNTRY | DYNAMIC DETROIT

Places

More, more, more – Michigan is the Midwest state that cranks it up. It sports more beaches than the Atlantic seaboard. More than half the state is covered by forests. And more cherries and berries get shoveled into pies here than anywhere else in the USA. Plus Detroit is one of the Midwest's most exciting cities, reinventing itself daily with street art and fresh architecture.

Michigan occupies prime real estate, surrounded by four of the five Great Lakes – Superior, Michigan, Huron and Erie. Islands – Mackinac, Manitou and Isle Royale – freckle its coast and make top touring destinations. Surf beaches, colored sandstone cliffs and trekkable sand dunes also woo visitors.

The state consists of two parts split by water: the larger Lower Peninsula (LP), shaped like a mitten; and the smaller, lightly populated Upper Peninsula (UP), shaped like a slipper. They are linked by the gasp-worthy Mackinac Bridge, which spans the Straits of Mackinac.

GETTING AROUND

Detroit has an enormously busy airport that serves as a Midwest hub. Within Detroit, the **QLine streetcar** *(qlinedetroit.com)* and the **People Mover** *(thepeoplemover.com)* provide some handy transport. Grand Rapids, Lansing and Traverse City have smaller air facilities. Amtrak stops throughout the Lower Peninsula's southern half, including in Detroit, Grand Rapids, Ann Arbor, New Buffalo and Holland. Megabus and Greyhound are faster and more widespread. Per usual, driving is fastest. I-75 is the only Interstate that enters the Upper Peninsula. Ferries to Isle Royale National Park sail from Houghton and Copper Harbor. On the west, the ferries that sail across Lake Michigan to/from Wisconsin dock in Muskegon and Ludington. On the region's eastern edge, Michigan has four border crossings to Canada, with the busiest at Detroit.

Detroit

MAP P96

Admire Rivera, Picasso and local artists

From fine art to street art, Detroit is a creative wonderland. First, **Detroit Institute of Arts** *(dia.org; adult/child $20/8)* holds one of the world's premier art collections, and its centerpiece is Diego Rivera's mural *Detroit Industry*, which fills an entire room and reflects the city's blue-collar labor history. Beyond it are Picassos, Caravaggios, suits of armor, modern African American paintings, puppets and troves more spread through 100-plus galleries. A 10-minute walk south, the **Museum of Contemporary Art Detroit** *(mocadetroit.org; adult/child $12/free)* is set in an abandoned, graffiti-slathered auto dealership. Heat lamps hang from the ceiling over peculiar exhibits that change every few months. Music and literary events take place regularly. The on-site cafe-cocktail bar is popular.

For street art, head to the **Lincoln Street Art Park**, an industrial site abutting a recycling facility where you'll see vivid graffiti, murals and sculptures made from found objects. It's a quintessential slice of urban-cool, DIY Detroit that's always changing, as local artists continue to add to it. DJ-fueled dance parties take place on occasion; keep an eye on its Facebook page.

TOP TIP

Don't leave Michigan without trying a pasty! Driving around the Upper Peninsula, you'll see plenty of shops selling the local meat-and-vegetable pot pies brought over by Cornish miners 160 years ago.

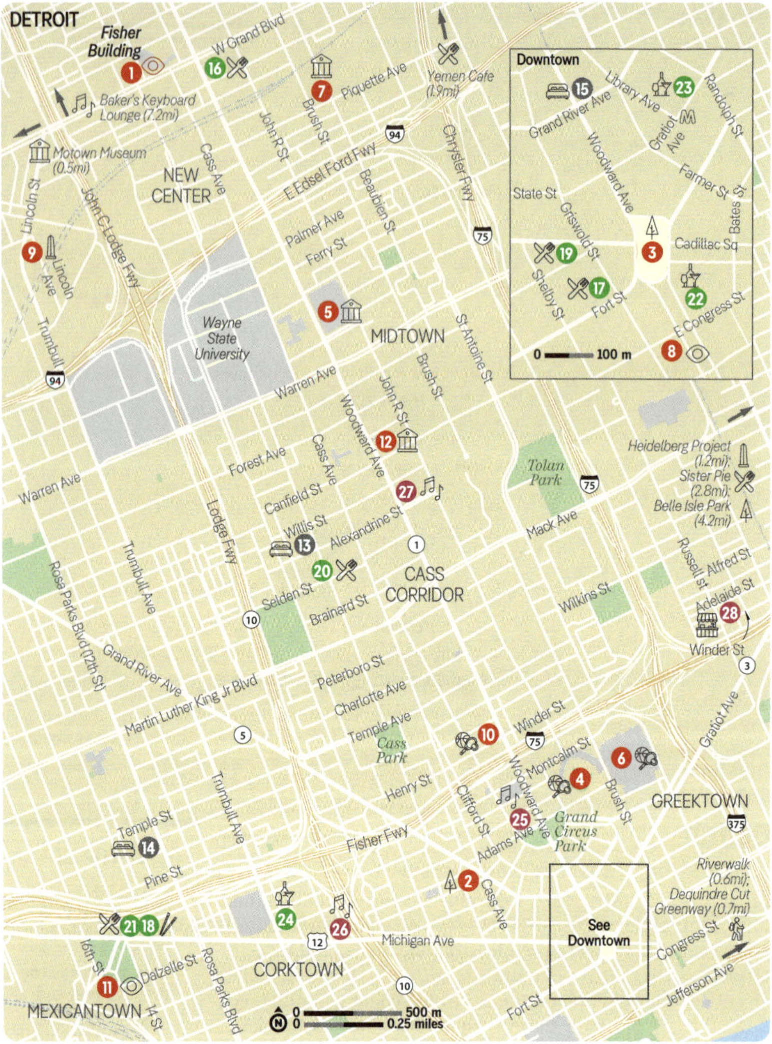

DETROIT

HIGHLIGHTS
1 Fisher Building

SIGHTS
2 Beacon Park
3 Campus Martius Park
4 Comerica Park
5 Detroit Institute of Arts
6 Ford Field
7 Ford Piquette Avenue Plant
8 Guardian Building
9 Lincoln Street Art Park
10 Little Caesars Arena
11 Michigan Central Station
12 Museum of Contemporary Art Detroit

SLEEPING
13 El Moore Lodge
14 Hostel Detroit
15 Shinola Hotel

EATING
16 Baobab Fare
17 Dime Store
18 Ima
19 Lafayette Coney Island
20 Selden Standard
21 Slows Bar BQ

DRINKING & NIGHTLIFE
22 Grand Trunk Pub
23 Standby
24 UFO Bar

ENTERTAINMENT
25 Cliff Bell's
26 Lager House
27 Magic Stick

SHOPPING
28 Eastern Market

And then there's the **Heidelberg Project**: polka-dotted streets, houses covered in Technicolor paint blobs, strange doll sculptures in yards – this is no acid trip, but rather a block-spanning art installation. It's the brainchild of artist Tyree Guyton, who wanted to beautify his rundown community and has been at it for nearly 40 years. It's an ever-evolving work in progress, and now it's undergoing a transformation from a founder-driven project to a community-focused one, celebrating emerging artists.

Eat your heart out at the Eastern Market

The sprawling, multi-shed **Eastern Market** *(easternmarket.org)* bills itself as the largest historic market district in the US, with more than 200 vendors. Whether it's produce, cheese, spices, flowers or beyond, you're sure to find nearly anything your heart desires. Saturday is the main market day, open 6am to 4pm year-round, but you can also turn up Monday through Friday to browse the specialty shops and cafes that flank the halls on Russell and Market Sts. In addition, from June through September, and in November and December, there are scaled-down markets on Tuesdays and craft markets on Sundays. Stop in at the Welcome Center for maps, directories, recipes and more information.

The sounds of jazz, Motown and beyond

Go on a musical tour of Detroit. By day, hit the **Motown Museum** *(motownmuseum.org; adult/youth/child $20/17/free; closed Mon)*, where you can take a tour of the row of modest houses where Berry Gordy launched Motown Records – and the careers of Stevie Wonder, Diana Ross, Marvin Gaye and Michael Jackson – with an $800 loan in 1959. Gordy and Motown split for Los Angeles in 1972, but you can still step into humble Studio A and see where the famed names recorded their first hits. Then by night, bask in the smooth sounds of two of Detroit's most historic jazz clubs, the legendary **Baker's Keyboard Lounge** *(bakerskeyboardloungedet.com)* and **Cliff Bell's** *(cliffbells.com)*. Continuously operating since 1934, Baker's is the world's oldest jazz club, a character-filled time capsule of a space with a small stage and curving art-deco bar, styled as piano keys. Cliff Bell's, meanwhile, is an elegant, candlelit space decked out in mahogany and brass, that started in 1935, before shuttering for a spell between 1985 and 2006. And if rap, rock and indie are more your jam, then **Magic Stick** *(majesticdetroit.com)* is the place for you.

MOTOR CAPITAL OF THE WORLD

French explorer Antoine de La Mothe Cadillac founded Detroit in 1701. Sweet fortune arrived in the 1920s, when Henry Ford began churning out cars. He didn't invent the automobile, as is sometimes mistakenly believed, but he did perfect assembly-line manufacturing and mass-production techniques. The result was the Model T, the first car the USA's middle class could afford to own. Detroit quickly became the motor capital of the world. General Motors (GM), Chrysler and Ford were all headquartered in or near Detroit (and still are). But Japanese competitors shook the industry in the 1970s. Detroit entered an era of deep decline, losing about two-thirds of its population.

EATING IN DETROIT: OUR PICKS

MAP P96

Sister Pie: Owner Lisa Ludwinski (a 2019 James Beard Award finalist) and her female bakers create amazing treats at this corner storefront. *10am-3pm Sat & Sun* $

Dime Store: A cozy, diner-esque venue with sandwiches, truffle mayo-dipped fries and eggy brunch dishes on the menu. *8am-3pm Mon-Tue & Thu-Sun* $

Slows Bar BQ: Southern-style barbecue in Corktown, with three-meat combo plates. Vegetarians have a couple of options, too. *11am-9pm, to 10pm Fri & Sat* $$

Selden Standard: Farm-to-table restaurant serving small plates, including fresh-caught fish, roasted vegetables and house-made bread and butter. *5-10pm* $$$

FROM MOTOWN TO ROCK CITY

Motown Records and soul music put Detroit on the map in the 1960s, while the thrashing punk rock of the Stooges and MC5 was the 1970s' response to that smooth sound. By 1976, Detroit was dubbed 'Rock City' by a Kiss song. In the early 2000s hard-edged garage rock pushed the city to the music-scene forefront, thanks to homegrown stars such as the White Stripes, Von Bondies and Dirtbombs, while Eminem gave Detroit its rap bona fides. And then there's techno, the electronic dance music that DJs in the city created in the mid-1980s; heavy on synthesizer melodies and complex machine rhythms, it became a global sensation. One of the world's largest electronic music festivals still takes place in the city annually in honor of the style.

Support the home team

Detroit is the only US city to host all its major league men's sports teams in the heart of downtown. What's more, they're all in the same neighborhood. If you're in Detroit for a game, spectating can be an affordable and fun way to experience the local sports fandom. Head to **Ford Field** to cheer on Detroit's National Football League (NFL) team, the Lions; **Comerica Park** for its Major League Baseball (MLB) team, the Tigers; and **Little Caesars Arena**, which hosts both the Pistons (National Basketball Association; NBA) and Red Wings (National Hockey League; NHL).

Appreciate architectural grandeur

From Michigan Central Station (the beaux-arts rail terminal designed by the architect of New York's Grand Central) to art-deco beauties like the Fisher and Guardian buildings, Detroit is full of architectural grandeur that harken back to its heyday.

In Corktown, take in the transformation of **Michigan Central Station** *(michigancentral.com; free)*, which after closing in 1988, was left to fall into decline, becoming a symbol of the city's shattered economy. In 2018, Ford Motor Company bought it, and in 2024, it reopened as a new innovation campus. The Station is the focal point of the broader Michigan Central, a 30-acre tech and culture hub with workspace, commercial space, restaurants, parks and plazas. Visitors can book a 90-minute tour journeying through the Station's restoration.

Downtown, the **Guardian Building** *(guardianbuilding.com)* was originally commissioned as a 'cathedral of finance.' Indeed, this distinctive, 40-story, redbrick building with green and white accents was the world's tallest masonry structure when it opened in 1929. The interior is a colorful explosion of marble, mosaic and murals that draw from Aztec, art deco and local influences. For a behind-the-scenes peek of the building's history, arrange a tour through **City Tour Detroit** *(citytourdetroit.com; adult/child $12/6)*.

North, in New Center, the **Fisher Building** *(fisherbuilding.city)* is a 1928 masterpiece from the man who built Detroit, Albert Kahn. Its imposing art-deco exterior is made from Minnesota granite and Maryland marble, while its interior rivals any Italian cathedral – from the soaring vaulted ceilings, featuring an array of intricate, hand-painted patterns, to the sparkling mosaics by Hungarian artist Géza Maróti and gleaming marble on the walls. **Pure Detroit** runs tours *(puredetroit.com; $15)*.

DRINKING IN DETROIT: OUR PICKS

MAP P96

Standby: Hiding in the Belt alleyway, an innovative resto-bar presenting creative cocktails. *5pm-1am Sun, Wed & Thu, to 2am Fri & Sat*

Lager House: Corktown staple: live music, extensive beer list, tasty New Orleans-style grub. *1pm-midnight Mon-Thu, to 2am Fri, 9am-2am Sat, 9am-midnight Sun*

Grand Trunk Pub: Once the Grand Trunk Railroad ticket hall. Vast food and drink menu. *11am-10pm Mon-Wed, to midnight Thu, to 1am Fri & Sat, 10am-10pm Sun*

UFO Bar: A hip hangout featuring cheap beer, grilled cheese sandwiches, indie music and retro vibes. *4pm-2am Tue-Sun*

EQROY/SHUTTERSTOCK

Guardian Building

The first Ford Model T

More than sand dunes, beaches and Mackinac Island fudge, Michigan is synonymous with cars. To trace the state's automotive history, begin in Detroit with a look at the **Ford Piquette Avenue Plant** *(fordpiquetteplant.org; adult/youth/child $20/10/free)*, the landmark factory where Henry Ford cranked out the first Model T. Admission includes a detailed tour by enthusiastic docents, plus loads of shiny vehicles from 1904 onward.

You can see other iconic vehicles in Dearborn, Kalamazoo (p100) and Lansing (p100).

Dearborn

Historical tour of vintage cars

In Dearborn, the quintessential **Henry Ford Museum of American Innovation** *(thehenryford.org; adult/youth/child $38/28.50/free, parking extra, discounted for paying online)* is loaded with vintage cars, including the first one Ford ever built, the 1896 gas-powered Quadricycle. The museum also contains a fascinating wealth of American culture, such as the chair Lincoln was sitting in when he was assassinated, the presidential limo in which Kennedy was killed, the hot-dog-shaped Oscar Mayer Wienermobile and the bus on which Rosa

DETROIT'S BEST PARKS, PLAZAS & PEDESTRIAN WAYS

Belle Isle Park: Floating in the Detroit River, parkland with trails, kayaking, a glass-domed conservatory, beach, aquarium and maritime museum.

Riverwalk: From Hart Plaza to Mt Elliott St, this 3-mile riverfront path passes several parks and outdoor theaters.

Beacon Park: Gathering place featuring food trucks, local vendors, and free concerts and yoga.

Campus Martius Park: In the heart of downtown, a plaza with a fountain, stage, restaurant and bar, plus an ice rink in winter and sandy beach in summer.

Dequindre Cut Greenway: Halfway along the Riverwalk, near Orleans St, a 1.5-mile path juts north, offering a pleasant passageway to Eastern Market.

EATING IN DETROIT: OUR PICKS

MAP P96

Lafayette Coney Island: A 'coney' is a hot dog smothered with chili and onions. It's a Detroit specialty. *9am-midnight, to 2am Fri & Sat* $

Yemen Cafe: Hamtramck favorite serving amazing Arabic food like slow-cooked lamb *haneeth*, *fahsah* (stew) and hummus. *8am-1am* $$

Baobab Fare: Mouthwatering Burundian restaurant. Signature dish is *nyumbani*: a slow-simmered beef and tomato sauce. *11am-9pm Tue-Sun* $$

Ima: Modern *izakaya* experience: outstanding ramen, udon, gyoza, sushi and more. Sake and beer as well. *11am-10pm Mon-Thu, to 11pm Fri, from noon Sat & Sun* $$

DETROIT'S BLACK ROLLER-SKATING CULTURE

Roller-skating remains a beloved pastime in Detroit, and the Black skating community has long been at the center of the city's unique and innovative skating style. In a time when skating rinks barred/limited Black skaters, one family broke barriers when they opened the first Black-owned skating rink, RollerCade, in 1955. In the late 1950s through early 1970s, Black skating culture grew hand in hand with Motown; Detroit-style skating characterized by synchronized movements that follow the beat. RollerCade is still in operation, and many other roller rinks, communities and events have popped up on the scene, like Motown Roller Club and Soul Skate Detroit. The biannual festival draws the world's best skaters and is next slated for May 2026.

PETERSPIRO/GETTY IMAGES

University of Michigan Union building

Parks refused to give up her seat. At the adjacent **Ford Rouge Factory Tour** *(adult/youth/child $26/19.50/free ; closed Sun)*, you can watch F-150 trucks roll off the assembly line; while in **Greenfield Village** *(adult/youth/child $41/30.75/free)*, you can ride in a Model T from 1923. Combination tickets are available. Across the parking lot, the separate interactive **Automotive Hall of Fame** *(automotivehalloffame.org; adult/youth/child $10/4/free; Thu-Sun)* focuses on the people behind notable cars, such as Mr Ferdinand Porsche and Mr Soichiro Honda.

Kalamazoo

Diner and drives

If you're on the car trail and you've got the time, head north of Kalamazoo along Hwy 43 to Hickory Corners and stop at the **Gilmore Car Museum** *(gilmorecarmuseum.org; adult/youth/child $20/12/free)*. Comprising some 20 buildings, this massive museum is filled with nearly 400 vintage autos, including 15 Rolls-Royces dating back to a 1910 Silver Ghost. Take a ride in a classic car, have a hot dog at the Blue Moon Diner and even stay overnight at a rented campsite. Check the calendar in advance, as there are lots of special car shows, seasonal festivals and live music events happening year-round.

Lansing

A riverside route through Michigan's capital

Tour Michigan's capital city by following the **Lansing River Trail** *(lansingrivertrail.org)*, a 16-mile route of paved paths and bridges that run alongside the Grand and Red Cedar rivers. Linking several parks, museums, a farmers market and a zoo, the trail system makes for a convenient way to explore some of the city's top attractions, either by bike or on foot.

Start at **Turner Dodge Park** and head south through **Old Town**, Lansing's arts and entertainment district, and stop at **Brenke Fish Ladder**, a peaceful sculpture-dotted park that's great for picnicking. Keep going and you'll reach the city's indoor farmers market, a science center and the **RE Olds Transportation Museum** *(reoldsmuseum.org; adult/youth/child $10/7/free)*. Featuring a whopping garage full of shiny vintage cars that date back nearly 140 years, the museum, closed Mondays, leads guided 45-minute tours every Friday and Saturday at 1pm *(free with admission)* and hosts the Car Capital Auto Show each summer.

Further south, where the Grand and Red Cedar rivers converge, head east to **Potter Park Zoo**. From there, continue to follow the Red Cedar River eastward toward **Michigan State University**, or opt to veer south and link up with Sycamore Creek. This is the most naturally scenic part of the trail network, with acres of wetlands, wildflower-blanketed meadows and woodlands. (**Fenner Nature Center** makes for a good place to take it all in.) And for those who can't get enough of RE Olds, his tombstone is nearby too, tucked within **Mount Hope Cemetery**.

Ann Arbor

Michigan's most popular college town

Spend some time in the liberal and bookish little city that's home to the **University of Michigan**. Ann Arbor's walkable downtown is loaded with free-trade coffee shops, bookstores and brewpubs. If it's Saturday, peruse the **Farmers Market**: a bounty of goods from the surrounding farms and orchards, offering up everything from spicy pickles to cider to mushroom-growing kits. Make a stop at **Zingerman's Delicatessen** for one of the best Reuben sandwiches you'll ever have. From there, head south toward campus, where you can check out, all for free, the **University of Michigan Museum of Art** – there's a nice collection of Asian ceramics, Tiffany glass and modern abstract works – and the **University of Michigan Museum of Natural History**. Finish with a stroll through **Nichols Arboretum**, a 123-acre oasis of greenery that features a restored prairie landscape and North America's largest peony garden.

Grand Rapids

Tour one of the USA's best beer cities

Once voted the USA's best beer city, Grand Rapids now has 40 craft breweries in and within a half-hour drive of town.

MORE OF MICHIGAN'S BEST MUSEUMS

Great Lakes Shipwreck Museum: Displaying the vestiges of the vessels that have sunk on 'Shipwreck Coast,' the UP stretch from Munising to Whitefish Point.

Broad Art Museum: A parallelogram of stainless steel and glass, designed by Zaha Hadid in East Lansing.

Arab American National Museum: In Dearborn, home to one of the largest Arab American communities, showcasing the artifacts of well-known Arab Americans.

Grand Rapids African American Museum & Archives: Commemorating the contributions of local African Americans to history and culture.

Grand Rapids Public Museum: Established in 1854, Michigan's oldest museum features history, science and a 1928 carousel.

EATING & DRINKING IN CENTRAL MICHIGAN: OUR PICKS

Downtown Market Grand Rapids: Stylish food hall. Standouts are Fish Lads and Love's Ice Cream. *11am-7pm Mon-Thu, to 8pm Fri, 10am-8pm Sat, 10am-7pm Sun* $

Chez Olga: A taste of the Caribbean in Grand Rapids; try curried goat, jerk chicken and creole tofu and more. Looks like a hobbit house! *5-9pm Mon, from 11am Tue-Sat* $$

Stella's Lounge: Grand Rapids restaurant. Award-winning stuffed burgers and other bar fare, including vegan options. *4pm-midnight Mon & Tue, from noon Wed-Sun, to 1am Fri & Sat* $

Naing Myanmar Family Restaurant: Lansing takeout spot. Traditional dishes from Burma, Malaysia and Thailand. Small grocery attached. *11am-8pm Tue-Sat* $

MORE DUNES IN MICHIGAN

They don't call Michigan's 300-mile western shoreline the Gold Coast for nothing.

Warren Dunes: Three miles of beachfront, with climbable dunes 260ft high.

Nordhouse Dunes: Within the Huron-Manistee National Forest, one of Lake Michigan's wildest stretches of shoreline.

Rosy Mound Natural Area: Boardwalk over wooded dunes to the lakeshore; interpretive signs along the way.

Silver Lake Dunes: Only dunes in Michigan where you're allowed to drive your own off-road vehicle.

Arcadia Dunes: Equipped with a universally accessible trail. The Baldy trailhead is here.

Saugatuck Dunes State Park: Dunes over 200ft tall, where visitors can book Saugatuck Dune Rides.

The **Beer City Brewsader app** *(experiencegr.com)* shows you where they are, and allows you to check in at each brewery you visit – when you reach eight, a free Brewsader T-shirt comes your way.

Top picks in Grand Rapids include **Vivant Brewery** for Belgian-style beers in an old chapel, the huge rock-and-roll-style **Founders Brewing Co**, **Mitten Brewing Company** and its wide-ranging brews in a cool old firehouse, and inventive neighborhood gem **Harmony Brewing Company**.

If you prefer a guided experience, book a tour through the popular **Grand Rapids Beer Tours** *(grbeertours.com; incl samples from $70)*. These van tours stop at three or four breweries, where a guide leads you through production facilities and tastings.

Charlevoix & Petoskey

Visit Hemingway's haunts

A number of writers have ties to northwest Michigan, but none are as famous as Ernest Hemingway, who spent the summers of his youth at his family's cottage on Walloon Lake. Go on a self-guided tour of the area to view the places that made their way into his writing. The **Michigan Hemingway Society** *(michiganhemingwaysociety.org)* has all the info you need. In Petoskey, stop at the **Little Traverse History Museum** *(petoskeymuseum.org; adult/child $5/free)* to see a collection that includes rare 1st-edition books the author autographed for a friend when he visited in 1947. Then head over to the nearby **City Park Grill** *(cityparkgrill.com)* to toss back a drink and enjoy some fresh-caught fish at the bar where Hemingway was reportedly a regular.

In Boyne City, there is the **Horton Bay General Store** *(hortonbaygeneralstore.com)*, which readers will recognize for its 'high false front' from Hemingway's short story *Up in Michigan*. The old-time shop now sells sandwiches, charcuterie, ice cream, spirits and wine on the 1st floor, and runs an inn on the 2nd floor. Next door, the **Red Fox Inn**, now listed on the National Register of Historic Places, is where Hemingway would stay with his fishing buddy Vollie Fox. It now operates a shop, with erratic hours, offering Hemingway books and memorabilia.

EATING ON THE GOLD COAST: OUR PICKS

Morning Star Café: Cooking up the best breakfast in Grand Haven. The Michigan blueberry pancakes are a winner. *6:30am-2:30pm* $

Spanglish: Mexican recipes made with Michigan ingredients in Traverse City, with lots of vegetarian and vegan options. *11am-6pm Tue-Sat* $

Paisley Grille: Fried chicken, burgers, fish and chips, and other fantastic gastropub fare at a Grand Haven favorite. *11am-9pm, to 10pm Fri & Sat* $$$

Chandler's: In Petoskey, upmarket fare – from sushi rolls to steak. Extensive wine list. Wine cellar seating available. *11am-9pm Mon-Thu, to 11pm Fri, 9am-9pm Sat & Sun* $$$

TOP EXPERIENCE

Sleeping Bear Dunes National Lakeshore

Extraordinary lake views from atop colossal sand dunes? Water blue enough to be in the Caribbean? Miles of unspoiled beaches? Secluded islands with mystical trees? All here at Sleeping Bear Dunes, along with lush forests, terrific day hikes and glass-clear waterways for paddling. The national park stretches from north of Frankfort to just before Leland, on the Leelanau Peninsula. Several cute towns fringe the area.

Empire Bluff Trail

Manitou Islands

The forest-cloaked **Manitou Islands** provide an off-the-beaten-path adventure. North Manitou is known for star-speckled backcountry camping, while South Manitou is terrific for wilderness-rich day trips. Kayaking and hiking are the big to-dos, especially the 7-mile trek to the Valley of the Giants, an otherworldly stand of cedar trees on South Manitou.

Dune Climb

The park's most popular attraction, this **climb** is up a 200ft-high dune to then run or roll down. Gluttons for punishment can keep slogging all the way to Lake Michigan, a strenuous 1½-hour trek one way.

Trails

The 22-mile paved **Sleeping Bear Heritage Trail** goes from Empire to Bohemian Rd (aka County Rd 669), and makes for a mostly gentle walk/bike ride – though there are some larger hills at the southern end. Trailheads with parking lots are located roughly every 3 miles; the one at Bar Lake Rd, near Empire, is a good place to embark.

The 1.5-mile round-trip **Empire Bluff Trail** rambles through peaceful beech-maple forest and eventually reaches a high bluff with grand views over Lake Michigan. Sunsets are awesome. It's moderately difficult, with a couple of sets of stairs to go up and down.

TOP TIPS

- If you're an America the Beautiful Pass holder, your entrance is already covered.
- This national lakeshore is cashless.
- Planning to camp in summer? Don't rely on first-come, first-served, as sites are likely to be sold out. Reserve online up to six months in advance.

PRACTICALITIES

- nps.gov/slbe
- 24hr
- 7-day pass per car $25

MICHIGAN'S BEST FESTIVALS

National Cherry Festival: A Traverse City tradition since 1931. Nearly 500,000 visitors watch parades, taste cherry pies and crown the National Cherry Queen each first week of July.

Movement: One of the world's largest electronic music festivals is held in Detroit over Memorial Day weekend.

Great Lakes Surf Festival: At Muskegon's Pere Marquette Beach in August, a day of surf lessons, yoga, art, music and more.

ArtPrize: Global artists display pieces throughout Grand Rapids over an annual 16-day period to win juried and popular-vote prizes.

Tulip Time: Holland blooms with millions of tulips – celebrated for nine days in early May, with Dutch food and cultural events at venues around town.

JOHN MCCORMICK/SHUTTERSTOCK

Holland

Tulips, windmills and more

You don't have to cross the ocean for tulips, windmills and clogs. Michigan's Holland has the whole kitschy package, plus a beautiful beach and a destination brewery. In early May, it's **Tulip Time** – the name of Holland's popular nine-day festival that takes over the town with parades, traditional clog dancing, a marketplace with Dutch foods and crafts, and other cultural events. If you haven't timed your trip with the festival, but the tulips are still in bloom, you can see them at **Veldheer Tulip Gardens** *(veldheer.com; adult/child $14/free)*. Outside of tulip season, it's free to check out the wooden-shoe factory, traditional blue-and-white pottery workshop and – somewhat oddly amid the Dutch items – a small buffalo herd.

From there, stop at **Windmill Island Garden** *(holland.org; adult/child $13/6)* to see an original working Dutch windmill, before enjoying lunch at the family-run **DeBoer's Bakkerij and Restaurant** *(deboerbakery.com)*, where the dishes are more Dutch-influenced than true Dutch, but nonetheless tasty. Klompen cakes (like pancakes with caramelized apple or other fruit added), eggs Benedict and croquettes star on the menu. It's touristy, but lots of locals eat here too. Finish with

DRINKING ON THE GOLD COAST: OUR PICKS

Pigeon Hill Brewing Company: In Muskegon, pale ales, IPAs and nitro stouts bubble from the taps. *11am-10pm Mon-Thu, to 11pm Fri & Sat, noon-9pm Sun*

Beards Brewery: A couple of home brewers opened Beards in Petoskey, and they know their stuff. Outside patio overlooking the bay. *11:30am-10pm Tue-Sun*

Odd Side Ales: Experimental suds in Grand Haven, like Tiramisu Bean Flicker and Imperial Mayan Mocha Stout. *11:30am-10pm Mon-Thu, to midnight Fri & Sat, to 9pm Sun*

Beer Church: In a former Methodist church in New Buffalo, signature brews include Pontius Pilate IPA and Crooked Cross cream ale. Wine and cocktails, too. *8am-midnight*

Holland tulip field

a pint at **New Holland Brewing Pub on 8th** *(newholland brew.com)*, known for its robust beers, such as Tangerine Space Machine and Dragon's Milk stout.

Michigan's Wine Country

Viticulture along the shore

Michigan has five main wine regions, aka American Viticulture Areas (AVAs) – Fennville, Lake Michigan Shore, Leelanau Peninsula, Old Mission Peninsula and Top of the Mitt – and four of them produce 95% of the state's wines. Those are Lake Michigan Shore, which actually encompasses Fennville; and Leelanau and the next door Old Mission peninsulas, near Traverse City. With so much great wine around, where to go? If you love a bold red, stick down south; if riesling is your thing, head up north; or, of course, there's nothing wrong with doing both.

Hop on the **Lake Michigan Shore Wine Trail** *(miwine trail.com)*, the stretch of I-94 and I-196 between New Buffalo and Saugatuck (and east to Kalamazoo) where about 15 member wineries are clustered.

Up in the Leelanau Peninsula AVA, there's the **Leelanau Peninsula Wine Trail** *(lpwines.com)* connecting 21 member wineries – go on a guided or self-guided bike tour with **Grand Traverse Bike Tours** *(grandtraversebiketours.com)*. Nearby, north of downtown Traverse City, the **Old Mission Peninsula Wine Trail** *(ompwinetrail.com)* links together 10 more. Tasting prices vary by winery, but range from $5 to $15 for four to six tastes.

MICHIGAN'S TOP SPOTS FOR WINTER ACTIVITIES

Eben Ice Caves: Fantastical caves form when snow melts and freezes over a cliff's edge, glowing green-yellow from the tannins.

Muskegon Luge Adventure Sports Park: One of the nation's only public luge tracks, with cross-country ski and snowshoe trails, too. Clinics and rentals available.

Boyne Mountain Resort: More than 400 acres of skiing in Boyne Falls, including 63 downhill trails and 11 lifts.

Porkies Winter Sports Complex: Downhill skiing with a 787ft vertical drop, plus 26 miles of cross-country trails. Beginner-friendly.

Munising Snowmobile Trail System: Billed as the 'Snowmobile Capital of the Midwest,' this city has 10 trails that cover 300 miles.

The M-22

One of Michigan's most scenic drives

Take a ride along the M-22, arguably Michigan's most scenic drive, with dramatic vistas over Lake Michigan. The pretty

NEED TO KNOW: THE UPPER PENINSULA

Residents of the UP, aka 'Yoopers,' consider themselves distinct from the rest of the state – they've even threatened to secede in the past. Rugged and isolated, with hardwood forests blanketing 90% of its land, the UP is edged by Lakes Huron, Michigan and Superior. Only 45 miles of Interstate highway slice through the trees, punctuated by a handful of cities, of which Marquette is the largest. The Keweenaw Peninsula is the UP's northernmost bit; its largest town Houghton is the jump-off to Isle Royale National Park, with ferries and seaplanes departing in summer. Further ahead on Hwy 26 is the turnoff for the Brockway Mountain Dr, which goes along the spine of the eponymous crag to reach the Copper Harbor, where another ferry sails for Isle Royale.

route goes from Manistee to Traverse City, hugging more than 100 miles of coastline, passing Sleeping Bear Dunes National Lakeshore (p103) and plenty of fun diversions along the way. Don't miss **Fishtown** *(lelandmi.org)*, a tiny commercial fishing village in **Leland** from the early 1900s and one of the few to be preserved on the Great Lakes shore. Wander among the shanties and see fish being cleaned and smoked, then pick up some to try at **Carlson's Fishery** *(carlsonsfishery.com)*.

Stop off for some grub in **Northport** – you can't go wrong at **Fischer's Happy Hour Tavern** *(fischershappyhour.com)*, a vintage tavern tucked in the woods, where the broasted (it combines broiling and roasting) chicken and fish are excellent – before stopping off for some suds in **Suttons Bay**. For beer, head to the outdoor beer garden at the **Hop Lot Brewing Company** *(hoplotbrewing.com)*; for cider, **Tandem Ciders** *(tandemciders.com)*.

At M-22's end in **Traverse City**, aka Michigan's 'cherry capital,' treat yourself to a slice of **Grand Traverse Pie Company's** top-selling cherry crumb pie (or one of its other seven or so pies with cherries). There are also guided kayak pub crawls via outfitters like **Paddle for Pints** *(paddleforpints.com; from $99)* or **Paddle TC** *(paddletc.com; from $69)*. Prices don't include the alcohol.

Mackinac Island

Ditch your car for two wheels

Mackinac's location in the straits between Lake Michigan and Lake Huron made this 3.8-sq-mile island a prized port in the North American fur trade, and a site the British and Americans battled over many times. To get here, catch the ferry from either Mackinaw City or St Ignace.

In 1898, cars were banned to encourage tourism, and 80% of the island is state parkland. Edging the island's shoreline is Hwy 185 (aka Lake Shore Rd), the only Michigan highway that doesn't permit cars. The best way to view the incredible scenery along this 8-mile road is by bicycle; bring your own or rent one at one of the many businesses. You can loop around the flat road in an hour. Along the way, you'll see the huge limestone **Arch Rock** *(mackinacparks.com)*, curving 150ft above Lake Huron and providing dramatic photo opportunities; and **Fort Mackinac** *(adult/child $17/10.25)*, built in 1780 by the British and one of the best preserved military forts in the country. Costumed interpreters, and cannon and rifle firings entertain the kids. Stop at the tearoom for a bite and

(continues on p109)

EATING IN THE UP: OUR PICKS

Syl's Cafe: In Ontonagon, breakfast is Syl's glory. Lunch and dinner don't disappoint either. The UP specialty (pasties) is available anytime. *7:30am-9pm* $

Falling Rock Cafe & Bookstore: New/used books, live music and wi-fi with your sandwich and coffee in downtown Munising. *8am-4pm, to 6pm Thu, to 8pm Fri & Sat* $

Jampot: In Eagle Harbor, bearded, black-robed monks from a nearby monastery sell homemade jams, coffee and pastries. *noon-4pm Tue-Thu, 10am-5pm Fri & Sat* $

Lake Superior Brewing Company: Whitefish and pizzas with house-made brews at this pub in Grand Marais. Also called the Dunes Saloon. *noon-midnight* $$

TOP EXPERIENCE

Isle Royale National Park

Totally free of vehicles and roads, Isle Royale National Park – a 210-sq-mile island in Lake Superior with 2000 moose roaming through the forest – is certainly the place to go for peace and quiet. It gets fewer visitors in a year than Yellowstone National Park gets in a day. The island is laced with 165 miles of hiking trails that connect dozens of campgrounds along Superior and inland lakes.

SANYA KUSHAK/GETTY IMAGES

Greenstone Ridge Trail

At 42 miles, Greenstone Ridge Trail is the longest on Isle Royale, a grand backpacking adventure that spans the entire length of the island from Rock Harbor in the east to Windigo in the west. You can hike it in either direction, but most people start in Rock Harbor and take five to seven days to complete the epic wilderness trek.

The moderately difficult route pays off big time with forest solitude, fab lookouts over the wave-based coast and abundant moose and red fox sightings. The only accommodations along the way are basic campgrounds with pit toilets, so you have to carry all food and gear. Whether you finish in Windigo or Rock Harbor, it's easy to arrange boat transportation back to your starting point.

Stoll Trail

This easy 4.4-mile loop begins at Rock Harbor Lodge (p137) and meanders through old-growth forest and along shoreline bluffs to Scoville Point, an outcrop that unfurls dramatic views of Lake Superior and the craggy landscape. Keep an eye out for moose and osprey.

TOP TIPS

- It may be more cost efficient for groups to purchase a season pass *($60)*, which covers the pass holder, plus three more adults.
- If you're an America the Beautiful Pass holder, you're already covered to enter Isle Royale.
- Pay entrance fees online in advance; otherwise, it's credit card only on-site.

PRACTICALITIES

- nps.gov/isro
- 24hr mid-Apr to Oct
- daily adult/child $7/free

TOP EXPERIENCE

Pictured Rocks National Lakeshore

Stretching along Lake Superior, Pictured Rocks National Lakeshore is a series of wild cliffs and caves, where blue and green minerals have streaked the red and yellow sandstone into a kaleidoscope of color. In between Grand Marais in the east to Munising in the west, you'll find lakeside hikes, kayak trips and boat tours that feature brilliant ways to take in the area's shipwrecks, waterfalls and artist's-palette geology.

Au Sable Point Light Station

TOP TIPS

- If you are an America the Beautiful Pass holder, you're already covered to enter Pictured Rocks.
- This national lakeshore is cashless.
- Cell service is spotty here, so be sure to download maps ahead of time.

Sights

Top sights (from east to west) include the c 1874 **Au Sable Point Light Station** and its surrounding shipwrecks; agate-strewn **Twelvemile Beach**, accessed via the campground; hike-rich **Chapel Falls**, **Chapel Rock** and **Chapel Beach**; and view-worthy **Miners Castle**, one of the lakeshore's most distinctive rock formations.

Cruises

Boats with both deck and enclosed seating glide along the shore for 40 miles, passing many of Pictured Rocks' most popular sights. Rides last between two and three hours – the sunset option is particularly lovely – and depart from Munising's city dock. Book through **Pictured Rock Cruises** *(picturedrocks.com)*; reserving ahead is wise.

Kayaking

Kayaking is popular in Pictured Rocks and no wonder, given that you paddle beneath sheer, color-stained bluffs with names like Lovers Leap, Flower Vase and Caves of the Bloody Chiefs. The duck's-eye view of the geologic features is awesome. Experienced paddlers can go it alone, but conditions are often wavy and windy. Newbies should go with a guide. Several operate out of Munising, with trips from just a few hours to all day. **Pictured Rocks Kayaking** *(picturedrockskayaking.com)* has good ones for beginners.

PRACTICALITIES

- nps.gov/piro
- 24hr
- 7-day pass per car $25

(continued from p106)
a million-dollar view of downtown and the Straits of Mackinac from the outdoor tables. The fort admission price also allows you entry to five other museums in town along Market St, including the **Mackinac Art Museum**, which houses Native American arts, historic maps and island photography.

Marquette

Outdoor adventures in nature's playground

The Upper Peninsula's largest (and snowiest) town, lakeside Marquette draws the outdoor enthusiasts. Forests, beaches and cliffs provide a playground spitting distance from downtown for skiing, hiking, biking, boating and beyond.

The easy **Sugarloaf Mountain Trail** and the harder, wilderness-like **Hogsback Mountain Trail** both have panoramic views, while the **Noquemanon Trail Network** *(noquetrails.org)* is highly recommended for mountain biking and cross-country skiing.

For water-sports enthusiasts, **Down Wind Sports** *(shopdownwindsports.com)* rents all kinds of gear and has the lowdown on kayaking, fly-fishing, surfing, ice climbing and other adventures.

In the city, on a peninsula jutting out into Lake Superior, the high bluffs of **Presque Isle Park** make a great place to catch the sunset.

Porcupine Mountains

Roam Michigan's largest state park

Michigan's largest state park, **Porcupine Mountains** *(michigandnr.com; per day $11)*, with 90 miles of trails, is a wilderness winner. 'The Porkies,' as they're called, are so rugged that loggers bypassed most of the range in the early 19th century, leaving the park with the largest tract of old-growth forest between the Rocky Mountains and Adirondacks. Along with 300-year-old hemlock trees, the Porkies are known for waterfalls, 20 miles of undeveloped Lake Superior shoreline, black bears lumbering about, and the view of the park's stunning Lake of the Clouds, the area's most photographed sight. After stopping at the **visitor center** to pay the park entrance fee, continue to the end of Hwy 107 and climb 300ft via a short path for the stunning view of the shimmering water. Lengthier trails depart from the parking lot.

MORE OF MICHIGAN'S TOP STATE PARKS

Tahquamenon Falls State Park: The Upper Falls' 50ft drop flows with hemlock-tinted waters, while the Lower Falls' series of small cascades swirl around an island.

Petoskey State Park: Beautiful beach featuring indigenous Petoskey stones (honeycomb-patterned fragments of ancient coral).

Grand Haven State Park: A 48-acre urban park that's all beach: popular in summer for swimming, a boardwalk and a tall red lighthouse.

Holland State Park: Has a Lake Michigan beach for sunset gaping, along with an inland Lake Macatawa beach where watercraft can be rented.

Ludington State Park: Once inside, simply pull over on the roadside and make a break for the beautiful beach. Trail system and lighthouse, too.

DRINKING IN THE UP: OUR PICKS

Keweenaw Brewing Company: In Houghton, quality pints, including Widow Maker black ale and Pick Axe blonde ale. *3-10pm Mon-Wed, 11am-midnight Thu-Sat, noon-8pm Sun*

Blackrocks Brewery: Set in a cool refurbished house in Marquette, making deliciously hoppy beers, heavy on American IPAs. *4-11pm Mon, from noon Tue-Sun*

Ore Dock Brewing Co: Across from the docks in downtown Marquette, with laid-back bar, sidewalk seating, often food trucks out front. *noon-11pm, to midnight Fri & Sat*

Drifa Brewing Company: South of downtown Marquette, a dog-friendly brewery with tasty pours, ample outdoor seating area, and food truck. *noon-10pm, to 11pm Thu-Sat*

Wisconsin

FUN TRADITIONS | BEER BONANZA | WATER ADVENTURES

Places

TOP TIP

Buy a Wisconsin state park annual pass. It costs $38 per vehicle, whereas a day pass costs $16 per vehcle, so if you're visiting for more than two days it pays off quickly. Buy it online or at any of the parks.

Wisconsin is cheesy and proud of it. Its cow-speckled farmland pumps out more cheddar, Gouda and other pungent wedges than any other US state, and local license plates read 'America's Dairyland' with udder dignity.

So embrace the cheese thing, because there's a good chance you'll be here for a while. Wisconsin has a ton to offer: exploring the rocky coastline and lighthouses of Door County, kayaking through sea caves at Apostle Islands National Lakeshore, touring Green Bay's football shrine of Lambeau Field and driving along the bluff-framed Great River Rd. Families soak up the Wisconsin Dells' kitschy water parks, while architecture buffs marvel at Frank Lloyd Wright's forever home. The state's two largest cities, Milwaukee and Madison, welcome by offering bountiful beer, markets and locavore eats. At week's end, the whole state throws a party known as the Friday night fish fry, a quintessential Wisconsin experience.

Milwaukee

MAP P112

Brewery tours in Brew City

Milwaukee's enduring relationship with beer is no accident. The city was settled by Germans in the 1840s, and many started breweries. A few decades later, the introduction of bulk-brewing technology turned beer production into a major industry here, with Pabst, Schlitz, Blatz and Miller leading the way.

GETTING AROUND

The main Interstates are I-94 (runs east-west, connecting Milwaukee to Chicago and Minneapolis), I-90 (runs east-west near Madison) and I-43 (runs north-south, connecting Milwaukee to Green Bay). Wisconsin has no toll roads. Note that roads into Door County and the Wisconsin Dells often get jammed on summer weekends.

Amtrak runs a popular train between downtown Milwaukee and Chicago seven times per day; the trip takes 1½ hours and is often faster than driving.

Going on a brewery tour is a beloved Milwaukee activity, and visits typically include several samples. Make all bookings in advance.

Historic **Miller Brewing Company** *(millerbrewerytour.com; tours $20)* is the granddaddy of the scene. Though the mass-produced beer may not be your favorite, the factory impresses with its sheer scale: you'll visit the packaging plant where thousands of cans are filled each minute and the warehouse where half a million cases await shipment. It's closed Tuesday and Wednesday.

Much-loved **Lakefront Brewery** *(lakefrontbrewery.com; tours $13-16)* puts on 50-minute tours daily. Guides have a

EATING IN MILWAUKEE: OUR PICKS

MAP P112

Pitch's Lounge & Restaurant: Retro spot that's been family-run since 1942. Don't miss the baby back ribs. *5-9pm Wed, Thu & Sun, to 10pm Fri & Sat* $$

Uncle Wolfie's Breakfast Tavern: The brunch crowd lines up for biscuits and gravy, French toast and Bloody Marys. *8am-2pm Tue-Thu, to 3pm Fri-Mon* $$

Comet Cafe: Locals of all types pile in for meatloaf smothered in beer gravy and some of Milwaukee's best mac and cheese. *9am-9pm* $$

Odd Duck: Boisterous room for inventive, locally sourced small plates and cocktails; lots of vegetarian options. Reserve ahead. *3pm-midnight Tue-Sat* $$$

HIGHLIGHTS
1 Milwaukee Art Museum

SIGHTS
2 America's Black Holocaust Museum
3 Bobblehead Hall of Fame and Museum
4 Bradford Beach
5 Bronze Fonz
6 Discovery World at Pier Wisconsin
7 Harley-Davidson Museum
8 Pabst Mansion

SLEEPING
9 Ambassador
10 Brewhouse Inn & Suites
11 County Clare Irish Inn

EATING
12 Comet Cafe
13 Milwaukee Public Market
14 Odd Duck
15 Pitch's Lounge & Restaurant
16 Swingin' Door Exchange
17 Uncle Wolfie's Breakfast Tavern

DRINKING & NIGHTLIFE
18 Best Place
19 Bryant's Cocktail Lounge
20 Central Standard Craft Distillery
21 Don's TV & Repair
22 Lakefront Brewery
23 Third Space Brewing

ENTERTAINMENT
24 German Fest
see 24 Irish Fest
see 24 Polish Fest
see 24 PrideFest
see 24 Summerfest

great sense of humor, and they take you right up to the bottling line. It's super-fun.

Pabst doesn't brew in Milwaukee anymore, but you can head to **Best Place** *(bestplacemilwaukee.com; tours $14-25)*, a dark-wood tavern in the former brewery headquarters, to tour the company's historic premises.

Chow down at a fish fry

Friday is the hallowed day of the 'fish fry' all over Wisconsin. This communal meal of beer-battered cod, French fries and coleslaw came about years ago, providing locals with a cheap meal to socialize around and celebrate the end of the working week. Milwaukee is a terrific place to take part in the convention, as it's still going strong at many local bars and restaurants.

Lakefront Brewery (p111) hosts a popular fish fry in its beer hall that includes a polka band letting loose. **Swingin' Door Exchange** *(swingindoorexchange.com)* goes beyond the norm with its throwback, dark-wood ambience and elevated side dishes like spicy vermouth carrots. At **South Shore Terrace** *(southshoreterrace.com)*, you'll eat your fish in a sprawling lakefront beer garden.

Renegade bikes at the Harley Museum

Celebrate more than a century of motorcycles at the **Harley-Davidson Museum** *(harley-davidson.com/museum; adult/child $25/11)*. The company was founded in Milwaukee in 1903 when schoolmates William Harley and Arthur Davidson built and sold their first motorcycle. This museum has hundreds of motorcycles that show the styles through the decades, including the flashy rides of Elvis and Evel Knievel and 'Serial Number One,' the oldest known Harley in existence. Even nonbikers will enjoy the interactive exhibits and leather-clad crowds.

Art inside and out

On the shore of Lake Michigan, the **Milwaukee Art Museum** *(mam.org; adult/child $27/free)* showcases more than 32,000 works, including fabulous folk and outsider art and a sizeable collection of paintings by Wisconsin native Georgia O'Keeffe.

The museum building is a work of art itself and features a stunning winglike addition by Spanish architect Santiago Calatrava. Called the Burke Brise Soleil, the moveable shade is made of 72 steel fins spanning 217ft, slightly larger than a Boeing 747's wings. They spread wide with the museum opening at 10am, flap at noon and close at 5pm (8pm on Thursdays). Head to the suspension bridge outside for the best view of the action.

Sights along the RiverWalk

Edged by Lake Michigan and crisscrossed by three rivers, Milwaukee was made for waterfront wandering. The RiverWalk path cuts through downtown along both sides of the Milwaukee River. Don't miss the **Bronze Fonz** on the RiverWalk's east side, just south of Wells St. The Fonz, aka Arthur Fonzarelli, was a character from the 1970s TV show *Happy Days*, which was set in Milwaukee. It's a quintessential photo op.

MILWAUKEE'S BEST FESTS

Summerfest: The 'world's largest music festival' brings 600 rock, blues, country and alternative bands over nine days in June and July.

German Fest: Get ready for the dachshund derby, oompah bands, lots of beer drinking and shouts of 'Prost!' in late July.

Irish Fest: In mid-August, crowds amass for corned beef and cabbage, fiddle music, step dancing and beer guzzling.

Polish Fest: Get your fill of vodka tastings, polka dancing and cooking classes over three days in mid-June.

PrideFest: Beer drinking, live music, a dance pavilion and a family stage are all part of the June festivities.

DRINKING IN MILWAUKEE: OUR PICKS

MAP P112

Bryant's Cocktail Lounge: Opened in 1938, Milwaukee's oldest cocktail bar has no menu, just knowledgeable bar staff who mix up magic. *hours vary*

Don's TV & Repair: Swig boozy shakes named after old gaming consoles, mimosas served in a cute little bathtub and huge old fashioneds. *hours vary*

Central Standard Craft Distillery: Creates its own vodka, brandy, bourbon and whiskey, best enjoyed on the 5th-floor rooftop. *hours vary*

Third Space Brewing: The huge beer garden is an excellent choice for summertime sips, often accompanied by live music. *hours vary*

MORE MILWAUKEE TO-DO'S

America's Black Holocaust Museum: Founded by a lynching survivor, the museum presents a moving story of Black resilience despite centuries of oppression.

Bobblehead Hall of Fame and Museum: You know the bouncy-noggin dolls that look like celebrities? More than 10,000 of them bob here.

Pabst Mansion: Tour the Gilded Age grandiosity of beer baron Captain Frederick Pabst.

Discovery World at Pier Wisconsin: The lakefront science and technology museum features aquariums and a cool Les Paul electric guitar exhibit.

Bradford Beach: Legions of locals swim, play volleyball and lick frozen custard at this sandy strand a few miles north of downtown.

Onward as you head south is the **Milwaukee Public Market** *(milwaukeepublicmarket.org)*, packed with local vendors selling cheese, sandwiches, beer and frozen custard each day.

Continue south along the path and you'll be in the heart of the **Third Ward**, an old warehouse district that's now a hub of galleries, boutiques and cool-cat dining venues powered by area farms, orchards and creameries. Pick a waterside bar or cafe to while away an afternoon or evening.

Racine

Unexpected architecture stop

By most accounts, the southeastern city of Racine is an unremarkable industrial town, but it has two key Frank Lloyd Wright sights. Start at the **SC Johnson Administration Building & Research Tower** *(reservations.scjohnson.com; tours free)*, where Wright designed several striking buildings. Ninety-minute tours cover the 1939 Admin Building, with tall, flared columns in its vast Great Workroom and 43 miles of Pyrex glass-tube windows letting in soft, natural light. You'll also see the 1950 Research Tower – where Raid, Off and other famous products were developed – which features 15 floors of curved brick bands and more Pyrex windows.

About 5 miles north, **Wingspread** *(reservations.scjohnson.com; tours free)* is the house Wright designed for HF Johnson Jr, one of the company's leaders. It's the last and largest of Wright's Prairie-style abodes, completed in 1939, with 500 windows and a 30ft-high chimney. Tours for both sights run Wednesday through Sunday (reduced in winter) and must be booked in advance.

Racine makes a great stop between Milwaukee and Chicago.

Bite into a mega pastry

Racine is a prime place to sample the tire-sized state pastry known as the 'kringle.' The oval-shaped confection consists of 32 or more layers of flaky dough filled with fruits and nuts and baked until golden brown. Racine became a hub for the treat in the late 1800s, when the recipe came over with the many Danish immigrants who settled in the city. The kringles at family-owned **O&H Danish Bakery** (*ohdanishbakery.com*) are addictive wonders in flavors such as cranberry cream cheese, chocolate pecan and almond.

Madison

Wander the college district for art, beer and books

Madison is a pretty combination of small, grassy state capital and liberal, bookish college town. But it's that college – the University of Wisconsin and its 50,000 students – that dominates the scene and invites an afternoon hangout (which may well lead to an evening hangout).

The **Memorial Union** *(union.wisc.edu)* is the gathering spot. The sun-splashed terrace, set on Lake Mendota, could not be more perfect for a pitcher of beer and brat (local parlance for bratwurst). You can rent kayaks and paddleboards,

YOUNGRYAND/SHUTTERSTOCK

State Street, Madison

or walk the trail around the lake. In winter the action moves indoors to the fireplace-warmed beer hall.

Nearby, the **Chazen Museum of Art** *(chazen.wisc.edu; free)* goes way beyond the norm for a university collection. The 3rd floor holds most of the genre-spanning trove: everything from the Old Dutch Masters to Picasso sculptures and Andy Warhol pop art.

State St links the campus to the Capitol. The mile-long, pedestrian-only road is lined with poets' cafes, parked bicycles and stores selling Free Tibet stickers through clouds of jasmine incense. Several locavore and international restaurants also fold in to the scene.

Graze through the Farmers Market

On Saturdays mornings from mid-April to early November, a food bazaar takes over Madison's Capitol Square. The **Dane County Farmers Market** *(dcfm.org; free)* is one of the nation's most expansive markets, famed for its artisan cheeses and breads. Keep your eyes peeled for Bleu Mont Dairy, which makes fantastic cheeses in a climate-controlled cave; and Stella's Bakery, which makes warm, pliable cheese bread. Street musicians and arts-and-crafts vendors add to the bohemian festival atmosphere. It gets crowded, but you can always find a tree-shaded grassy spot for respite.

WISCONSIN'S BEST TRAILS

Ice Age Trail: Zigzags 1200 miles up and down the state, revealing icy springs, pine woods and bluff-top views. *iceagetrail.org*

400 State Trail: Gentle 22-mile cycling path between Elroy and Reedsburg that rolls through a farm-studded river valley.

Elroy-Sparta State Bike Trail: This 33-mile rail-trail meanders up hills, through old tunnels and alongside pastures; connects to the 400 State Trail.

Oak Leaf Trail: a 135-mile paved path that takes in parks, forests and lakefront vistas around Milwaukee.

CAMBA Trail System: The Chequamegon Area Mountain Bike Association has 250 miles of northern Wisconsin trails for beginners and experts.

EATING IN MADISON: OUR PICKS

Mickie's Dairy Bar: Diner near campus that's been slinging breakfast for generations. Try the cinnamon roll French toast. *7am-2pm Wed-Sun* $

Tipsy Cow: Popular spot near Capitol Square for hobnobbing over burgers and beers from small-batch producers. *11am-10pm Mon-Sat* $

Lucille: Concocts inventive pizzas and cocktails across three stylish floors. *3-11pm Mon-Wed, 11am-11pm Thu & Sun, 11am-1am Fri & Sat* $$

Old Fashioned: Woodsy, retro spot for eating walleye, cheese soup and other Wisconsin specialties. *11am-9pm Mon-Thu, to 10pm Fri & Sat* $$

BEST WEIRD WISCONSIN SIGHTS

House on the Rock: Abode stuffed to mind-blowing proportions with wonderments, like whirring music machines, an enormous carousel and glass-walled 'infinity room.'

National Mustard Museum: Born of one man's ridiculously intense passion, it houses around 6000 mustards and kooky condiment memorabilia.

Dr Evermor's Sculpture Park: Found objects welded into a hallucinatory world of futuristic birds, dragons and other bizarre structures.

Cow Chip Throw: In September in Prairie du Sac, 800 competitors fling dried manure patties.

Concrete Park: A lumberjack's extraordinary folk art, featuring 200-plus whimsical, life-size sculptures.

If you're in town on a nonmarket day, get your fix at **Fromagination** *(fromagination.com)*, a shop that carries loads of hard-to-find local cheeses.

Wisconsin Dells

Water parks, both constructed and natural

About an hour's drive north of Madison, the **Wisconsin Dells** *(wisdells.com)* is an epicenter of kitschy diversions, including more than 20 water parks, water-skiing thrill shows, epic mini-golf courses and Ripley's Believe It or Not oddities. Practically every Midwestern family has splashed through a weekend here.

But beyond the carnival-like attractions, the Dells offers a nature fix amid limestone gorges and rushing rivers. **Dells Boat Tours** *(dellsboats.com; adult/child $40/20)* glide into the scenery; the Upper Dells trip is particularly lovely. Or head to nearby **Mirror Lake State Park** *(dnr.wisconsin.gov; vehicle day pass $16)* to hike amid sandstone bluffs that surround a glassy lake where you also can rent kayaks and pontoon boats. In winter, cross-country skiers glide over 18 miles of groomed trails, and ice fisherfolk set up on the lake. Even architecture buffs get a thrill here: Frank Loyd Wright's Seth Peterson Cottage is tucked in the woods, and visitors can rent it if they get on the waiting list two years in advance.

Spring Green

Explore Frank Lloyd Wright's Taliesin

Renowned architect Frank Lloyd Wright chose the rolling green hills and valleys of southwestern Wisconsin for his dream home. He built **Taliesin** *(taliesinpreservation.org; tours from $35)* in 1911 in his signature Prairie style using low horizontal lines and local materials like limestone and river sand. Tours take you inside the house (actually the third Taliesin incarnation, after fires burned the first two), resplendent with warm, natural light and his clever custom-built decor. Longer jaunts go to other parts of the 800-acre estate, such as the Hillside Studio where he taught his apprentices. Wright lived at Taliesin on and off for almost 50 years.

Buy tickets in advance. Park at the visitor center. A shuttle bus takes you to the house. Even if you're not going on a tour, you can park and walk on the public trails that depart from the visitor center. Taliesin is an hour's drive east of Madison.

See a play in the woods

So you're in Spring Green to see Frank Lloyd Wright's mega sight. Why not stay into the evening for a magical show at **American Players Theatre** *(americanplayers.org; tickets from $66)*? The critically acclaimed troupe stages classical productions at an outdoor amphitheater in the woods. There's nothing like seeing *A Midsummer Night's Dream* under a silvery moon. Bring a picnic – it's tradition to hang out and nibble before the show. **Wander Provisions** *(wanderprovisions.com)* is a good place to stock up.

ROLLING ON THE GREAT RIVER ROAD

The Mississippi River forms Wisconsin's southwestern border, and alongside it runs the timeless, cheese-and-pie-laden Great River Rd.

START	END	LENGTH
Ellsworth Cooperative Creamery	La Crosse	105 miles; 5 hours

The Great River Rd follows Old Man River throughout its 2300-mile flow from Minnesota to Louisiana. Wisconsin's sections are among the prettiest. Start inland at 1 **Ellsworth Cooperative Creamery**, the state's largest cheese-curd producer. Bite a curd, and hear it squeak: a Wisconsin rite of passage.

Head south 15 miles to WI-35. Now you're on the River Rd, curving past bluffs until you reach 2 **Stockholm Pie & General Store**. Study the blackboard: double lemon, triple chocolate pecan, butterscotch cream? The slice will fuel you 6 miles to Pepin, where *Little House on the Prairie* fans can stop at the 3 **Laura Ingalls Wilder Museum**, and foodies at renowned, book-stuffed 4 **Harbor View Cafe**.

Stay on WI-35 a short distance to the 5 **Nelson Cheese Factory**. The shop carries a stash of Wisconsin cheese and rich ice cream. Take the bridge across the river to Wabasha, MN, where the 6 **National Eagle Center** gives the lowdown on the mighty birds, about 100 of which flock here each winter.

From Wabasha, stay on Hwy 61 on the Minnesota side for 60 miles, passing bucolic farms and green hills. Cross the bridge to La Crosse, WI. Get your camera ready for the 7 **World's Largest Six-Pack**, then explore the bars and shops of La Crosse's historic downtown.

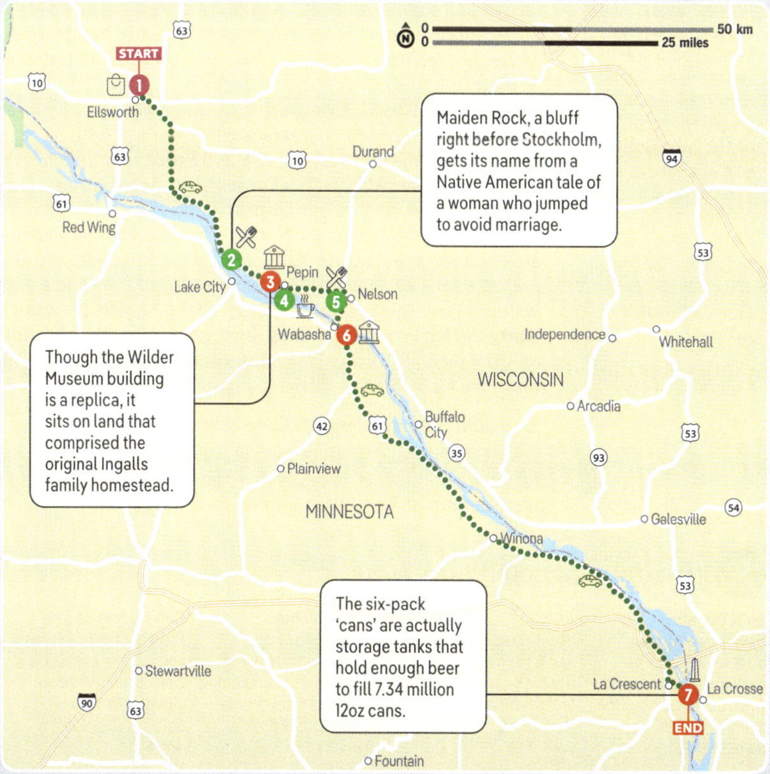

Maiden Rock, a bluff right before Stockholm, gets its name from a Native American tale of a woman who jumped to avoid marriage.

Though the Wilder Museum building is a replica, it sits on land that comprised the original Ingalls family homestead.

The six-pack 'cans' are actually storage tanks that hold enough beer to fill 7.34 million 12oz cans.

DOOR COUNTY ORIENTATION

Door County spreads across a narrow peninsula jutting 75 miles into Lake Michigan. Sturgeon Bay, at the southern end, is the county seat and its only real city. Going north, the side of the peninsula that borders Lake Michigan is the more scenic 'quiet side,' and home to the communities of Jacksonport and Baileys Harbor. The side that borders Green Bay is busier, where villages such as Egg Harbor, Fish Creek, Ephraim and Sister Bay brim with bars, restaurants and shops. The sun rises on the lake side and sets on the bay side. The scene slows down in winter, when cold and snowy weather sets in. Roughly half of local businesses close from November to May.

RANDY KOSTICHKA/SHUTTERSTOCK

Lambeau Field, Green Bay

Door County

Hike, bike and paddle the parks

With its rocky coastline, picturesque lighthouses, cherry orchards and small 19th-century villages, Door County is lovely. Sure, you can simply poke around the clapboard hamlets and enjoy the scenery. But it's even better to get out into the slew of parks for a day or two of adventures.

Peninsula Kayak Company *(peninsulakayakcompany.com; half-day tour $65)* in Jacksonport leads paddling tours around the cliffs and caverns at **Cave Point** (beginners welcome). Next door, **Whitefish Dunes State Park** entices with a sandy, mile-long swimming beach and short hiking trails through the wooded dunes. North in Fish Creek, vast **Peninsula State Park** features bluff-side hiking and cycling trails, and Nicolet Beach for swimming and kayaking (bikes and watercraft rentals available on-site). Further north, **Newport State Park** has tranquil hiking, bird-watching and stargazing (it's an official Dark Sky Park). Information for the parks is at *dnr.wisconsin.gov*; a vehicle day pass costs $16.

Fish boil: fiery meal meets live show

Touristy but fun, the fish boil is a Door County tradition held up and down the peninsula from mid May to late October. Scandinavian lumberjacks started the custom, in which

EATING IN DOOR COUNTY: OUR PICKS

Wild Tomato: Family-friendly, wood-fired pizza joint that gives back to the community when customers buy the monthly specialty pie. *11am-8pm* $$

AC Tap: A glowing Pabst beer sign hangs out front and leads the way into this cash-only pub known for its terrific burgers. *11am-2am* $

White Gull Inn: Generations of diners have come for heaping breakfast dishes featuring the famed local cherries. *7:30am-2pm & 5pm-varies* $$$

Chives: Fork into French-influenced plates and sublime pastries in a rustic room with lake views. *4-9pm Mon & Thu-Sat, 9am-2pm & 4-9pm Sun* $$$

whitefish, potatoes and onions are cooked in a cauldron over an open flame outdoors. Stand around the firepit while the 'boil master' prepares the ingredients and shares local lore. Then they douse the flames with kerosene, and whoosh! A fireball creates the requisite 'boil over' (which gets rid of the fish oil), signaling dinner is ready. Several restaurants host dinnertime fish boils. The **Old Post Office Restaurant** *(oldpostoffice-doorcounty.com; adult/child $28.50/18)* in Ephraim puts on a lively one, with a bonus of great sunset views.

Sail to Washington and Rock islands

If Door County starts to feel crowded, steer to its tip for your getaway. Hop aboard the **Washington Island Ferry** *(wisferry.com; adult/child/car $15/8/30)* at Northport Pier for the 30-minute crossing. The time-warped little isle, settled by Icelandic villagers in the 1800s, beckons with some 700 residents, lavender fields, rugged beaches and small resorts. You'll need a car (or bicycle) to get around. The ferry sails year-round. While the crossing is generally smooth, it does go through the strait known as 'Death's Door,' so named by Native Americans and early French explorers due to the treacherous currents that sank many a ship in past centuries. That's where Door County gets its moniker. Modern navigation aids have rendered the strait far less threatening today.

More remote is teeny Rock Island, which has no roads or facilities. It's a true escape for forest hiking and bird-watching. You also can explore the 1858 lighthouse, where volunteers offer free tours daily. The **Rock Island Ferry** *(wisferry.com; adult/child $15/6)* makes the trip from Washington Island's Jackson Harbor in 15 minutes, sailing from late May to mid-October. Leave your car in the parking lot by the dock. It's possible to visit both islands in one long day trip. Bring cash for small purchases like snacks or souvenirs.

Green Bay

Tour fabled Lambeau Field

The Green Bay Packers are legendary as the National Football League's smallest-market team but one of its most successful, winning 13 league championships and four Super Bowls (so far). The franchise is unique as the only community-owned nonprofit team in the NFL; perhaps pride in ownership is what makes the fans so die-hard.

The Packers' storied history makes a half-day visit to Lambeau Field worthwhile even if you aren't a hard-core supporter.

STELLAR SUNSETS

Betsy Riley, co-owner of Square Rigger Lodge (p137) in Jacksonport, shares top spots to see Door County's famous sunsets.

Stabbur Beer Garden at **Al Johnson's** Swedish restaurant is a fun place to watch the sky ignite. Or walk across the street to the waterfront park for a closer view. My grandparents would go there often in the evening. They'd plan their day around the sunset.

Shipwrecked Brew Pub has an outdoor patio and sits above the water, so you have a great lookout over Green Bay and boats in the marina.

Ellison Bluff County Park feels off the beaten path – there are never many people there – but it's near the highway. With no buildings around, it's a gorgeous wide-open place to see the sun drop.

DRINKING IN DOOR COUNTY: OUR PICKS

Pearl Wine Cottage: Cute-as-a-button white bungalow serving European wines alongside cheeses and charcuterie. *4-9pm Thu-Sun mid-May-Oct*

Mink River Basin: Tucked-away bar that's been around for ages with fun games (Pac-Man!) and good beers, whiskies and food. *noon-2am*

Peach Barn Farmhouse & Brewery: Sprawling outdoor space to play lawn games and hear live music while sipping sours and lagers. *11am-8pm*

Bayside Tavern: Locals and visitors mix it up over burgers and beers in this festive, time-honored pub with a lively patio. *11am-2pm*

WHY SO CHEESY?

Wisconsin produces 3.5 billion pounds of cheese per year – a quarter of America's hunks. That's thanks to 5000 state dairy farms and their 1.3 million cows, according to the Department of Agriculture.

Most farming and cheesemaking happens in Wisconsin's hilly southwest. Here, in what's known as the Driftless Region, glaciers did not flatten the landscape as elsewhere in the state, but left hills, valleys and limestone-rich soil – poor for crop farming but perfect for roaming dairy herds that produce distinctive sweet milk.

Immigrants from Germany, Switzerland and Scandinavia who settled in Wisconsin in the 1800s put their old-country cheesemaking skills to work. The state has been America's Dairyland ever since.

DANITA DELIMONT/GETTY IMAGES

The hour-long 'classic' **stadium tour** *(lambeaufield.com; adult/child $23/14)* takes in the luxury boxes and lets you walk through the tunnel out onto the field. Guides provide great stories of Packers lore. Tours happen daily year-round (except on game days). Afterward mosey around the Titletown district adjacent to Lambeau, which has live music, markets and other free events open to the public.

Apostle Islands

Kayaking and sea-cave adventures

Forested and windblown, trimmed with cliffs and caves, **Apostle Islands National Lakeshore** *(nps.gov/apis; free)* floats off Wisconsin's northern tip in Lake Superior. Kayaking around the 21-isle archipelago is very popular, paying off with stacks of red-rock arches and pillars rising from the water. Sea caves along the mainland near Meyers Beach and the craggy shores of Devils and Sand islands are the showstoppers. Conditions get rough and winds strong, so it's wise to go with a guide. Reputable companies offering half- and full-day outings include **Lost Creek Adventures** *(lostcreekadventures.org; tours from $80)* and **Trek & Trail** *(trek-trail.com; tours from $75)*.

The resort town of Bayfield has everything you need. The **National Lakeshore Visitors Center** *(nps.gov/apis)* downtown can help with camping permits. The islands themselves have no facilities. June through September is prime time to paddle.

Take a boat tour or hike

You don't have to be in a kayak to enjoy the Apostle Islands. Hop on a sightseeing boat with **Apostle Islands Cruises** *(apostleisland.com; tours adult/child $55/34)* instead. The

Devils Island, Apostle Islands National Lakeshore

three-hour 'grand tour' sails to sea caves and lighthouses, and you can bring your own wine and snacks on-board.

Or hike the first 2 miles of the Lakeshore Trail near **Meyers Beach**, which has terrific sea-cave views from land. Brave souls also can swim at Meyers Beach, but the water is breathtakingly cold. It's near Cornucopia, west of Bayfield, along Hwy 13.

Day trip to Madeline Island

The **Madeline Island Ferry** *(madferry.com; return adult/child/car $21/10/38)* makes the 25-minute trip multiple times per day from downtown Bayfield to bohemian **Madeline Island** and its walkable village of La Pointe. To go beyond, bring your car or rent a bicycle from **Motion to Go** *(motion-to-go.com; per hr $12)* by the dock. Pedaling around the island is pure joy.

Big Bay State Park *(dnr.wisconsin.gov; vehicle day pass $16)* beckons with a pretty beach, cliff-view hiking trails and stargazing. Or walk and forage for mushrooms in lovely **Madeline Island Wilderness Preserve** *(miwp.org; free)*.

SUPPER CLUBS

Supper clubs are a type of time-warped restaurant, common in the upper Midwest. They took off in the 1930s, after Prohibition ended and people once again sought places to socialize over a drink. Most supper clubs today retain a retro vibe. Hallmarks include a woodsy location, mounted fish on the walls, a radish-and-carrot-laden relish tray on the table, a surf-and-turf menu and a mile-long, unironic cocktail list topped by the brandy old-fashioned (brandy, bitters, sugar, soda water, orange slice and cherry). Wisconsin has the most supper clubs by far, though Minnesota and Michigan also uphold the tradition. See *wisconsinsupperclubs.com* for locations around the state.

EATING & DRINKING IN BAYFIELD: OUR PICKS

Hoop's Fish & Chips Dockside: Fresh fish, beer and wine served alfresco, plus live music on weekends. *11am-7pm Mon-Sat, to 6pm Sun* $

Manypenny Bistro: Diner-esque venue for breakfast sandwiches, burgers, lake fish, wood-fired pizzas and Turkish kebabs. *7am-9pm* $$

Fat Radish: Farm-to-table meat, fish and veg dishes in a log cabin in Washburn, just south of Bayfield. *11am-8pm Wed & Thu, to 9pm Fri & Sat* $$$

Copper Crow Distillery: Tasting room on Native land for cocktails with house-made vodka and rum. *3-7pm Thu & Fri, 1-7pm Sat, noon-4pm Sun*

Minnesota

WILDERNESS TRAILS | LAKES | ROCK STARS

Places

TOP TIP

The state is nicknamed 'Minnesnowta' for a reason. It's not uncommon for it to snow in late April or even early May. Then again, it can swing the other way and boil in summer. Moral of the story: bring layered clothing options.

Minnesota really is the land of 10,000 lakes (and then some). All that water is a boon for travelers. Adventurous types can wet their paddles in the Boundary Waters, where nighttime brings a blanket of stars and the lullaby of wolf howls. Voyageurs National Park unfurls another remote landscape, where roads vanish and the boreal backcountry is accessible only by boat. Hwy 61 slices into the cliffy, falls-filled North Shore. For a state with such vast tracts of unspoiled wilderness, Minnesota flies under the radar as an outdoor adventure hub. But that it is.

Urban explorers get the prize of Minneapolis, the biggest, coolest town on the prairie, with swanky art museums, rowdy rock clubs, progressive dining establishments and edgy theaters. It's always happenin,' even in winter. And for those looking for middle ground – a cross between the big city and big woods – the dramatic, ship-laden port of Duluth beckons.

Minneapolis

MAPS P124, P126

Follow Prince's purple path

Minneapolis' most famous former resident is the music star Prince. Even before his death in 2016, visitors flocked to town to follow his trail.

Hot spots include First Avenue (p127), the downtown music club that featured in the film *Purple Rain*. Nearby, a 100ft-tall

GETTING AROUND

The main Interstates are I-94 (runs east–west, connecting Minneapolis to Milwaukee and Chicago), I-90 (runs east–west through southern Minnesota) and I-35 (runs north–south, linking the Twin Cities and Duluth). Minnesota does not have toll roads, though express lanes on Twin Cities highways charge a fee for use. Hwy 61, the scenic road along Lake Superior north of Duluth, gets jammed on summer weekends. Amtrak trains go twice daily to Chicago and Milwaukee.

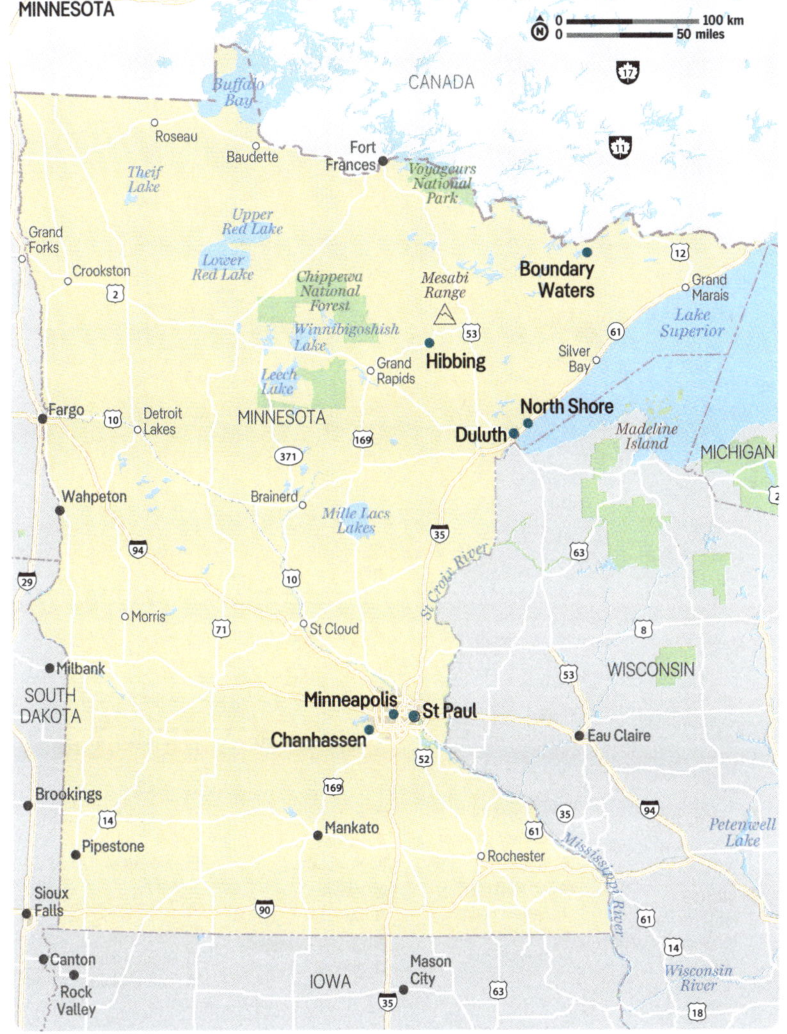

mural of Prince rises on the wall of a parking ramp. Hardcore fans can also seek out Prince's childhood home and more using the city's 'purple path' map *(minneapolis.org/princes-minneapolis)*.

The mega sight for fans is Paisley Park (p128), Prince's mansion in Chanhassen, 20 miles southwest of Minneapolis, complete with the Prince Tribute Tunnel.

Go on an art bender

Minneapolis takes its art seriously. Near downtown, the **Walker Art Center** *(walkerart.org; adult/child $18/free)* is one of

MINNEAPOLIS

HIGHLIGHTS
1 Minneapolis Institute of Art

SIGHTS
2 Mill Ruins Park
3 Minneapolis Sculpture Garden
4 Prince Mural
5 Walker Art Center
6 Weisman Art Museum

ACTIVITIES
7 Endless Bridge
8 St Anthony Falls Heritage Trail

SLEEPING
9 Hewing Hotel
10 Hotel Alma

EATING
11 Owamni

ENTERTAINMENT
12 Armory
13 Bunker's Music Bar & Grill
14 First Avenue & 7th St Entry
see 7 Guthrie Theater

SHOPPING
15 Electric Fetus
16 Twelve Vultures

EATING IN MINNEAPOLIS: CIVIC-MINDED RESTAURANTS

MAPS P124, P126

Owamni: Sun-splashed venue that only uses indigenous ingredients like corn, beans, wild game and native plants. *11am-9pm Tue-Fri, from 10am Sat & Sun* **$$$**

Mama Safia's Kitchen: Somali restaurant serving chicken, goat and spiced rice; it was rebuilt by the community after 2020's civil unrest. *7am-10pm* **$$**

Trio Plant-Based: Breezy vegan soul-food place decorated with photos of civil-rights heroes. *noon-6:45pm Tue-Thu, to 7:15pm Fri & Sat* **$$**

All Square: It's all about grilled cheese sandwiches at this little spot that helps recently incarcerated people get back on their feet. *11am-8pm Tue-Sat* **$**

the nation's top five for modern works. Most of the permanent collection is post-1960, heavy on Andy Warhol soup-can prints and Jasper Johns flag images. It's free on Thursday evenings. The **Minneapolis Sculpture Garden** *(walkerart.org; free)* sits next door, where Claes Oldenburg's beloved *Spoonbridge & Cherry* presides over the 11-acre grounds alongside a whimsical blue rooster and the Robert Indiana *Love* monument. It's delightful to meander.

South of downtown, the **Minneapolis Institute of Art** *(new.artsmia.org; free)* spans centuries and continents, with everything from Tibetan tangkas to Rembrandt paintings to 2000-year-old Mexican jade masks in its warren of galleries. You could spend the entire day here. The **Weisman Art Museum** *(wam.umn.edu; free)* on the University of Minnesota campus is smaller but equally impressive, thanks to its gleaming, Frank Gehry–designed building. It holds a quick-browse mash-up of ceramics, Korean furniture and 20th-century American art. Note: most museums are closed on Monday and Tuesday.

For the local art scene, check out the **Northeast Minneapolis Arts District** *(northeastminneapolisartsdistrict.org)*. Located north of downtown, the area teems with artist lofts and open-house events.

George Floyd Square: site of history and healing

George Floyd was killed by police in May 2020 outside a convenience store at the corner of E 38th and Chicago Aves in south Minneapolis. His death, which became a symbol for racial injustice and police brutality, sparked worldwide protests. Since then, the site – now known as **George Floyd Square** – has become a place to reflect and pay respects to Mr Floyd. People bring rocks, paintings, dolls, candles, beads, flowers and poems as offerings to the ever-changing memorial that has taken over the intersection. Murals, raised fist sculptures and raw art installations in locals' lawns extend for a block in each direction and add to the sobering feel. The square itself is a pedestrian-only zone.

Say Their Names Cemetery, another community-built memorial, lies a few blocks northwest, near where E 37th St and Columbus Ave meet. White cardboard headstones rise up in an empty lot and pay homage to everyone from Floyd to Emmett Till, Breonna Taylor and more than 100 other Black Americans killed by police.

Late morning or afternoon are good times to visit, though the sights are always open.

MINNEAPOLIS: GET YOUR BEARINGS

Minneapolis is relatively spread out. Neighborhoods include the North Loop (stylish warehouse district abutting downtown), Uptown (lively area south of downtown near Bde Maka Ska and other popular lakes), Northeast (art studios, breweries and dive bars northeast of downtown), East and West Banks (home to University of Minnesota's 50,000-plus students near downtown) and Powderhorn (where Floyd Square is in south Minneapolis). St Paul lies 10 miles east of Minneapolis, while the airport and Mall of America lie 10 miles south.

Handy Blue Line trains connect the mall, airport and downtown Minneapolis. Green Line trains connect Minneapolis to St Paul. A Metro Transit *(metrotransit.org)* day pass costs $4.

EATING IN MINNEAPOLIS: OUR PICKS

MAP P124, P126

Hola Arepa: Margaritas and Venezuelan-style arepas. Colorful, festive ambience. *4-10pm Tue-Thu, to 11pm Fri, 10am-11pm Sat, to 10pm Sun* **$$**

Heather's: Bright cafe whipping up from-scratch French toast, burgers, vegan tofu bowls and more. *9am-9pm Mon-Sat, to 8pm Sun* **$$**

Young Joni: Hip industrial space that fuses two seemingly unrelated types: pizza and Korean food. There's a hidden bar in back. *hours vary* **$$**

Creekside Supper Club: Retro knotty pine walls, vintage signs and classic fare like prime rib and martinis. *4-9pm Tue-Fri, 10am-2pm & 4-9pm Sat & Sun* **$$$**

SIGHTS
1 George Floyd Square
2 Minnehaha Falls
3 Say Their Names Cemetery

EATING
4 All Square
5 Creekside Supper Club
6 Heather's
7 Hola Arepa
8 Mama Safia's Kitchen
see 2 Sea Salt Eatery
9 Trio Plant-Based

DRINKING & NIGHTLIFE
see 5 Sidecar at the Tap
10 Troubadour Wine Bar

ENTERTAINMENT
see 9 Jungle Theater
11 Lake Harriet Band Shell
12 Luminary Loppet

SHOPPING
13 Tropes & Trifles

TRANSPORT
14 Wheel Fun Rentals

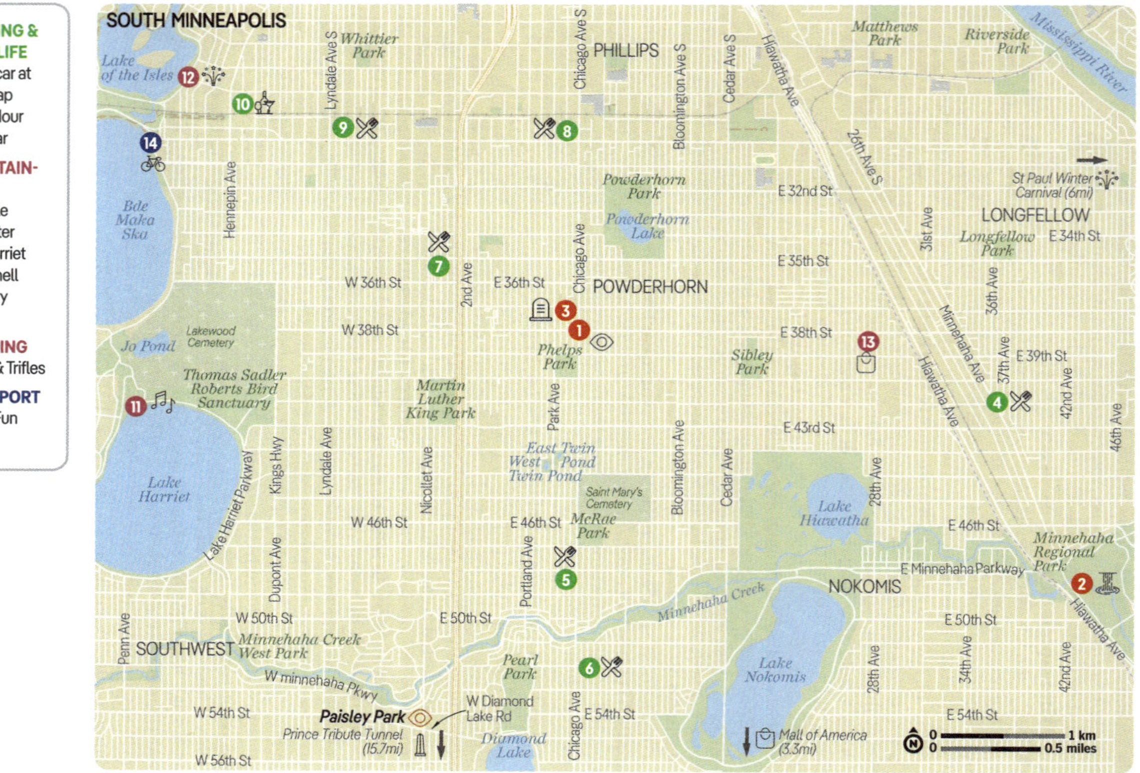

Riverfront views: mill ruins, a waterfall and more

The Mississippi River slices through downtown Minneapolis, flanked by parkland and a waterside trail. Join the many locals who are out for a stroll.

The cobalt-blue **Guthrie Theater** *(guthrietheater.org)* is a striking place to start. Check to see if the building is open (closed Mondays and most mornings) and then make your way up the escalator to the **Endless Bridge**. The cantilevered walkway juts out over the river and offers a knockout view. Onward along the water is brooding **Mill Ruins Park**, steeped in history from when Minneapolis led the world in flour milling. From here, pick up the **St Anthony Falls Heritage Trail**, a 1.8-mile path that crosses the car-free Stone Arch Bridge, providing a terrific view of cascading St Anthony Falls.

Jump in a lake

Minnesota is dubbed the land of 10,000 lakes, and Minneapolis claims over 22 of them. **Bde Maka Ska** (a Dakotan name) and **Lake Harriet** are among the most popular, where everyone flocks to revel in the summer sunshine. Both have beaches, cafes, walking and cycling paths, and kayaks and stand-up paddleboards from **Wheel Fun Rentals** *(wheelfunrentals.com; per hr $15-25)*. The castle-like **Lake Harriet Band Shell** is always abuzz with free concerts and films. Both lakes are conveniently located a short distance southwest of downtown.

Further north **Lake of the Isles** and **Cedar Lake** are two quieter neighborhood lakes, surrounded by grand historic homes that make for some astonishing scenery.

Summer is the busiest time, but locals are out in all seasons. Autumnal walks around the lakes are particularly marvelous.

Catch a show

The city buzzes with creative energy that spills over into an active nightlife. Downtown's **First Avenue & 7th St Entry** *(first-avenue.com)* – where native son Prince grooved in *Purple Rain* – is the epicenter of the music scene. It's two venues in one: First Avenue is the main room featuring national acts; smaller 7th St Entry is for up-and-comers who play a stage-dive away from the crowd. Stars painted on the building's exterior show the famed names who've rocked here over the years.

The historic **Armory** *(armorymn.com)* pops on the weekends with punk, metal and alt-rock bands downtown. Nearby in the North Loop, **Bunker's Music Bar & Grill** *(bunkersmusic.com)* is a scruffy winner that puts funk, blues or reggae bands on stage six nights a week (closed Mondays).

Theater buffs should see what's on at the **Guthrie Theater** *(guthrietheater.org)*, where Minneapolis' top-gun troupe mounts bold-themed classic and new works downtown. **Jungle Theater** *(jungletheater.org)* offers a more intimate experience, staging high-quality productions in Uptown.

Urban escape to Minnehaha Falls

It's hard to believe a 53ft-tall waterfall crashes down into a limestone gorge just 15 minutes from downtown Minneapolis. But **Minnehaha Falls** *(minneapolisparks.org; free)*

WINTER FESTS

Krista Westendorp, writer, outdoor enthusiast and 40-year Twin Cities resident, shares her favorite winter events.

St Paul Winter Carnival: Cold and snow don't stop locals from being outside. The St Paul carnival has been going for 140 years. It starts in late January, with ice-carving competitions, snow sculptures, parades, winter biking and more over 10 days. It's an annual highlight.

Luminary Loppet: This enchanted evening walk (held every February) goes around Lake of the Isles, lit by 1200 candle luminaries, past intricate ice sculptures. Hot cocoa and s'mores are served along the trail, and the walk ends at a party with food trucks, music and beer. Other parks also host candlelit trail events throughout winter with bonfires and refreshments.

BEST TWIN CITIES SHOPPING

Mall of America: The USA's largest shopping center goes beyond stores with a zipline, mini-golf course and amusement park inside.

Electric Fetus: Prince used to browse at this indie record store, with a great selection of local music and cool gifts.

Twelve Vultures: Theatrical curiosity shop where shelves hold taxidermy foxes, moose antlers, antique-framed insect specimens and more.

Birchbark Books: Native-owned indie bookstore that's a cozy community hub, with creaking wood floors and handwritten staff recommendations.

Tropes & Trifles: Dedicated to romance novels; lots of cheeky gifts supplement the spicy book selection.

does exactly that. Gawp over the ledge from the top or take the stairs down to the bottom and explore the cascade from a different angle. It's particularly stunning in winter when it freezes over and you can walk right around it.

The sublime waterfall sits in the middle of a park with 193 acres of woodlands, bluffs and riverside trails to roam around. Afterward, angle for a seat at **Sea Salt Eatery** *(seasaltmpls.com)*, an open-air seafood spot right by the falls that's open daily April through October. Fish tacos, raw oysters, crab-cake sandwiches and pitchers of beer are available to help you replenish.

Chanhassen

Pay tribute to Prince at Paisley Park

Paisley Park *(paisleypark.com; tours from $75)*, Prince's mansion in Chanhassen, is a stark white building at the highway's edge, and looks like an unsexy office building outside, but inside is a different story. Ninety-minute tours take in the recording studio, soundstage and music club where he hosted his famous late-night bashes.

Outside the building, the **Prince Tribute Tunnel** is an underpass beneath the highway that leads directly toward Paisley Park, which is behind a wire fence. Along the fence, fans have affixed purple love locks, purple guitars, purple flowers, poems and other offerings. The underpass itself is covered in purple drawings and graffiti. It's all quite moving. To reach the tunnel, it's easiest to park at Lake Ann Park and follow the pedestrian path under the road, which heads to Riley Creek Tunnel (its official name).

St Paul

F Scott Fitzgerald's early haunts

St Paul, Minnesota's capital city, is smaller and quieter than its twin to the west, Minneapolis. Strolling through its historic neighborhoods is a delightful way to spend a morning or afternoon.

St Paul's most celebrated literary son is *The Great Gatsby* author F Scott Fitzgerald (1896–1940). The genteel area around Cathedral Hill – named for the colossal church that marks the spot – is his old stomping ground. The **Fitzgerald birthplace**, a Pullman-style apartment, is on Laurel Ave. Nearby, the brownstone at **599 Summit Ave** is where he lived when he

DRINKING IN MINNEAPOLIS: OUR PICKS

MAP P124, P126

Surly Brewing: Family-friendly beer hall with outdoor, dog-friendly beer garden. *3-10pm Mon-Thu, to midnight Fri, 11am-midnight Sat, 11am-11pm Sun*

Troubadour Wine Bar: Low-lit charmer for globally sourced reds and whites amid soulful live music. *5-10pm Mon-Thu, to midnight Fri & Sat*

Dogwood Coffee: Neon-clad industrial space to fuel your day with an espresso and game of ping-pong. *7am-7pm Mon-Fri, 8am-6pm Sat & Sun*

Sidecar at the Tap: Casually chic room for cocktails made with attention to detail. *4-11pm Tue & Wed, to midnight Thu-Sat, to 10pm Sun*

STEVE SKJOLD/SHUTTERSTOCK

Paisley Park

published *This Side of Paradise*. Both are private residences, so you can't go inside. Plaques mark the sites.

From here, continue along Summit Ave toward the cathedral to gape at the Victorian homes rising from the tree-lined street. Gilded Age vibes abound. Walk another half-mile or so toward the Mississippi River for more in the Irvine Park district, which is replete with fountains, gardens and turreted manors. It's next to W 7th St, an eating and drinking hub.

Learn to curl

For those uninitiated in northern ways, curling is a winter sport that involves sliding a 42lb granite stone (sort of like a jumbo hockey puck) down the ice toward a bull's-eye. It's popular in Minnesota, and there are rinks all over the state. The friendly folks at the **St Paul Curling Club** *(stpaulcurlingclub.org)* don't mind if you stop in to watch the action. Heck, they'll probably invite you to share a microbrew in the upstairs bar. It's the USA's largest club, and open daily in the evening from mid-October to late May.

CULINARY SPECIALTIES

Hearty comfort foods hit the tables in Minnesota. Keep an eye on local menus for walleye, Minnesota's state fish, which offers a mild, white meat. Nutty-tasting, native wild rice often turns up in breads and soups. The Jucy Lucy appears in pubs around the Twin Cities. It's a burger stuffed with a molten core of American cheese, made by pinching two patties around the yellow slices and grilling to greasy perfection. A 'hot dish' (aka casserole) typically includes ground beef, potatoes or pasta, green beans or corn, and a canned cream soup. Tater tots commonly top it. Lutefisk, dried cod that's rehydrated with lye and then cooked, is popular during the winter holidays. The gelatinous dish is an acquired taste.

EATING & DRINKING IN ST PAUL: OUR PICKS

Cecil's Deli: Kosher, family-run classic where locals devour huge sandwiches and matzo-ball soup at close-packed tables. *9am-8pm* $$

Hyacinth: Intimate, date-night restaurant serving modern takes on pasta, risotto and other buttery Italian dishes alongside cocktails. *5-9pm Tue-Sun* $$$

Nina's Coffee Cafe: In a rambling historic building full of nooks and crannies beloved by writers and cardamom-infused-latte fans. *6:30am-5pm*

Emerald Lounge: Sip creative cocktails (including alcohol-free ones) in plush seats amid vintage, green-toned decor. *4-10pm Tue-Thu, to 11pm Fri & Sat*

BEST QUIRKY MINNESOTA SIGHTS

Spam Museum: Learn all about the peculiar blue-tinned meat that has fed armies and inspired legions of haiku writers.

Darwin Twine Ball: The 'World's Largest Built by One Person': Francis A Johnson wrapped the 17,400lb whopper over 29 years.

Paul Bunyan Statue: The lofty lumberjack and his blue ox, Babe, tower over Bemidji's visitor center, which displays Paul's giant toothbrush inside.

Greyhound Bus Museum: See buses from yesteryear in an art deco–style terminal in Hibbing, where Greyhound Lines originated.

Mary Tyler Moore Statue: Photo op with the beloved 1970s TV character who put Minneapolis on the pop-culture map.

TAMMI MILD/GETTY IMAGES

Duluth

Freighter-filled, eclectic port town

Duluth is a brawny shot-and-a-beer port town that immerses visitors in its storied history as a major shipping center. Start downtown at the **Aerial Lift Bridge**, Duluth's landmark that raises its mighty arm to let horn-bellowing freighters into the harbor. About 900 vessels per year glide through. Pop in to the **Maritime Visitor Center** *(lsmma.com; free)*, next to the bridge, where computer screens tell what time the big ships come and go. Cool model boats and exhibits on Great Lakes shipwrecks also make it a top stop. From here you're a block from **Vikre Distillery** *(vikredistillery.com)*, which makes gin with Northwoods-foraged botanicals. Free tours take place on Monday and Friday (reserve ahead), while the festive tasting room is open every afternoon. Or hop on the Lakewalk outside the maritime center and amble along the paved path that edges Lake Superior. It's part of the long-distance Superior Hiking Trail (p132).

For a hip scene of indie breweries, cider makers and restaurants, ramble through the Lincoln Park Craft District, west of downtown.

EATING & DRINKING IN DULUTH: OUR PICKS

OMC Smokehouse: Buzzing industrial space for revered, slow-cooked meats and local craft brews; try the pulled pork. *11am-9pm Sun-Thu, to 10pm Fri & Sat* **$$**

New Scenic Cafe: Fork into refined meat and fish dishes in a cozy wood-paneled room with partial lake views. *11am-9pm Wed-Sun* **$$$**

Ursa Minor Brewing: Lively indoor-outdoor taproom serving pilsners, hazy IPAs, fruited sour ales and pizzas. *11am-10pm Sun-Thu, to 11pm Fri & Sat*

Duluth Cider: Choose among 14 hard ciders in this cool taproom carved from an old livery. *noon-10pm Mon-Thu, to 11pm Fri & Sat, 11am-8pm Sun*

Gooseberry Falls State Park

TALL TALES

While the legend of Paul Bunyan is heard throughout the northern USA, it's particularly prevalent in Minnesota. Stories of the giant lumberjack with superhuman strength were told in logging camps in the late 1800s and gained widespread popularity in the early 20th century when companies began using the character in ads. Famous feats by Paul and his trusty blue ox, Babe, are myriad. For instance, Paul scooped out the Great Lakes when Babe was thirsty and needed water. And Babe created the Mississippi River when his tank wagon leaked while paving icy logging roads, with the trickle forming the Mississippi. Minnesota leads the USA in Bunyan statues with 11, including the 2.5-ton colossus in Bemidji.

North Shore

Highway 61: nature at Lake Superior's rugged edge

Hwy 61 traces Lake Superior's shoreline, winding through red-tinged cliffs and towering firs from Duluth to Canada's edge. Several state parks dot the way, offering spectacular gorges, waterfalls and pine-scented hiking trails, much of it easily accessible from roadside parking lots. The route is 150 miles, drivable in three hours, but most folks make a weekend out of it, overnighting in little towns that speckle the landscape. Crowds amass on summer weekends.

After Duluth and Two Harbors, Hwy 61 ramps up its riches. First, there's pie at **Rustic Inn Cafe**, which wafts berry crumb, lemon meringue and a dozen other flaky-crust flavors from its log cabin at road's edge. **Gooseberry Falls State Park** appears a few miles onward. It's always busy, thanks to its five cascades, scenic gorge and easy trails, including the 2-mile Gooseberry River Loop. Another gorgeous landscape arrives 41 miles later at **Temperance River State Park**, where the waterway roars through a twisting gorge a short hike from the road.

Grand Marais (p132) has good eats, drinks and a lighthouse before hitting **Judge CR Magney State Park**. Here you can view Devil's Kettle, the famous falls where the Brule River splits around a huge rock. Half of the flow drops 50ft in a typically gorgeous North Shore gush, but the other half disappears down a hole and flows underground. Where it goes is a mystery – scientists have never been able to determine the water's outlet. It's a moderately breath-sapping 1.1-mile walk each way.

The road nears its end at **Grand Portage National Monument** *(nps.gov/grpo; free)*, a reconstructed 1788 trading post

MINNESOTA'S UNOFFICIAL STATE BIRD

Look in any souvenir shop up north, and you'll see a postcard or T-shirt that says 'Minnesota State Bird' with an image of a big, nasty mosquito underneath. These bloodsuckers are relentless in summer. They're drawn to carbon dioxide and body heat, which is why they feast on hikers and paddlers. But mosquitos aren't the only biters in action: black flies sink their teeth into your skin with a sharp pinch. No amount of swatting keeps them away. They annoy mostly in May and June, a bit earlier in the season than mosquitos. Both pests buzz throughout Minnesota, but they're most brutal in the north, where forests and wetlands provide ideal breeding grounds. Use repellent and a net hat to deter them.

CRAIG HINTON/SHUTTERSTOCK

Grand Marais Lighthouse

and Ojibwe village. The site is impressively lonely and windblown, open in summer only. **Isle Royale Ferries** *(isleroyaleboats.com; adult/child $100.50/90.50)* also depart from Grand Portage for the 90-minute ride to Isle Royale National Park.

Information for the state parks is at *dnr.state.mn.us*. A vehicle day pass costs $7. An annual pass costs $35. Much of the hiking in the parks is along the Superior Hiking Trail.

Superior Hiking Trail adventure

The 300-mile **Superior Hiking Trail** *(shta.org)* follows the lake-hugging ridge line between Duluth and the Canadian border. Along the way it passes dramatic red-rock overlooks and the occasional moose and black bear. Trailheads with parking lots pop up every 5 to 10 miles, making it ideal for day hikes. The **Superior Shuttle** *(superiorhikingshuttle.com)* makes life even easier, picking up trekkers anywhere along the route as needed (reserve ahead). Overnight hikers will find 94 backcountry campsites and several lodges to cushion the body come nightfall; the trail website has details. The whole footpath is free, with no reservations or permits required. It's easiest to start in the south, where the terrain is more gentle. Thru-hikes take two to four weeks.

GETTING TO ISLE ROYALE

While you can get to **Isle Royale National Park** (p107) from Minnesota, there is greater access from Michigan, which is the state that Isle Royale is officially part of.

Artsy getaway to Grand Marais

Pretty little Grand Marais beckons toward the northern end of Hwy 61 (p131). It makes an excellent base for exploring the parks and trails along Lake Superior, as well as for venturing into the Boundary Waters. Several bars, restaurants, art galleries and antique shops in the tidy downtown give it a 'big city' feel.

Grand Marais' artistic pretensions are genuine. The **Grand Marais Art Colony** *(grandmaraisartcolony.org)* started in 1947 and exists to this day, luring painters, potters and print makers. Do-it-yourself enthusiasts can learn to build boats, sail a schooner and forage for mushrooms at the **North House Folk School** *(northhouse.org)*. If nothing else, make time for the 20-minute walk along the breakwater to **Grand Marais Lighthouse**. The path departs adjacent to **Artist's Point**, a dramatic-looking flat-rock area that is especially luminous as the sun sets.

Gunflint Trail scenic drive

The **Gunflint Trail** *(gunflinttrail.com)*, aka County Rd 12, slices inland through the pines from Grand Marais to Saganaga Lake. The paved, 57-mile-long byway dips into the Boundary Waters area and presents excellent hiking, picnicking and moose-viewing opportunities. It takes 1½ hours to drive one way, but you'll want longer to make stops at roadside pull-offs like the **Moose Viewing Trail**, a 0.3-mile walk to a lake where antlered pals sometimes gather. There aren't any towns along the route, but there are several lodges tucked in woods if you want to grab a meal or snack.

Hibbing

Explore the Iron Range

An area of red-tinged scrubby hills rather than mountains, the ore-rich Iron Range stretches across northeastern Minnesota. Hibbing is the largest town in the region with a couple of claims to fame. For one, Bob Dylan grew up here. See the papier-mâché Bob and small collection of memorabilia at the **Hibbing Public Library** *(hibbingmn.gov)*. It also provides a free walking tour map to find sites like his **Boyhood Home**, where he lived from 1948 to 1959, when he left for Minneapolis. It's privately owned, but good for a discreet photo.

The **Hull Rust Mine Viewpoint** *(hibbingmineview.org)* is the other must-see. Follow the signs that lead a few miles north of town, and behold the enormous, 3.5-mile-wide, open-pit mine spread below. The mind-blowingly huge display trucks give a sense of scale; go ahead and climb up. It's one of the largest iron-ore mines in the world.

Boundary Waters

Canoeing unspoiled wilderness to sleep under the stars

Legendarily remote and pristine, the Boundary Waters Canoe Area Wilderness is one of the world's premier paddling regions.

BOB DYLAN'S MINNESOTA ROOTS

Robert Zimmerman was born in Duluth in 1941. His family moved to Hibbing when he was still quite young. As a teenager he listened to radio stations from Chicago and Little Rock, which played the kind of music that few people in Hibbing knew. His first group, the Golden Chords, won a mere second prize at the local talent show. Bobby made frequent trips to big-city Minneapolis, where he hung around the university area, going to jazz joints and coffeehouses. He enrolled at the University of Minnesota for a year, but dropped out and headed to New York City's folk scene. By 1962 he had legally changed his name to Bob Dylan and never looked back.

EATING & DRINKING IN GRAND MARAIS: OUR PICKS

Fisherman's Daughter at Dockside Fish Market: The morning boat's fresh haul is your fish and chips by lunchtime. *11am-8pm* $$

My Sister's Place: Tuck into sandwiches, burgers and fish dishes in this woodsy spot with an old-time saloon atmosphere. *11am-8pm* $$

World's Best Donuts: Staff nobly arrive at 3am to fry and glaze; join the queue for the chocolatey, cream-filled results. *7am-3pm Thu-Mon* $

Voyageur Brewing Co: Brewpub with a lake-view deck for knocking back sturdy stouts and ales. *11:30am-9pm Sun-Wed, to 10pm Thu-Sat*

TOP EXPERIENCE

Voyageurs National Park

Northern Voyageurs National Park, which marks the border between the USA and Canada, is a mosaic of land and water. Get ready for boating in summer, snowmobiling in winter and starry dark skies year-round. You'll have much of the landscape to yourself, as this is one of the USA's least-visited parks.

PER BREIEHAGEN/GETTY IMAGES

TOP TIPS

- Visit late July to mid-August for warmest lake temperatures and fewest biting insects.
- Boat tours operate mid-June to September; reserve at *recreation.gov*.
- Evening boat tours are often timed to coincide with stargazing tours; check *nps.gov/voya*.

Summer Action

During the late May to September peak season, people come to Voyageurs to boat, fish, swim and spot wildlife. Moose, wolves and black bears prowl the forest. Visitor centers at Rainy Lake (open year-round), Kabetogama Lake, Crane Lake and Ash River (all open seasonally) have the lowdown on programs and boat tours. The 2½-hour **Rainy Lake Grand Tour** *(adult/child $50/25)* gives a feel for the scene, as does the **North Canoe Voyage** *(adult/child $15/7.50)* aboard a 26ft birchbark vessel like 17th-century fur traders (aka voyageurs) once paddled. For a true park experience, many visitors rent a houseboat from **Ebel's Voyageur Houseboats** *(ebels.com)* or **Voyagaire Houseboats** *(voyagaire.com)*.

Dark Skies & Winter Fun

Voyageurs is an International Dark Sky Park. The upper parking lot at **Rainy Lake Visitor Center** is an excellent place to stargaze. You might even glimpse the green-draped northern lights (more common in winter). Also prevalent in winter: snowmobiling. Voyageurs is a hot spot for the sport, with 110 miles of staked and groomed trails slicing through the pines. Snowshoeing and cross-country skiing on the trails also are popular.

PRACTICALITIES

- nps.gov/voya
- open year-round
- free

More than 1000 lakes and streams speckle the piney, 1.1-million-acre expanse, rich in wildlife and sweeping solitude. If you're willing to dig in and canoe for a while, it'll just be you and the moose, bears, wolves and loons that roam the landscape.

The area draws hard-core outdoor adventurers, with most coming for at least four or five days to get away from it all. But it's possible to glide in for a day, too.

However long you plan to stay, know that this is real-deal backcountry and you need to be prepared. Outfitters can help. Ely (pronounced *ee*-lee), the main gateway into the Boundary Waters, has scores of them. The super-knowledgeable folks at **Piragis Northwoods Company** *(piragis.com)* have been around for decades and can set you up with canoes and gear for day trips, overnight stays, guided trips and more. **Ely Outfitting Company** *(elyoutfittingcompany.com)* is another good one.

Entry into the Boundary Waters requires a permit. Day-trip permits are free and can be obtained from the kiosk wherever you enter, no advance booking needed. Overnight permits *(recreation.gov; per trip adult/child $16/8, plus reservation fee $6)* are issued by the US Forest Service and best obtained in advance online. They're limited, and paddlers start snapping them up in January when they are released for the year. It gets a bit complex, as permits are for a specific entry location, of which there are many throughout the vast expanse, some of which require advanced paddling skills. Check *friends-bwca.org* for info. Outfitters are a good resource to help with this, too.

Late May through September is the paddling season, with July and August the peak times. Besides Ely, you can also access the Boundary Waters from Grand Marais by following the Gunflint Trail.

Meet a Boundary Waters rebel

Dorothy Molter lived for 56 years in a cabin in the Boundary Waters' midst, 18 miles from the nearest road. When the Forest Service tried to obtain her land, she refused to move, sparking a long legal battle. Dorothy won and remained in her cabin, paddling, hiking and fishing for whatever she needed. She became famous for providing medical assistance (she was trained as a nurse) and homemade root beer to anyone who dropped by. She died at age 79 (while hauling firewood!) and her friends brought her homestead by dogsled to Ely. It's now a root-beer-selling **museum** *(rootbeerlady.com; adult/child $7/4.50)* that lets you look around her badass abode.

WILDLIFE SPOTTING

Minnesota's northern region, including the Boundary Waters and Voyageurs National Park, holds the star wildlife. Between 13,000 and 18,000 black bears roam the local forests, according to the Department of Natural Resources (DNR). They're relatively common to spot, especially in the fall. Moose are more elusive. The DNR estimates around 4000 rustle through the north woods. Early morning or evening is the best time to see them. Minnesota has the largest population of wolves in the lower 48 states, with some 2900 prowling the area. They're rare to see, but you might hear their eerie howl at night. The loon, Minnesota's state bird, hangs out in the multitude of lakes in summer. Their haunting wail often is heard at night.

Places We Love to Stay

$ Budget $$ Midrange $$$ Top End

Chicago

MAPS P55, P60, P65

HI-Chicago $ Chicago's most stalwart hostel is immaculate and adds a staffed information desk, lounge and stocked kitchen to the mix.

Hampton Inn Chicago Downtown/N Loop $$ Features the chain's much-loved amenities in retro environs.

Publishing House Bed & Breakfast $$ Vintage West Loop building with 11 mid-century modern rooms named after Chicago writers.

Robey $$ Sunny rooms stack a 12-story, art-deco tower in Wicker Park, complete with rooftop swimming pool.

Acme Hotel $$ Industrial-chic fills this energetic, 130-room Near North hotel.

Illinois

Inn at 835 (Springfield) $$ Rooms of the four-poster bed, claw-foot bathtub variety occupy a 1908 arts-and-crafts-style luxury apartment building.

Shawnee Forest Cabins (Herod) $$ Settle into a cozy log cottage, with hot tub and firepit, in the peaceful woods.

Indiana

Pepin Mansion (New Albany) $ Standing supremely along New Albany's historical Mansion Row, this 1851 Italianate abode features ornate hand-painted ceilings, original hardwood flooring and gas chandeliers.

Riverboat Inn & Suites (Madison) $ Parts of this historic inn on the river date back to 1929 (it was a former button factory). Riverfront patio bar and free breakfast.

Hotel Broad Ripple (Indianapolis) $$ This Scandinavian-accented boutique hotel is a cozy getaway in hip Broad Ripple, offering spacious rooms right along the Monon Trail.

Story Inn (Nashville) $$ This former general store dating to 1851 (tin roof and metal facade still intact!) drips with countrified rustic charm, offering rooms, cottages and a farm-to-table restaurant.

Riley's Railhouse (Chesterton) $$ Occupying a decommissioned 1914 freight station, this is a railway-themed boutique B&B with rooms inside a renovated depot and railcars. Train enthusiasts will love it – 86 pass per day!

Oliver Inn (South Bend) $$ Elegant nine-room B&B in a Queen Anne–style home dating to 1886. Corner turrets, curved-glass bay windows, claw-foot tubs, and spindles and balustrades abound.

Ironworks Hotel (Indianapolis) $$$ With design touches forged from industrial parts from an abandoned Wisconsin iron foundry, this hotel has several restaurants, a gym and 120 fantastic rooms.

Ohio

Symphony Hotel (Cincinnati) $ Nine rooms in a traditional Italianate building, each named after a classical composer, and each chock-full of period antique decor. Breakfast included.

Clifford House B&B (Cleveland) $$ If you don't like animals, this beautiful Ohio City B&B isn't for you. If you do, Henry the dog and Connie the cat are ready for you! Jim the human cooks up a scrumptious breakfast and is great fun to chat with. Free parking.

Inn at Brandywine Falls (Cuyahoga Valley) $$ An 1848 Greek Revival country home situated in a gentle sweep of pastoral prettiness. Six rooms, of which the Granary suite is particularly lovely. Breakfasts are delicious.

Inn at Honey Run (Millersburg) $$$ In Amish Country, 25 rooms occupy the lodge-like main building, while 12 'honeycomb' rooms are built right into the hillside Frank Lloyd Wright–style. Adults only.

Metropolitan at the 9 (Cleveland) $$$ Upscale Marriott-branded property with 156 good-sized rooms, a rooftop bar and a subterranean cocktail lounge set in the building's old bank vaults.

Hotel Kilbourne (Sandusky) $$$ Near the ferry dock, a boutique hotel complete with rooftop bar, a Mexican restaurant and a gift shop, all on-site.

Michigan

MAP P96

Hostel Detroit (Detroit) $ An old building rehabbed using recycled materials and painted in vivid colors inside and out. Dormitories, private rooms and shared bathrooms and kitchens.

Landmark Inn (Marquette) $$ This elegant, six-story hotel fills a historic lakefront building and has a couple of resident ghosts.

El Moore Lodge (Detroit) $$ A unique option in Midtown with a friendly vibe, its 11 rooms occupy a turreted 1898 building that's been renovated;

reclaimed wood and tiles feature in the interior.

Shinola Hotel (Detroit) **$$$** Detroit's homegrown brand known for luxury watches extends to this stylish hotel downtown. The 129 rooms have mid-century modern decor, big windows and Bluetooth speaker systems.

Perry Hotel (Petoskey) **$$$** Grand historic place where Hemingway once stayed (in 1916 after a hiking trip in the region). Count on comfy beds, vintage furniture and a cozy on-site pub.

Grey Hare Inn (Traverse City) **$$$** An intimate, three-room B&B on a working vineyard, with French-style decor and bay views. Free wine tastings.

Glen Arbor B&B (Sleeping Bear Dunes) **$$$** The owners renovated this century-old farmhouse into a sunny, French country inn with eight themed rooms.

Burnt Toast Inn (Ann Arbor) **$$$** Colorful house with a lovely garden, big porch and five rooms that mix sturdy antiques with edgy art. On a leafy street walkable to downtown. Free parking and breakfast.

Rock Harbor Lodge (Isle Royale) **$$$** The island's sole lodge, offering 60 rooms with lake views in the main building, as well as 20 cabins with kitchenettes.

Wisconsin

MAP P112

Julie's Park Cafe and Motel (Door County) **$** Long-standing, crowd-pleasing budget option in Fish Creek right next door to Peninsula State Park.

Ambassador (Milwaukee) **$$** Renovated art-deco gem near Marquette University, chock-full of polished marbled floors, bronze elevator doors and more period details.

County Clare Irish Inn (Milwaukee) **$$** Rooms have a snug cottage feel, with four-poster beds, white wainscot walls and whirlpool baths; there's an on-site pub.

Hotel Ruby Marie (Madison) **$$** A 19th-century railroad hotel retrofitted with modern conveniences while retaining vintage charm; free breakfast and happy-hour drinks.

Graduate Madison (Madison) **$$** Near State St's action, this 72-room hotel wafts a hip academic vibe with its mod-meets-plaid decor and book-themed artwork.

Square Rigger Lodge (Door County) **$$** Guests return year after year to this Jacksonport motel winner that features a private sand beach.

Beachfront Inn (Door County) **$$** Cute Bailey's Harbor lakefront motel that earns extra points for its pool, nighttime beach bonfires and nearby pubs.

Charmant Hotel (La Crosse) **$$** Sweet renovation of a 1898 candy factory into 67 rooms with exposed brick walls, wood floors and industrial-cool charm.

Brewhouse Inn & Suites (Milwaukee) **$$$** A 90-room hotel set in the old Pabst Brewery complex. The large chambers have steampunk-type decor.

Old Rittenhouse Inn (Bayfield) **$$$** Looking for lace, creaky floorboards and a romantic escape? This inn fills two Victorian homes atop a hill with lake views.

Minnesota

MAP P124

Mountain Inn (Lutsen) **$** Well-run motel with spacious rooms that are nothing fancy, but they're great value for the Lake Superior area.

Adventure Inn (Ely) **$** A blue ribbon to the cute tidy motel rooms, which are walkable to eats and drinks in downtown Ely.

Canopy Mill District (Minneapolis) **$$** Ornamental historic building downtown, where contemporary rooms have high, timbered ceilings and exposed brick.

Hewing Hotel (Minneapolis) **$$** Rustic-vibe chambers feature wood-beam ceilings, deer-print wallpaper and plaid wool blankets; near downtown's action.

Celeste of St Paul (St Paul) **$$** Located downtown, this lovingly restored former convent offers 72 smart, lofty rooms and a bouncy bar.

Hungry Hippie Farm & Hostel (Grand Marais) **$$** Pretty farmhouse 8 miles east of Grand Marais, with six rustic-chic private rooms that share bathrooms.

Northern Rail Traincar Inn (Two Harbors) **$$** It doesn't get much cooler than 14 rooms built into renovated train boxcars.

Ash Trail Lodge (Orr) **$$** Family-owned business that offers little cabins and great home cooking right next to Voyageurs National Park.

Hotel Alma (Minneapolis) **$$$** Seven light-wood, Nordic-style rooms set above Alma (the Beard Award–winning restaurant-cafe); delicious breakfast pastries provided.

Researched and curated by
Lauren Keith and Amy C Balfour

Great Plains

SURPRISING CITIES AMID PRISTINE PRAIRIE

The Great Plains are happy to transition you between east and west, but don't you dare dismiss this as flyover country.

If you slow down, the Heartland invites you in and shares some of the country's finest history, scenery and adventure. Each of its seven states has enough to stop you in your tracks; the only hard part is figuring out how to experience as much as possible in this vast region that makes up 15% of the country.

The USA's two longest rivers, the Missouri and the Mississippi, cut through the Plains, and many of the region's cities got their start along these mighty routes. Dams have tamed them since then, but wild – and federally protected, thanks to their outstanding scenery – waterways can still be found in Missouri's Ozarks and Nebraska's Niobrara Valley. Other gripping landscapes include the dreamy colors of the badlands in the Dakotas and the bison-studded prairies also found there, as well as in Kansas and Oklahoma. Meanwhile, the Great Plains cities are quietly cool and self-confident – many have been undergoing a renaissance as they spruce up former warehouse districts and embark on new infrastructure projects that make it easier to travel here.

Does this region have the national parks of Utah, the coastline of California or the big cities of the East? No, but if you've come this far, you know that's not why you're here. Open your mind in these wide-open spaces, and you're bound to be captivated by what you discover.

RIVERNORTHPHOTOGRAPHY/GETTY IMAGES

THE MAIN AREAS

For places to stay in the Great Plains, see p212

ALEX CIMBAL/SHUTTERSTOCK

Bison, Custer State Park (p209)

IOWA
Heartland beauty and a cycling hot spot. p184

NORTH DAKOTA
Explore the grasslands that inspired Theodore Roosevelt. p195

SOUTH DAKOTA
Mt Rushmore, bison and badlands. p199

Find Your Way

Distances in the Great Plains are vast, and having your own wheels is the best way to rack up the miles. Interstates crisscross the region; the smaller state and federal highways are slower but more scenic.

TRAIN

Amtrak *(amtrak.com)* runs four long-distance routes across the Great Plains. Arriving by train (particularly from the hub city of Chicago) is an option, but getting around is not, with the exception of the *Missouri River Runner* between St Louis and Kansas City.

CAR

A car is essential for getting around the Great Plains, as well as within its cities, which lack comprehensive public transport networks. Car rental companies usually have locations in airports and downtown districts.

AIR

The major cities in each of the Great Plains states have airports, including **St Louis**, **Kansas City**, **Omaha**, **Oklahoma City** and **Des Moines**. However, they generally connect to larger hubs like Denver, Chicago and Dallas instead of one another.

North Dakota, p195

Find the celebrity woodchipper in Fargo, mingle with dinosaurs in Chamberlain, and hike the landscapes that Theodore Roosevelt called 'the romance of my life.'

South Dakota, p199

Squint at presidents at Mt Rushmore then drive past shaggy bison, granite spires and ponderosa pines in the Black Hills. National parks spotlight caves and badlands.

Iowa, p184

Admire architectural treasures in Des Moines and Mason City, cycle statewide trails, follow Lewis and Clark, and soak up the bucolic scenery that inspired American Gothic.

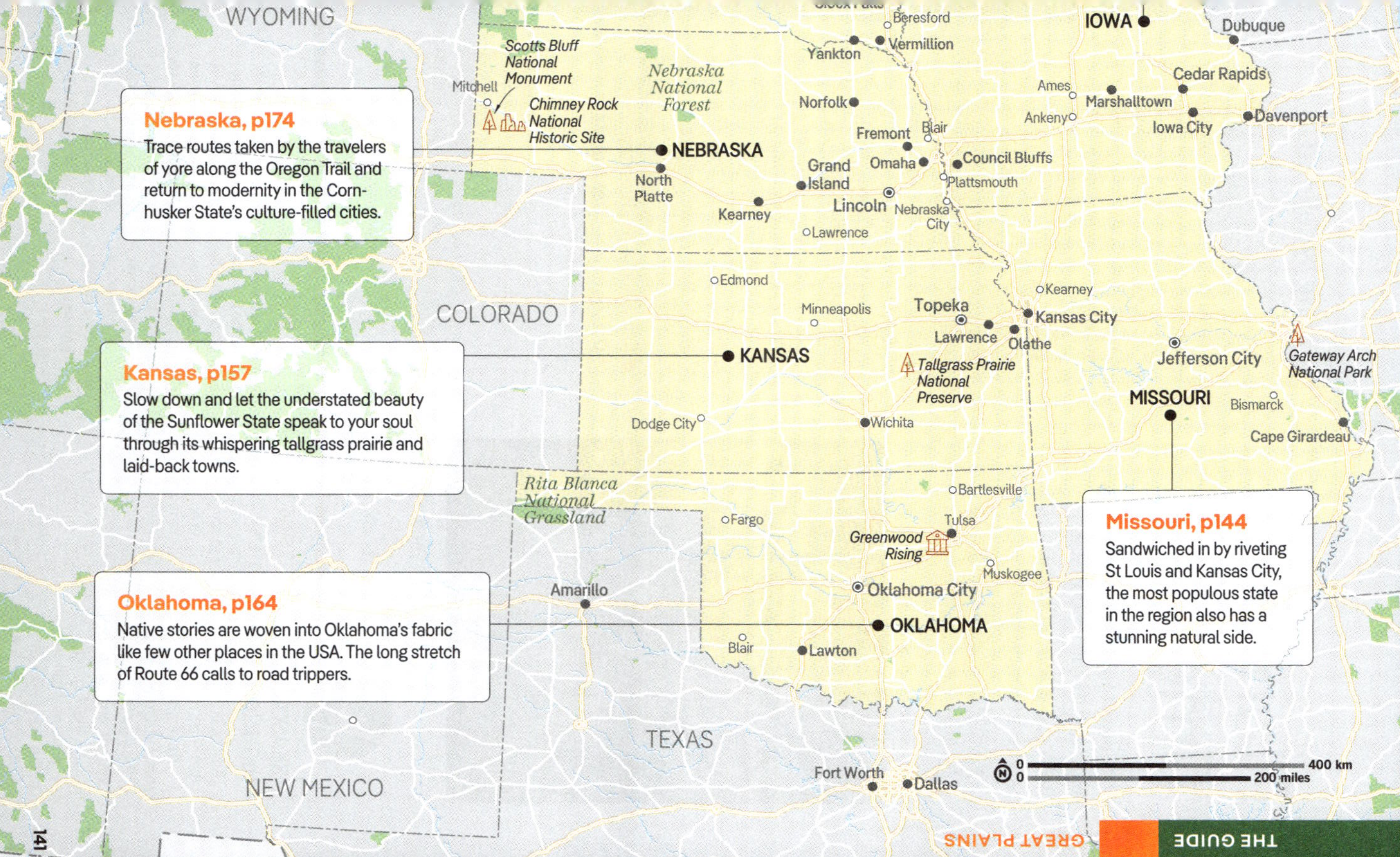

Nebraska, p174

Trace routes taken by the travelers of yore along the Oregon Trail and return to modernity in the Cornhusker State's culture-filled cities.

Kansas, p157

Slow down and let the understated beauty of the Sunflower State speak to your soul through its whispering tallgrass prairie and laid-back towns.

Oklahoma, p164

Native stories are woven into Oklahoma's fabric like few other places in the USA. The long stretch of Route 66 calls to road trippers.

Missouri, p144

Sandwiched in by riveting St Louis and Kansas City, the most populous state in the region also has a stunning natural side.

Plan Your Time

The Great Plains cover a huge expanse of the country. Be strategic about how much you can bite off and how much time you want to spend in the car.

KIT LEONG/SHUTTERSTOCK

Meramec Caverns (p147)

A Long Weekend

- Arrive in **St Louis** (p144) and ride the 1960s tram to the top of the **Gateway Arch** (p150). Unleash your inner child (or actual children) at **City Museum** (p144) and check out the museums and family-friendly attractions dotted around **Forest Park** (p148).

- Drive or take Amtrak's *Missouri River Runner* to **Kansas City** (p151) to go full glutton on some **barbecue** (p151). When you're full up, dig into the trenches of history at the **National WWI Museum** (p151) and peruse the galleries of the **Nelson-Atkins Museum of Art** (p151). After dark, head to the historic Black district of **18th and Vine** (p153) for drinks and jazz.

- If time allows, add on a trip to **Omaha** (p176) or **Des Moines** (p190), both about a three-hour drive from KC.

SEASONAL HIGHLIGHTS

This region mostly hibernates in winter (November to February). Other times of the year bring out vibrant, only-here festivals that highlight the quirks and culture of the Great Plains.

FEBRUARY

Bird-watchers flock to Nebraska's Platte River to witness half a million honking sandhill cranes make a stop on their northerly migration. Conservation organizations in Grand Island and Kearney run **tours** (p180).

MARCH

Tornado season starts, but we hope the only whirlwind you see is the inside of a Lawrence, Kansas, sports bar, cheering on the University of Kansas Jayhawks basketball team during **March Madness**.

MAY

Truman Day (May 8) is a Missouri state holiday, and entry to the **Harry S Truman Presidential Library** (p154) in Independence is free. Some bars and restaurants offer a third off your bill in honor of the 33rd president.

A Week in the Plains

- After a few days in **St Louis** (p144), snake up the Mississippi River to Iowa along the **Great River Road**, stopping in **Dubuque** and **Davenport** (p185). Pause in the folksy **Amana Colonies** (p188), established as 19th-century German religious communes, with a museum, shops and a boutique hotel.

- Take the back roads or hop on I-80 to **Des Moines** (p190) for art and architecture. Cross the state line to **Omaha** (p176) to explore shops, bars and restaurants in the **Old Market** (p176).

- Leave city life behind on your way to **Badlands National Park** (p200) and **Mt Rushmore** (p208) in South Dakota, stopping in Nebraska to float the Niobrara River near **Valentine** (p183) or just having lunch at **Monowi Tavern** (p183), run by the town's sole resident.

Route 66

- Marking its 100th anniversary in 2026, Route 66 is one of the USA's most iconic road trips. The Mother Road clocks up many miles through three Plains states. Spend a week or more checking out the cool cities and oddball small towns along the way.

- After seeing the sights of **St Louis** (p144), have a concrete at **Ted Drewes** (p147) and hit the road. **Meramec Caverns** (p147), the largest commercial cave in Missouri, is a classic stop.

- **Kansas** (p157) contains just 13 miles of the Mother Road but has diversions aplenty.

- Budget most of your time for Oklahoma. Stop at roadside attractions like the **Blue Whale** (p168) and get waylaid in **Tulsa** (p164), the 'capital of Route 66,' then carry on through **Oklahoma City** (p170) toward Texas.

JUNE

School's out, and summer fun is starting. Get weird on the water at Wichita's **Riverfest** (p159), celebrate **Pride** in cities across the region and mark **Juneteenth** on Tulsa's Black Wall Street (p164).

JULY

Road-tripping families scoot across Missouri, Kansas and Oklahoma along historic Route 66, while cyclists set off on **RAGBRAI** (p194), a weeklong non-competitive 470-mile bike ride that traverses Iowa.

AUGUST

The **Iowa State Fair** (p190) in Des Moines is legendary, even inspiring a Broadway musical. More than a million visitors come to eat deep-fried Twinkies, coo over farm animals and check out the famous butter sculptures.

OCTOBER

Admire prismatic fall foliage along the **Great River Road** (p190), which traces the Mississippi River along Iowa's eastern edge through quaint waterfront towns. Peak leaf-peeping times are in mid- to late October.

Missouri

FINGER-LICKING BARBECUE | COOL MUSEUMS | WILD RIVERS

Places

With more forest and fewer farm fields than neighboring states, Missouri might not seem like a natural fit in the Great Plains. Limestone canyons, more caves than anywhere else in the country and glacial-blue springs that feed undammed rivers aren't what many travelers expect, but the Show Me State deserves to brag about its outdoor attractions, as well as its cities.

The most populous Plains state likes to mix things up. St Louis (STL) and Kansas City (KC) are on opposite ends of the state, both with excellent museums, must-devour foods, and diversions for music fans and sports nuts. Expect to spend at least a few days soaking up the sights in each.

From St Louis, Route 66 cuts its way diagonally across the state, delivering hokey roadside detours. No matter where you go, you're sure to find an adventure worthy of Missouri native Mark Twain as you explore the state.

TOP TIP

Which state is Kansas City in? Well, both Kansas (KCK) and Missouri (KCMO). Don't get it wrong like many national politicians and musicians shouting it on stage. We include Kansas City in Missouri in this book, but we've noted when places are on the Kansas side of the state line.

St Louis

Run wild at the City Museum

City Museum *(citymuseum.org; $20)*, perhaps St Louis' most boring-sounding attraction, is one of the coolest things to do in the entire region, so don't you dare let the dull name put you off. The Ferris wheel and school bus on the roof surely hint at the hilarity inside this museum gone maximalist.

GETTING AROUND

International airports in Kansas City and St Louis bookend Missouri, making the state the easiest entry point by air into the Great Plains. You can travel between these two cities aboard Amtrak's *Missouri River Runner*, but if you're going further afield, you'll need a car.

Often congested, I-70 connects St Louis and Kansas City, while I-44 paved over much of Route 66 between St Louis and the Kansas–Oklahoma border. Roads in the Ozarks are often scenic, winding, two-lane roller coasters.

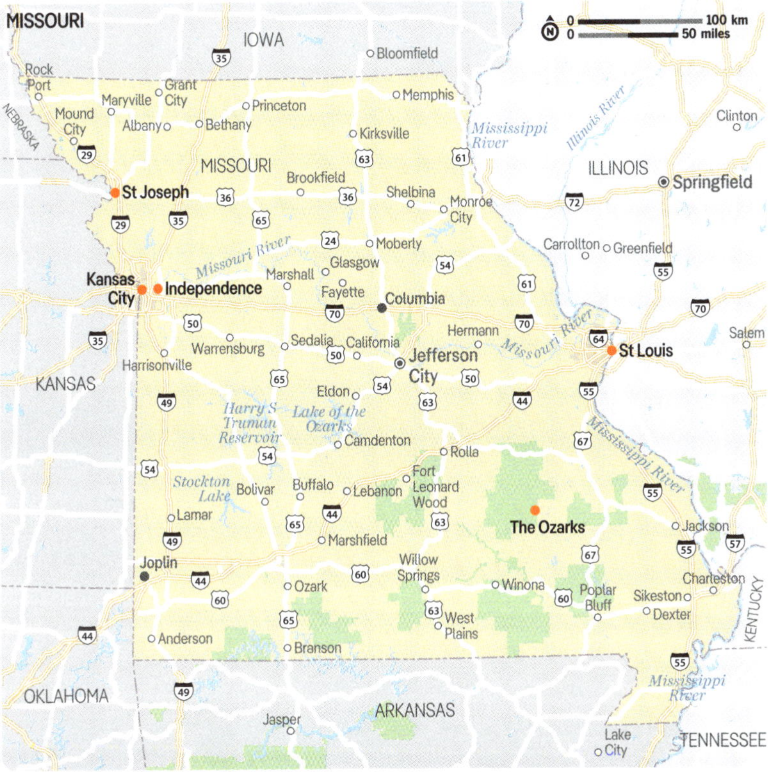

Part playground, part architectural salvage, part art installation, this fun house is a wild ride – literally. Seven- and 10-story slides cascade through the industrial building, a century-old former warehouse for the International Shoe Company. Relics from demolished buildings – many designed by architect Louis Sullivan, the 'father of skyscrapers' and mentor to Frank Lloyd Wright – are portals to other floors (and maybe even other worlds).

It costs $8 extra to visit the roof, but it's worth it. The modern art is sure to crack a smile, from a 'sausage man' made of bronze to *Bop Bear*, a punching bag resembling a bear-shaped honeypot that first debuted at Burning Man and is now a hit with kids.

EATING IN ST LOUIS: OUR PICKS

City Foundry: Upscale food hall with 17 globe-trotting stalls, plus shops, mini-golf and escape rooms, in an old motor factory. *10am-9pm* **$$**

Blood & Sand: This former members-only club has opened to us commoners with a signature tasting menu and killer cocktails. *5-11pm Mon-Sat* **$$$**

Broadway Oyster Bar: Suck down crawfish and other Cajun treats at this New Orleans–style joint that's part bar, part live-music venue, but all restaurant. *11am-10pm* **$$**

Katie's Pizza & Pasta: Phenomenal Italian food right outside Busch Stadium in Ballpark Village. *11am-10pm Mon-Thu, from 10am Sat & Sun* **$$**

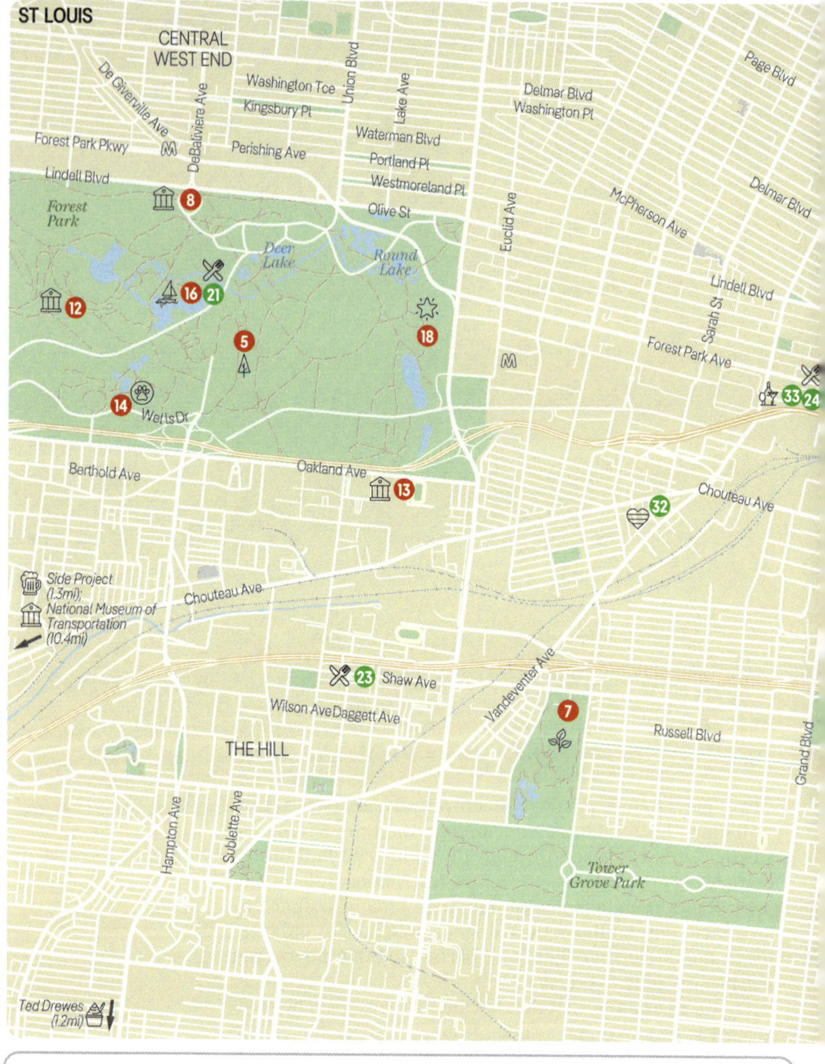

HIGHLIGHTS
1 City Museum

SIGHTS
2 Busch Stadium
3 Energizer Park
4 Enterprise Center
5 Forest Park
6 Gateway Arch National Park
7 Missouri Botanical Garden
8 Missouri History Museum
9 Museum at the Gateway Arch
10 National Blues Museum
11 Old Courthouse
12 St Louis Art Museum
13 St Louis Science Center
14 St Louis Zoo
15 Union Station

ACTIVITIES
16 Big Muddy Adventures
17 Gateway Arch Riverboats
18 Steinberg Skating Rink

SLEEPING
19 St Louis Union Station Hotel

EATING
20 Blood & Sand
21 Boathouse at Forest Park
22 Broadway Oyster Bar
23 Charlie Gitto's
24 City Foundry
25 Imo's
26 Katie's Pizza & Pasta
27 Pappy's Smokehouse
28 Park Avenue Coffee

DRINKING & NIGHTLIFE
29 4 Hands Brewing Co
30 Anheuser-Busch Brewery
31 Blueprint Coffee at High Low
32 Just John Club
33 None of the Above

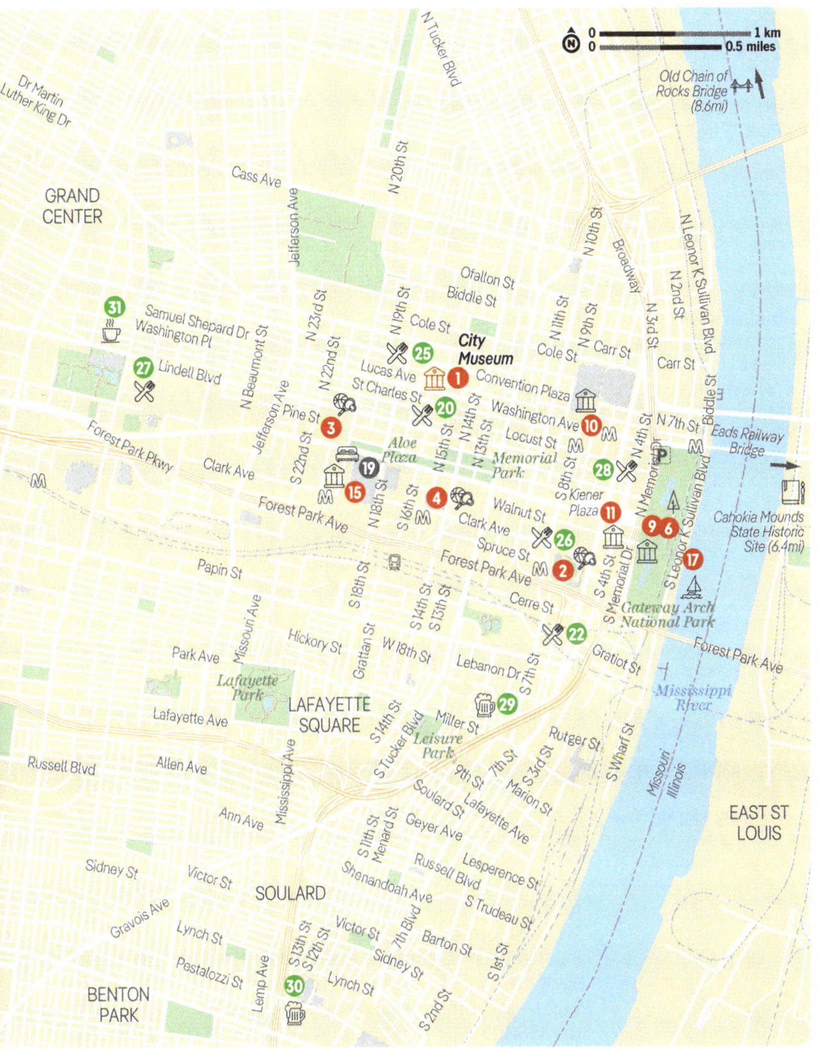

ROUTE 66 STOPS IN MISSOURI

Old Chain of Rocks Bridge: Now open only to pedestrians and cyclists, this mile-long span over the Mississippi River north of St Louis opened in 1929.

Ted Drewes: Save room for a concrete, a cup of thick frozen custard, invented at this St Louis institution in 1959. *(teddrewes.com)*

Meramec Caverns: Hugely popular and totally corny, these caves are filled with stalactites and Civil War history. *(americascave.com; adult/child $29.50/16)*

Uranus Fudge Factory: No pun is left unexcreted at this shameless roadside attraction. *(uranusgeneralstore.com)*

WHERE TO WATCH SPORTS IN STL

The love of the game runs deep in St Louis, which has been named one of the best sports cities in the country.

Busch Stadium: The Cardinals play baseball in this fun downtown stadium. The team has won the World Series 11 times, second only to the New York Yankees. *(mlb.com/cardinals)*

Enterprise Center: The St Louis Blues hockey team won the Stanley Cup in 2019 and makes frequent appearances in the playoffs. *(nhl.com/blues)*

Energizer Park: In 2023, STL got its first Major League Soccer team – St Louis City SC – along with a new purpose-built downtown stadium. *(stlcitysc.com)*

Seek justice at the Old Courthouse

Part of Gateway Arch National Park (p150), the 19th-century **Old Courthouse** *(nps.gov/jeff; free)* marks a pivotal point – and a huge step backwards – in the conversation about slavery in the United States. Auctions to sell enslaved people took place on its steps, and the courthouse is also where more than 300 Black people, including Dred and Harriet Scott in 1847, sued for their freedom. Their case reached the Supreme Court, which ruled that American citizenship did not extend to Black people of African descent, so they did not have constitutional rights.

Reopened in May 2025 after a two-year renovation, the Old Courthouse has overhauled galleries that explain the Scott case, as well as the design of the building, Black life in St Louis and the relevance of the judicial system. You are free to wander on your own or join a ranger-led tour at 2:15pm daily.

Tour the Anheuser-Busch Brewery

Some of the best-selling beers in the United States hail from St Louis. Opened in the 1850s by German immigrants looking to create a beer that appealed to the entire nation's taste buds, the **Anheuser-Busch Brewery** *(budweisertours.com; tours from $15)* is a huge red-brick complex that still brews and bottles Budweiser, Bud Light and dozens of other brands as it has for more than a century, with more than a few expansions and technological upgrades since its founding. Sign up for a tour to see the famous huge-hooved Clydesdale horses and ornate architecture, then sample the suds on tap.

Find your space in Forest Park

Clocking in at 1371 acres – almost 45% larger than Central Park in New York City – **Forest Park** *(forestparkforever.org)* is the green heart of St Louis. Once the grounds for the 1904 World's Fair, Forest Park remains a cultural hub of St Louis, thanks to the array of free-to-visit museums, as well as having plenty of family-friendly attractions and activities for sporty types.

The **St Louis Art Museum** *(slam.org; free; closed Mon)* is located inside a grand beaux-arts building that was originally built for the fair. Art lovers could spend an entire day admiring the 34,000-piece collection. Dive deeper into the legacy of the World's Fair at the nearby **Missouri History Museum** *(mohistory.org; free; closed Mon)*, whose showcase exhibit is

EATING IN ST LOUIS: ICONIC STL FOODS

Charlie Gitto's: Said to be the spot that invented toasted ravioli in 1947 when a chef dropped them in oil instead of water. *5-9pm Sun-Thu, to 10pm Fri & Sat* $$$

Imo's: This local chain is a prolific purveyor of St Louis–style pizza: cracker-thin, square-cut crust topped with Provel cheese. *10am-11pm or later* $

Park Avenue Coffee: Treat yourself to a slice of gooey butter cake. This cafe does them in several flavors, such as red velvet and pumpkin caramel. *7am-2pm Mon-Fri* $

Pappy's Smokehouse: Food Network called these the best BBQ ribs in the country, and our sticky fingers agree. *11am-4pm or later Wed-Mon* $

Forest Park

a scale model of the 1904 grounds. The museum's gift shop is one of the best places in town for STL souvenirs you never knew you needed, like a toasted ravioli fridge magnet.

Kids will be more drawn in by the critters at the **St Louis Zoo** *(stlzoo.org; free)* and the interactive displays and demonstrations at the **St Louis Science Center** *(slsc.org; free; closed Tue & Wed)*. From mid-November to early March, lace up your ice skates to glide on the **Steinberg Skating Rink** *(steinbergrink.com)*, the largest in the Midwest.

Fuel up for a big day out at the **Boathouse at Forest Park** *(boathousestl.com)*, the park's waterside cafe, where you can dine outdoors next to the ducks. Next door, rent paddle boats, canoes, kayaks, stand-up paddleboards – or bikes for landlubbers – from **Big Muddy Adventures** *(paddleforestpark.com)*.

MORE STL SIGHTS

Missouri Botanical Garden: Walk around a 14-acre Japanese garden, a Victorian-style hedge maze and the geodesic Climatron. *(missouribotanicalgarden.org; adult/child $16/free)*

National Blues Museum: Explore the deep history of this influential music genre. *(nationalbluesmuseum.org; adult/child $15/10)*

National Museum of Transportation: Huge railroad locomotives, historic cars cooler than your rental and more that moves. *(tnmot.org; adult/child $16/8)*

Union Station: Family-friendly attractions in this former train station include a 200ft-tall Ferris wheel, a shark-filled aquarium and a ropes course. Adults can watch the light show in the Grand Hall, now a hotel bar (p212). *(stlouisunionstation.com)*

DRINKING IN ST LOUIS: OUR PICKS

4 Hands Brewing Co: STL's largest craft brewery is down the road from big brother Bud, with a lively taproom. *11am-10pm or later Mon-Sat, to 8pm Sun*

Side Project: Hopheads must visit this suburban brewery that's been ranked as one of the best in the world multiple times. *4-8pm Mon, Wed & Thu, from 1pm Fri-Sun*

None of the Above: Sleek speakeasy below City Foundry (p145) started by a James Beard–winning chef. Look for the red light. *5pm-1am Wed-Mon*

Blueprint Coffee at High Low: This 'literary cafe' serves live music, art exhibitions and a creative atmosphere alongside coffee and pastries. *8am-4pm*

TOP EXPERIENCE

Gateway Arch National Park

The world's largest arch soars 630ft above the smallest national park in the United States. Set within a green space near the Mississippi River, long an unofficial divider between east and west, the Arch is a symbol of St Louis, promoting the city's historic role as the 'Gateway to the West.' The museum presents nuanced views on manifest destiny and white western migration.

FIIPHOTO/SHUTTERSTOCK

TOP TIPS

- Save $3 on tram tickets with the **America the Beautiful** national park pass. Combo tickets for cruises also net small savings.
- Going through airport-style security is required to visit the museum and take the trams.
- Tram tickets often sell out; book online in advance.

PRACTICALITIES

- gatewayarch.com; nps .gov/jeff
- museum free; tram ride from $12
- museum and tram open 9am-6pm; grounds 5am-11pm

Museum at the Gateway Arch

The fascinating, free-to-visit **Museum at the Gateway Arch** will take up the majority of the time you spend at this national park. It's filled with interactive exhibits that detail the history of St Louis, provide updated perspectives on westward expansion, and dive into the architectural and engineering feats required for the arch's construction.

Tram to the Top

A visit to the Gateway Arch isn't complete without whizzing to the top in one of the small trams that feel like 1960s space capsules straight out of *The Jetsons*. They take four minutes to trundle to the top, releasing passengers into a narrow viewing area with windows that provide unbeatable views over the city.

Gateway Arch Riverboats

Churn up the 'Big Muddy' (the Mississippi River) on replica 19th-century steamboats on a narrated cruise with **Gateway Arch Riverboats**. Unfortunately, this stretch of river isn't particularly scenic, but it's still a fun way to see the city, and it's the only way to get on the fast-flowing water of the country's most fabled river.

Kansas City

Remembering the Great War

The United States' congressionally designated national museum of the Great War isn't in Washington, DC, but in the heart of the country in Kansas City. Enter the impressive, modern **National WWI Museum** *(theworldwar.org; adult/child $19.50/11.50; closed Mon Sep-May)* on a glass walkway over a field of red poppies, the symbol of remembrance of WWI. Through detailed and engaging displays, learn about a war that is almost forgotten by many Americans.

Outside, the **Liberty Memorial** towers nearly 270ft above the lawn, and you can ride an elevator to the top (for an extra $6) to see the city from on high. The view of Union Station (p149) from the top of Liberty Memorial and the courtyard below is the most photographed angle of Kansas City. The courtyard is free for all to access – you don't have to visit the museum.

Artsy outing at Nelson-Atkins

One of the top galleries in the region, the **Nelson-Atkins Museum of Art** *(nelson-atkins.org; free; closed Tue & Wed)* is a cherished city treasure and a must-visit for culture vultures. The globe-trotting collection spans continents, showing off ancient Egyptian coffins, Chinese bronzes and works by European masters (including pieces by Monet and Caravaggio).

But the most iconic pieces aren't in the museum at all – they are outside on the lawn. Four 18ft-tall badminton shuttlecocks playfully plunge into the grass on either side of the museum building, which represents the net, and they feature on countless KC souvenirs.

Nearby, the smaller **Kemper Museum of Contemporary Art** *(kemperart.org; free; closed Mon & Tue)* has edgy rotating exhibitions and an excellent cafe.

Track down KC's best barbecue

Kansas City was once home to some of the largest stockyards in the country, second only to Chicago, and smoked meat is still big business. KC's status as one of the best places in the USA to eat barbecue is thanks to Henry Perry, a Black pitmaster who opened a restaurant in the early 1900s. Although Perry's restaurant no longer exists, he trained apprentice pitmasters who carried on his craft at the thriving institutions of **Gates Bar-B-Q** *(gatesbbq.com)* and **Arthur Bryant's** *(arthurbryantsbbq.com)*.

WHERE TO WATCH SPORTS IN KC

Kansas City is the smallest city to host the 2026 World Cup games. To say that this place is sports mad is an understatement.

Arrowhead Stadium: Even before Taylor Swift, the Kansas City Chiefs were hitting the headlines, winning the Super Bowl three times between 2020 and 2024. *(chiefs.com)*

Kauffman Stadium: The Royals baseball team hits homers at The K. *(mlb.com/royals)*

CPKC Stadium: The first arena in the world purpose-built for a professional women's sports team opened for the KC Current's soccer stars in 2024. *(kansascitycurrent.com)*

Children's Mercy Park: Sporting KC, the men's soccer team, plays on the Kansas side. *(sportingkc.com)*

EATING IN KANSAS CITY: OUR PICKS

Antler Room: Local ingredients go global in seasonal small plates, which might include fresh pasta, potato gyoza or grilled octopus. *5-10pm Wed-Sun* $$

Baba's Pantry: Nowhere else in town does hummus, falafel and chicken shawarma as good as this Palestinian-American deli. *11am-7pm Mon-Sat* $

Green Dirt on Oak: The charcuterie boards are works of art and mostly sourced from its own farm in Weston, about 30 miles northwest. *10am-10pm Wed-Sun* $$

Corvino: Sit in the darkened dining room for a decadent New American dinner, starting with the signature seaweed doughnuts. *5-10pm Sun-Thu, to 11pm Fri & Sat* $$$

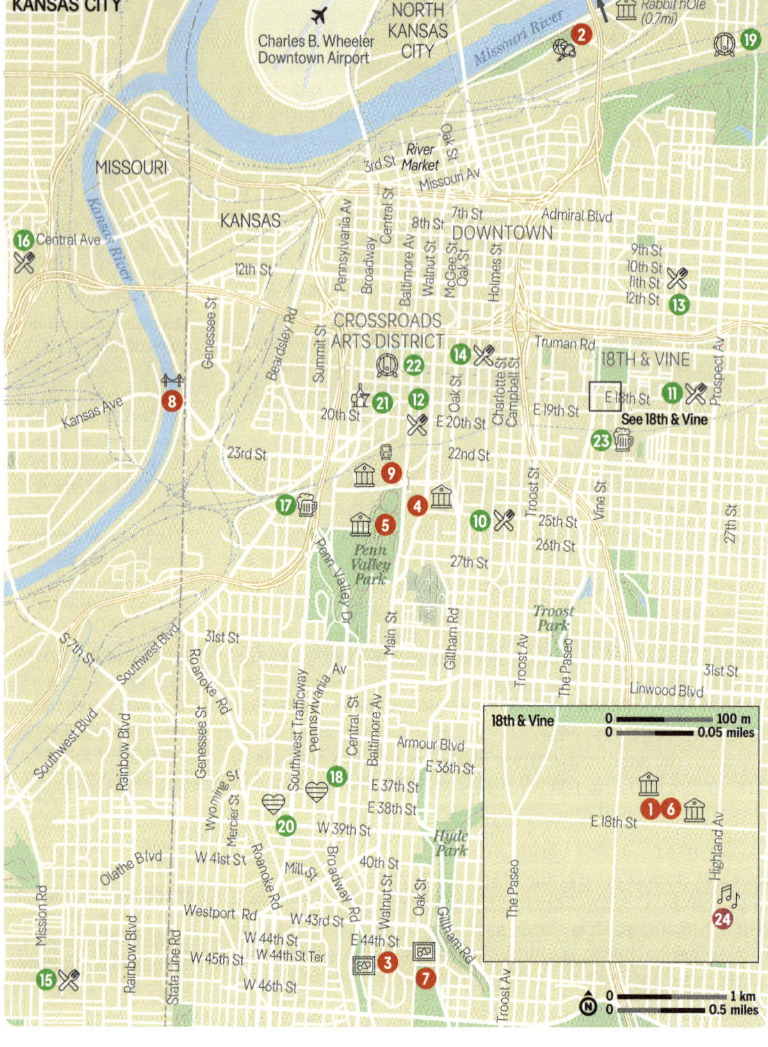

SIGHTS
1 American Jazz Museum
2 CPKC Stadium
3 Kemper Museum of Contemporary Art
4 Museum of BBQ
5 National WWI Museum
6 Negro Leagues Baseball Museum
7 Nelson-Atkins Museum of Art
8 Rock Island Bridge
9 Union Station

EATING
10 Antler Room
11 Arthur Bryant's
12 Corvino
13 Gates Bar-B-Q
14 Green Dirt on Oak
15 Joe's Kansas City Bar-B-Que
16 Slap's BBQ

DRINKING & NIGHTLIFE
17 Boulevard Brewery
18 Hamburger Mary's
19 J Rieger
20 Missie B's
21 Swordfish Tom's
22 Tom's Town
23 Vine Street Brewing Co

ENTERTAINMENT
24 Mutual Musicians Foundation

Kansas City barbecue has deep roots but continues to evolve, with a new generation of pitmasters firing up the smokers for their own takes on tradition. The Z-Man sandwich (sliced brisket, smoked provolone cheese and onion rings on a Kaiser roll) from **Joe's Kansas City Bar-B-Que** *(joeskc.com)* holds legendary status, best devoured at its original location in a gas station on the Kansas side of the state line. Vegetarians should try the version with portobello mushroom. Elsewhere in KCK, **Slap's BBQ** *(slapsbbqkc.com)*, well, slaps. (Its name is actually an acronym that stands for 'Squeal Like a Pig.') Burnt ends – the fatty charred ends of brisket, like smoked beef crackling – are a Kansas City invention and a must-order here and at any spot worth its sauce.

Before you fill your stomach, feed your mind at the world's first **Museum of BBQ** *(museumofbbq.co; $12)*, opened in March 2025. It dissects the history of KC barbecue and other major regional styles. More importantly, it has a 'bean' ball pit.

Feel the soul of Black Kansas City

The historic Black district of **18th and Vine** was a cradle of jazz music and is still a focal point of Black culture in KC.

Learn about musicians – including Kansas City native Charlie 'Bird' Parker – instruments and styles at the **American Jazz Museum** *(americanjazzmuseum.org; adult/child $10/6)*, which also has an jazz club called the **Blue Room** for live performances throughout the week, some of which are free. Jazz-loving night owls should head to **Mutual Musicians Foundation** *(themutualmusiciansfoundation.com; midnight-5am Fri & Sat)*. When performers wrap up their evening shows elsewhere, they head to Mutual Musicians to jam. Sessions don't get going until midnight or later, and Mutual Musicians is the only place in the entire state that's allowed to sell alcohol all night, thanks to a special exemption from the Missouri legislature.

Next to the American Jazz Museum, the **Negro Leagues Baseball Museum** *(nlbm.com; adult/child $10/6; closed Mon)* covers the lesser-known history of Black teams, such as the KC Monarchs and New York Black Yankees, that flourished until baseball became fully integrated.

Vine Street Brewing Co *(vinestbrewing.com; closed Tue)*, Missouri's first Black-owned brewery, opened in 2023 and is already a neighborhood staple. Sip a pint of Jazzman, a black lager that's the brewery's signature pour, at its premises in a graffitied limestone former public-works building.

This district has been undergoing major and much-needed improvements, including a new pedestrian plaza for better

KC WITH KIDS

Rabbit hOle: Tumble into the magic of children's literature at this one-of-a-kind art-filled celebration of kids' books. *(rabbitholekc.org; $16)*

Union Station: It's still a working train station, but it also contains Science City, a planetarium and a five-story-tall movie screen. *(unionstation.org)*

Kansas City Zoo & Aquarium: Colorful fish, sharks and a giant Pacific octopus fill a 650,000-gallon aquarium opened in 2023. *(kansascityzoo.org; from $20)*

Wonderscope: Children's museum best suited for under-10s. *(wonderscope.org; $16)*

Deanna Rose Children's Farmstead: Pet farm animals and bottle-feed baby goats in the Kansas-side suburb of Overland Park. *($5)*

DRINKING IN KANSAS CITY: OUR PICKS

Swordfish Tom's: KC's best cocktail bar is hiding down an alleyway. Descend the stairs into a darkened basement boiler room. *4pm-1:30am Tue-Sat*

J Rieger: This historic distillery was closed during Prohibition but resurrected a century later by the founder's great-great-great-grandson. *3-10pm Wed-Sat*

Tom's Town: Distillery named for a 1930s political boss with an art deco–style bar and a weekend-only speakeasy. *4-10pm or later Mon-Fri, noon-midnight Sat*

Boulevard Brewery: A conglomerate now owns KC's original craft brewer, but locals still love sipping Boulevard Wheat. *noon-9pm Mon-Sat, 10am-6pm Sun*

INDEPENDENCE TO THE FRONTIER

Nicknamed the 'Queen City of the Trails,' Independence was a major launching point for the Santa Fe, California and Oregon Trails.

National Frontier Trails Museum: This free museum covers the history of the three main trails, as well as the Mormon Trail. Mormons still have a major presence in Independence, which church leader Joseph Smith declared as Zion. *(ci.independence.mo.us/nftm)*

SantaCaliGon Days: Named after the three trails, this late-summer fun fair brings amusement park rides and food vendors to Independence's historic square. *(santacaligon.com)*

Pioneer Trails Adventures: Tour the main sites of Independence in a covered wagon. *(pioneertrailsadventures.com)*

walkability, renovations of the century-old Boone Theater – set to become a Black Movie Hall of Fame – and a planned expansion of the Negro Leagues Baseball Museum to include more exhibit space, a seven-story hotel and rooftop bar.

Independence

Get to know the only president from Missouri

Harry Truman, the 33rd US president, grew up in **Independence**, a suburb east of Kansas City. Reopened in 2021 after a $29 million update, the **Harry S Truman Presidential Library and Museum** *(trumanlibrary.gov; adult/child $12/5; closed Sun)* is a behind-the-scenes look at his life, legacy and the world at large in the 1940s and '50s. Exhibits include somber artifacts, such as the safety plug from the atomic bomb dropped on Nagasaki, Japan, to more lighthearted items like the famous 'The Buck Stops Here!' sign.

Join a National Park Service ranger on a tour of the **Harry S Truman National Historic Site** *(nps.gov/hstr; free; 9am-4pm Wed-Sun)* to see the simple life Harry and his wife, Bess, lived in their basic but charming wood house. The former president lived here from 1919 to 1972, and it's furnished with their original belongings. Visits are by a 30-minute tour only, and you must pick up a first-come, first-served free ticket from the **Harry S Truman National Historic Site Visitor Center**, about half a mile away.

St Joseph

From the Pony Express to psychiatry

St Joseph (usually abbreviated to St Jo) was another major departure point for westward-bound 19th-century pioneers headed for the goldfields of California or the Oregon territory. No matter their origin or final destination, travelers converged in St Jo, once the westernmost American city accessible by rail and a river port for steamboats.

As the eastern terminus of the Pony Express, which first set off from here in April 1860, St Jo served as a lifeline that connected east and west. The **Pony Express National Museum** *(ponyexpress.org; adult/child $10/5)* is located in the stables from which the horse riders once departed. Time your visit for June for the annual **Re-Ride**, when riders gallop along the historic route and still carry letters in a leather mochila.

Nearby, the imposing 1858 **Patee House** *(ponyexpressjessejames.com; adult/child $8/5)* was a luxury hotel and the Pony

EATING & DRINKING IN INDEPENDENCE: OUR PICKS

Dixon's Famous Chili Parlor: Open since 1919, Dixon's is a diner that served Truman; wonder if he got the chili or all-you-can-eat tacos. *10am-9pm Mon-Sat* $

Clinton's Soda Fountain: Little has changed from when Truman got his first job. Come for ice cream and phosphate sodas. *11am-5pm Tue-Sat* $

3 Trails Brewing: This welcoming brewery is a hub for the community and hosts lots of events. *4-10:30pm Wed & Thu, to midnight Fri, noon-midnight Sat, to 7pm Sun*

Sentinel Room: Top-notch cocktail bar with a huge whiskey selection in a former newspaper office. *3-10pm Tue-Thu, to midnight Fri, noon-midnight Sat*

Ethnic Enrichment Festival

Express headquarters. It now showcases the city's rich story with exhibits full of historic memorabilia. Behind it is the modest house of notorious outlaw **Jesse James** *(extra $5/3)*. He was murdered here, and the bullet hole is still visible in the wall.

Continue the dark tourism trend at the **Glore Psychiatric Museum** *(stjosephmuseum.org; adult/child $12/8)*. Housed in the former State Lunatic Asylum No 2, this museum gives a frightening and fascinating look at lobotomies, the 'bath of surprise' and other discredited mental health treatments.

The Ozarks

Hike the hills and float in wild rivers

Ozark hill country spreads across southern Missouri and extends into northern Arkansas and eastern Oklahoma. Flashy Branson receives the lion's share of tourists, but the region's true charms lie not in town but further afield in the rolling hills and deep clefts where spring-fed rivers carry legions of happy campers floating downstream.

Two wild rivers, the Current and the Jacks Fork, wind through 80,000 acres of raw natural beauty in the **Ozark National Scenic Riverways** *(nps.gov/ozar; free)*, the first national park established to protect a waterway. Numerous natural springs feed the river; the most famous and accessible is **Big Spring**, which releases some 286 million gallons a day. **Blue Spring** is harder to get to but even more stunning, with surreal cerulean waters that almost look glacial. Swimming in the springs isn't allowed, but you can jump in the river nearby.

Another scenic swimming spot is **Johnson's Shut-Ins State Park** *(mostateparks.com; free)*, where the Black River swirls through canyon-like gorges (shut-ins). Find outfitters and rental services for river activities in the towns of **Van Buren** and **Eminence**. Summer weekends get busy and boisterous.

Hikers can tackle portions of the 430-mile **Ozark Trail** *(ozarktrail.com)*, parts of which follow the Current River. For a good half-day hike, head to **Taum Sauk Mountain State Park** *(mostateparks.com; free)*, where you can scale the state's

BEST MISSOURI FESTIVALS

National Tom Sawyer Days: Head to Hannibal, the childhood hometown of Mark Twain, to watch competitive fence painting and more in July. *(hannibaljaycees.org)*

Mardi Gras: The second-largest Mardi Gras celebrations in the country take place in the St Louis neighborhood of Soulard. *(stlmardigras.org)*

Ethnic Enrichment Festival: Diverse clubs in KC set up booths to share their food and culture in August. *(eeckc.org)*

Birthplace of Route 66 Festival: The nation's largest celebration of the Mother Road takes place every August in Springfield. *(route66festivalsgf.com)*

Maifest: Celebrate spring in the German-heritage town of Hermann in May. *(maifesthermann.org)*

LGBTIQ+ MISSOURI

In 2024, Missouri ranked last – along with 23 other states – in a Human Rights Campaign survey of LGBTIQ+ equality, but that doesn't necessarily mean queer travelers should avoid the state.

St Louis and Kansas City have the most welcoming attitudes and dedicated gay bars. Try **Hamburger Mary's** *(hamburgermarys.com)* and **Missie B's** *(missiebs.com)* in KC, and **Just John Club** *(justjohnnightclub.com)* and other nearby LGBTIQ+ bars in the Grove neighborhood of STL. The college town of Columbia, home to the University of Missouri, was the first Missouri city to ban conversion therapy for LGBTIQ+ youth. These three cities, along with Springfield, have Pride festivities in June.

LAUREN KEITH /LONELY PLANET

Blue Spring (p155)

highest peak, 1772ft Taum Sauk Mountain (a flat walk from the already elevated parking lot) and see the state's tallest waterfall, 132ft Mina Sauk Falls.

See Branson's artificial and natural amusements

Hokey, family-friendly **Branson** is an unabashedly shameless tourist resort. The main attractions are **Silver Dollar City** *(silverdollarcity.com; 1-day pass adult/child $92/82)* – a huge Old West–themed amusement park – and the more than 45 theaters hosting country music, magic and comedy shows. **Branson's Famous Baldknobbers** *(baldknobbers.com; adult/child from $46/23)* is the musical comedy show that started it all in 1959. Three generations of the Mabe family – and a lot of 'friends' – cover country and gospel tunes, dance and offer up cornball comedy.

Drive just a few minutes out of town and you'll find yourself close to the Ozark wilderness again, though in a more manicured form. Man-made **Table Rock Lake** is a popular destination for boating and fishing, and you can rent motorboats and pontoons from multiple marinas. Much of the conserved land around Branson is thanks to Johnny Morris, the Missouri-born CEO of Bass Pro Shops. **Top of the Rock** *(bigcedar.com/top-of-the-rock; adult/child from $45/20)* lets you drive a golf cart along limestone cliffs and into a cave (which, of course, has a bar inside), while **Dogwood Canyon** *(dogwoodcanyon.org; adult/child from $19/14)* offers opportunities for hiking, cycling, horseback riding, fishing and hopping onto a trailer for nature tour.

EATING IN BRANSON: OUR PICKS

Keeter Center: Staffed by students at the College of the Ozarks, this country-chic farm-to-table restaurant gets top marks. *10:30am-8pm Mon-Sat* $$

Gettin' Basted: Grilled by award-winning pitmasters, brisket, pulled pork and burnt ends are the stars at one of the best places to eat on Branson's '76 Strip.' *11am-9pm* $

Full Throttle Distillery: Devour barbecue and comfort food at this motorcycle-themed spot that makes its own moonshine. *7am-10pm or later* $$

Pie Safe: Kitschily charming Victorian-styled cafe serving miniature pies and other baked goods alongside flavored lattes. *10am-6pm Mon-Sat* $

Kansas

PRESERVED PRAIRIE | AVIATION HISTORY | OUTSIDER ART

Wicked witches, yellow-brick roads and tornadoes powerful enough to erase entire towns are popular images of Kansas, but visions of amber waves of grain spreading as far as the eye can see are closer to reality.

What Kansas might lack in mind-boggling scenery, it makes up for in quirky, soul-stirring stops. The rolling hills and limitless horizons have an evocative, understated beauty, particularly evident in places like the beguiling Tallgrass Prairie National Preserve. Gems abound, from the superb space museum in Hutchinson to the college-town cool of Lawrence.

The largest city in the state is Wichita, a 19th-century cow town that became the 'Air Capital of the World' as a major aircraft manufacturer. This transformation is emblematic of how the whole state continues to reinvent itself in weird and wonderful ways while still drawing on history and tradition – no matter where you go in Kansas, it's unlikely to be at all what you expected.

Places

TOP TIP

For discounts on tolls on the Turnpike, request a free K-TAG online *(ksturnpike.com)* before your trip, which will be mailed to you. Toll tags from some other states, such as Best Pass, Pikepass, EZ TAG and SunPass, can also be used here. Tolls cannot be paid with cash.

Atchison

Birthplace of America's finest female aviator

Famed flier Amelia Earhart broke many barriers and records. She was the first female pilot to fly solo nonstop across the Atlantic, and she disappeared in 1939 attempting to become the

GETTING AROUND

You need a car to get around Kansas. Two interstates cross the state in different directions, coming together near Kansas City: I-35, linking Wichita and Kansas City; and I-70, which shoots through Lawrence, Topeka and points west. Sections of both interstates are toll roads, called the Kansas Turnpike.

Wichita Dwight D Eisenhower National Airport is the busiest airport in Kansas (Kansas City's airport is in Missouri) and has services from regional hubs, such as Dallas, Denver and Chicago. Amtrak's *Southwest Chief*, which runs from Chicago to Los Angeles, stops in Lawrence, Topeka and Dodge City.

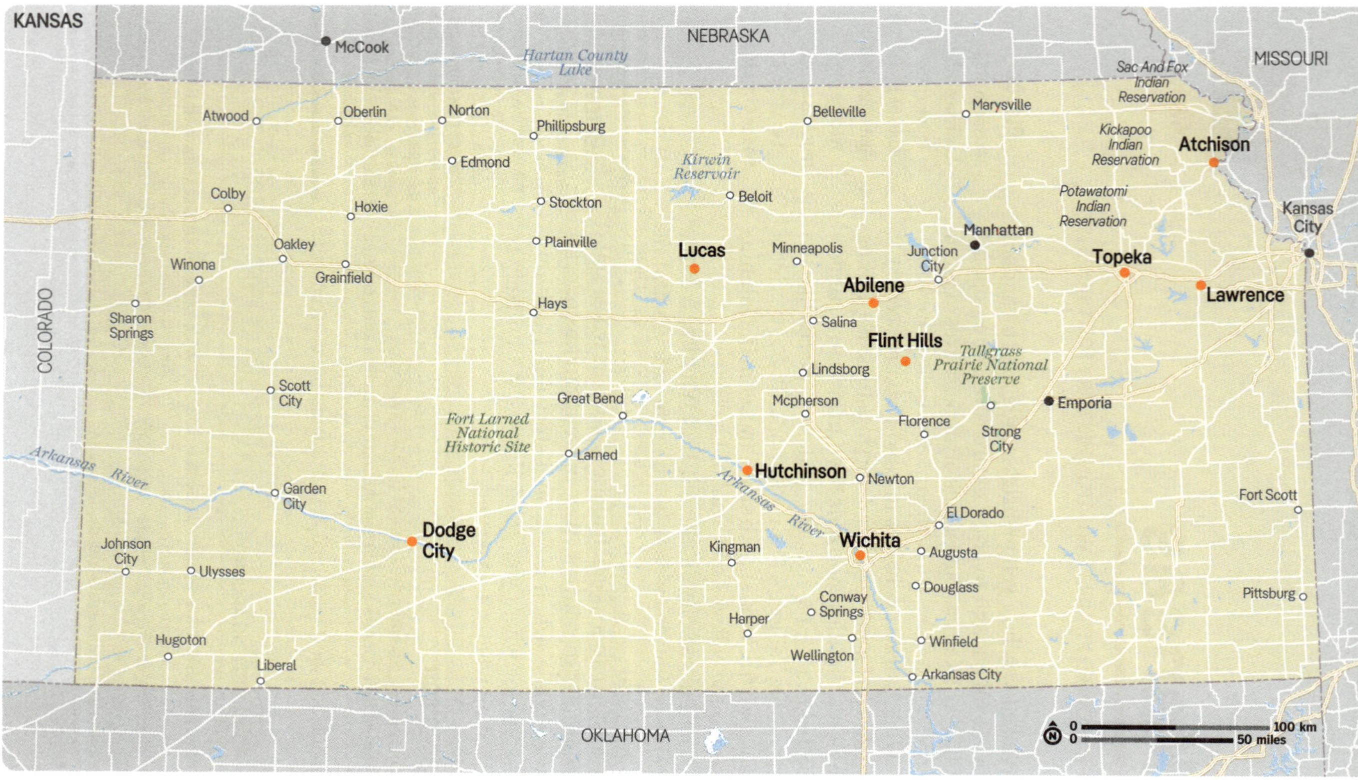
KANSAS
McCook
NEBRASKA
Hartan County Lake
MISSOURI
Sac And Fox Indian Reservation
Atwood
Oberlin
Norton
Phillipsburg
Belleville
Marysville
Kickapoo Indian Reservation
Atchison
Edmond
Kirwin Reservoir
Colby
Hoxie
Stockton
Beloit
Potawatomi Indian Reservation
Kansas City
Manhattan
Oakley
Plainville
Lucas
Minneapolis
Junction City
Topeka
Winona
Grainfield
Abilene
Lawrence
Sharon Springs
Hays
Salina
COLORADO
Flint Hills
Tallgrass Prairie National Preserve
Lindsborg
Scott City
Great Bend
Mcpherson
Emporia
Fort Larned National Historic Site
Florence
Strong City
Larned
Arkansas River
Hutchinson
Newton
Garden City
Fort Scott
El Dorado
Dodge City
Wichita
Johnson City
Ulysses
Kingman
Augusta
Douglass
Conway Springs
Pittsburg
Harper
Winfield
Hugoton
Wellington
Liberal
Arkansas City
OKLAHOMA
0 100 km
0 50 miles

first woman aviator to circumnavigate the globe. She championed gender equality and women pursuing male-dominated careers in engineering and science. Her body and plane were never found, which fuels speculation to this day.

Aptly located at Atchison's tiny airport, the **Amelia Earhart Hangar Museum** *(ameliaearharthangarmuseum.org; adult/child $15/8; closed Mon & Tue)* opened in 2023 and shows off *Muriel,* the only surviving Lockheed Electra 10-E plane, exactly like the one Earhart flew on her final voyage.

You can also visit the **Amelia Earhart Birthplace Museum** *(ameliaearhartmuseum.org; guided/self-guided tour $15/12),* the 1861 Gothic Revival home where she grew up.

Lawrence

College-town vibes in Kansas' coolest city

Lawrence has been an island of progressive politics since its inception. Founded by East Coast abolitionists in 1854, it became a battlefield in the clash between pro- and antislavery factions. The city's free-thinking spirit continues, fueled in no small part by the huge student body at the University of Kansas (KU). It's one of the country's most vibrant college towns.

The appealing downtown centers on **Massachusetts St** (abbreviated to Mass), lined with historic buildings home to the city's best restaurants, coffee shops, bars and stores. It's an excellent place to spend an afternoon shopping and bar-hopping.

The KU campus is at the top of Mt Oread, aka 'the Hill,' and it's worth stopping by the **Spencer Museum of Art** *(spencerart.ku.edu; free; closed Sun & Mon)* to check out the exhibitions, and globe-trotting and century-spanning works.

Topeka

The push to desegregate public schools

Kansas' vital role in the country's race relations is documented in the otherwise humdrum state capital of Topeka. Set in the former Monroe Elementary School, one of Topeka's four segregated primary schools for Black students, **Brown v Board of Education National Historical Park** *(nps.gov/brvb; free; closed Sun & Mon)* tells the story of the famous 1954 Supreme Court case that threw out the 'separate but equal' doctrine, in the context of the wider Civil Rights movement.

BEST KANSAS FESTIVALS

Riverfest: Wichita's biggest festival includes a city-wide scavenger hunt, 'cowboy bathtub' races and a cardboard boat regatta in June. *(wichitariverfest.com)*

Walnut Valley Festival: This September bluegrass festival near Winfield draws more visitors than the town's population. *(wvfest.com)*

Water Wars: Everyone in Humboldt participates in a town-wide water fight in August. *(facebook.com/waterwars.humboldt)*

Lawrence Busker Festival: Fire breathers, dancers, magicians and other street performers take over downtown Lawrence in May. *(lawrencebuskerfest.com)*

Louisburg Ciderfest: Celebrate all things apple in late September. *(louisburgcidermill.com)*

EATING & DRINKING IN LAWRENCE: OUR PICKS

Free State Brewing: Opened in 1989 as the first brewery in Kansas since Prohibition, with pints and pub grub. The cheddar ale soup is classic. *11am-9pm* $$

715: Classy but laid-back Italian-influenced restaurant with a neighborhood feel on Mass St. A happy hour favorite. *3-9pm Tue & Wed, to 10pm Thu-Sat* $$

Barker: Out-of-this-world pastries from a James Beard–nominated chef. Go early lest they sell out. *7am-8pm Mon-Fri, 8am-2pm Sat & Sun* $$

John Brown's Underground: The best cocktail bar in town is named for the famed abolitionist and Kansas hero. *5pm-midnight Wed-Sat*

BEST KANSAS SMALL TOWNS

Humboldt: A brewery, a boutique hotel with a cool cocktail bar, and lakeside cabins have put tiny Humboldt on the map in a big way. *(abolderhumboldt.com)*

Lindsborg: Its Swedish heritage shines with events like Våffeldagen (Waffle Day) and a Midsummer's Festival. *(visitlindsborg.com)*

Nicodemus: Formerly enslaved people founded Nicodemus in 1877 as the first Black town west of the Mississippi. The National Park Service has restored the town hall and church. *(nps.gov/nico)*

Council Grove: Main St was the Santa Fe Trail, and historic businesses, including Hays House, the oldest continuously operating restaurant west of the Mississippi, line the route. *(councilgrove.com)*

Climb to the top of the Kansas State Capitol

The grand **Kansas State Capitol** *(kansashistory.gov/capitol; free; closed Sun)*, made of state-sourced limestone, took 37 years to complete after its cornerstone was laid in 1866. You can take a guided or self-guided tour of the building – either way, don't miss *Tragic Prelude* on the east side of the 2nd-floor rotunda. This fiery mural by Kansas-born artist John Steuart Curry depicts a raging, oversized John Brown, a famous abolitionist who was later convicted of treason, holding a Bible in one hand and a rifle in the other. Brown stands in front of sparring Union and Confederate Civil War soldiers with a tornado and a prairie fire engulfing the background. Guided tours depart on the hour between 9am and 3pm, except at noon, Monday to Friday, and 10am, 11am, 1pm and 3pm on Saturday.

The Kansas Statehouse is one of the few where you can climb up into the huge copper dome on a guided tour. Brace yourself for the 296 steps; there's no elevator. Dome tours take place at 15 minutes past the hour.

Abilene

Make like Ike in Eisenhower's childhood home

In the late 19th century, Abilene was a rowdy cow town at the end of the Chisholm Trail. Today, its compact core of historic brick buildings and well-preserved neighborhoods seems perfectly appropriate for the birthplace of Dwight D Eisenhower, the 34th president.

The **Dwight D Eisenhower Presidential Library and Museum** *(eisenhowerlibrary.gov; adult/child $20/15)* includes Ike's boyhood home, a museum and library, and his and his wife's graves. Interactive exhibits cover the Eisenhower presidential era (1953–61) and his role as the Supreme Allied Commander in Europe in WWII. Don't miss the original script for his landmark 1961 speech in which he famously warned of the military-industrial complex.

Flint Hills

Pieces of the last surviving tallgrass prairie

Prairie once covered more than 30% of North America – some 170 million acres – but was decimated by agriculture and urban development. Only a tiny sliver remains today, mostly in Kansas' Flint Hills, which were never plowed because the soil is too rocky.

Run by the National Park Service, the 11,000-acre **Tallgrass Prairie National Preserve** *(nps.gov/tapr; free; buildings 8:30am-4:30pm, trails 24hr)* protects one of the last stands of this ecosystem that's symbolic of the center of the country. Walking trails meander along gently rolling hills, including through a pasture where reintroduced bison roam, as well as to the **Lower Fox Creek School**, a one-room limestone schoolhouse that drew in students from 1882 to 1930.

Near the visitor center, the impressive 1881 **Spring Hill Ranch House** was surprisingly sophisticated for its remote

LAUREN KEITH / LONELY PLANET

Tallgrass Prairie National Preserve

location in the rural countryside, built in Second Empire style with a mansard roof, a grand walnut staircase, and ornate woodwork and ceiling medallions. Find the preserve 2 miles northwest of tiny Strong City or 23 miles west of Emporia, a larger city that sits on I-35. A scenic way to get here is on the **Flint Hills National Scenic Byway**, where grasses and wildflowers wave you on through the timeless landscape that looks much the same as it did when the Native Kaw, Osage, Pawnee and Wichita people called it home.

If you're driving I-70 through Kansas, a closer option is the **Konza Prairie Biological Station** *(nature.org; free)* near the college town of Manhattan, home to Kansas State University. It's smaller and doesn't have bison, but its three looped hiking trails are just as evocative. Remember that these areas are grassland, so you won't find shade from trees. Sun protection and timing your hikes for cooler parts of the day are musts.

In March or April every year, prescribed burns set 2.2 million acres of the Kansas prairie on fire. This process, now started by humans instead of naturally by lightning, preserves the ecosystem and is a sight to see.

Wichita

A family-friendly, history-filled day out

The **Museums on the River** district could occupy a day or more of your time in Wichita. Note that here the name of the Arkansas River is pronounced 'OUR-Kansas,' not like the state of Arkansas.

A hit with kids and history-lovers, the **Old Cowtown Museum** *(oldcowtown.org; adult/child $12/10; closed Mon & Tue)* recreates the Wild West. This mini city is complete with dirt

ROUTE 66 IN KANSAS

The Sunflower State holds a mere 13 miles of the Mother Road (less than 1% of the total), but it still has a lot to see. It's also the only part of Route 66 that hasn't been overwritten by the interstate.

Entering from Missouri, you pass through mine-scarred **Galena**, where a rusty old tow truck inspired Pixar animators to create the character Mater in *Cars*. Look for the original outside **Cars on the Route** *(facebook.com/CarsOnTheRoute)*, a restored gas station.

West of Galena, stop at the red-brick **Old Riverton Store** *(oldrivertonstore.com)* and stock up on sandwiches and Route 66 memorabilia. Continue to the 1923 **Rainbow Bridge** and then to the **Kansas Route 66 Visitor Center** *(baxtersprings museum.org)* in **Baxter Springs**.

MORE WICHITA ATTRACTIONS

Frank Lloyd Wright's Allen House: Completed in 1918, with more than 30 pieces of Wright-designed furniture and original art glass windows. *(flwrightwichita.org; $22)*

Original Pizza Hut Museum: In 1958, two Wichita State University students borrowed $600 to start a pizza restaurant. A few exhibits are inside the tiny building. *(free)*

Kansas Aviation Museum: This museum inside the city's first airport shows off aviation artifacts and aircraft such as the 1920 Laird Swallow, the first built in Wichita. *(kansasaviationmuseum.org; adult/child $10/6)*

Hatman Jack's: Famed hat shop that's outfitted Hollywood celebrities. *(hatmanjacksict.com)*

streets and a significant number of authentic 1800s buildings from Wichita and around Kansas, which were saved from demolition and relocated here. Don't miss the opportunity to sip a sarsaparilla in the saloon. From April to October, costumed cowboys, blacksmiths, newspaper printers and schoolmarms wander the grounds to bring history to life, and gunfights are known to break out.

Another kid favorite is **Exploration Place** *(exploration.org; adult/child from $12/10)*, an architecturally striking children's museum that has no end of cool exhibits, including a tornado chamber where you can feel 75mph winds and a sublime erosion model that shows water creating a new little Kansas. A 6-acre playground is set to open in spring 2026.

On the other side of the river, the **Mid-America All-Indian Museum** *(theindianmuseum.org; adult/child $7/3; closed Sun & Mon)* features Native art from its 3000-piece collection, particularly those of Kiowa-Comanche artist Blackbear Bosin – his 44ft-tall **Keeper of the Plains sculpture** stands outside at the river confluence. The Keeper is an icon of the city, and every night a 'ring of fire' is lit around the base of the statue for 15 minutes, starting at 9pm in spring and summer and 7pm in fall and winter.

For a dose of culture and color, head to **Botanica** *(botanica.org; adult/child $12/10)*, the city's botanical gardens including a children's area with a carousel, and the **Wichita Art Museum** *(wam.org; free; closed Mon & Tue)*, which greets you with the vibrant glasswork of Dale Chihuly.

Hutchinson

Below ground and above the atmosphere

About 50 miles northwest of Wichita, Hutchinson has two incredible sights that are worth a detour.

Possibly the most surprising sight in the state, the amazing **Cosmosphere** *(cosmo.org; adult/child $16.50/13.50)* captures the race to the Moon better than any other museum on the planet. Absorbing displays and artifacts such as the *Apollo 13* command module and entire rockets will enthrall you for hours. You'll come to realize why the museum is regularly called in to build props for Hollywood movies portraying the space race, including *Apollo 13*.

Speaking of Hollywood props, a surprising number are stored nearby at **Strataca** *(underkansas.org; adult/child from $25/18; closed Mon)*, a salt mine 650ft underground,

EATING & DRINKING IN WICHITA: OUR PICKS

Doo-Dah Diner: A model for diners everywhere; regularly named Wichita's favorite restaurant. *7am-2pm Tue-Fri, from 8am Sat & Sun* $

Georges French Bistro: Wichita's first appearance on a James Beard list came in 2025 thanks to this classy spot. *11am-10pm Mon-Sat, 10am-2pm Sun* $$$

Central Standard Brewing: Our favorite brewery in town is this chilled-out spot with mid-mod furniture. *3-10pm or later Mon-Fri, noon-midnight Sat, to 5pm Sun*

Lava & Tonic: Speakeasy-style tiki bar with drinks in appropriately retro ceramicware. *5-11pm Wed & Thu, 4pm-12:30am Fri & Sat, 4-10pm Sun*

including the original camera negatives of *Gone with the Wind,* and Batman and Mr Freeze costumes. Why are they here? Stable temperatures, low humidity and the fact that salt doesn't catch on fire. Visits are by tour, which includes a tram ride through some of the 150 miles of tunnels.

Lucas

Get weird in the grassroots art capital of Kansas

Nothing is too off the wall for tiny Lucas, population 333, a hub of 'outsider' art made by self-taught creators.

If you only have time for a bathroom break, **Bowl Plaza** is the place to stop. These public restrooms have a toilet-shaped entrance and are covered in mosaics and trinkets.

Also on Main St are the **Grassroots Art Center** *(grassrootsart.net; adult/child $9/5),* an intriguing collection of 'outsider' works, and the **World's Largest Collection of the World's Smallest Versions of the World's Largest Things** *(worldslargestthings.com; free),* a museum that perfectly encapsulates the spirit of Lucas.

A few blocks east is the **Garden of Eden** *(gardenofedenlucas.org; adult/child $9/4),* the former home of Civil War veteran SP Dinsmoor, who decorated his yard with kooky concrete sculptures of bankers, politicians and biblical figures. He even prepared his own mausoleum, where you can see his moth-munched remains under a glass-topped coffin.

Dodge City

Relive the cowboy days in the 'queen of the cow towns'

Dodge City – where famous lawmen Bat Masterson and Wyatt Earp tried, sometimes successfully, to keep law and order – had a notorious reputation during the 1870s and 1880s. The **Boot Hill Museum** *(boothill.org; adult/child $20/14)* brings it roaring back to life with gunslingers and cancan dancers along reconstructed Front St, Dodge City's historic main street, with some original buildings, including the 1865 Fort Dodge jail.

Today, Dodge City is still a cow town, but of a different sort. Along with nearby Garden City and Liberal, Dodge City is home to multiple cattle slaughterhouses, which 'process' up to 5800 cows a day each. The stench might make you want to get the hell out of Dodge, but if you want a view over the enormous cattle pens, visit the **Feed Yard Overlook** off Wyatt Earp Blvd.

SIGHTS ON THE SANTA FE TRAIL IN WESTERN KANSAS

Unlike the later California and Oregon Trails, the Santa Fe Trail (1821–80) was primarily for commerce, not emigration. On this route, traveling traders moved goods between Missouri and Mexico.

Santa Fe Trail Tracks: See evidence of the thousands of 50in wooden prairie-schooner wagon wheels that carved their way through the Plains about 10 miles west of Dodge City, off US 50.

Fort Larned National Historic Site: A remarkably well-preserved 1860s fort in an evocative setting. It's well worth the trip, about 60 miles northeast of Dodge City, to learn about the turbulent history of the Indian Wars era. *(nps.gov/fols; free)*

EATING & DRINKING IN DODGE CITY: OUR PICKS

Central Station Bar & Grill: Dine on steak or Mexican food in an extension of the train station or an old railroad car. *11am-10pm Mon-Fri, from 4pm Sat* $$

Gollo Grande: About 65% of Dodge City's residents are of Hispanic descent, and this is one of the top Mexican joints. *10:30am-9pm or later Wed-Mon* $

Boot Hill Distillery: Three farmers run and supply the grains at this soil-to-sip distillery. Ask about the prickly ash bitters. *3-11pm Wed-Sat*

Dodge City Brewing: Southwest Kansas' first craft brewery serves its own excellent beers plus brick-oven pizza. *4-10pm Wed-Fri, from 11am Sat, 11am-8pm Sun*

Oklahoma

NATIVE STORIES | COWBOY LORE | COOL CITIES

Places

Oklahoma gets its name from Choctaw words meaning 'brave people.' With 39 tribes located in the state – many forcibly relocated to the unwanted 'Indian Territory' in the 19th century – it remains a place of deep Native heritage that has withstood the onslaught of centuries of assimilation and erasure that the word brave hardly begins to cover.

On the other side of the Old West coin, cowboys also figure prominently in the Sooner State, and there's still a great sense of the open range, interrupted only by urban Oklahoma City and Tulsa. Both cities, but Tulsa in particular, feel as if they are on the up, with so many new attractions, restaurants, breweries and bars that you're destined to find yourself adding extra days to your itinerary.

Oklahoma's share of Route 66, the second-longest of any state, links some of the Mother Road's iconic highlights and atmospheric old towns.

TOP TIP

If you're in Oklahoma to visit its hard-hitting, top-notch museums, leave your visit for later in the week. Many are closed on Mondays or Tuesdays – or both.

Tulsa

Remembering Black Wall Street

On May 30, 1921, a Black male teenager and a white female teenager were alone in an elevator in downtown Tulsa when she screamed. The how and why have never been answered, but the incident sparked three days of race riots that engulfed the neighborhood of Greenwood, nicknamed 'Black Wall Street'

GETTING AROUND

Highways crisscross the state, including Route 66 (mostly overtaken by I-40 west of OKC). Several of the US highways and interstates are toll roads that can't be paid for with cash. It's worth ordering a Pikepass *(pikepass.com)* in advance for discounts of up to 50%. Passes used for toll roads in Kansas (K-TAG; *ksturnpike.com)* and Texas (EZ TAG, TollTag, TxTag) are also valid on Oklahoma highways.

Parking is paid in downtown Tulsa and OKC. Download ParkMobile *(parkmobile.io; $1/hour)* in Tulsa and Flowbird *(flowbirdapp.com; $2/hour)* for OKC.

OKLAHOMA

COLORADO
KANSAS
MISSOURI
NEW MEXICO
TEXAS
ARKANSAS
OKLAHOMA
Cimarron River
Hooker
Guymon
N Canadian River
Laverne
Waynoka
Great Salt Plains Reservoir
Ponca City
Pawhuska
Bartlesville
Lake of the Cherokees
Oologah Lake
Clayton
Texhoma
Fort Supply Reservoir
Perryton
Enid
Keystone Lake
Claremore
Lake Hudson
Beaver Lake
Tulsa
Stillwater
Canton Lake
Arkansas River
Dalhart
Cushing
Fort Gibson Reservoir
Tahlequah
Dumas
S Canadian River
Muskogee
Tenkiller Ferry Reservoir
Black Kettle National Grassland
Oklahoma City
Lake Meredith
Canadian River
Pampa
Weatherford
Elk City
N Canadian River
Arkansas River
Canadian River
Panhandle
North Fork Red River
Sayre
Moore
Shawnee
Eufaula Lake
Amarillo
Shamrock
Chickasha
Ouachita Mountains
Wichita Mountains
Mcalester
Buffalo Lake
Hereford
Talihina
Pauls Valley
Fort Still
Lawton
Altus
Marlow
Duncan
Kiamichi Mountain
Frederick
Walters
Comanche
Muleshoe
Plainview
Ardmore
Vernon
Waurika
Lake Texoma
Hugo
Broken Bow
Ryan
Red River
Wichita Falls
Red River
Lake Kemp
Lake Arrowhead
Nocona
Lubbock
Brazos River
Seymour
Archer City
Bowie
0 100 km
0 50 miles

TULSA'S MUSICAL HERITAGE

Woody Guthrie Center: This impressive museum explains the life and music of this 1930s folk artist. *(woodyguthriecenter.org; adult/child $12/free)*

Bob Dylan Center: Walk through the long career of one of the greatest songwriters of all time at this museum, opened in 2022. *(bobdylancenter.com; adult/child $15/free)*

Cain's Ballroom: Legendary live music venue where Sid Vicious of the Sex Pistols punched a hole in the wall. *(cainsballroom.com)*

Guthrie Green: Urban park with a full schedule of concerts and events. *(guthriegreen.com)*

Jazz Depot: Tulsa's Union Station is under renovation but will feature a Jazz Hall of Fame and live gigs when it reopens. *(jazzdepotlive.com)*

because of its wealth. The aftermath of one of the worst episodes of racially motivated violence in the country? Up to 300 dead, more than $2 million in property damage, 1256 houses burned down, 191 businesses destroyed and 10,000 Black Tulsans left homeless.

The harrowing but extraordinary **Greenwood Rising** *(greenwoodrising.org; adult/child $15/8; closed Mon)* unflinchingly lays this history bare in five galleries of multimedia presentations that put the story of this neighborhood in the wider context of centuries of Black oppression in the United States. A few blocks northwest, **John Hope Franklin Reconciliation Park** has outdoor plaques and statues, and is a good place for reflection.

Tracking down Tulsa's art deco architecture

In the early 20th century, the land around Tulsa was the largest oil-producing area on the planet, and this wealth fueled a boom in art deco architecture downtown. Start a visit of architectural admiration not downtown, but on Route 66 at **Decopolis** *(decopolis.net),* part art deco museum and part bonkers souvenir shop that's set to expand to a new location in 2026. Peek at the exhibits and then ask at the counter for the free walking-tour map, which starts you off about a mile away at the stunning 1931 **Philcade Building**. Grab a coffee at art-deco-inspired **Topeca** *(topecacoffee.com)* for a taste of the interior, which is otherwise off limits. Across 5th St is another architectural highlight, the 1928 **Philtower Building**, which combines art deco and Gothic Revival. Wander into the lobby to check out the intricate fan-vaulted ceiling, marble floors and brass elevator doors.

At the southern end of downtown, the 1929 **Boston Avenue United Methodist Church** *(bostonavenue.org)* is a showpiece of religious art deco architecture designed by female artist Adah Robinson. Ask inside at the information desk for an architecture brochure or stop by on Sundays at 12:15pm for a guided tour.

For deeper insights and access to lobbies closed to the public, including the Philcade's, sign up for a walking tour with **Tulsa Tours** *(tulsa.tours; $45)*. The **Tulsa Foundation for Architecture** *(tulsaarchitecture.org; $20)* runs architecture-focused tours in downtown and beyond on the second Saturday of each month.

Must-sees along Route 66

Officially designated the 'capital of Route 66' in 2024, Tulsa boasts 28 miles of the Mother Road right through town, where

EATING IN TULSA: OUR PICKS

Tavern: Elevated comfort food like sriracha devilled eggs and bacon popcorn served in a beautiful pub. *11am-1pm Sun-Thu, to 1am Fri & Sat* $$

Daigoro: Romantic riverside spot opened in 2025. The pan-Asian menu also peppers in local flavors, like brisket fried rice. *5-10pm Tue-Fri, from 11am Sat* $$

Vault: Brunch, pasta and more in a mid-mod space that was once the world's largest 'autobank' with six drive-thru lanes. *11am-10pm Mon-Sat, 10am-3pm Sun* $$

Andolini's Pizzeria: Top-notch pizza in the historic Cherry St District delivered in an old dining room with a pressed-tin ceiling. *11am-10pm Sun-Thu, to 11pm Fri & Sat* $$

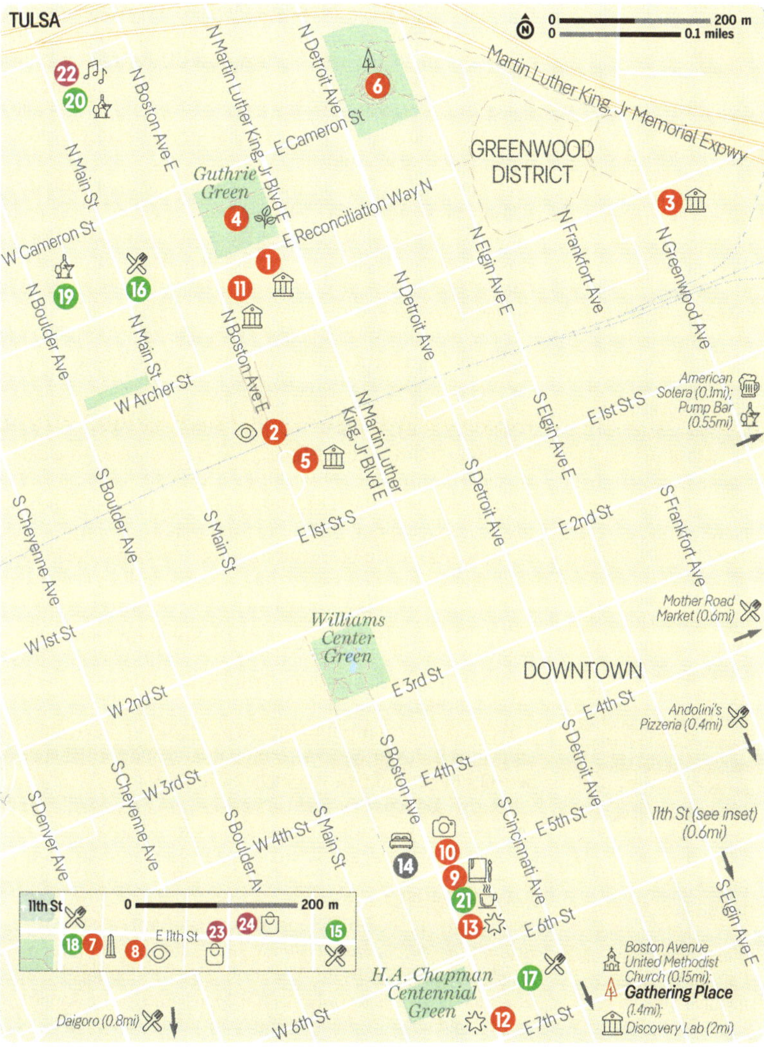

SIGHTS
1 Bob Dylan Center
2 Center of the Universe
3 Greenwood Rising
4 Guthrie Green
5 Jazz Depot
6 John Hope Franklin Reconciliation Park
7 Meadow Gold Mack
8 Meadow Gold Sign
9 Philcade Building
10 Philtower Building
11 Woody Guthrie Center

ACTIVITIES
12 Tulsa Foundation for Architecture
13 Tulsa Tours

SLEEPING
14 Mayo Hotel

EATING
15 Ike's Chili
16 Tavern
17 Vault
18 Wildflower Cafe

DRINKING & NIGHTLIFE
19 Saturn Room
20 Soundpony Lounge
21 Topeca

ENTERTAINMENT
22 Cain's Ballroom

SHOPPING
23 Buck Atom's Cosmic Curios on 66
24 Decopolis

TOP ROUTE 66 STOPS IN OKLAHOMA

Oklahoma has more miles of the original alignment than any other state.

Blue Whale: One of the most photographed Route 66 landmarks is the 80ft-long Blue Whale, the centerpiece of a long-gone water park in Catoosa.

Pops 66: A 66ft LED soda bottle near Arcadia lures you into buying some of the hundreds of varieties of pop from around the world. *(pops66.com)*

Oklahoma Route 66 Museum: If you take time for just one museum, make it this engagingly designed exhibition in Clinton. *(okhistory.org/sites/route66; adult/child $7/4)*

Pony Bridge: The 38-truss, 0.75-mile-long Pony Bridge crosses the Canadian River in rhythmic style.

it's called 11th St. The **Meadow Gold District** *(meadowgolddistrict.com)* is one of the most interesting stretches, so called because of the 1930s neon-lit **Meadow Gold sign**. Originally a promo for a dairy company, this Route 66 landmark was saved from demolition by preservationists and moved a few blocks from its original location. It now sits atop an open brick structure built specifically for it.

Look nearby for the three 20ft-tall 'muffler men' sculptures – **Meadow Gold Mack** *(meadowgoldmack.com)*, the friendly lumberjack; and space cowboy Buck Atom and gunslinging cosmic cowgirl Stella Atom outside **Buck Atom's Cosmic Curios on 66** *(buckatomson66.com)*, a teeny former gas station turned souvenir shop.

For more neon nostalgia, the glowing beacon of the **Route 66 Neon Sign Park** *(free)* is on the way out of town if you're driving west to Oklahoma City.

Take the family to the country's favorite city park

The 66-acre **Gathering Place** *(gatheringplace.org)* is a model for parks worldwide – since it opened in 2018, it's ranked at the top of lists of the best green spaces in the USA. Multiple themed playscapes designed for different age groups include a 5-acre adventure playground and Slide Vale (which has a slide that goes underground), plus a skate park and courts for pickleball, basketball, volleyball and street soccer.

Parents, don't hold back – you can join in the fun, too. The boathouse, with views of downtown and the Arkansas River, rents out free pedal boats and canoes, and tons of events take place on the huge lawn and stage.

Accessibility is built into the park so that kids of all abilities can enjoy it. It's fully ADA-compliant and offers quiet spaces, sensory bags, and free wheelchairs to rent.

Nearby, **Discovery Lab** *(discoverylab.org; $14)*, a huge science-centric children's museum, is an ideal indoor alternative when the weather isn't cooperating for a park visit.

Arty attractions

South of town, the **Philbrook Museum of Art** *(philbrook.org; adult/child $18/8; closed Mon & Tue)* is housed in an oil magnate's converted 1920s Italianate villa that's just as much a work of art as the pieces it contains. It displays fine Native American works, and classic and contemporary international art.

Northwest of downtown, the superb **Gilcrease Museum** *(gilcrease.org)* is another gem in Tulsa's cultural crown, but it's undergoing a huge renovation and reconstruction project and is

EATING IN TULSA: OUR PICKS ON ROUTE 66

Tally's Good Food Cafe: Let the neon signs lure you into this bustling chrome-and-vinyl diner dishing up Americana on a plate. *6am-11pm* $

Ike's Chili: Serving chili for more than 110 years. Get it straight, in a Frito pie (a Midwest fave), or atop a hot dog, fries or spaghetti. *10am-2:30pm Mon-Sat* $

Mother Road Market: This sprawling food hall attracts joyous groups who feast on the plethora of creative offerings. *11am-9pm Tue-Sun* $

Wildflower Cafe: A brunch staple with made-from-scratch waffles, biscuits and gravy, and a line out the door on weekends. *7am-3pm* $

BD IMAGES/SHUTTERSTOCK

Meadow Gold sign

set to open in fall 2026. It's named for Thomas Gilcrease of the Muscogee (Creek) Nation, who discovered oil on his allotment.

Pawhuska

Hear Osage stories

The Hollywood spotlight shone on the Osage Nation (Ni Okašką, 'People of the Middle Waters') in a big way with the 2023 release of *Killers of the Flower Moon*, detailing the true story of a series of murders after oil was discovered on their reservation. The town of Pawhuska was the center of the movie's production. Its historic main street, Kihekah Ave, was covered in dirt, and the old brick storefronts were restored to their original looks, traces of which remain. Stop for a 'cowboy coffee' (dark roast with sarsaparilla syrup) or a bite to eat at **Pioneer Woman Mercantile** *(themercantile.com)*, started by Food Network star Ree Drummond.

At the **Osage Nation Visitors Center** *(osageculture.com; closed Sat & Sun)*, staff can help you plan your visit, and you can browse a few history and art exhibits. The small **Osage Nation Museum** *(free; closed Sun & Mon)* is in an old stone chapel and is the country's oldest tribal museum.

Get a sense of the land's majestic sweep and what many Osage must have seen at the **Joseph H Williams Tallgrass Prairie**

BEST OKLAHOMA FESTIVALS

Red Earth Festival: A three-day celebration of Native culture in OKC, with an art market, tribal dance performances and a powwow in March. *(redearth.org)*

Paseo Arts Festival: This late-May event shows off the galleries and restaurants of its namesake neighborhood in OKC. *(thepaseo.org)*

Fried Onion Burger Day Festival: Watch the world's largest fried onion burger – 850lb – get cooked, and feast on this Depression-era classic in El Reno in May. *(facebook.com/elrenoburgerday)*

Tulsa Juneteenth Festival: Experience this federal holiday that marks the end of slavery in Greenwood (p166), Tulsa's Black Wall Street, with food trucks, vendors and games. *(tulsajuneteenth.org)*

DRINKING IN TULSA: OUR PICKS

American Solera: Sip award-winning craft beer in this brewery's laid-back industrial-mod space. *4-9pm Mon-Thu, noon-10pm Fri & Sat, to 6pm Sun*

Soundpony Lounge: A sticker-covered dive bar par excellence with welcoming bartenders, live music and karaoke nights. *3pm-2am*

Saturn Room: Find the 'tropics of Tulsa' at this adorable tiki bar with a light-strung patio. It pours knock-out drinks with just the right amount of rum and fire. *4pm-2am*

Pump Bar: A 1960s gas station morphed into a kitschy vintage bar with great drinks and snacks like 'trashy tots.' *11am-10pm Tue-Thu & Sun, to midnight Fri & Sat*

TRAIL OF TEARS

In the 1830s, white farmers in the southeastern US wanted to expand onto land occupied by more than 125,000 Native people. President Andrew Jackson used the army to remove tribes from their homelands and forced them to walk upwards of 1000 miles to Indian Territory, present-day Oklahoma.

Tens of thousands of people from the Cherokee, Chickasaw, Choctaw, Muscogee (Creek) and Seminole nations – the 'five civilized tribes' – made the journeys. A third are thought to have died along the way. Don't miss the **Five Civilized Tribes Museum** *(fivetribes.org; adult/child $6/3)* in Muskogee or the many museums in **Tahlequah**, the capital of the Cherokee Nation since 1839.

Preserve *(nature.org; free)*, the world's largest remaining protected area of its kind that's home to 2500 free-range bison. Enthusiastic staff can talk you through the nature exhibits in the small visitor center, and you can get out into nature on three looped hiking trails, ranging from a half-mile to 2 miles.

Oklahoma City

Myths and truths about the American West

Oklahoma has the highest proportion of Native people of any state (14.2% of residents), and the **First Americans Museum** *(famok.org; adult/child $15/5; closed Tue)* tells the stories of the 39 tribes that call this place home – many because of forced government migration along the Trail of Tears. With a collection largely sourced from the storage rooms of the Smithsonian's National Museum of the American Indian in Washington, DC, this museum, opened in 2021, is perhaps the best Native cultural institution in the country. The 2nd floor shows off the Smithsonian's goods, on long-term loan and returned to Oklahoma for the first time in a century, while the ground floor details the long history of Native life on this land, moving through deceitful US government 'deals' and laws, and into the present, explaining it all from a Native perspective in evocative multimedia displays. Outside, the free-to-visit 90ft-high mound is reminiscent of Cahokia in Illinois, and one of the three daily docent-led tours heads there. Save time for a meal made with traditional ingredients, such as bison, chokecherries and hominy, at **Thirty-Nine Restaurant**, the museum's on-site eatery, helmed by Loretta Barrett Oden, a member of the Citizen Potawatomi Nation.

Native history is often overshadowed by white cowboys and romantic – and unrealistic – Westerns, but the **National Cowboy and Western Heritage Museum** *(nationalcowboymuseum.org; adult/child $20/12)* does a more multifaceted deep dive into this background. It has some displays of Native artifacts, along with an excellent collection of historic and contemporary paintings and sculptures depicting life in the West, including works by underrepresented Native and female artists. Kids love walking through the mock cow town and running amok in the huge outdoor playground with recreated Native cliff dwellings, tipis and sod houses.

Get a combination ticket to visit both museums for $30, saving $5.

Remembering the 1995 OKC bombing

The story of the United States' worst incident of domestic terrorism is laid out in sobering hour-by-hour detail at the poignant **Oklahoma City National Memorial and Museum** *(memorialmuseum.com; adult/child $18/15)*. Outside is a free-to-visit area with 168 empty chair sculptures, one for each of the people killed in the attack; the 19 small ones are for the children who perished in the daycare center.

Park at the Memorial Parking Garage at the northeast corner of 6th and Harvey for free parking with a museum ticket purchase.

SIGHTS

1 Centennial Land Run Monument
2 First Americans Museum
3 Myriad Botanical Gardens
4 Oklahoma City National Memorial & Museum
5 Oklahoma History Center
6 Oklahoma State Capitol
7 Stockyards City

ACTIVITIES

8 Bricktown Water Taxi

SLEEPING

9 Classen Inn
10 Colcord Hotel
11 The National

EATING

12 Cattlemen's Steakhouse
13 Cheever's Cafe
14 Ma Der Lao Kitchen
15 Nonesuch
16 Sunnyside Diner

DRINKING & NIGHTLIFE

17 Good for a Few
18 Later Bye
19 Prairie Artisan Ales
20 Skydance Brewing Co

SHOPPING

21 Langston's
22 National Saddlery

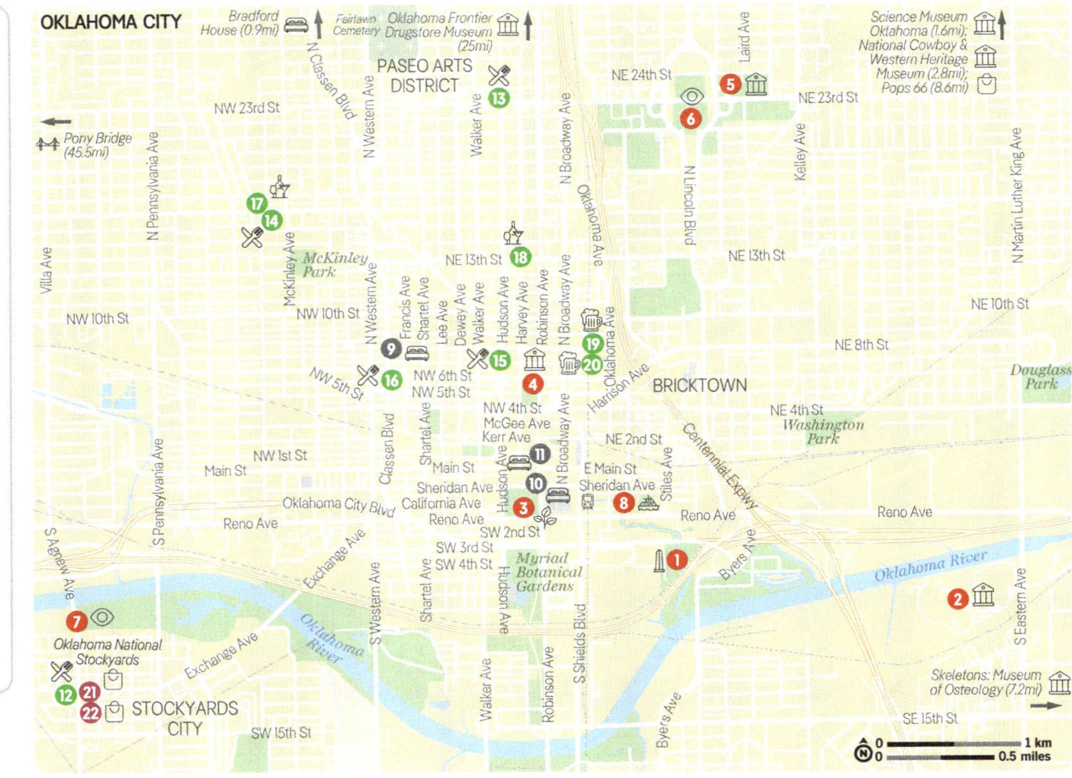

ODDBALL OKLAHOMA

Center of the Universe: It's said that noise made inside this 8ft circle of bricks in downtown Tulsa is loudly echoed, but people standing outside the circle can't hear it.

Oklahoma City Underground: Art and history exhibits line a mile of color-coded corridors below downtown OKC. *(downtownokc.com/underground)*

Skeletons: Museum of Osteology: Flesh-eating beetles help prepare the bones of dead animals for a new life on display. *(skeletonmuseum.com; adult/child $14/12)*

Oklahoma Frontier Drugstore Museum: A kooky museum in Guthrie that shows the remedies (like jars of leeches) offered at an Old West pharmacy. *(drugmuseum.org; adult/child $5/4)*

Tip your hat to Stockyards City

A sign spanning Agnew Ave welcomes you to **Stockyards City** *(stockyardscity.org)*, still home to the Oklahoma National Stockyards, the world's largest feeder and stocker cattle market. Cows are auctioned off every Monday and Tuesday, an event open to the public.

Most people come here to shop, though perhaps not for live cows – Western-wear shops abound. Favorites include **Langston's** *(langstons.com)* and **National Saddlery** *(nationalsaddlery.com)*. Across the street, **Cattlemen's Steakhouse** *(cattlemensrestaurant.com)* is the oldest continually operating restaurant in OKC, feeding cowpokes and city slickers big breakfasts and steaks since 1910.

Cruise Bricktown's canal

Modeled after San Antonio's **River Walk**, OKC's **Bricktown** *(bricktownokc.com)* is an industrial-turned-entertainment district. Much of it is geared toward families and can feel touristy, but it's worth a wander. **Bricktown Water Taxi** *(bricktownwatertaxi.com; adult/child $15/12)* runs hour-long boat trips on the canal past historic buildings and public art, culminating at the **Centennial Land Run Monument**. Covering the size of a football field, 45 larger-than-life bronze horsemen and wagon drivers capture the chaos and drama of the 1889 land rush that settled a large part of the future state – and dispossessed Native people from their lands.

Fort Sill

Find remnants of the Indian Wars in western Oklahoma

Constructed in 1869, **Fort Sill** *(sill-www.army.mil; free; closed Sun)* was a frontier post that remains an important military base today. The history is still on display for visitors, particularly around the Old Post Quadrangle, which is surrounded by original stone buildings. Start your visit at the **Interpretive Center** on its southern side, which has old-school museum displays and staff who can help you find other points of interest. Many travelers come to see the eagle-topped **grave of Geronimo** (Goyahkla), an Apache warrior and shaman who fought the Mexicans and Americans trying to confine his nomadic tribe to reservations. He died at Fort Sill as a prisoner of war in 1909. The **US Army Artillery Museum** is another draw for those interested in historic and modern weaponry.

EATING IN OKC: OUR PICKS

Nonesuch: Slide into one of just 22 seats for a foodie adventure in Oklahoma flavors via a multicourse tasting menu. *5:30-9pm Tue-Sat* **$$$**

Ma Der Lao Kitchen: A Laotian restaurant in OKC? Yes, and a damn good one, too. The crispy rice salad is a must-order. *11am-10pm Tue-Thu, to 11pm Fri & Sat* **$$**

Cheever's Cafe: Upscale cafe in an art deco former flower shop with excellent Southwestern-style fare. *11am-9pm Mon-Thu, to 10pm Fri-Sun* **$$**

Sunnyside Diner: This cheerful cheapie doles out the best breakfasts in town, from fresh blueberry pancakes to Okie poutine. *6am-2pm* **$**

ZACK FRANK/SHUTTERSTOCK

Bison, Wichita Mountains Wildlife Refuge

Fort Sill is still an active Army base, so visitors without a Department of Defense license require a background check before entering. Speed up the process by giving your details on the Visitor Pre-Registration System online in advance. Non-US citizens aren't allowed on base unless they know someone stationed there.

Wichita Mountains

Hiking and wildlife-watching off the grid

West of Oklahoma City, the state opens into expansive prairies, nowhere as beautifully as in the Wichita Mountains. The 59,020-acre **Wichita Mountains Wildlife Refuge** *(fws.gov/refuge/wichita-mountains; free)* protects bison, elk, longhorn cattle and prairie dogs.

Displays at the **visitor center** highlight the refuge's flora and fauna, and it has large picture windows for views of prairie grasslands. For elevated views, drive to the top of **Mt Scott**, the highest peak in the refuge at 2464ft. For a short but scenic hike, try the **Kite Trail**, which climbs above the West Cache Creek and has access points to small waterfalls. Your best bet for food and accommodations is in **Medicine Park**.

MORE OKC ATTRACTIONS

Myriad Botanical Gardens: Elaborate landscapes with thousands of plants right in the city center. The IM Pei-designed conservatory holds a tropical wonderland. *(myriadgardens.org; grounds free, conservatory adult/child $10.50/5.50)*

Oklahoma State Capitol: Built in 1917, the Capitol building has stained-glass windows, rotating art exhibits and even on-site oil wells. Free walk-up tours at 11am and 1pm weekdays.

Science Museum Oklahoma: Family-friendly galleries filled with planes, dinos and a planetarium *(sciencemuseumok.org; adult/child $23/18)*.

Oklahoma History Center: Focuses on the people of the Sooner State through interactive exhibits; good Native galleries *(adult/child $12.50/9)*.

DRINKING IN OKC: OUR PICKS

Prairie Artisan Ales: Craft-beer spot run by a fourth-generation brewer in the Automobile Alley district. Bomb, a stout, is its flagship pint. *11am-10pm*

Skydance Brewing Co: Only 0.4% of craft breweries are Native-owned, and Skydance showcases Indigenous stories. *noon-10pm Sun-Thu, to midnight Fri & Sat*

Good for a Few: Magic mixologists pour incredible creations in this moody cocktail bar, semi-hidden in a burger restaurant. *4pm-midnight Wed-Sat*

Later Bye: This cozy 31-seat neighborhood cocktail bar can do no wrong. Pair drinks with Italian or Spanish small plates. *3pm-midnight Mon-Thu, to 1am Fri & Sat*

Nebraska

PIONEER TRAILS | FRONTIER FORTS | BIRD-WATCHING

Places

Travelers have traversed Nebraska for millennia: Native tribes; transcontinental settlers coming by covered wagon, railroad and automobile on the USA's first country-belting routes; thousands-strong flocks of sandhill cranes on their seasonal migration; and dinosaurs and other extinct prehistoric wildlife. You can still follow their trails, but do more than just make tire tracks through the Cornhusker State.

Alongside the state's sprinkling of cute towns, Nebraska's two main cities are culture-driven and artful. Omaha, the state's biggest urban center, is home to the brick-street Old Market district of revamped warehouses, a booming riverfront, and several museums and family-friendly attractions. Just an hour's drive away, the state capital of Lincoln is anything but stuffy, thanks to the students at the University of Nebraska who know how to have a good time.

Nature calls in the remote Nebraska Panhandle, where stark rock formations stand sentinel over the prairie, and in the lush Niobrara Valley, a federally protected scenic river.

TOP TIP

Nebraska ranks second in the country (after Texas) as the state raising the most cattle, so if you're an omnivore, sampling the steak is a must. Committee Chophouse (p178) in Omaha is a top pick. Its summer-only 'steak flights' offer four perfectly prepared slabs sourced from Nebraska ranches.

GETTING AROUND

You need a car to get around Nebraska. I-80 is the state's main access point by car, and Nebraska's biggest cities are dotted along it.

The interstate allows you to zip across Nebraska for 455 miles at 75mph, but the real way to enjoy the countryside is to take the smaller roads. Some I-80 alternatives include US 6 between Omaha and Lincoln, US 30 between Omaha and Grand Island, and US 34 between Grand Island and Lincoln. US 30, the Lincoln Hwy, is particularly historic. Opened in 1913, it was the first transcontinental highway specifically for cars.

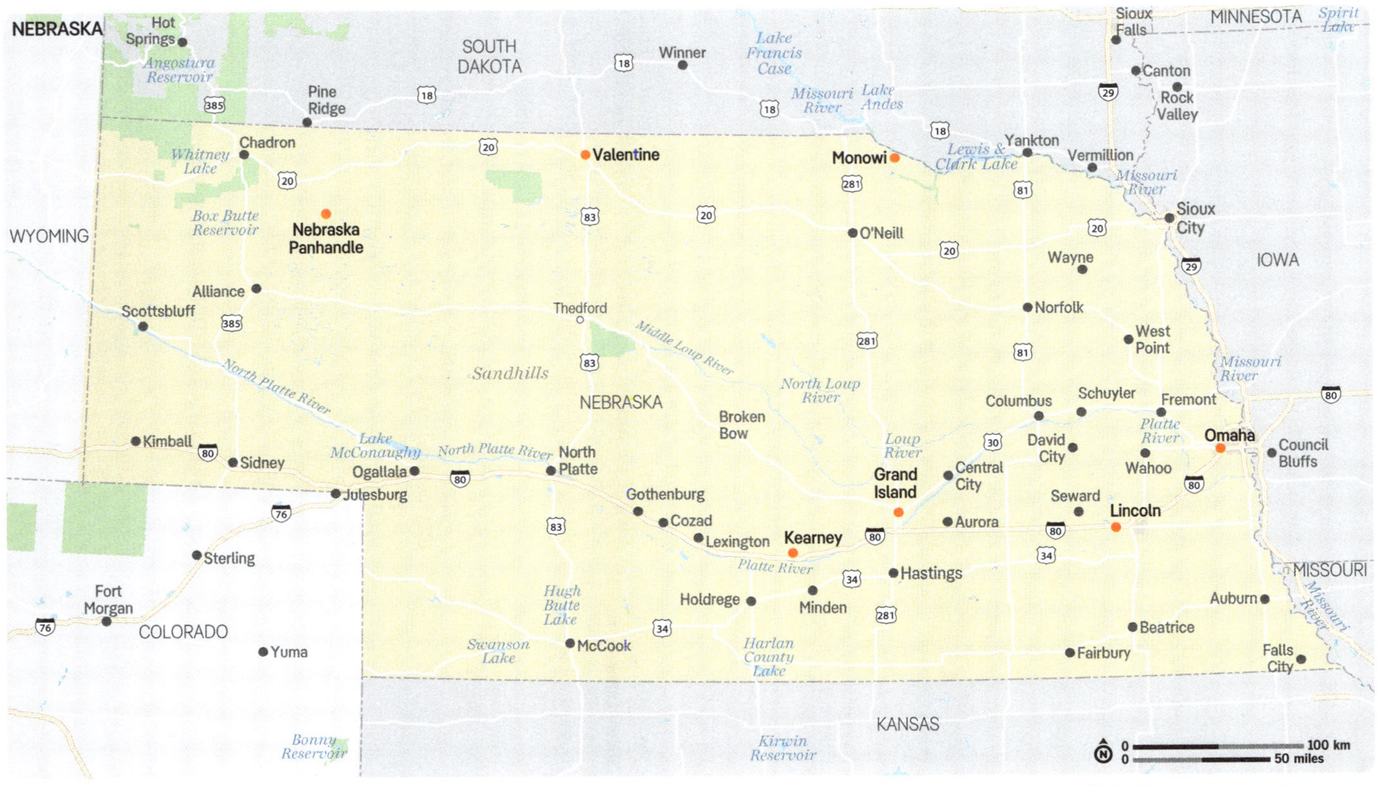
NEBRASKA
SOUTH DAKOTA
MINNESOTA
IOWA
MISSOURI
KANSAS
COLORADO
WYOMING
NEBRASKA
Hot Springs
Angostura Reservoir
Pine Ridge
Winner
Lake Francis Case
Missouri River
Lake Andes
Sioux Falls
Spirit Lake
Canton
Rock Valley
Chadron
Whitney Lake
Valentine
Monowi
Lewis & Clark Lake
Yankton
Vermillion
Sioux City
Box Butte Reservoir
Nebraska Panhandle
O'Neill
Wayne
Alliance
Scottsbluff
Thedford
Middle Loup River
Norfolk
West Point
Sandhills
North Loup River
North Platte River
Columbus
Schuyler
Fremont
Platte River
Omaha
Council Bluffs
Broken Bow
Loup River
David City
Wahoo
Kimball
Sidney
Lake McConaughy
Ogallala
North Platte
Grand Island
Central City
Julesburg
Gothenburg
Cozad
Lexington
Kearney
Aurora
Seward
Lincoln
Sterling
Hastings
Holdrege
Minden
Hugh Butte Lake
Fort Morgan
Auburn
Beatrice
Fairbury
Falls City
Yuma
Swanson Lake
McCook
Harlan County Lake
Bonny Reservoir
Kirwin Reservoir
385
18
29
20
83
281
81
30
80
34
76
0
100 km
0
50 miles

OMAHA WITH KIDS

Omaha's Henry Doorly Zoo & Aquarium: Consistently ranked as the best in the country, Omaha's zoo features the world's largest indoor desert, the country's largest indoor rainforest and much more that you could spend a full day exploring. *(omahazoo.com; adult/child $32/25)*

Omaha Children's Museum: Let the little ones loose to take over a recreated city, splash in the fountains, create art or run science experiments. Set to move to a new space on the RiverFront in 2027. *(ocm.org; $17)*

Kiewit Luminarium: This hands-on science museum makes learning a blast for kids and kids at heart. *(kiewitluminarium.org; adult/child $25/20)*

Omaha

Eat, drink, shop and stroll the Old Market

The heart of the action in Omaha is the **Old Market** *(oldmarket.com)*, a revitalized 19th-century warehouse district that covers a square of city blocks bounded by 10th, 13th, Farnam and Jackson Sts. Restaurants, bars and quirky shops – mostly local and full of personality – have taken over brick-walled, ghost-sign-covered industrial buildings, but if you're here for a taste of the history, sign up for a 1½-hour walking tour with **River City History Tours** *(durhammuseum.org/river-city-history-tours; $26, includes entry to the Durham Museum; 10am Sat May-Oct)*. Otherwise, you can track down cool spots like the plant-filled **Passageway** yourself. Lovers of antiques and vintage fashion will find no shortage of distractions, while **Made in Omaha** *(madeinomaha.com)* is a great spot to pick up locally crafted souvenirs.

Kid-tastic parks along the Missouri River

Flowing along the Missouri River, the country's longest waterway, Omaha's **RiverFront** *(theriverfrontomaha.com)* is an elongated family-friendly park that's an excellent place to walk, ride a bike or let the kids run loose. Spanning the river is the 3000ft-long, architecturally impressive **Bob Kerrey Pedestrian Bridge** *(visitomaha.com/bob)*, better known as 'Bob the Bridge,' a landmark so beloved that it has its own social media presence. The river is the border between Nebraska and Iowa, and a marker on the bridge lets you know when you're straddling the state line.

Nearby, the **Lewis and Clark National Historic Trail Visitor Center** *(nps.gov/lecl; free)* is more of an info point and gift shop than museum, but it's a good place to stop for advice from the park rangers if you're planning to take on the 4900-mile route of the 19th-century Louisiana Purchase explorers. To the south is **Lewis and Clark Landing**, which has an excellent playground, sand volleyball courts, an 'urban beach' (a sand pit that doesn't touch the water) and sculptures on the riverfront. Further south still, the **Heartland of America Park** has walking trails that encircle a lake with a large fountain. Heading west into downtown, **Gene Leahy Mall**, partially set below street level, has intriguing modern sculptures and water features, and a cooler, more urban feel than the other RiverFront areas.

The best way to explore is on foot or by downloading the Heartland B-cycle app *(heartland.bcycle.com; 24-hour pass*

EATING & DRINKING IN THE OLD MARKET: OUR PICKS

Boiler Room: Industrial chic meat-focused New American restaurant helmed by a multi-time James Beard nominee. *5:30-10pm Tue-Sat* $$$

La Buvette: Daily changing menu of French-influenced specials that pair perfectly with wine and people-watching on the patio. *10am-10pm Mon-Sat* $$

Mr Toad's Pub: Pull up a literal pew in this lively dive bar decked out in stained-glass windows and old books. *2pm-2am Sun-Fri, from noon Sat*

Berry & Rye: Well-stocked craft cocktail bar pouring inventive drinks to patrons sinking into velvety magenta seats. *5pm-2am Sun-Thu, from 3pm Fri & Sat*

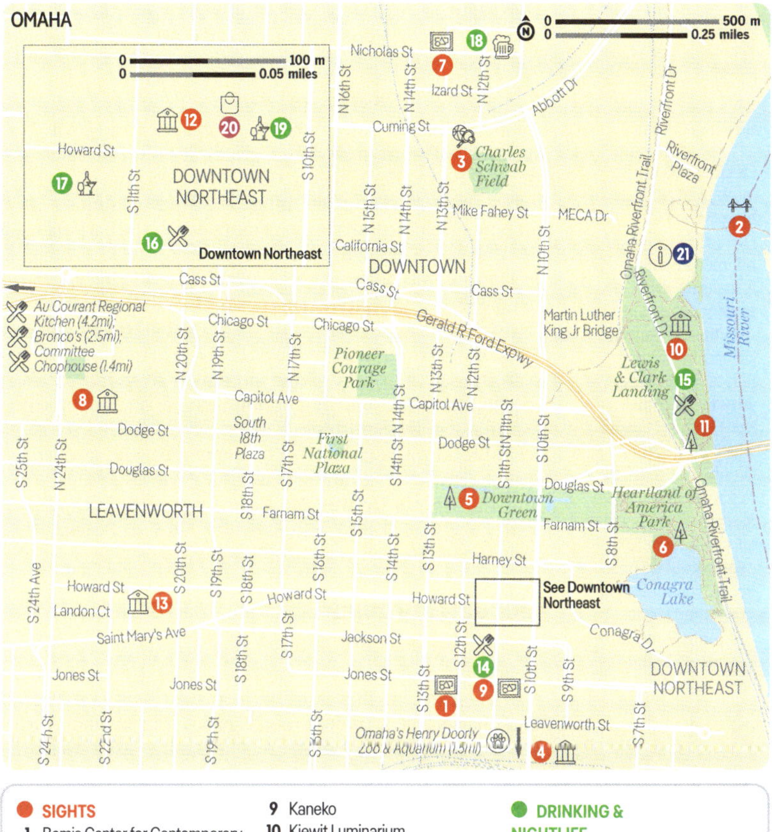

SIGHTS
1 Bemis Center for Contemporary Arts
2 Bob Kerrey Pedestrian Bridge
3 Charles Schwab Field
4 Durham Museum
5 Gene Leahy Mall
6 Heartland of America Park
7 Hot Shops Art Center
8 Joslyn Art Museum
9 Kaneko
10 Kiewit Luminarium
11 Lewis & Clark Landing
12 Old Market Passageway
13 Omaha Children's Museum

EATING
14 Boiler Room
15 Fig
16 La Buvette

DRINKING & NIGHTLIFE
17 Berry & Rye
18 Kros Strain Draft Works
19 Mr Toad's Pub

SHOPPING
20 Made in Omaha

INFORMATION
21 Lewis & Clark National Historic Trail Visitor Center

$16.05) and checking out one of the docked e-bikes. Bicycles are allowed in most RiverFront areas, while e-scooters are not. Fuel up first at **Fig** *(figomaha.com)*, a sun-filled cafe overlooking the river.

All aboard for history at the Durham Museum

Though trains no longer stop here, Omaha's soaring art deco Union Station, now the **Durham Museum** *(durhammuseum.org; adult/child $15/8)*, is a sight to behold with its cathedral windows, geometric chandeliers, ornate ceilings and reliefs of railroad workers carved into the facade. Admire it from the old-school soda fountain while drinking a phosphate pop.

OMAHA STREETCAR

Omaha is on the move, and Nebraska's biggest city is currently constructing a 3-mile streetcar line *(omahastreetcar.org)* to connect downtown with the Blackstone District in Midtown. Similar to the modern streetcar line in Kansas City, Missouri, which opened in 2016, Omaha's will be free to ride. It's scheduled to open in 2028, with services every 10 minutes during peak hours. The route has 13 planned stops and loops through downtown before running east–west along Farnam and Harney Sts.

The project is not without its detractors, including Warren Buffett, Omaha's most famous resident and the fifth-richest man in the world, who said that the $306 million plan is too expensive and that residents deserved to vote on it.

Downstairs is an extensive local history and transportation museum that has floor-to-ceiling windows to watch freight trains roll by.

Get creative in Omaha's galleries

Reopened in 2024 after a $100 million expansion, the **Joslyn Art Museum** *(joslyn.org; free)* is firmly on the list of the region's best galleries. More than 100 new acquisitions were added to the 12,000-piece collection, which contains a good amount of classic European art, but head to the halls focused on American Regionalism first if you're short on time. Pieces by historic and contemporary Native artists add much-needed perspectives to traditional scenes of the West.

If you prefer your art hands-on, visit the **Hot Shops Art Center** *(hotshopsartcenter.com),* where artists create, display and sell their works from more than 50 studios in a former mattress factory. Sign up for a course on glassblowing, ceramics or silversmithing.

Find rotating exhibitions of contemporary and modern art in huge brick warehouses at **Kaneko** *(thekaneko.org; free)* and the **Bemis Center for Contemporary Arts** *(bemiscenter.org; free).* Check online before you visit because they sometimes close between exhibitions.

Lincoln & Around

Learn Nebraska state history

Nebraska's capital isn't its largest city, but it is a big college town, home to the University of Nebraska's main campus. You don't have to be a student to get schooled in Lincoln, where several cultural institutions tell the state's story. Near the college, the **Nebraska History Museum** *(history.nebraska.gov/museum; adult/child $5/3; closed Sun and Mon)* begins the narrative 13,000 years ago, and its three floors of displays carry on to the present.

Less than a mile south, the 400ft-high **Nebraska State Capitol** *(capitol.nebraska.gov; free)* is architectural eye candy. Completed in 1932, its art deco interiors could be mistaken for a soaring cathedral. For deeper insights, join the free guided tours that depart from the north end of the 2nd floor on the hour *(9am-4pm Mon-Fri, from 10am Sat, from 1pm Sun),* or you can wander up on your own to the 14th-floor observation deck.

EATING & DRINKING IN OMAHA: OUR PICKS

Committee Chophouse: The summertime 'steak flight' from Nebraska ranches is an indulgent treat at this suave, low-lit steakhouse. *5-10pm* $$$

Bronco's: Classic 1950s local fast-food joint with an iconic neon sign. Burgers are made from state-sourced ground beef. *9am-10pm* $

Au Courant Regional Kitchen: Farm-fresh artful plates of New European cuisine in the Benson neighborhood west of downtown. *5-10pm Thu-Sun* $$

Kros Strain Draft Works: Sip the flagship Fairy Nectar IPA inside the industrial taproom in a former furniture warehouse or on the patio. *hours vary; closed Mon*

ROBERT HARDING VIDEO/SHUTTERSTOCK

Nebraska State Capitol

Back to school at UNL

The University of Nebraska has its main campus in the middle of Lincoln. Nebraska doesn't have any major-league sports teams, so everyone in the state pins their hopes on the Huskers. In fall, football games kick off at **Memorial Stadium** *(huskers.com),* and the 85,000 seats often sell out.

A pigskin throw away, the **University of Nebraska State Museum** *(museum.unl.edu; adult/child $12.50/6.75; closed Mon)* has fascinating, though somewhat dated, displays of dinos, many of which were found in the Agate Fossil Beds (p181) in the Nebraska Panhandle. The museum's icon is Archie, the world's largest Columbian mammoth skeleton, which stands 15½ft tall. The newer top-floor Cherish Nebraska exhibit details the state's ecology and changing environment.

On the East Campus, agriculture majors hand-make and sell cheese and ice cream at the **UNL Dairy Store** *(dairystore.unl.edu).* Cones come in more than a dozen delicious seasonal flavors, including sweet corn and white chocolate lavender.

MORE ATTRACTIONS IN & AROUND LINCOLN

International Quilt Museum: Elevates the humble quilt to an exquisite art form. *(internationalquiltmuseum.org; adult/child $8/4)*

Sunken Gardens: In the 1930s, a former neighborhood dump was transformed into this pocket park.

Lincoln Children's Museum: Kids can run free in this 23,000-sq-ft space with prairie dog–style tunnels, a three-story climbing structure and even a miniature Runza (p180). *(lincolnchildrensmuseum.org; adult/child $13/16)*

Strategic Air Command & Aerospace Museum: Massive hangars contain an example of every significant US bomber, from the B-17 to the B-52. Between Lincoln and Omaha on I-80. *(sacmuseum.org; adult/child $12/6)*

EATING & DRINKING IN LINCOLN: OUR PICKS

Dish: Lincoln's top restaurant presents inventive New American seasonal plates with locally sourced ingredients. *5-8:30pm or later Tue-Sat* $$

Hub Cafe: This creative cafe is a brunch-time favorite, best enjoyed from the sunny, park-facing seats. *7:30am-9pm Tue-Sat, to 2:30pm Sun* $

Other Room: Perhaps the best cocktail bar in the state hides behind a heavy metal door in the historic Haymarket district. *5pm-1am*

Boiler Brewing Co: A highly awarded former homebrewer now pours pints, often high-ABV, for the thirsty public. *3-10pm Mon-Thu, noon-midnight Fri & Sat, to 8pm Sun*

RUNZA

Nebraska's most iconic food is the runza, a rectangle of yeast-dough bread filled with ground beef and onions. This meaty sandwich was brought to the US by 19th-century Volga German immigrants who settled in Nebraska and Kansas (where the dish is called bierock).

The ubiquitous fast-food chain called Runza is the easiest place to try one. The first Runza opened in Lincoln in 1949, and though the original restaurant no longer exists, more than 80 other locations have popped up around the state, as well as a handful in Colorado, Iowa, Kansas and South Dakota. The classic flavor is still on the menu, but you can also order versions with mushroom and Swiss cheese, barbecue and bacon, or Southwest ranch and taco seasoning.

Pioneers on the prairie

The Homestead Act of 1862 forever altered the landscape and demographics of the western US territories, converting public land (which was Native land before the Indian Removal Act of 1830) to private ownership. Immigrants, formerly enslaved people, women and anyone else who could farm 160 acres for five years got the land cheap in exchange for back-breaking work.

The first plot of land claimed through the Homestead Act is now encompassed by **Homestead National Historical Park** *(nps.gov/home; free)*, 45 miles south of Lincoln. Start at the **Heritage Center**, which puts the Homestead Act into context, and then head outside to visit the **gravesite of Daniel Freeman**, said to have filed his homestead claim 10 minutes after midnight on the day the Act went into effect. None of the Freeman family's buildings still exist, but the 1867 **Palmer-Epard Cabin** behind the Heritage Center is from the era, originally constructed about 14 miles away. The Heritage Center closes at 5pm daily, but the trails around it through the tallgrass prairie are open until dusk.

Grand Island & Kearney

The changing face of the West

For an engaging look at the lives of the homesteaders, head to the **Stuhr Museum** *(stuhrmuseum.org; adult/child $14/12)* in Grand Island. More than 60 buildings from the 1800s were moved to this huge outdoor living-history museum, where reenactors in period dress feed the farm goats, work in the blacksmith shop and roam the wooden boardwalks. The museum gives a nod to the land's original inhabitants with a Pawnee Earth Lodge and a small bison enclosure.

Witness the sandhill crane migration

During their spring migration (mid-February to early April), more than 500,000 sandhill cranes – 80% of the world population – touch down along 80 miles of the Platte River in central Nebraska in one of the country's most spectacular wildlife events. Just off I-80 southwest of Grand Island, the **Crane Trust Nature and Visitor Center** *(cranetrust.org; closed Sun)* runs migration season tours on foot and by bus. East of Kearney, the **Iain Nicolson Audubon Center at Rowe Sanctuary** *(rowe.audubon.org; closed Sun and Mon)* also puts on guided tours. Reserve tours in advance; bookings open in January.

EATING & DRINKING IN GRAND ISLAND & KEARNEY: OUR PICKS

Coney Island Lunch Room: Old-school diner in downtown Grand Island offering hot dogs, burgers and malts. *8:30am-5pm Mon-Fri, to 3pm Sat* $

Archives: 2024-opened speakeasy below the tourism office in a historic building in Grand Island's adorable downtown. *4-11pm Thu, 6pm-1am Fri, from 1pm Sat*

Cunningham's Journal: Laid-back spot in downtown Kearney with a lengthy menu of pub grub and local beer. *11am-1am Mon-Sat, to midnight Sun* $$

Platte Valley Taphouse: The place to go for good IPAs and pizza in Kearney. Eat, drink and play cornhole in the beer garden. *3-11pm Mon-Wed, 1pm-1am Thu-Sat*

ZACK FRANK/SHUTTERSTOCK

Agate Fossil Beds National Monument

Outside migration season, both free-to-see visitor centers welcome travelers with informational displays and riverfront hiking trails to spot other waterfowl.

Converging trails around Kearney

The first outpost established to protect travelers on the California and Oregon Trails, the 1848 **Fort Kearny** *(outdoornebraska.gov/fortkearny; per vehicle $14, visitor center adult/child $5/1)* still sits among lonesome prairie about 9 miles southeast of Kearney. Today's two 1960s reconstructions are a little disappointing, but if you're here during the sandhill crane migration season, the park is a good place to see the birds.

To get a bigger-picture view of the trails under your feet, visit the **Archway** *(archway.org; adult/child $15/7)*, a museum that bends over the top of I-80 east of Kearney. An audio device leads you through hand-painted exhibits that you might think would border on hokey given the location of this attraction, but they actually do a decent job of telling colorful tales about the people who've passed this way, from pioneers in covered wagon trains to drivers zipping down the interstate.

Connect with Nebraska art

For a cultural stop in Kearney, check out the small but mighty **Museum of Nebraska Art** *(mona.unk.edu; free; closed Mon)*, the state's official art gallery. It's half set in modern premises that reopened in May 2025 after a four-year, $36.5-million expansion, and half in a neoclassical 1911 post office. Nearly two centuries of artwork, predating statehood, trace Nebraska's visual history through the creations of artists who were born, lived or worked in the state.

ROAD TRIP STOPS IN WESTERN NEBRASKA

Pony Express Station: Original log-built 1860 Pony Express stop in Gothenburg. *(ponyexpressstation.org; free)*

Buffalo Bill Ranch State Historical Park: Tour the home of Bill Cody, the father of rodeo and the famed Buffalo Bill's Wild West Show that ran for 30 years from 1883. *(park pass per vehicle $14, plus mansion tour adult/child $5/1)*

Carhenge: A faithful Stonehenge replica made of 39 wrecked cars. Kooky roadside art at its finest, 3 miles north of Alliance. *(carhenge.com; free)*

Agate Fossil Beds National Monument: Some 20 million years ago, this part of Nebraska was like the Serengeti in Africa today: a gathering place for a rich variety of creatures, now fossilized. *(nps.gov/agfo; free)*

HISTORIC TRAILS THROUGH NEBRASKA

Oregon Trail (1846–69): Nearly half a million settlers traveled this 2170-mile route in the largest voluntary mass migrations in human history.

California Trail (1841–69): Few settlers took to this 1600-mile trail until 1848, when gold was discovered near Sacramento, California.

Mormon Trail (1846–69): Fleeing religious persecution, members of the Church of Jesus Christ of Latter-day Saints packed up their lives in Illinois and made the journey to Utah, then not part of the United States.

Pony Express (1860–61): Express mail on horseback cut down the time to receive a message to 10 days. Operational for only 18 months before the telegraph took over.

Nebraska Panhandle

See iconic rock formations on the prairie

The remote and little-visited Nebraska Panhandle is perhaps the most evocative part of the state. Stark vistas stretch to the horizon in lands little changed in millennia, and rocky bluffs that can be seen from miles around rise out of the prairie.

At **Chimney Rock National Historic Site** *(history.nebraska.gov/rock)*, a 300ft-tall stone spire was so striking to travelers on the Oregon, California and Mormon Trails that it's estimated that 97% of pioneers mentioned it in their journals. The small **Chimney Rock Museum** *(adult/child $8/4; 9am-4pm)* has updated displays but isn't worth the admission fee. Instead, set off on the easy 2-mile loop trail *(free; dawn-dusk)* that gets closer to the base of the formation.

About 25 miles northwest, **Scotts Bluff National Monument** *(nps.gov/scbl; free)* was another important waypoint on the pioneer trails. The **visitor center** *(8am-6pm mid-May–Aug, to 4:30pm Sep–mid-May)* contains exhibits and the largest collection of original paintings and photos by William Henry Jackson, a Civil War veteran famous for his scenes of the American West. Walk in the footsteps of history on the mile-long **trail** *(dawn-dusk)* west of the visitor center, which follows the original path of the Oregon Trail and even has some swales – deep indentations in the dirt compressed by hundreds of thousands of wooden wagon wheels. Drive the **Summit Road** *(9am-5pm mid-May–Aug, to 4pm Sep–mid-May)* or hike the 3.2-mile **Saddle Rock Trail** to the top of the bluff for sweeping views.

War and peace at Fort Robinson State Park

The turbulent past of **Fort Robinson** *(outdoornebraska.gov/location/fort-robinson; per vehicle $14)* belies its peaceful atmosphere today. Guards killed Lakota chief Crazy Horse (Tȟašúŋke Witkó) here in 1877 when it served as the Red Cloud Indian Agency, brigades of Black troops known as Buffalo Soldiers were formed for the Civil War and it was a POW camp for Germans in WWII. Understand the complex history at the **Fort Robinson Museum** *(adult/child $5/3)*. Several of the old buildings are open to wander around, and you can even stay overnight in former officers' and soldiers' quarters from 1909. Bugle wake-up call not included.

EATING & DRINKING IN THE NEBRASKA PANHANDLE: OUR PICKS

Mixing Bowl: This Gering cafe's specials tap into the area's German immigrant history. *6am-3pm Wed-Fri, from 7am Sat & Sun* $

Gering Bakery: Fuel a day of hiking with doughnuts from this neon-signed spot in Gering, open since 1950. *5:30am-5:30pm Mon-Fri, to 1pm Sat* $

Flyover Brewing Company: Everyone in this attractive Scottsbluff brewery is enjoying a better brew (and view) than those at 40,000ft. *11am-11pm Tue-Sun*

Mark Ferrari Specialty Coffees: Find an unexpected taste of aloha in tiny Oshkosh, population 884. *8:30am-2pm Mon-Fri, to 12:30pm Sat*

ROBERT WALTMAN/SHUTTERSTOCK

Scotts Bluff National Monument

Valentine

Raft the Niobrara National Scenic River

Kayaking, canoeing or inner-tubing down the Niobrara (pronounced nigh-oh-BRAH-rah) draws scores of people to north-central Nebraska in summer. Sheer limestone bluffs, lush forests and more than 200 spring-fed waterfalls along the banks shatter any 'flat Nebraska' stereotypes.

Most float tours start from the town of Valentine. **Brewers Canoers and Tubers** *(brewerscanoers.com)* is one of the original outfitters in the area and was the first to introduce tubing on the Niobrara River. You can rent canoes, kayaks or tubes with them or arrange shuttles to and from launch and landing sites.

Monowi

Eat in Nebraska's smallest town

If you don't think a ghost town can have a strong sense of community, you haven't been to Monowi. Its lone resident is nonagenarian Elsie Eiler, who runs **Monowi Tavern** *(closed Mon)*. The bar and grill is a one-woman show, where Elsie cooks burgers, fries and steaks for a surprising number of customers. Her family has operated the tavern since 1971, and in addition to working as the cook and bartender, she's also Monowi's mayor. Farmers and people from all over the county sit down to catch up and share gossip, and travelers are welcomed just as warmly.

BEST NEBRASKA FESTIVALS

NCAA College World Series: The top Division I baseball teams head to Omaha's **Charles Schwab Field** every June. *(cwsomaha.com)*

Star City Pride: Lincoln turns rainbow with pride at this LGBTIQ+ parade in June. *(starcityprideevents.org)*

Kool-Aid Days: The sugary drink was invented in Hastings in 1927, and it's celebrated with boat races and a Kool-Aid drinking contest in August. *(kool-aiddays.com)*

Oregon Trail Days: In Gering, the state's oldest festival includes a street dance party and a chili cook-off. *(oregontraildays.com)*

Nebraska Star Party: Spy on the night sky in July at Merritt Reservoir, the state's only Dark Sky Park. *(nebraskastarparty.org)*

Iowa

HEARTLAND BEAUTY | FANTASTIC CYCLING | INNOVATIVE ARCHITECTURE

Places

TOP TIP

Get off the interstates and spend time on Iowa's backroads, which pass the farms and fields that comprise America's heartland. The state is home to 14 national and state scenic byways *(iowadot.gov)*, and you'll find at least one in every region. Slow down and soak up the pastoral beauty!

You'll come to appreciate the rumble strips that keep you alert while driving across Iowa's rural backroads, where miles and miles of fields and farmhouses cast a hypnotic spell – and stop signs pop up unexpectedly at lonely crossroads. Stretching east from the soaring Loess Hills across swaths of rolling farmland, the Hawkeye State packs in the pastoral beauty before bumping into bluffs along the Mississippi River. In the middle? The writers' town of Iowa City, the tradition-loving Amana Colonies, art-minded Des Moines and architecturally impressive Mason City. A network of biking trails link the state's picture-perfect towns.

Iowa emerges from slumber every four years as the make-or-break state for presidential hopefuls. The Iowa Caucus opens the national election battle, and wins by George W Bush in 2000 and Barack Obama in 2008 stunned many pundits and launched their victorious campaigns. Another statewide highlight is RAGBRAI, an annual multi-day bike ride that draws thousands of cyclists.

GETTING AROUND

You'll need a car to explore greater Iowa. I-80 runs east-west across the state, linking Des Moines with Chicago to the east and Omaha, NE, to the west. I-35 travels north-south, connecting Des Moines with Minneapolis to the north and Kansas City to the south. Iowa has a fantastic network of cycling trails, and they are a pretty option for exploring urban areas and beyond.

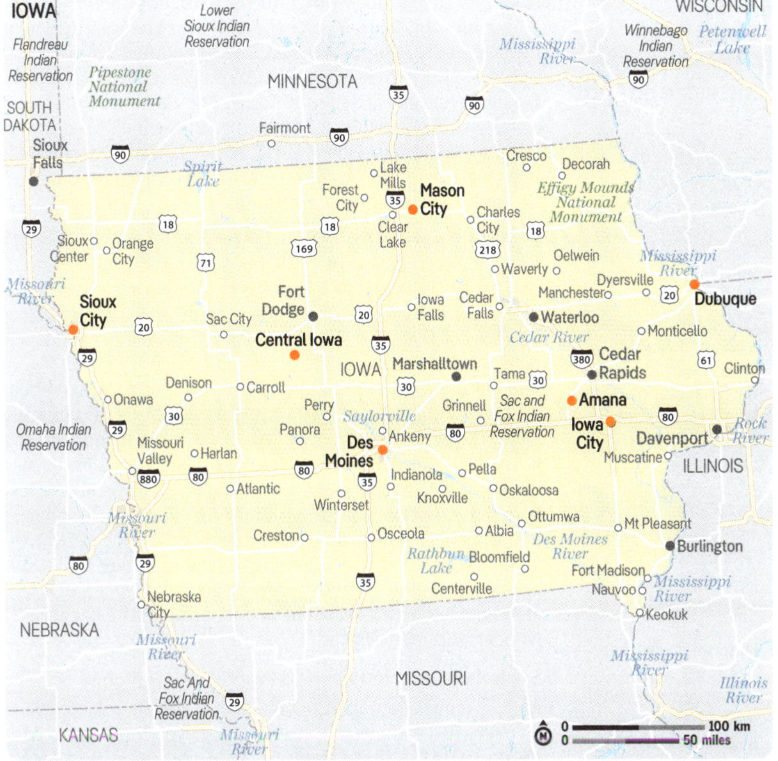

Dubuque & Around

Strolling the river cities

The historic city of **Dubuque**, with its 19th-century Victorian homes lining narrow streets between the Mississippi River and seven steep limestone hills, is a fine base for Great River Road explorations. Stroll the 9-mile path along the waterfront and explore neighborhoods in the midst of an urban revitalization that's drawing national acclaim. Don't miss the redeveloped Millwork District immediately north of downtown past 6th St. Its old wood-working factories are now home to great restaurants and nightlife. Red-brick walls are splashed with spectacular **murals** *(voicesproductions.org)* across downtown.

Davenport is the largest and most appealing of the Quad Cities about 70 miles south of Dubuque (the other three are Bettendorf in Iowa and Moline and Rock Island in Illinois). It has a grand riverfront setting with a vast network of walking and biking trails.

Ride the Fenelon Place Elevator

Stepping into Dubuque's tiny **Fenelon Place Elevator** *(fenelonplaceelevator.com; adult/child $2/1 roundtrip)* at 8:30am, especially if traveling solo, is a leap of faith. The sign

AMERICAN GOTHIC

It may be impossible to find a state more proud of a homegrown artist than Iowa is of Grant Wood. You know Wood. He painted *American Gothic* (1930), which depicts a pitchfork-holding Iowa farmer and his daughter (not his wife) standing resolutely before their tiny farmhouse.

While you can find plenty of Wood works in Iowa (p188), his most iconic painting hangs in the Art Institute of Chicago. But you know what's better? The actual *American Gothic* farmhouse, located in the town of Eldon about 100 miles southeast of Des Moines. The house sits beside the **American Gothic House Center** *(americangothichouse.net; $5)*, which interprets the painting that sparked a million parodies. It even has loaner costumes so you can make your own parody selfie (for no fee) in front of the house.

says 'Pull the cord.' So you pull the cord, and then *whee!* It's a four-minute climb up the shortest and steepest funicular railway in the United States. At the top of the bluff, step out, pay the fare then soak up the expansive view of downtown Dubuque and the Mississippi River. The elevator, also known as the 4th St Elevator, was constructed in 1882 for a downtown businessman who wanted to get home quickly for his lunchtime nap! The elevator is on 4th St and open from April through November (8am to 10pm).

Aquariums, touch tanks and river otters

Kids are pretty talkative while peering into the aquariums at the vast **National Mississippi River Museum** *(rivermuseum.org; adult/child $26/20)* in Dubuque, and if you can't find the alligator or the American eel, there's a sharp-eyed youngster ready to help you look in just the right place. The West Building spotlights the Mississippi River. Here you'll learn about backwater marshes, alligator habitats and birds that migrate along the Mississippi flyway. The river otters aquarium is a hotspot for the elementary school set. The East Building celebrates all of America's rivers, and the Riverways History Gallery here shares background about the Indigenous tribes, explorers and traders who depended on the country's major waterways.

Start your visit at the Journey Theater, where two alternating 20-minute movies – *Mississippi Journey* and *River of Dreams* – are an excellent introduction to the beauty and wonder of the Mississippi.

Exploring caves between Davenport and Dubuque

As you crouch low...and lower...and lower, to walk through Dancehall Cave, you might wonder if your detour to **Maquoketa Caves State Park** *(iowadnr.gov; free)* was such a great idea. Don't worry, it was, especially if you're traveling with kids. And the ten-minute walk through the multi-room Dancehall is a highlight of a visit to this fun state park, where excited kids don headlamps before wiggling into small, marked caves. Two short loop trails, which pass 13 designated caves, link up at the vast Dancehall – where locals did indeed hold dance parties back in the day. The park is just off US 61 between Davenport and Dubuque, about 35 miles west of the Mississippi River.

Have a catch at the Field of Dreams

Several nights each week in summer the 'ghosts' of legendary baseball players step onto the **Field of Dreams** *(fieldofdreamsmoviesite.com; $20 donation)* baseball diamond from the

EATING & DRINKING AROUND DUBUQUE: OUR PICKS

Brazen Open Kitchen: Heavenly seasonal New American cuisine, plus inventive cocktails and a sizable wine list in the Millwork District. *4:30-9pm Mon-Sat* **$$**

L May Eatery: The creative thin crust pizzas are delicious at this chic downtown cafe. Works well for solos and celebratory couples alike. *hours vary* **$$**

Monk's: Every town needs a joint like Monk's: friendly folks in a creaky old house serving coffee in the morning and local beer at night. *7am-11pm most days*

Textile Brewing Co: Occupies an old sewing factory in Dyersville 30 miles west of Dubuque. Giant pretzels, fantastic flatbreads and tasty beer. *11am-9pm most days*

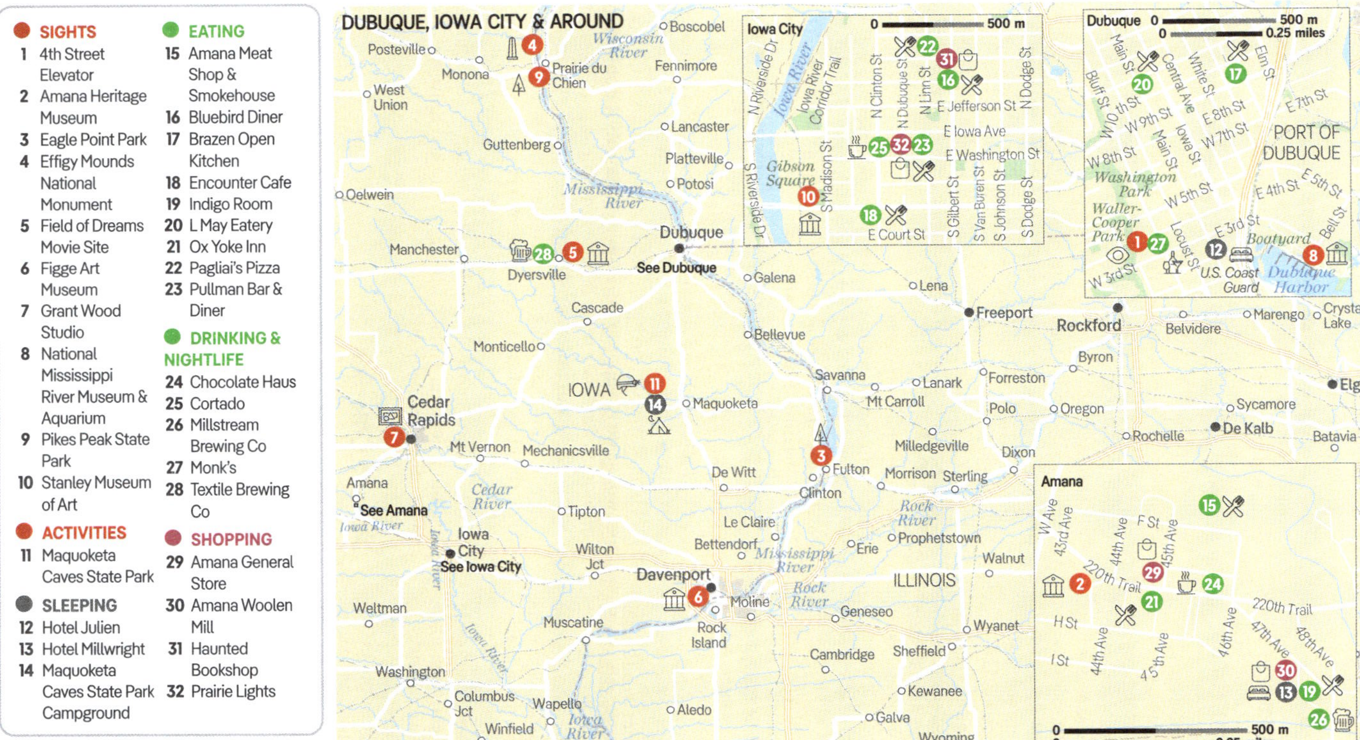
DUBUQUE, IOWA CITY & AROUND
SIGHTS
1 4th Street Elevator
2 Amana Heritage Museum
3 Eagle Point Park
4 Effigy Mounds National Monument
5 Field of Dreams Movie Site
6 Figge Art Museum
7 Grant Wood Studio
8 National Mississippi River Museum & Aquarium
9 Pikes Peak State Park
10 Stanley Museum of Art
ACTIVITIES
11 Maquoketa Caves State Park
SLEEPING
12 Hotel Julien
13 Hotel Millwright
14 Maquoketa Caves State Park Campground
EATING
15 Amana Meat Shop & Smokehouse
16 Bluebird Diner
17 Brazen Open Kitchen
18 Encounter Cafe
19 Indigo Room
20 L May Eatery
21 Ox Yoke Inn
22 Pagliai's Pizza
23 Pullman Bar & Diner
DRINKING & NIGHTLIFE
24 Chocolate Haus
25 Cortado
26 Millstream Brewing Co
27 Monk's
28 Textile Brewing Co
SHOPPING
29 Amana General Store
30 Amana Woolen Mill
31 Haunted Bookshop
32 Prairie Lights
Postevillle
Monona
Prairie du Chien
Boscobel
Wisconsin River
Fennimore
West Union
Lancaster
Guttenberg
Platteville
Potosi
Oelwein
Mississippi River
Dubuque
See Dubuque
Manchester
Dyersville
Galena
Lena
Freeport
Rockford
Belvidere
Marengo
Crystal Lake
Cascade
Bellevue
Monticello
Byron
Elgin
Savanna
Lanark
Forreston
IOWA
Maquoketa
Mt Carroll
Polo
Oregon
Sycamore
Cedar Rapids
Mt Vernon
Mechanicsville
Milledgeville
Rochelle
De Kalb
Batavia
Dixon
Fulton
Clinton
De Witt
Morrison
Sterling
Amana
See Amana
Cedar River
Tipton
Rock River
Iowa River
Iowa City
See Iowa City
Le Claire
Prophetstown
Bettendorf
Erie
Wilton Jct
Walnut
Davenport
ILLINOIS
Moline
Geneseo
Weltman
Rock Island
Wyanet
Muscatine
Cambridge
Sheffield
Washington
Columbus Jct
Wapello
Kewanee
Aledo
Galva
Winfield
Wyoming
Alexis
0 50 km
0 25 miles
Iowa City
0 500 m
N Riverside Dr
Iowa River
Iowa River Corridor Trail
N Clinton St
N Dubuque St
N Linn St
E Jefferson St
N Dodge St
E Iowa Ave
E Washington St
Gibson Square
S Madison St
S Riverside Dr
S Gilbert St
S Van Buren St
S Johnson St
S Dodge St
E Court St
Dubuque
0 500 m
0 0.25 miles
Main St
Central Ave
White St
Elm St
Bluff St
W 10th St
W 9th St
E 8th St
E 7th St
W 7th St
Iowa St
PORT OF DUBUQUE
W 8th St
Washington Park
W 5th St
E 4th St
E 5th St
Waller-Cooper Park
Locust St
E 3rd St
Boatyard
Bell St
W 3rd St
U.S. Coast Guard
Dubuque Harbor
Amana
W Ave
43rd Ave
44th Ave
F St
45th Ave
220th Trail
H St
I St
44th Ave
45th Ave
46th Ave
47th Ave
48th Ave
0 500 m
0 0.25 miles

LANDSCAPES THAT INSPIRED GRANT WOOD

You can admire Grant Wood's (p186) Midwestern Regionalist works across eastern Iowa, as well as experiencing the landscapes that influenced him.

Figge Art Museum: This Davenport museum holds many of Wood's works. *(figgeartmuseum.org; adult/teen/child $14/10/8)*

Stanley Museum of Art: Look out for the strangely mesmerizing *Plaid Sweater* (1931) in Iowa City. *(stanleymuseum.org; free)*

Grant Wood Studio: Head to Cedar Rapids to see the spot where Wood painted *American Gothic* and other works. *(crma.org; free)*

Grant Wood Scenic Byway: If you're not a fan of museums, simply take a drive on this road, which ribbons through the rolling farmland that inspired Wood's work.

surrounding cornfield during a game or event, echoing a scene from Kevin Costner's classic movie. And just like Shoeless Joe, these ghosts also interact with spectators.

But no worries if you miss one of these 'Ghost Nights.' The field, which is 4 miles northeast of Dyersville off US 20, is open to visitors during the day. Come play catch with mitts, baseballs and bats stashed beside the diamond and tour the white clapboard farmhouse seen in the movie. After on-site construction projects are completed, the complex plans to host one Major League Baseball game annually. And the corn? They'll tell you it's 'knee-high by the 4th of July,' and at its tallest in August.

Drive to Dyersville for an enormous pizza-style pretzel and an easy-drinking Dyersville Lager at **Textile Brewing Co** (p151; *textilebrews.com*). There's a nice *Field of Dreams* mural one block east.

Iowa City

Books, art and hawkeyes

The vibe in downtown Iowa City is youthful and artsy thanks to the University of Iowa campus, which spills across both sides of the Iowa River beside the charming downtown. The school's writing programs are renowned, and Iowa City was named a UNESCO City of Literature in 2008. For a sharp parody of the town and school, read Jane Smiley's *Moo*.

Bibliophiles should beeline to **Prairie Lights** *(prairielights.com)*, a multi-level bookstore with an entire section dedicated to 'Writing in Iowa.' The small cafe serves baked goods, coffee and teas plus wine and beer. You'll find used books and a cat or two inside the appropriately creaky **Haunted Bookshop** *(thehauntedbookshop.com)*. Refuel with a coffee and croissant (delicious!) at **Cortado** *(cortadoic.com)*.

Opening its doors on the campus of the University of Iowa in 2022, the glossy **Stanley Museum of Art** *(stanleymuseum.org; adult/child $8/3)* is a whirlwind of spectacular art, most of it displayed across 12 small galleries. Don't miss *Mural*, a seminal Jackson Pollock work gifted to the university by Peggy Guggenheim in 1951.

Amana Colonies

Crafts, religion and a spiffy hotel

In the late 1800s the Amana woolen mill was a hub of industry within the greater Amana Colonies, a collection of historic

EATING IN DOWNTOWN IOWA CITY: OUR PICKS

Pullman Bar & Diner: Attentive service and decadent, upscale diner fare beside Prairie Lights. *8am-10pm Mon-Thu, to 10:30pm Fri & Sat, to 9pm Sun* $$

Encounter Cafe: Enjoy panini sandwiches, salads and made-from-scratch pastries. *7am-2:30pm* $

Bluebird Diner: Diner fare has a worldly spin at this busy, long-time downtown joint. *7am-9pm Mon-Sat to 8pm Sun* $

Pagliai's Pizza: Serving delicious pies cooked in stone-hearth ovens since 1957. *4-10pm* $$

SANDRA FOYT/SHUTTERSTOCK

Prairie Lights

German religious villages located 25 miles northwest of Iowa City. In 2020 the old mill welcomed its first guests under a brand new name and identity: the **Hotel Millwright**. An adaptive re-use project, this 66-room boutique hotel celebrates the stories and craftsmanship of the mill workers. It has also revitalized the villages, which have been a shopping and dining destination long known for its craft stores and family-style German restaurants.

If you're driving across Iowa on I-80, the colonies are a convenient stop just north of the interstate. Most attractions are located in the village of Amana, which is home to the **Amana Heritage Museum** *(amanaheritage.org; adult/child $10/5)*. The museum shares a good overview of the history of the colonies. Don't skip the short introductory film.

For books, toys, gifts and a variety of preserves, stop by the **Amana General Store** *(amanaheritage.com)*. Buy locally produced cheeses and smoked meats around the corner at the **Amana Meat Shop & Smokehouse** *(amanameatshop.com)*. Amana-made blankets, throws and scarves catch the eye at

HISTORY OF THE AMANA COLONIES

Seven villages are stretched along a 17-mile loop just north of I-80 west of Iowa City. All were established as German religious communes between 1855 and 1861 by Inspirationists who lived a utopian life with no wages paid and all assets communally owned. Communal kitchens served daily meals to all. During the Great Depression the community voted to end the communal way of living, although the Amana Church continues. Unlike the Amish and Mennonite religions, Inspirationists embrace modern technology (and tourism).

Today the well-preserved (and discreetly tasteful) villages offer a glimpse of this unique culture, and there are lots of arts, crafts, cheeses, baked goods and wines to buy.

EATING & DRINKING IN THE AMANA COLONIES

Ox Yoke Inn: Bratwurst, schnitzels and fried chicken. Family-style meals have refillable entrees and sides for all. *11am-7pm Mon-Thu, to 8pm Fri & Sat, 9am-6pm Sun* $

Indigo Room: Bustling restaurant with a cocktail bar inside Hotel Millwright. Enjoy elevated small plates and a few mains. *4-8pm Mom, to 9pm Tue-Sun* $$

Chocolate Haus: Sells delicious artisanal truffles and fudge as well as chocolate-y coffee drinks. Wonderful frappuccinos. *10am-5pm Mon-Sun, 11am-5pm Sun*

Millstream Brewing Co: Listen to German oom-pah-pah while sipping innovative craft beer beside the mill race near Hotel Millwright. *11am-7pm most days*

TOP SIGHTS ALONG IOWA'S GREAT RIVER ROAD

Iowa's Great River Road mostly hugs the Mississippi River along the state's eastern edge. It links with numerous country byways and passes through beautiful riverfront towns.

Effigy Mounds National Monument: Hundreds of Native American burial mounds sit in the bluffs above the Mississippi in northeast Iowa.

Pikes Peak State Park: A nature reserve at the confluence of the Wisconsin and Mississippi Rivers.

National Mississippi River Museum & Aquarium: Learn about life along the length of the Mississippi in Dubuque.

Eagle Point Park: Beautiful bluff-top park in Clinton with river views and elaborate 1930s stonework.

Figge Art Museum: This glass-walled museum in Davenport sparkles above the River Road, and is now illuminated at night.

the **Amana Woolen Mill** *(amanawoolenmill.com)*, which is located in the original weaving building beside the hotel.

Des Moines

Butter cows and fried Twinkies on a stick

Much more than just country music and butter sculpture, the **Iowa State Fair** *(iowastatefair.org; adult/child $16/10)* draws more than one million visitors over its 11-day run in early August. Fairgoers can admire award-winning farm animals, and they have their pick of more than 50 food items, from deep-fried Twinkies to bacon-cheddar pretzel dogs, that are shoved on a stick. It's the setting for the Rodgers and Hammerstein musical *State Fair* and the 1945 film version. The fairgrounds are 3.5 miles east of downtown Des Moines.

If you're not in Iowa for the fair, try instead **Des Moines' Downtown Farmers Market** *(facebook.com/downtownfarmersmarket)*. Held Saturday mornings from May though October, this popular market – which began in 1975 – hosts hundreds of vendors selling produce, prepared foods, baked goods, meals, snacks and crafts.

A gold dome and top-drawer digs

You're looking pretty impressive there, **Iowa State Capitol** *(iowa.gov; free)*. Perched on a hill overlooking an enormous green lawn, this is one state capitol that is worth a closer look. Topped by a sparkling gold dome, the building soars 275ft. The bling-heavy interior is also a wonder, from the stained glass in the library to the spiral staircases. While exploring the 1st floor, be sure to look up to see the interior artistry of the dome. On the first floor you'll also find an intricate model of the USS *Iowa*. The enormous *Westward* mural, completed in 1905, draws you in for a closer look – are those angels protecting a wagon train? – while climbing from the 1st to the 2nd floor.

Parking is free in front of the building, and there's a public entrance under the front steps. After you're screened by security, walk straight ahead to the information desk for a self-guided tour pamphlet, or ask when the next guided tour departs. Tours last 90 minutes, but it's okay to spin off early.

Art and architecture in Des Moines

From its nondescript name to its ho-hum entry sign, the **Des Moines Art Center** *(desmoinesartcenter.org; free)* doesn't knock it out of the park when it comes to first impressions. But don't skip it. Three of the greatest architects of the modern era – Eliel Saarinen, IM Pei and Richard Meier – designed separate buildings within the complex. For visitors, it's easy to walk between them, and the varied architectural styles complement the collection's different artistic genres in striking ways. Matisse, Hopper, Rodin, Warhol and Basquiat are a few of the names represented.

From most points downtown it's an easy walk to the museum's satellite location, the **Pappajohn Sculpture Park**, where Jaume Plensa's enormous *Nomade* is particularly compelling. Grab a coffee near the park at eco-minded **Horizon Line**, where your to-go drink is served in a recyclable jar.

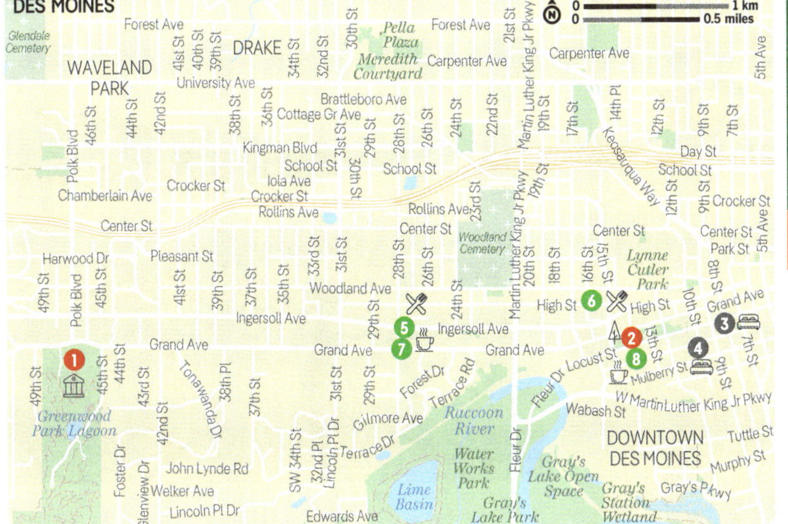

Indie shops in West Des Moines

There's not a chain store in sight in **Valley Junction** *(valleyjunction.com)*, a former village that has been swallowed up by West Des Moines. This five-block commercial corner unfurls along Fifth St, which is lined with locally owned shops, cafes and antique stores housed in attractive old brick buildings.

Don't miss **Bozz Prints** *(bozzprints.com)*, a print shop selling a colorful array of Iowa-promoting stickers, magnets, shirts and postcards. Prints also celebrate the Midwest and national parks. You'll find Iowa-made products a few doors down at **Heart of Iowa Marketplace** *(heartofiowamarketplace.com)*. Writers won't leave **Quill & Nib** *(valleyjunction.com)* empty-handed – it's pens and journals galore.

SIGHTS
1 Des Moines Art Center
2 Pappajohn Sculpture Park

SLEEPING
3 Des Lux Hotel
4 Hotel Fort Des Moines

EATING
see 5 Harbinger
5 Lachele's Fine Foods
6 Lua Brewing

DRINKING & NIGHTLIFE
7 Chain & Spoke
8 Horizon Line Coffee

Central Iowa

Silos, biker bars and black dirt

It's hard to miss the **High Trestle Bridge** *(inhf.org)* at night. Forty-one steel frames, illuminated by colorful LED lights, form a tunnel over the span, which soars 13 stories above the Des Moines River Valley. With its overlooks, interpretive signage and great birdwatching, the bridge is nearly

EATING & DRINKING IN DES MOINES: OUR PICKS

Lachele's Fine Foods: Construction workers and ladies who lunch converge at this tiny joint for delicious smash burgers. *11am-9pm Tue-Sat, 10am-3pm Sun* $

Harbinger: James Beard nominee Joe Tripp elevates Asian street food at this chic number. Many veggie options. *4-8pm Sun-Thu, to 9pm Fri & Sat* $

Lua Brewing: Nationally acclaimed brewpub has excellent beers, welcoming staff and delicious gourmet pub fare. *11am-10pm most days* $$

Chain & Spoke: What? A friendly bike shop? Yep, drop by for local cycling advice and fine coffee. *8am-5pm Mon-Fri, to 3pm Sat & Sun*

BICYCLE RIDES FROM SLATER

Taylor Christensen is the mayor of Slater and cofounder of Local Spokes.

Why is Slater a good starting point for a half-day bike ride in Iowa? We sit at the T of both the Heart of Iowa Nature Trail and the High Trestle Trail.

Who can ride the High Trestle Trail? It is perfect for novices or experienced cyclists. It's very clear and has a level grade – less than 2%. About every 7 miles there's a town. We will get families, with kids five to seven, to some very serious bikers.

What are some recommended stops for food and good cheer? In Madrid we have the **Flat Tire**, right on the trail. In Woodward they have the **Whistlin' Donkey**. All the bars do a great job of hosting, with live music and entertainment.

JIM PACKETT/SHUTTERSTOCK

as compelling in the daylight. It's also a fantastic final stop for cyclists pedaling the High Trestle Trail, a paved 25-mile walking and cycling path that links five small towns in central Iowa just north of Des Moines.

If you decide to take a half-day ride, you'll pass silos, fields and a few convivial trailside restaurants and bars. You'll likely see chipmunks, squirrels and rabbits, with frogs croaking songs of love (or is it hunger?) along the way. The trail, which links Ankeny and Woodward, is paved, mostly level and well marked. It's popular with families, and it links up with other long biking trails. For an e-bike rental, try **Local Spokes** *(thelocalspokes.com; half-day rental $50)* in Slater.

To see the illuminated bridge at night, you can park and hike a short distance to the span west of Madrid (*traveliowa .com/trails*).

Mason City

Frank Lloyd Wright and The Music Man

There's a lot going on in Mason City, and though it's not on the way to anywhere, this quirky place in north-central Iowa is a highly recommended stop if you are interested in

EATING & DRINKING IN MASON CITY: OUR PICKS

Three on the Tree Coffee & Cafe: Wake up with a pastry and coffee downtown before checking out the architecture. *7am-3pm* $

Birdsall's Ice Cream Co: Pause beneath the red-and-strip awning for a scoop, a sundae or a malt. Around since 1931. *noon-9pm* $

LD's Filling Station: All-American breakfast and lunch fare fueling the heartland, with decor embracing classic cars. *7am-8pm Wed-Fri, to 1pm Sat & Sun* $

Northwestern Steakhouse: Renowned statewide for its Greek-style broiled steaks. Order the spaghetti as your side. *4:30-9pm Mon-Sat* $$$

Stockman House

Prairie School architecture and, well, musicals. Architectural bona fides? The only remaining hotel designed by Frank Lloyd Wright, the **Historic Park Inn Hotel** *(historicparkinn.com)*, is downtown. The hotel is open for overnight guests and for those who just want to poke around and admire his vision. Don't miss the wonderful gift shop. You can also tour the **Stockman House** *(stockmanhouse.org; tour adult/child $15/5)*, a Prairie-style home also designed by Wright.

A self-guided walking tour passes a slew of nearby Prairie School, Usonian and Arts & Crafts–style homes designed by prominent architects in the early 1900s. Pick up a free walking tour map at the downtown **visitor center** *(visitmasoncityiowa.com)*.

Mason City was also the boyhood home of Meredith Willson, who wrote the Broadway musical *The Music Man*. The play was later turned into a Warner Brothers movie of the same name. The entire **Music Man Square** *(themusicmansquare.org)*, as seen in the movie, was recreated in Mason City and often hosts music events. Theater kids, join me now... *You got trouble, right here in River City...*

And take note: Mason City's cute downtown is anchored by a festive town square. If you're not careful with your planning, you might find yourself bumping elbows with the musical masses during the **North Iowa Band Festival**, the largest free marching-band competition in the Midwest.

Bil Baird and the Sound of Music puppets

Known globally in the mid-1900s for his modernist puppets and marionettes, puppeteer Bil Baird was a native of Mason City. His puppets made numerous appearances in Broadway productions and on television variety shows. His most famous creations are probably the Lonely Goatherd puppets, which made a memorable appearance in the movie *The Sound of*

CYCLING IOWA

With more than 2500 miles of paved cycling trails, Iowa is a top destination for cyclists. Trails cater to a variety of ages and skill levels, and they are often dotted with public art, festive bars and welcoming towns. The state is known internationally for its RAGBRAI ride (p194) in July.

Recommended trails include the Cedar Valley Trails, which link Cedar Falls with Waterloo in eastern Iowa; the High Trestle Trail in Central Iowa; and the Raccoon River Valley Trail, which connects small towns with the suburbs of Des Moines. A 9-mile extension to the High Trestle Trail in 2024 linked it to the Raccoon River route, forming a 120-mile loop.

WHAT THE HECK IS RAGBRAI?

Cyclists the world over are familiar with **RAGBRAI** *(ragbrai.com)*, a one-week bike ride across the state of Iowa every July. The ride, which always starts on the western side of the state, is non-competitive, and cyclists camp at eight host communities along the way. The total distance is around 470 miles.

The event attracts about 20,000 registered riders and is the best-attended cycling tour in the world. The name is an acronym for *Register*'s Annual Great Bicycle Ride Across Iowa; two reporters for the *Des Moines Register* took the first ride for a newspaper story in 1973.

SAXTON STUDIO/SHUTTERSTOCK

RAGBRAI riders

Music. Today, you can see the goat, one little girl in a pale pink coat, her gloating mama and the dancing couple at the **MacNider Art Museum** *(macniderart.org)* in Mason City. We're not sure where the goatherd went off to. Oh ho lay-dee odl lee o!

Sioux City

On the trail of Lewis and Clark

As they journeyed west along the Missouri River toward the Pacific Northwest, the Lewis and Clark expedition stopped near present day Sioux City. It was during this stop, on August 20, 1804, that Sgt Charles Floyd, a member of the corps, became ill and died, probably from appendicitis. He was the only person to die during the entire trek. You can learn much more about this event and other aspects of the journey at the **Lewis & Clark Interpretive Center**, which is beside the Missouri River. Inside, animatronic characters tell the story of the expedition. The information is geared toward younger visitors, but most everyone will learn something new from the exhibits, which can be fully explored in under an hour. Take exit 49 off I-29.

A bluff-top **obelisk** marks the final resting spot of Sgt Floyd, the first United States soldier to die west of the Mississippi River. A short drive from the interpretive center, his memorial is a tranquil spot to view the Missouri River and reflect on the bravery of the corps.

The iconic **Tastee Inn & Out** *(tasteeinnandout.com)* was not around when Lewis and Clark came through, but this retro drive-thru on the way to the Sergeant Floyd Monument has been around since 1955. There are two specials here: the Tastee, an Iowa loosemeat sandwich (a regional specialty that combines loose ground beef, onions and orange cheese), and onion chips, which are battered and fried.

North Dakota

BADLANDS BEAUTY | DINOSAUR FOSSILS | FARGO FUN

North Dakotans have a 'We're all in this together' charm that is pleasantly disarming after miles and miles of lonely driving. And oh, those drives. Fields of grain stretch beyond every horizon. Except for the rugged 'badlands' of the far west, geographic relief is subtle; often it's just a pond – known as a prairie pothole – creeping up against the interstate or a ruined homestead that break up the vista.

This is one of the least-visited states in the US. The lack of visitors, however, doesn't mean the state is sleepy. The Bakken oil boom (named for geologic formations beneath the surface) transformed the northwest quadrant into one vast drilling site. At night, fires burning off waste gas give the landscape hellish views. Though the boom has leveled off, once-quiet towns like Williston and Watford City have become industrial warrens.

Near the Montana border you'll find natural beauty that justifies a trip while the Missouri River is dotted with sights tied to the Lewis and Clark Expedition.

Places

GETTING AROUND

You'll need your own vehicle to explore the state. The only interstate is I-94, which runs east-west. North Dakota's main airports are in Bismarck, Fargo and Minot. Cities served by Amtrak's *Empire Builder* train include Fargo, Grand Forks, Minot and Williston. Jefferson Lines *(jeffersonlines.com)* runs limited bus services to Bismarck, Dickinson, Fargo and Grand Forks.

TOP TIP

The southwest quarter of North Dakota, including Medora, uses Mountain Time, which is one hour earlier than the rest of the state's Central Time.

Fargo

Pose by the Woodchipper

Visitor centers can be a little ho-hum. But that's amusingly not the case in Fargo. At the engaging **Fargo-Moorhead Visitors Center** you'll find the actual **woodchipper** from the 1996 movie *Fargo*. It was used in the scene where Gaear feeds the last of Carl's body into its maw and is discovered by Marge. You can reenact the scene – although not the results – while wearing Fargo-style hats and jamming in a fake leg (both provided). There's a reproduction out front. You'll find the visitor center off exit 348 on I-94 southwest of downtown.

Celebrate like nice Vikings

Step into the enormous **Brewhalla** *(brewhalla.com)* – an indoor/outdoor beer hall and market with loads of personality. Here you'll walk past bars slinging craft beer, families

TOP EXPERIENCE

Theodore Roosevelt National Park

Future president Theodore Roosevelt retreated from New York to this remote spot in his early 20s after losing both his wife and mother in a matter of hours. It's said that his time in the Dakota badlands inspired him to become an avid conservationist, and he set aside 230 million acres of federal land while in office. His North Dakota legacy is this beautiful 110-sq-mile national park.

ZAKZEINERT/SHUTTERSTOCK

TOP TIPS

- If escape is your goal, visit the remote, low-key Elkhorn Unit, where Roosevelt lived.
- Short on time? A quick stop at the free Painted Canyon Visitor Center off I-94 at exit 32 is recommended. View scenic badlands, hike trails and, possibly, see buffalo.

PRACTICALITIES

- nps.gov/thro
- admission $30/25 vehicle/motorcycle 7-day pass
- the park has three units: North, South and remote Elkhorn

Scenic Drives

Green prairie grasses frame rock formations streaked with red, yellow, brown, black and silver minerals in two units of the park. The colors of these badlands change with the moods of nature and time of day. The bison, elk, pronghorn and prairie dogs strutting about are clearly living their best lives. To maximize sightseeing, many visitors drive the 36-mile scenic loop (U-shaped due to construction when we visited) in the South Unit. Make the short hike up **Buck Hill** and soak up the spectacular stillness. It's also well worth the journey to the North Unit for the 14-mile one-way drive to the **Oxbow Overlook** and its wide views into the vast and colorfully striated river canyon.

Hiking & Camping

In the South Unit, the 0.4-mile **Wind Canyon Trail** leads to a dramatic viewpoint over the Little Missouri River, especially scenic at sunset. In the North Unit, the 1.5-mile **Buckhorn Trail** passes a lively Prairie Dog Town. The **Caprock-Coulee Loop** is a 4.1-mile hike across a grassy butte into the badlands. Camp at **Cottonwood Campground** in the South Unit or **Juniper Campground** in the North Unit. For a good adventure, hike or cycle the 96-mile Maah Daah Hey Trail between the two units.

chilling by fire pits and communal areas buzzing with groups playing board games. You might even muscle past a cluster of conventioneers attending the Hel's Fury Tattoo Fest. This industrially hip space is anchored by **Drekker Brewing Co**, which has a slew of innovative draft beers on tap across the market, where you'll also find food stalls selling woodfired pizzas, noodle dishes and smashburgers. Small retail shops here stay local. The vibe is welcoming and friendly – if this is the future of third places in America, we like it.

Take an art break downtown

If you're staying downtown, stroll over to the ambitious **Plains Art Museum** *(plainsart.org; free)*. Exhibits are housed in a renovated International Harvester warehouse. The permanent collection includes contemporary works by Native American and African artists. Temporary exhibits spotlight 20th- and 21st-century art.

The skybridge linking the museum with the adjacent Burgum Center for Creativity is a piece of art in its own right. Along the length of the span, a pretty screen print captures the delicate beauty of the tallgrass prairie. Look for big and little bluestems, a Harvester mouse and gray wolf tracks as you walk.

BIG SCULPTURES, QUIET PLAINS

Between Fargo and Theodore Roosevelt National Park on I-94, you can break up the drive by veering off the highway at exit 72. The exit marks the northern start of the **Enchanted Highway**, a 32-mile stretch that passes a series of enormous whimsical sculptures by local artist Gary Greff. The 75-ton **Geese in Flight** soars above exit 72.

EATING & DRINKING IN FARGO: OUR PICKS

Wurst Bier Hall: German-style beer hall downtown ups the stakes with inventive sausage sandwiches, exotic meats and more than 35 beers on tap. *hours vary* $

Shack: A beloved local diner known for its pancakes and – queue *Fargo* accent – eggs. *6am-2pm Sat-Tue, to 8pm Wed-Fri* $

Rosewild: Elevated American fare for breakfast, lunch and dinner inside the new Hotel Jasper. Cocktails too. *7am-10pm* $$

Sky Prairie: Seasonal cocktail bar *(May-Sep)* atop Hotel Donaldson (p213) with views of downtown. *4-9pm Sat & Sun*

BEST FOR LAST CLUB

Folks who keep track of the states they've visited often leave North Dakota for last thanks to it remote location. But its status as the 50th state doesn't bother North Dakota, and they now encourage travelers to save the best for last. Visitors can celebrate this accomplishment by joining the **Best for Last Club** – just walk into the **Fargo-Moorhead Visitors Center** (p195) and tell them you've hit 50. After you sign a form, they'll take your photo in front of the Best for Last banner and hand you a certificate. There are currently 7,300 members. Does induction include North Dakota swag? You betcha.

Bismarck

Brake for dinosaurs

Be warned. If anyone in your group is obsessed with dinosaurs and fossils, you will find yourselves hanging out at the excellent **North Dakota Heritage Center & State Museum** *(statemuseum.nd.gov; free)* far longer than originally planned. An enormous mastodon skeleton in the entranceway atrium sets the stage for the wonders to come, which include a fossilized dinosaur bone that still has its skin and soft tissue attached! This 67-million-year-old rarity was discovered in North Dakota's Hell Creek Formation, an extended rock layer southwest of Bismarck and a paleontologist's jackpot. The adjacent *Adaptation Gallery: Geologic Time* houses full-size replicas of various ancient beasts.

In addition to geology and paleontology, galleries spotlight early peoples, North Dakota history and fine art. Kids get a kick out of smelling a buffalo hide. There is a small **cafe** on-site.

Bismarck is the **state capitol**, and the museum is located on the grounds of the capitol complex. The museum is easily accessed from exit 159 on I-94.

Medora

Say 'howdy!' near the national park

As you mosey past the old wooden buildings in tiny Medora, which lounges beside the entrance to Theodore Roosevelt National Park (p196), look for the jaunty statue of the park's namesake. Roosevelt spent time in Medora and this pocket of North Dakota in the late 1800s. As the plaque here notes, Roosevelt once claimed, 'It was here that the romance of my life began.'

Today, this gateway community treads a fine line between real cowboy town and hokey modern interpretation. We'll give a nod to the former thanks to the dusty cowboy we saw who strolled into the Farmhouse Cafe with boots clomping and spurs a jingling.

For travelers, comfortable lodgings are available across all budgets and there are a handful of places to eat. Check *medora.com* for details about historic sites and family-focused activities. The much-anticipated **Theodore Roosevelt National Library** is set to open in Medora in July 2026. Note that many businesses close from October through May.

EATING & DRINKING IN MEDORA: OUR PICKS

Medora Convenience & Liquor Store: The fresh breakfast biscuits are regional legends at this friendly gas station and store. They start selling 'em early. *5:30am-9pm* $

Farmhouse Cafe: Pancakes, omelets, chicken-fried steaks and endless coffee. Nice staff. Lunch offerings too. *7am-11am* $

Theodore's Dining Room: Don your cleanest shirt for bison *osso bucco* and pan-seared walleye at the fanciest joint in town. Excellent pork-belly cobb salad. *hours vary* $

Little Missouri Saloon: This old-timey saloon will whip you back to the Wild West. Live music in summer. Open year-round. *11am-1am*

South Dakota

BLACK HILLS | SCENIC BYWAYS | ROAMING WILDLIFE

More than two million visitors walk the Avenue of Flags each year, squinting upward as they approach the iconic Mt Rushmore and its four presidential visages. And these attendance numbers are justified – it's a remarkable sight. But it's the unbound beauty of South Dakota that will likely stick with you. From the pine forests of the Black Hills to the ephemeral colors of the badlands to the windswept bluffs of the Missouri River, the natural beauty is rich and varied. And no one will forget their first sighting of a buffalo roaming prairie grasslands. The state's many scenic byways ribbon past these gorgeous landscapes as well as a crackerjack collection of old-school roadside attractions.

Historic and educational sites are abundant too, with mastodon fossils, old mining towns and abandoned missile silos all jostling for attention. The state is also the home of nine Native American tribes, and their stories and traditions are increasingly shared statewide.

Sioux Falls

Relax at Falls Park

It's hard to take a bad photo of the rambling waterfall that anchors **Falls Park** and the city of Sioux Falls. Paved trails frame the rocky cascades, and overlooks perch on the prettiest points. Our favorite spot? The footbridge over the Big Sioux River. The park has a perfectly placed cafe, and picnic tables are scattered about. You can also climb the five-story observation tower for high-elevation views of the action. Between mid-November and mid-January the park becomes a winter wonderland with 338,000 twinkling lights.

Continued on p203

TOP TIP

Roughly the western third of South Dakota – including the Black Hills and everything west of I-90 exit 177 and west of the Missouri River north of Pierre – uses Mountain Time, which is one hour earlier than Central Time in the rest of the state.

Places

GETTING AROUND

Driving is the most efficient way to explore the state. I-90 links Sioux Falls in the east with Rapid City in the west. These cities have South Dakota's two main airports. Each has services to major American hubs. I-29 runs north–south and links Sioux Falls with Fargo, ND, to the north and Sioux City, IA, to the south. Jefferson Lines *(jeffersonlines.com)* buses stop in Rapid City, Wall, Mitchell and Sioux Falls along I-90.

ABSTRACT ARTIST USA/SHUTTERSTOCK

TOP EXPERIENCE

Badlands National Park

The scenic wonders begin almost immediately along the Badlands Loop Rd, where the corrugated walls and crumbly spikes of an ancient floodplain shimmer ethereally in the afternoon light. It was understandably named *mako sica* (badland) by Native Americans, but the landscape is more secretive than bad – those geologic formations protect a motherlode of fossils. Above ground, buffalo roam the park's mixed-grass prairie.

DON'T MISS

- Ben Reifel Visitor Center
- Badlands Loop Rd
- Big Badlands Overlook
- Notch Trail
- Hay Butte Overlook
- Sheep Mountain Table

Park Overview

For those in a rush, the North Unit of the park is easily viewed on a one-hour drive along the **Badlands Loop Rd (Hwy 240)**. If you have an extra hour, however, several short hiking trails along the route will sling you right into the earthen wonderland here.

The park sprawls across grasslands south of I-90. The Pinnacles Entrance can be reached from exit 110, which is also the Wall Drug exit. You can access the Northeast Entrance from

PRACTICALITIES

● nps.gov/badl ● admission $15–30 for 7-day pass ● park open 24hrs ● visitor center hours vary

exit 131. The park's less accessible South Unit, also known as the Stronghold Unit, is on the **Pine Ridge Indian Reservation** and sees fewer visitors.

The **Ben Reifel Visitor Center** *(8am-5pm May-Aug, 9am-4pm Sep-Apr)* is located just south of the Northeast Entrance and is open year-round. Spend time here to check out the good exhibits. Don't miss the on-site **paleontology lab** *(mid-Jun–mid-Sep)* where you can watch staff prepare fossils. The **White River Visitor Center** is a small summer-only information outlet in the Stronghold Unit.

Badlands Loop Rd (Hwy 240)

The 39-mile Badlands Loop Rd stretches from the town of Cactus Flat west to the town of Wall, curving into the North Unit along a narrow ridge of rock formations known as the Badlands Wall. Carved by the White River, the wall separates the upper (to the north) and lower prairie. There are 12 overlooks and picnic areas along the way. For the best lighting and the most vibrant colors along the wall, make the drive before sunrise or sunset. The **Big Badlands Overlook** just south of the northeast entrance is particularly pretty at dawn.

Sage Creek Rim Road

This gravel road extends west from the Badlands Loop Rd, passing scenic overlooks and prairie-dog towns. Seeing buffalo is also a possibility. This drive is less traveled than the Badlands Loop Rd, and it is where most backcountry hikers and campers go to escape the crowds. There is almost no water or shade here, so don't strike out into the wilderness unprepared. For a quick introduction to scenery along the road, pull off at **Hay Butte Overlook** just west of the Badlands Loop Rd.

Hiking

Several short trails shoot into the badlands north of the Ben Reifel Visitor Center. The surreal **Door Trail** and its boardwalk lead to a scenic gap in the Badlands Wall. Take sunrise photos here. The **Notch Trail** twists through a canyon, scampers up a wooden ladder then curves along a crumbly ridge line to an expansive view of grasslands and more serrated walls. Both trailheads are accessed from the same parking lot.

Lodging & Camping

The cosy cabins at **Cedar Pass Lodge** *(mid-Apr–mid-Oct)* have air-conditioning, heat, microwaves and mini-fridges. The onsite restaurant serves breakfast, lunch and dinner. **Cedar Pass RV & Campground** *(late Mar–mid-Oct; campsites $37-47)* is the most popular place to pitch a tent in the park. Open year-round, **Sage Creek Campground** is primitive but also popular. Campsites are free.

SHEEP MOUNTAIN TABLE

For solitude and spectacular views of sweeping badlands, drive to **Sheep Mountain Table**, a plateau on the border of the North and South Units. The unpaved road to the overlook here is ideally tackled in a 4WD vehicle, but it shouldn't be too bad if the weather has been clear. The road beyond the overlook, however, is appropriate for 4WD and high-clearance vehicles only, but you can walk along the table from the overlook and soak up the otherworldly views.

TOP TIPS

- Hwy 44, which bisects the North and South Units, is a scenic route linking the Badlands and Rapid City. If you have extra time, take it to soak up the views and to avoid I-90.
- Keep at least 100ft from wildlife in the park. The animals may look approachable, but if they notice you, you are definitely too close.
- The park recommends two quarts of water per person for a two-hour hike.
- Do not collect fossils, plants, rocks or artifacts while exploring the park.

TOP EXPERIENCE

Wind Cave National Park

Home to the sixth-largest cave system in the world, Wind Cave is a sprawling treasure. But its wonders are not confined to its subterranean passages. It is also a haven for wildlife in the grasslands and forests south of Custer State Park. The namesake cave is laced with 167 miles of mapped passages. Cave tours, hikes and scenic drives are the primary activities.

CHERI ALGUIRE/SHUTTERSTOCK

TOP TIPS

- Reserve your tour before your visit. Tours are extremely popular and do sell out. You can book 30 days ahead.
- If you wing it, plan to arrive before the visitor center opens to join the line waiting to nab a ticket, particularly from March through October.

Boxwork Formations

The cave's foremost feature is its collection of 'boxwork' calcite formations – 95% of all that are known to exist are here. The boxwork looks like honeycomb and dates back 60 to 100 million years.

Cave Tours

Three tours are offered year round: the easy Garden of Eden Tour, the family-friendly Natural Entrance Tour, and the strenuous Fairgrounds Tour. The unique boxwork formations can be seen on all three. The Candlelight Tour and the Wild Cave Tour are available from June through early August. Expect a lot of crawling on the Wild Cave Tour, and be aware that you will have to wriggle through a space that is 10 inches high and 3ft wide! The 30-minute Accessibility Tour is open to visitors in wheelchairs.

PRACTICALITIES

- nps.gov/wica
- open 24hr, tour times vary
- free admission
- tours $7-$17 at recreation.gov

Hiking & Camping

More than 30 miles of trails navigate the grasslands and ponderosa pines that blanket the park. Keep watch for bison, elk, pronghorns and prairie dogs as you walk. The southern end of the 111-mile **Centennial Trail**, which links to Bear Butte State Park, begins on Hwy 87 north of the visitor center. Tucked in the pines beside the prairie, **Elk Mountain Campground** has 62 reservable spaces *($12–24 per site)*; backcountry camping *(free with permit)* is allowed in limited areas.

Continued from p199

For a fantastic meal, drive south from the park into downtown and take a seat at **MB Haskett Delicatessen** *(mbhaskett.com; hours vary)*. This retro cafe serves brilliant food throughout the day.

Scramble over quartzite at Palisades State Park

Ancient quartzite formations soar above Split Rock Creek at **Palisades State Park** (*gfp.sd.gov, vehicle $10-15*), a compact state park on the prairie about 20 miles northeast of Sioux Falls. As your kids clamber at the base of the quartzite, you might see experienced climbers rappeling down the face of a nearby cliff. And geologists take note: the quartzite here is 1.2 billion years old! Swimming is allowed, but no jumping from the rocks.

Roadside attractions between Sioux Falls and Wall Drug

Roadside attractions along I-90 keep boredom at bay as you cruise west across South Dakota.

First up is the cavernous **Corn Palace** (*cornpalace.com; free*) in Mitchell. Close to 300,000 ears of corn are used annually to create new murals on the outside of the building. Head inside to learn how the facade has evolved since its creation in 1892. And please, don't eat the murals – fresh popcorn is for sale inside if you're hungry.

Continue 70 miles to the bluff-top **Lewis & Clark Interpretive Center** and rest area near exit 263 south of Chamberlain. There are worthwhile exhibits here about the intrepid duo and their voyages on the Missouri River below, but the highlight is the staggering **Dignity: of Earth & Sky** statue. Framed by sky and prairie, this 50ft-tall rendering of a Sioux woman – her magnificent quilt held against the wind – honors the Lakota and Dakota tribes. The diamond-shaped LED lights in her quilt sparkle at night.

HELLO SIOUX FALLS!

Parked in the southeastern corner of South Dakota, the state's largest city lives up to its name at **Falls Park** (p199), where the Big Sioux River plunges through a long series of rock faces. Just south lies a buzzing downtown district with a burgeoning foodie scene and some of the best eats in the region. You'll find more than 80 outdoor sculptures along downtown's **SculptureWalk**. Park on S Phillips Ave to start your explorations. Several hotel chains cluster downtown near the river while a slightly cheaper collection of accommodations line I-29 and I-229.

BEST SCENIC DRIVES IN SOUTHERN SOUTH DAKOTA

Spearfish Canyon Scenic Byway: Dotted with waterfalls, this curvaceous 20-mile road (US 14A) cleaves into the heart of the hills from Spearfish.

Iron Mountain Rd: Enjoy a 16-mile roller coaster of wooden bridges, tight turns, narrow tunnels and stunning vistas. Drive it north for views of Mt Rushmore.

Needles Hwy: This 14-mile drive twists past granite spires, pine trees, aspens and beautiful Sylvan Lake.

Wildlife Loop Rd: You might see bison, prairie dogs and pronghorn on this 18-mile drive in Custer State Park.

Native American National and State Scenic Byway: Drive along the Missouri River, passing through tribal lands and prairies with a dramatic pause beside *Dignity: of Earth & Sky* (p203).

CHERI ALGUIRE/SHUTTERSTOCK

Hotel Alex Johnson

About 140 miles west, the 1909 **Prairie Homestead** and its outhouse sit just a few miles from a missile silo. It's a wild juxtaposition, highlighting the rapid development of US technology in the span of 60 years. The **Minuteman Missile National Historic Site** *(nps.gov/mimi)* holds one of 1000 Minutemen II intercontinental ballistic missiles housed across the Great Plains during the Cold War (and now retired). The sod house and the Minuteman Missile site's visitor center are reached from exit 131. Tours of the Delta-01 Minuteman Missile Launch Facility *(tours adult/child $12/8)* begin off exit 127.

Shimmering mineral deposits await at Badlands National Park (p200) at exit 131. And then, at exit 110, there it is, after miles of signs: Wall Drug.

Wall

Get lost at South Dakota's wackiest roadside attraction

Only a curmudgeon could ignore all the signs along I-90 encouraging drivers to stop at **Wall Drug** *(walldrug.com)*. Fortunately this warren of kitsch, which opened in 1931, does have a few worthwhile charms behind its Old West facade: 5¢ coffee, free ice water, good doughnuts, public restrooms and loads of diversions. Amid the fudge and knickknackery is a superb bookstore with great regional titles. There's also a store selling quality cowboy boots. Out back, ride the mythical jackalope and check out the historical photos. And yes, you can still buy aspirin in the drugstore.

Pine Ridge Reservation

Exploring Lakota history and culture

Home to the Oglala Lakota Sioux, the Pine Ridge Reservation sits within beautiful prairies and badlands south of Badlands National Park. Residents face systemic hardships, from crime to unemployment, and more than half the population lives below the poverty line.

Despite being at times a jarring dose of reality, it is also a place welcoming to visitors. Tune in to KILI (90.1FM), which often plays traditional music. For an introduction to the reservation, stop by the **Red Cloud Heritage Center** *(mahpiyaluta.org; free)*. This well-curated art museum has traditional and contemporary works, and a craft shop with locally made artisan goods. The center hosts the **Red Cloud Indian Art Show** from June to early August. It's 4 miles north of the town of Pine Ridge on Hwy 18.

It helps to read up on the history before you visit the **Wounded Knee Massacre Site**, 16 miles northeast of Pine Ridge town. The mass grave sits atop the hill near a church above the massacre site. Small memorials appear daily amid the stones listing dozens of names. You can park below the hill and walk up, or tackle the rutted road to the top in your car. It's a desolate place, with sweeping views. You may encounter locals selling jewelry as well as locals looking for donations. For more details about Wounded Knee, visit nearby **Oglala Lakota College Historical Center** *(olc.edu/about-olc/historical-center; 9am-5pm Mon-Fri; free)* or the **White River Visitor Center** (p201) at Badlands National Park.

Black Hills

Presidents, artwork and shopping in downtown

An appealing capital for the Black Hills region, **Rapid City** has a cosmopolitan air best appreciated in the lively downtown where well-preserved brick buildings, filled with quality shopping and dining, make 'Rapid' a good urban base. From a shifty-eyed Nixon to a triumphant Harry Truman, lifelike **statues of America's presidents** dot street corners throughout downtown. According to lore, they are 9/10s the size of their counterparts – so they all seem just a little too small. The info center on Main St is the current home of the Trump statue.

Out back, ponder the difference between graffiti and art on a stroll through colorful **Art Alley**. For more art, step into **Prairie Edge Trading Co & Galleries**, a three-story shop with a truly mesmerizing collection of art, furniture and home goods made by members of the Northern Plains tribes. You'll find books and art supplies here too. Just across the street is **Main Street Sq**, a pleasant place to relax amid sculptures and fountains. Pop into the grand lobby at the **Hotel Alex Johnson** for its hunt-lodge vibes. Pause by the wall of photos of former celebrity guests – we see you Jerry Seinfeld!

WHAT ARE THE BLACK HILLS?

They call the Black Hills an evergreen island in a sea of high-prairie grassland. This stunning region on the Wyoming–South Dakota border lures scores of visitors with its winding canyons and wildly eroded 7000ft peaks. The region's name – the 'Black' comes from the dark ponderosa pine-covered slopes – was conferred by the Lakota Sioux. In the 1868 Fort Laramie Treaty, they were assured that the hills would be theirs for eternity, but the discovery of gold changed that and the Sioux were shoved out to low-value flatlands six years later. The 1990 film *Dances with Wolves* covers some of this period. You'll need several days to explore the byways, caves, bison herds, forests, Deadwood, and Mt Rushmore and Crazy Horse monuments.

EATING & DRINKING IN DOWNTOWN RAPID CITY: OUR PICKS

Sour: Nationally acclaimed, this slick bakery serves delicious breads and pastries, with a few daily sandwiches. *7am-2pm Wed-Sun* $

Harriet & Oak: Top-notch bakery, cafe and coffee bar with fun boho vibe. Creative sandwiches too and good draft microbrews. *7am-4pm Tue-Sat, 8am-2pm Sun* $

Tally's Silver Spoon: Savor upscale diner fare at this chic cafe and bar. Breakfasts are good; creative regional fare served nightly. *7am-2pm, 4-9pm* $$

Independent Ale House: Changing lineup of the best microbrews from the region served at the 'Indie' and its vintage-style bar. *11am-9pm most nights*

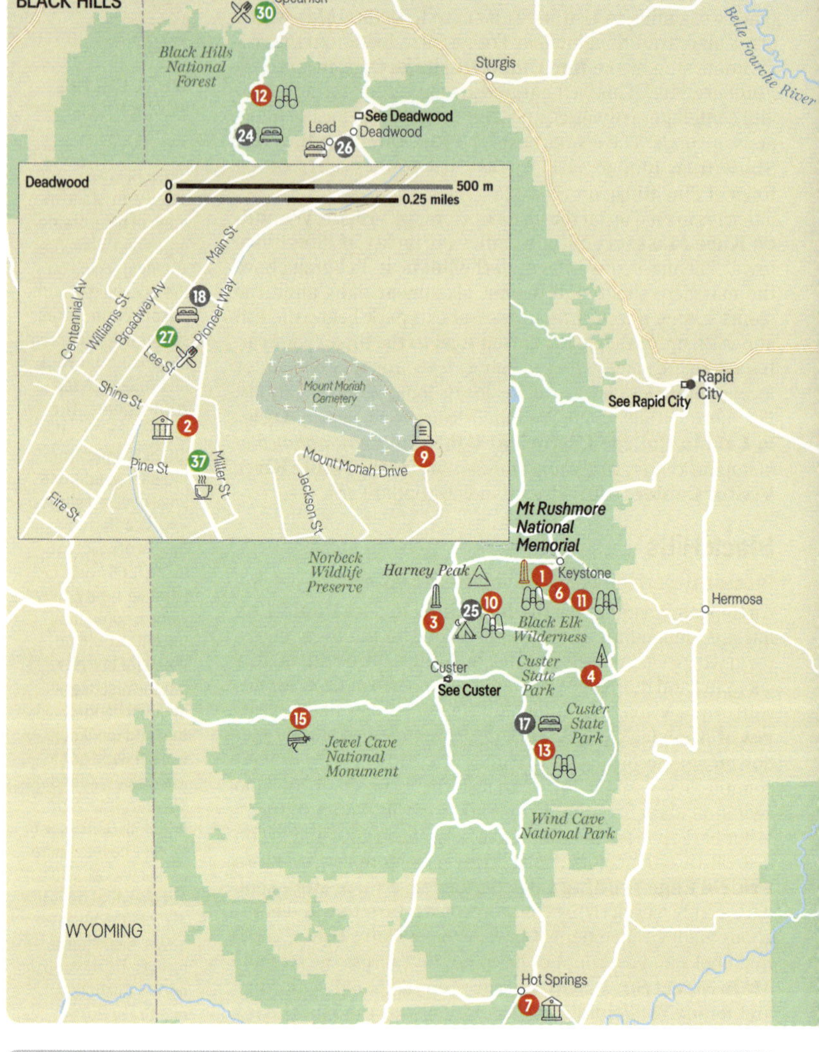

HIGHLIGHTS
1 Mt Rushmore National Memorial

SIGHTS
2 Adams Museum
3 Crazy Horse Memorial
4 Custer State Park
5 Hay Butte Overlook
6 Iron Mountain Rd
7 Mammoth Site
8 Minuteman Missile National Historic Site
9 Mount Moriah Cemetery
10 Needles Hwy
11 Peter Norbeck Scenic Byway
12 Spearfish Canyon Scenic Byway
13 Wildlife Loop Rd

ACTIVITIES
14 Door Trail
15 Jewel Cave National Monument
16 Notch Trail

SLEEPING
17 Blue Bell Lodge
18 Bullock Hotel
19 Cedar Pass Campground
20 Cedar Pass Lodge
21 Hotel Alex Johnson
22 Rocket Motel
23 Sage Creek Campground
24 Spearfish Canyon Lodge
25 Sylvan Lake Campground
26 Town Hall Inn

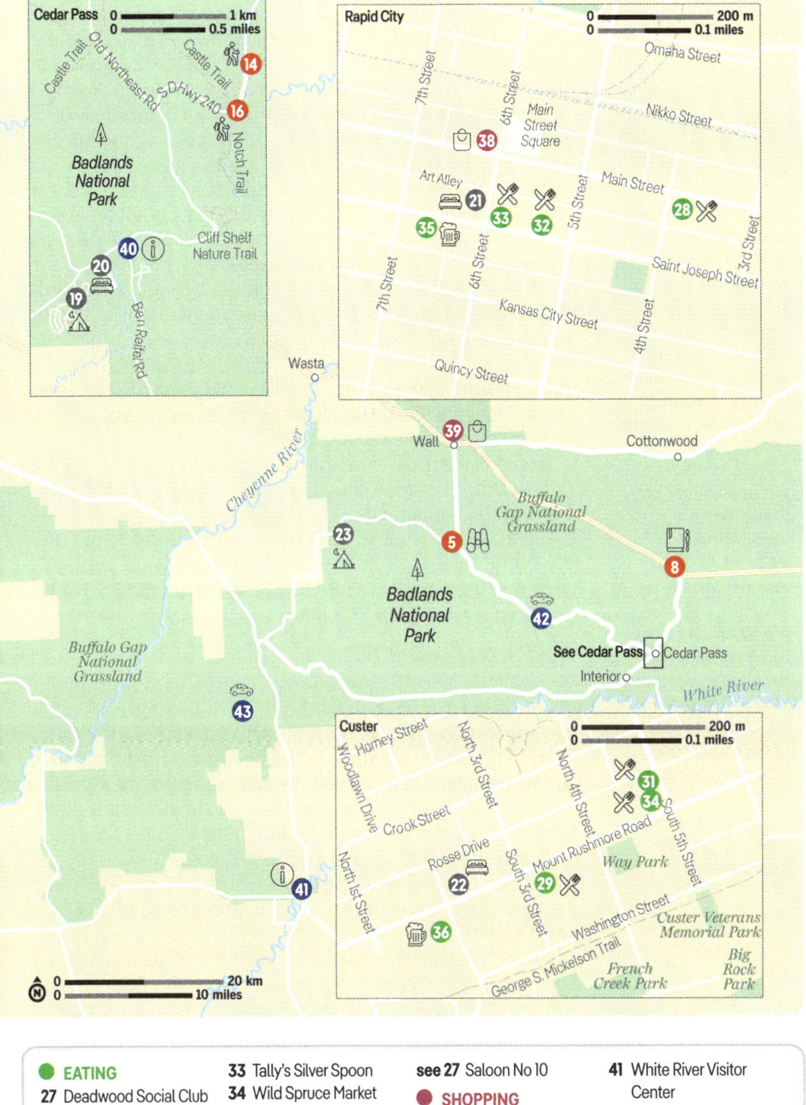

EATING
27 Deadwood Social Club
28 Harriet & Oak
29 Hjem AM
30 Killian's
31 Skogen Kitchen
32 Sour
33 Tally's Silver Spoon
34 Wild Spruce Market

DRINKING & NIGHTLIFE
35 Independent Ale House
36 Mt Rushmore Brewing Co
37 Pump House
see 27 Saloon No 10

SHOPPING
38 Prairie Edge
39 Wall Drug

INFORMATION
40 Ben Reifel Visitor Center
41 White River Visitor Center

TRANSPORT
42 Hwy 240 Badlands Loop Rd
43 Sheep Mountain Table

THE STORY OF WOUNDED KNEE

In 1890 the new Ghost Dance religion became popular and Lakota followers believed it would both bring back their ancestors and eliminate the white man. This struck fear into the area's soldiers and settlers, and the frenetic circle dances were outlawed. The 7th US Cavalry rounded up a band of Lakota people under Chief Big Foot and brought them to the small village of Wounded Knee.

On December 29, as the soldiers began to search for weapons, a shot was fired (nobody knows by whom), leading to the massacre of more than 250 men, women and children, most of them unarmed. It's one of the most infamous atrocities in US history. Twenty-five soldiers also died.

Admire presidential rockstars at Mt Rushmore

Glimpses of Washington's nose from the roads leading to this popular **monument** *(nps.gov/moru, parking $10)* never cease to surprise, and they are but harbingers of the full impact of this mountainside sculpture once you're up close (and past the dreary parking area). George Washington, Thomas Jefferson, Abraham Lincoln and Theodore Roosevelt each iconically stare into the distance in 60ft-tall granite glory.

Despite the crowds, there is something inspirational about the **Avenue of Flags**. Lined with the flags of all 50 states plus six districts and territories, this corridor of patriotism frames the presidents quite photogenically. If crowds are too thick, you can escape the hoopla on the 0.6-mile **Presidential Trail**. On this loop you can pause between the pines, in relative peace, to marvel at the artistry of sculptor Gutzon Borglum and the immense labor of the workers who created the memorial between 1927 and 1941. The trail also accesses the worthwhile **Sculptor's Studio**, which conveys the drama of how the monument came to be.

The official Park Service information centers have excellent bookstores. The main museum shares the story of the creation of the monument.

Mt Rushmore is a half-hour drive southwest of Rapid City via US 16. For rock-framed views of the presidents, approach via Iron Mountain Rd . The Crazy Horse Memorial is 16 miles south via Hwy 244 and US 365.

See the Crazy Horse Memorial

The world's largest **monument** *(crazyhorsememorial.org; $15-35 admission)* is this 563ft-tall work-in-progress (with a lot of work to go). When finished it will depict the Sioux leader astride his horse, pointing to the horizon saying, 'My lands are where my dead lie buried.' No one is predicting when the sculpture will be complete (the face was dedicated in 1998). Although you can see the mountain in the distance, you need to pay another $5 for a van ride to get close.

The memorial is a huge tourist draw, attracting more than one million visitors annually, but a trip here can feel underwhelming. Exhibits about Native Americans can seem haphazard and are often poorly contextualized. The focus of the place seems to be more on its Polish-American sculptor Korczak Ziolkowski and his family than the Lakota. For these reasons and others, the sculpture has drawn controversy (p210).

A scenic drive through the Black Hills

Driving the **Peter Norbeck Scenic Byway** is like flirting with a brand new crush: always exhilarating, occasionally challenging and sometimes you get a few butterflies. Named for the South Dakota senator who pushed for its creation in 1919, the oval-shaped byway is broken into four roads linking memorable destinations in the Black Hills.

Iron Mountain Rd (Hwy 16A) is the most diverse of the four, beloved for its pig-tailing loops, Mt Rushmore–framing tunnels and one gorgeous glide through sun-dappled pines. Tackle it early to avoid caravans of cars. The 14-mile **Needles**

Bison, Custer State Park

Hwy (Hwy 87) swoops below majestic granite spires, careens past rocky overlooks and slings through a super-narrow tunnel. The other two roads within the byway are Hwys 244 and 89.

And remember, there's no right way to drive the Black Hills, and the beauty of the place is evident no matter the byway. But there can be lots of traffic, and it can be confusing figuring out where you are when driving between sites – mostly on twisty two-lane roads with intermittent cell service. Plot out your route the night before, and note that splitting your time over two or three days is better than cramming everything into one frenzied day.

Driving times are often much longer than expected due to slow-moving traffic. RV drivers: visit *custerresorts.com* for tunnel measurements.

Wildlife-watching in Custer State Park

Your first animal sighting in **Custer State Park** *(gfp.sd.gov/parks; 7-day vehicle pass $25)* will likely be a white-tailed deer loping through the ponderosa pines that blanket the surrounding Black Hills. But soon after you turn onto the 18-mile **Wildlife Loop Rd** (p194), which swoops over untouched grasslands, the animal sightings grow thrillingly diverse. Watch bison lumber beside the road. Squint at pronghorns in

SOUTH DAKOTA'S TRIBAL NATIONS

There are nine Native American tribes in South Dakota. Their members constitute 15% of the state's population, and their tribal lands, or reservations, are scattered across tallgrass prairie, rolling grasslands, pine-dotted hills and remote badlands. The US government named the Lakota tribe the Sioux in 1825, and this term has come to apply to the Lakota, Dakota and Nakota peoples and their various bands.

Learn more at the engaging **Akta Lakota Museum & Cultural Center** at St Joseph's Indian School in Chamberlain. Visitors are welcome on reservations but should always ask for permission before taking photos, sketching or making audio and video recordings. Do not remove artifacts or disturb devotional sites.

EATING & DRINKING IN CUSTER: OUR PICKS

Skogen Kitchen: A James Beard nominee; a delicious global menu with luxury toppings like morels, caviar and sprinkles of pretension. *5-8:30pm Tue-Sat* **$$$**

Wild Spruce Market: Gourmet market with dips, specialty cheeses, produce and local bison beef. Buy drinks at the coffee and beer bar. *8:30am-6pm most days* **$**

HJEM AM: From the folks behind Skogen, HJEM serves decadent gourmet breakfasts. Reservations recommended. *8am-11am Wed-Fri, to noon Sat & Sun* **$$**

Mt Rushmore Brewing Co: The Rail Splitter Porter and other flagship beers give a nod to American history at this complex with two fine-dining restaurants. *11am-9pm*

CRAZY HORSE MEMORIAL REVISITED

Never photographed or persuaded to sign a meaningless treaty, Crazy Horse was chosen for a monument (p208) that Lakota Sioux elders hoped would balance the presidential focus of Mt Rushmore 16 miles north. In 1948 a Boston-born sculptor, Korczak Ziolkowski, started blasting granite. His family has continued the work since his death in 1982, and the monument has indeed become a counterpoint to Mt Rushmore.

On the flip side, some Lakota oppose the monument as a desecration of sacred land. Other concerns include the introductory film at the visitor center, which spotlights the Ziolkowski family with seemingly less emphasis on the stories of the Lakota. Native American exhibits and artifacts in the museums may be in need of better organization.

the misty distance. And listen for the 'chirps' of prairie dogs as they scamper between burrows.

To put it succinctly, this place is wonderful. The only reason this 111-sq-mile state park isn't a national park is that the state grabbed it first. What's here? One of the largest free-roaming bison herds in the world (about 1450) as well as elk, bighorn sheep, the famous 'begging burros' (donkeys seeking handouts) and more than 200 bird species.

Pick up the free Tatanka visitor guide at the entrance station for details about hiking, fishing and camping. It also includes a list of the park's daily programs. Don't miss the new **Bison Center**, where large video screens envelope you in the sights and sounds of a buffalo stampede. The corrals for the annual **buffalo round-up** are steps away. Another highlight is boulder-flanked **Sylvan Lake**; admire it from the Sylvan Lakeshore Trail.

Lodging options rival those of national parks. We're fond of the cabins and modern-rustic style of **Blue Bell Lodge**.

Admire rare underground crystals

If you visit only one Black Hills cave, **Jewel Cave** *(nps.gov/jeca; tours $6-45)* would be a good choice. It's 13 miles west of Custer and is so named because colorful calcite crystals line many of its walls. More than 200 miles have been surveyed (about 3% of the passageway), making it the third-longest known cave in the world.

You can only enter the cave on guided tours. One unique option is the **Historic Lantern Tour**; your path is illuminated by handheld lanterns. Tours can be reserved 30 days in advance at *recreation.gov*. To avoid disappointment, advance reservations are highly recommended.

Mammoth-bone bonanza

Kids who love fossils – and anyone who thinks paleontology is cool – will 'dig' the **Mammoth Site** *(mammothsite.com; adult/child $15/12)* in the town of Hot Springs. About 26,000 years ago, hundreds of animals perished in a sinkhole here. Today you can walk around their exposed tusks and bones, which were discovered during a construction project in 1974. So far 61 mammoths – two woolly, 59 Columbian – have been found. The site is the largest left-as-found mammoth fossil display in the country and an active dig.

The self-guided tour around the bone bed pauses by a lab where assistants are happy to answer your questions. Bones of a dire wolf and giant sloth are displayed in the adjacent Great Hall.

Hot Springs is about 60 miles south of Rapid City.

Relaxing in hot springs

Empty your water bottles before heading into Hot Springs, an unhurried town south of the main Black Hills circuit. The big natural attraction here is the warm mineral springs feeding the Fall River. You can relax weary muscles in one of six outdoor pools at the stylish **Moccasin Springs Natural Mineral Spa** *(moccasinsprings.com; 2hr soak pass $31.80)*, where the water temperature ranges from 80 to 105 degrees. The onsite **Dragonfly** restaurant serves salads, sandwiches and shareable nibbles.

The best water you'll drink in the Black Hills flows freely from Kidney Springs, just down the road from Moccasin Springs. It's not cold, but it's also not so hot you'll regret it on a sultry day. An old gazebo marks the spot along the pretty Hot Springs River Walk, across the narrow Fall River from the heart of town. Fill up your water bottles at the faucet. And you might want to stick around – downtown is home to ornate 1890s red sandstone buildings that glow at sunset.

Deadwood

Step into the past

Settled illegally by gold rushers in the 1870s, Deadwood is now a National Historic Landmark. Its atmospheric streets are lined with gold-rush-era buildings lavishly restored with gambling dollars. The lyrically foul-mouthed *Deadwood* HBO series and subsequent 2019 movie brought celebrity status.

You'll likely be greeted by a docent when stepping into the refreshingly quirky **Adams Museum** *(deadwoodhistory.com; suggested donation adult/child $5/3)*, home to artifacts including a two-headed calf and a big lumpy gold nugget. These exhibits are part of a larger cabinet of curiosities originally curated by pioneer businessman WE Adams in the 1930s.

For more Wild West history, stroll casino-lined Historic Main Street. Don't miss **Saloon No 10** *(saloon10.com)*, where stuffed game and old photographs recall rowdier days. Wild Bill Hickok was shot and killed while playing cards at the bar's original location across the street. Fans of *Deadwood* will recall the conflicted but upstanding sheriff Seth Bullock. He opened the **Bullock Hotel** *(historicbullock.com)* in 1895, and this creaky place still welcomes guests – and maybe a few ghosts.

A short but steep drive climbs from downtown to **Mount Moriah Cemetery** *(cityofdeadwood.com; admission $2; cash only)*, where Calamity Jane, Wild Bill and Potato Creek Johnny, a colorful prospector, rest side by side.

WIND CAVE OR JEWEL CAVE?

Um, excuse me. A cave is not just a cave, and if you've seen one, you certainly have not seen them all. One problem for travelers in the Black Hills is that two extended cave systems, both managed by the federal park service, are open for tours. How to pick?

It's win-win. Jewel Cave is a 'wet' limestone cave filled with classic formations like stalactites and stalagmites. It also has sparkling calcite crystals clustered into unusual shapes. Wind Cave (p202) is a 'dry' cave with fewer of these classic favorites. Wind Cave does, however, hold 95% of the world's known boxwork, which is a rare, honeycomb patterned calcite. Wind Cave also has outdoor hiking trails.

EATING & DRINKING AROUND DEADWOOD: OUR PICKS

Deadwood Social Club: In the historic Saloon No 10 in Deadwood, this busy restaurant offers crowd-pleasing Italian fare plus steaks. *hours vary Mon-Sat* $$

Saloon No 10: Legendary bar in Deadwood with dark walls, sawdust floors and knickknackery galore. *9am-2am*

Pump House: Drink a cup of locally roasted coffee or craft beer in this old Texaco gas station in Deadwood. Good sandwiches too. *7am-5pm*

Killian's: Enjoy a gouda jalapeño burger or ahi club in Spearfish before driving the Spearfish Canyon Scenic Byway. Vegan options. *11am-10pm Sun-Wed, to 11pm Fri & Sat* $$

Places We Love to Stay

$ Budget $$ Midrange $$$ Top End

St Louis

MAP P146

Angad Arts Hotel $$ The art-filled rooms are eye candy, as are the expansive views from the rooftop bar.

St Louis Union Station Hotel $$ The hotel lobby bar is tops, set in the 1894 barrel-vaulted train station. Good downtown location, but rooms could use a refresh.

21c Museum Hotel $$$ Our favorite hotel in St Louis has taken over a 1920s YMCA, filling it with plush rooms and an art gallery partly in the old basketball court.

Kansas City

Crossroads Hotel $$ Hip hotel with comfy rooms, excellent rooftop and lobby bars, a walkable location and an inventive Italian restaurant on the ground floor.

Hotel Kansas City $$ This downtown Gothic Revival stunner feels just as sleek as when it opened as a private members' club in the 1920s.

Truitt $$ Feel right at home at one of KC's few locally owned accommodation options. This stately 1916 converted mansion has just eight uniquely decorated rooms near the Nelson-Atkins (p151).

Branson

Ozarker Lodge $$ This reinvented roadside motel has mid-mod touches, cedar soaking tubs overlooking a creek and firepits for s'more roasting.

Tulsa

MAP P167

Campbell Hotel $ Restored to its 1927-era Route 66 splendor, this historic hotel east of downtown has 26 rooms with hardwood floors and oversized furniture.

Mayo Hotel $$ When this hotel, once Oklahoma's tallest building, opened in 1925, it was the height of luxury, and it's still one of Tulsa's top stays. Excellent choice for art deco architecture admirers.

Oklahoma City

MAP P171

Classen Inn $ Well-priced mid-century motel near downtown that's had a mod makeover.

Bradford House $$ Built in 1912 as a luxury apartment house, it's now a boutique hotel with eccentric interior design and modern, comfortable rooms.

The National $$$ Our favorite historic stay in the region is in this 1930s bank. Have a drink in the gasp-worthy lobby bar in the former banking hall with marble floors, columns and huge murals.

Omaha

Kimpton Cottonwood Hotel $$ Built as a hotel in 1915 and reimagined for modern travelers. Fantastic pool area and a knock-out **steakhouse** (p178).

Hotel Deco $$ Alice in Wonderland meets art deco detailing in this 14-story 1930s building within walking distance of the Old Market. Once you've settled into your room, track down the Wicked Rabbit, the hotel's speakeasy.

Hotel Indigo $$$ The bold accents and mismatched prints hint at the quirky personality of this modern hotel in a beautiful historic brick building downtown.

Lincoln

Kindler Hotel $$ The capital city's first indie boutique hotel is this downtown gem within walking distance of the historic Haymarket district.

Graduate by Hilton $$ Your college years never go out of fashion at this retro kitsch hotel that caters to the permanent student in every grad. It has a tiki bar, old-school pinball machines in the lobby and eclectic room decor that's part luxe, part rumpus room.

Dubuque & Around

MAP P187

Maquoketa Caves State Park Campground $ Camp beneath the pines near caves and trails at this family friendly spot between Dubuque and Davenport.

Hotel Julien $$ Built in 1915, this spiffy eight-story hotel in Dubuque was once a refuge for Al Capone. Some rooms have Mississippi River views.

Amana Colonies

MAP P187

Hotel Millwright (p189) $$ Decor inside this historic woolen mill gives a nod to the textile industry. Rooms have smart, contemporary appeal.

Des Moines

MAP P191

Hotel Fort Des Moines $$ A storied haunt for 20th-century powerbrokers and celebrities, this revamped number celebrates its roots with modern style.

Des Lux Hotel $$$ Luxurious downtown hotel with 51 rooms and loads of eclectic modern touches. A lavish hot breakfast is included.

Mason City

Historic Park Inn Hotel (p193) $$ Sleep inside a work of art at the only remaining hotel designed by Frank Lloyd Wright. Beside a lovely downtown square.

North Dakota

Juniper Campground (p196) $ Sites are first come, first served at this pleasant campground set beneath junipers in Theodore Roosevelt National Park's wildlife-filled North Unit.

Rough Riders Hotel $$ Old West meets New West at this upscale lodge in Medora, near the South Unit of Theodore Roosevelt National Park. Each room comes with a Teddy bear.

Hotel Donaldson $$ Well-appointed rooms are each decorated by a regional artist. In Fargo; don't miss the rooftop Sky Prairie for cocktails with a city view.

Sioux Falls & Around

King Campground (p159) $ Northeast of Sioux Falls, this new campground in Palisades State Park sprawls across a scenic plain close to trails, a creek and cool quartzite formations.

Black Hills

MAP P206

Sylvan Lake Campground $ All of the campgrounds in Custer State Park are recommended, but this one is set in the forest a short walk from a uniquely gorgeous rock-fringed lake.

Rocket Motel $ The neon sign is a jaunty welcome to this old-style motor court – a 'blast' from the past! – in Custer. Located in the center of town and well maintained.

Town Hall Inn $ Near Deadwood in Lead, this 12-room inn occupies the 1912 Town Hall and has spacious suites named and themed for their former governmental purpose.

Spearfish Canyon Lodge $$ Along a scenic byway, this Black Hills retreat sits near trails, streams and waterfalls in a gorgeous setting. Modern pine-y rooms are cozy.

Hotel Alex Johnson (p205) $$$ The design of this 1927 classic in Rapid City magically blends Germanic Tudor architecture with traditional Lakota Sioux symbols.

Blue Bell Lodge (p210) $$$ Chic cabins, ponderosa pines and buffalo stomping grounds in Custer State Park. Restaurant on-site and horseback trail rides nearby.

MICHAEL GORDON/SHUTTERSTOCK

Rough Riders Hotel

TOOLKIT

The chapters in this section cover the most important topics you'll need to know about in Midwest USA. They're full of nuts-and-bolts information and valuable insights to help you understand and navigate Midwest USA and get the most out of your trip.

The Loop, Chicago (p54)

Arriving

The largest city in the Midwest, Chicago is a hub for travel for both airlines and long-distance Amtrak trains. Chicago's airports, O'Hare (ORD) and Midway (MDW), are bases for United *(united.com)* and American *(aa.com)*, as well as low-cost carriers Frontier *(flyfrontier.com)* and Spirit *(spirit.com)*. Other major airports in the Midwest include Minneapolis–St Paul (MSP) and Detroit (DTW).

Visas

Citizens of many countries are eligible for the Visa Waiver Program, which requires prior approval via the Electronic System for Travel Authorization (ESTA). Fill out the online form at least 72 hours before departure.

ATMs

Choose wisely when selecting an ATM at the airport. It's better to go with machines linked to a bank rather than currency-exchange ATMs, which tend to charge higher fees.

Wi-Fi

All major airports provide free wi-fi, but long-distance Amtrak trains do not. Hotels, restaurants, cafes and public libraries have free wi-fi, and some cities and towns offer free public wi-fi hotspots.

SIM Cards

Major airports have stores and vending machines that sell SIM cards for travelers. Verizon and T-Mobile have the largest networks; Verizon tends to have the best coverage in rural areas.

Transportation from the Airport

	Chicago O'Hare (ORD)	Chicago Midway (MDW)	Minneapolis –St Paul (MSP)
PUBLIC TRANSIT	$5	$2.50	$2.50
UBER/ TAXI	$50	$35	$30
SHUTTLE	$25	$15	n/a

BRINGING ITEMS INTO THE USA

The US has fairly strict rules regarding what you can bring into the country, so plan carefully before you travel. In general, you're not allowed to bring agricultural products (food, vegetables, plants) into the country. Bakery items and prepared foods (coffee, tea, honey) are permitted. You can bring in 1L of alcohol for personal use (unless you're under 21). Although recreational or medical marijuana is legal in some Midwest states, it is illegal to bring marijuana and cannabis-infused products into the US. The exception is CBD oil with less than 0.3% THC on a dry weight basis.

FROM LEFT: FUSE/GETTY IMAGES, GOGLIK83/GETTY IMAGES

Getting Around

The car is king in the Midwest, especially for covering long distances. Outside of Chicago, relying on public transportation to get around can be challenging.

TRAVEL COSTS

Chicago transit fare
$2.50

Car rental
$40 per day

Gas
from $3 per gallon

Chicago to Kansas City flight
from $220

Road-Tripping

The Midwest is all about wide-open spaces, and taking a road trip (p36) is the best way to transport yourself. Car rentals are easily available at airports. Road conditions around the region are generally good. Federal and state highways tend to be more scenic than the interstates, but most are two lanes, so you might get stuck behind slow-moving semis or farm equipment.

Public Transit

Chicago has the most comprehensive public transportation network, and a few cities, such as Minneapolis and St Louis, have light-rail systems. More places are investing in modern streetcars to make it easier to get around downtowns and surrounding areas, including a network expansion in Kansas City set to open in late 2025 and a new system in Omaha slated to start operations in 2028.

TIP

Payment is required to park downtown in most Midwest cities. Some use apps like ParkMobile *(parkmobile.io)*, but others still require feeding a meter with change.

TOLL ROADS

It costs to drive on sections of the Midwest's interstates – particularly around Chicago, part of I-35 through Kansas and I-44 in Oklahoma. Tolls are now generally paid online by license plate. Get discounts on tolls by requesting a free transponder pass, such as I-Pass, E-ZPass, Pikepass or K-TAG, online in advance.

Amtrak Trains

Amtrak *(amtrak.com)* is the USA's only national passenger train service. Many medium- and long-distance routes branch out from Chicago, including to Minneapolis, Detroit, St Louis, Kansas City and Omaha. Trains are rarely the quickest, cheapest, timeliest or most convenient option, but they are a relaxing, social and scenic all-American experience.

Long-Distance Buses

Bus travel is cheaper than car rental, flying or taking the train. However, problems sometimes arise (late buses, breakdowns, troubled fellow passengers). Bus companies include Greyhound *(greyhound.com)*, FlixBus *(flixbus.com)*, Jefferson Lines *(jeffersonlines.com)* and Trailways *(trailways.com)*.

Flights

Chicago has good flight connections to cities across the Midwest, but other places in the region don't tend to have direct connections to one another. That means you'll often have a layover in Chicago or further afield, which can add a lot of time onto a trip. Driving – or in some cases, taking the train – is usually a better option for city-hopping.

DRIVING ESSENTIALS

Drive on the right

Speed limit is 30mph to 40mph on city roads and 55mph to 75mph on highways

.08
The blood alcohol limit is 0.08%

Money

CURRENCY: US DOLLAR ($)

Credit Cards vs Cash

Credit cards are widely accepted throughout the Midwest, and they are required for hotel reservations and car rentals. More restaurants and bars are starting to charge an additional fee of up to 4% to pay by card. Some restaurants and bars in rural areas remain steadfastly cash only.

Tipping

Tipping in the US is not optional, and 20% is the minimum standard amount in restaurants. Tip at least $1 per drink at a bar (or 20% for fancier cocktails). Tipping for hotel housekeeping and at counter-service cafes is a gray area, though many card payment terminals guilt you into it.

ATMs

ATMs are ubiquitous in towns and are also found in some cash-only bars. Most charge for withdrawals if you don't have the bank's card.

Sales Tax

Taxes vary by state, but add up to 10% to the sticker price of retail goods, prepared food and beverages. Additional taxes at hotels tack on 2% to 10.5%.

HOW MUCH FOR A...

Museum ticket
free–$35

State park day entry
free–$14

Chicago architecture boat tour
$56

Road toll
$1–18

HOW TO... Save Money

The Midwest is one of the cheaper regions of the country to visit, but the US economy has been a roller coaster since 2020. Cut expenses by using public transportation instead of driving where available and overnighting in smaller towns instead of big cities. Inexpensive state parks are a great way to immerse yourself in nature, and some museums and art galleries offer free admission.

MOBILE PAYMENTS

No card? No problem. Many shops, cafes and restaurants – and some transit systems – accept mobile payments such as Apple Pay and Google Pay, so you can pay by tapping your phone.

WHY GAS COSTS SO MUCH IN CHICAGO

If you've rented a car or driven to Chicago, you likely noticed gas prices spiked when you got to town. Chicago has the second-highest gas taxes in the US, adding about 85¢ to the price of every gallon. The price of gas in Chicago includes federal, state and local fuel taxes, fees and sales tax. Illinois is one of the few states that charges a sales tax on gasoline and on fuel taxes, effectively collecting taxes on taxes. Only drivers in California pay higher gas taxes.

Accommodations

Historic Hotels

Many Midwest cities are breathing new life into their formerly abandoned or industrialized urban cores, and sleek hotels in historic digs are helping to transform the scene. **The National** (p212) in downtown Oklahoma City is set in a grand 1930s bank, while Bottleworks Hotel in Indianapolis has taken over a former Coca-Cola bottling plant.

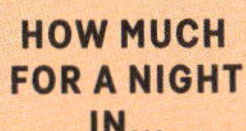

At Home in a B&B

In smaller towns and some major cities, intimate, family-run guesthouses are often contained in historic or architecturally interesting homes. Accommodations and amenities vary widely, from simple and rustic to luxurious (and prices range accordingly). Many B&Bs require a minimum stay of two or three nights during high season, and some places do not welcome children.

Camping Under the Stars

Camping options abound in state and national parks, and on privately owned land and farms. States and counties typically have their own reservation systems, while reservable campsites in national parks and forests can be booked up to six months in advance on recreation.gov. The most basic spots have portable toilets and no amenities beyond incredible views, while others have glamping options and pools.

Tracking Down Hostels

Hostels haven't ever had much of a foothold in the Midwest – or the US in general – and the few that were once open have started disappearing. Chicago still has a healthy collection, and some have survived in a few college towns around the Great Lakes.

HOW MUCH FOR A NIGHT IN...

a hotel
$150–400

a B&B
$150–250

a campsite
$20–50

Save Money in a Motel

Budget travelers in the Midwest often opt for motels. Many are generic, slightly dumpy chains along highway exits or on the outskirts of towns. Check online reviews carefully for safety and bed bug concerns. Some traditional motels are 1960s roadside classics that have been revamped from tired digs to kitsch-but-cool, neo-mid-century stays, particularly along Route 66.

HOUSE RENTALS & AIRBNBS

Across the Midwest, thousands of houses are available as short- and long-term rentals. Companies like Airbnb *(airbnb.com)* and Vrbo *(vrbo.com)* make it easy to find unique places to stay, but not everyone is thrilled with the rise of these platforms, which have taken long-term rentals intended for residents off the market and driven up housing prices in some places. Whether it's ethical to stay in Airbnb-type accommodations is a complicated question, but look for options that offer local experiences and stick more closely to the platform's original 'spare room' roots.

CLOCKWISE FROM TOP LEFT: XRISTOFOROV/SHUTTERSTOCK, LIUDMILA CHERNETSKA/GETTY IMAGES, SOMCHAI SOM/SHUTTERSTOCKK

Family Travel

The Midwest might be one of the most fun places in the world to be a kid, and it's a great place to simply slow down and enjoy time as a family. Epic zoos and plenty of parks and playgrounds let little ones unleash their inner animals, while dedicated children's museums are designed for endless adventures.

Fun by the Water

Pencil in water activities to keep everyone cool, especially during the scorching Midwest summer. Some large cities have huge water parks with mega-tall slides and lazy rivers, and even small towns have a local pool to cool off in. The Wisconsin Dells is a good choice, with more than 20 water parks, and Chicago, on the shores of Lake Michigan, has 22 beaches with summertime lifeguards.

Car Seats & Strollers

The Midwest's car-centric culture makes it easy for families to get around. Laws vary from state to state, but in general, children up to three years require federally approved car seats (rear-facing until one year old or 20lb). Children four to five years old need booster seats. Urban areas generally have decent sidewalks and are fine for strollers. Bathrooms with changing facilities are common, as are family bathrooms.

Family Discounts

Family admission to attractions across the Midwest is often discounted or in some cases is free for kids under a certain age. The definition of a 'child' varies, but usually means under 12 years old.

Kids' Menus

Kids' menus are common in chain restaurants and at many hotels, some of which allow children under 12 to dine for free (at least at breakfast) with a paying adult. Menu options typically include kid favorites, such as mac 'n' cheese and chicken nuggets.

BEST ATTRACTIONS FOR FAMILIES

City Museum, St Louis (p144)

A rooftop Ferris wheel and a 10-story slide at a former shoe warehouse.

Gathering Place, Tulsa (p168)

Voted one of the best parks in the country.

Omaha's Henry Doorly Zoo & Aquarium (p176)

The USA's favorite zoo boasts the world's largest indoor desert and much more.

Rabbit hOle, Kansas City (p153)

This artsy world brings children's literature to life.

Children's Museum of Indianapolis (p76)

The world's largest kids' museum.

BE A JUNIOR RANGER

Aimed at five to 12 year olds, the National Park Service's Junior Rangers program gets kids excited about natural history and the environment through a range of activities, typically presented in an activity book of questions and games that's available for free at visitor centers. Kids complete the activities in the booklet and then pledge to protect and respect national park lands. Afterward, they are rewarded with a special badge and the title of Junior Ranger. Some parks have a range of activities for younger vs older kids, as well as specialties such as nighttime stargazing, paleontology or sound exploration.

Health & Safe Travel

MEDICAL INSURANCE

International visitors should strongly consider buying travel insurance that includes medical coverage in the USA. Medical care and prescription drugs can be shockingly expensive, and emergency room visits without insurance can cost thousands of dollars. Travel insurance policies might also cover theft-related expenses, lost luggage or delayed travel. Read the fine print to ensure you understand what's covered.

Tornadoes

Tornadoes are common in the Midwest in spring and early summer. They can strike overnight and with little notice, so monitor weather alerts. A tornado watch means that conditions are such that a tornado is likely to occur, while a tornado warning means that an active tornado has been seen on the ground or indicated on radar.

Temperature Extremes

In summer, make sure you're prepared for heat and high humidity. Temperatures regularly shoot above 90°F. Nature spots in the Great Plains have few trees, and therefore little shade. In winter, dress for the bitter cold, layering clothing and wearing sturdy boots with solid traction in snow. Avoid driving in ice and snowstorms.

LEGAL MARIJUANA

Illinois, Michigan, Minnesota, Missouri and Ohio have legalized recreational marijuana. However, in neighboring states like Kansas and Iowa, it remains illegal.

COMMON POISONOUS PLANTS

Poison Ivy

Found in all Midwest states. Remember: 'leaves of three, leave it be'.

Poison Sumac

Lives in swampy clay soils around the Great Lakes states.

Poison Oak

Found in the southern states of the Great Plains.

Lyme Disease

Ticks (pictured, not to scale, typically the size of a sesame seed) are present in grasslands and wooded areas, so check yourself carefully after going outdoors. Some ticks carry the bacteria that cause Lyme disease, a potentially lifelong affliction of arthritis, body aches, fatigue and memory issues. Wear long pants and sleeves when outdoors, use bug repellent that contains DEET, and pre-treat outdoor clothing and gear with permethrin.

THOUSANDS WITHOUT HOMES

Despite billions spent annually to combat the country's homelessness crisis, the number of people living on the streets in the US continues to grow. Mental health issues, including substance abuse disorders, are major contributors to this issue. Other people are simply down on their luck, a side effect of the country's limited social safety net.

FROM LEFT: VALENTIN VALKOV/SHUTTERSTOCK, SARAH2/SHUTTERSTOCK

Food, Drink & Nightlife

When to Eat

Breakfast (7am to 10am) Ranges from on-the-go grub like bagels to pancakes and eggs at a diner.

Lunch (11:30am to 1:30pm) Often consists of one-item dishes such as a sandwich, burrito or burger.

Happy hour (4pm to 6pm) Some bars serve reduced-price snacks and drinks.

Dinner (5pm to 9pm) Typically heavier than lunch and often complemented with appetizers and desserts.

Where to Eat

Cafes and bakeries Open during the day, cafes are good for casual meals, sweet treats or coffee.

Food halls Typically six or more vendors offering a variety of diverse cuisines.

Food trucks Kitchens on wheels parked where hungry pedestrians are found; often at breweries.

Diners Breakfast all day, a menu of comfort foods and cozy vinyl booths.

Restaurants Have an excellent meal at a tiny neighborhood spot or indulge in an expensive Michelin-star tasting menu.

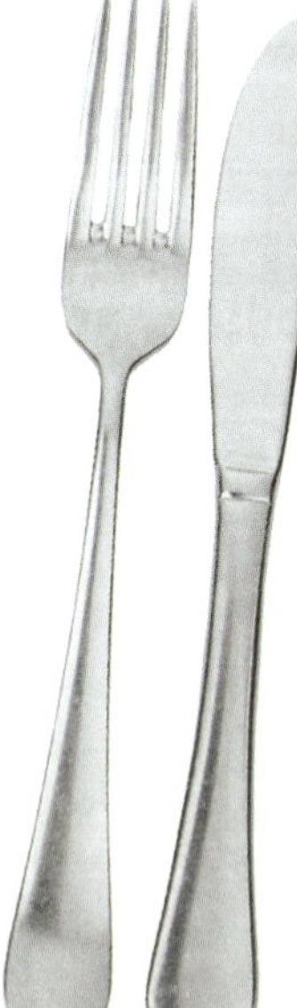

MENU DECODER

Entrée The main course.

Biscuit A slightly salty quick bread, similar to a scone, that's typically served with white sausage or mushroom gravy or jam at breakfast. Not to be confused with a cookie.

Deep dish A uniquely Chicago style of pizza with several layers of toppings and lots of cheese.

Chicago dog A hot dog topped with chopped white onions, sweet pickle relish, a dill pickle spear, tomato slices, peppers, celery salt and yellow mustard. Ketchup is frowned upon.

Brisket Beef that's been slow cooked for hours over a low-heat fire.

Burnt ends The charred point end of brisket, a Kansas City specialty.

Grits Ground corn cooked to a porridge-like consistency that's popular in Southern-style restaurants and some Great Plains states.

HOW TO... Drink Malört

The sleek tasting room at Chicago's **CH Distillery** (p59) would never give away the fact that it also produces Malört, the Windy City's unique liquor that's famous for tasting awful. Carl Jeppson, a Swedish immigrant who moved to Chicago in the 1880s, marketed Malört as medicinal bitters during Prohibition as a tonic for stomach worms to sidestep the draconian liquor laws.

Today, practically every bar in Chicago and other major Midwest cities stocks it, and drinkers have described it variously as the flavor of pencil shavings, canal water, cleaning fluid and sweaty socks. (Its taste comes from wormwood.) Downing a shot is a rite of passage, often in the form of a Chicago Handshake: a shot of Malört with an Old Style beer. Some bars add it to cocktails, such as a Malört-blended mai tai, or infuse it with herbs, pickles and even pumpkin spice in fall.

FROM LEFT: SERGIY KUZMIN/SHUTTERSTOCK, SOPHIE_MARIE/SHUTTERSTOCK

HOW MUCH FOR A...

Diner breakfast
$10–15

Chicago deep dish pizza
$25

Steak at a fancy steakhouse
$50–100

Small cappuccino
$5

Pint of craft beer
$6–10

Taco
$2–4

Craft cocktail
$12–20

Barbecue meal
$15–30

HOW TO... Order Kansas City Barbecue

For locals, eating Kansas City barbecue is not a special occasion, once-a-year event – it's a frequent ritual that you need zero excuse to indulge in. Ordering at a barbecue joint can be overwhelming for first-time feasters, given the number of choices.

Most places have online menus that are helpful to look through before you arrive, particularly if you go to **Gates Bar-B-Q** (p151), where staff shout, 'Hi, may I help you?' as soon as you walk in the door. Barbecue restaurants are always open for lunch and usually for dinner, but popular cuts and KC specialties such as burnt ends can sell out, so go early. Lines are often long at counter service spots like **Joe's Kansas City Bar-B-Que** (p153), so eating at off-times, such as right when the restaurant opens or mid-afternoon between the lunch and dinner rushes, means less time waiting.

Take your pick from the menu, perhaps brisket (flavorful beef, smoked or braised), pulled pork (shredded, slow-cooked pork shoulder), sausage, smoked chicken or ribs (pork, beef or lamb, served with sauce). If the meat is sold by weight, most adults eating solo will want a third- to a half-pound. Save room for sides, which might include cheesy corn, cornbread, baked beans, coleslaw, mac 'n' cheese, or French fries. Some barbecue joints have decent vegetarian options, but ask whether the side dishes are cooked in animal fat.

Stockyard Cities

Chicago once had the USA's largest stockyards – the second-biggest were in Kansas City – and they processed more meat than anywhere else on the planet, earning Chicago the title of 'hog butcher for the world'.

FOOD TRADITIONS

The upper Midwest has some fantastic foodie traditions worth seeking out on your visit.

Supper clubs are restaurants that are stuck in the past in a delightfully retro way. Their roots date from the 1930s, following the end of Prohibition, when diners were once again heading out to meet friends for a few drinks. How do you know when you've encountered a supper club? Look for wood-paneled walls mounted with fish, a relish tray filled with carrots and radishes on the table, and an extensive cocktail list that starts with an old-fashioned (brandy, bitters, sugar, soda water, orange slice and cherry). Wisconsin has the largest number of supper clubs, but they are also found in Michigan and Minnesota.

It doesn't have to be Lent and you don't have to be Catholic to indulge in a **Friday fish fry**, a year-round Wisconsin treat. Milwaukee's restaurants and breweries are good places to join in this communal meal of beer-battered cod, French fries and coleslaw, which has given locals a cheap dinner for socializing and celebrating the end of the work week for generations.

In Indiana, **cafeterias** are institutions where diners pick up a tray, slide it along a metal railing, and load it up with plates of hot and cold dishes, such as meatloaf, fried chicken and catfish, and roast beef Manhattan (an open-faced sandwich of roast beef on white bread). Cafeterias are particularly known for their pies, especially sugar cream pie, a custard-filled pastry that's Indiana's unofficial state pie.

Responsible Travel

Climate Change & Travel

It's impossible to ignore the impact we have when travelling; Lonely Planet urges all travellers to engage with their travel carbon footprint, which will mainly come from air travel. While there often isn't an alternative, travellers can look to minimise the number of flights they take, opt for newer aircrafts and use cleaner ground transport, such as trains. One proposed solution—purchasing carbon offsets—unfortunately does not cancel out the impact of individual flights. While most destinations will depend on air travel for the foreseeable future, for now, pursuing ground-based travel where possible is the best course of action.

The **UN carbon footprint calculator** shows how flying impacts a household's emissions.

The **ICAO Carbon Emissions Calculator** allows visitors to analyse the CO2 generated by point-to-point journeys.

Stay Longer

Hotels use significant amounts of water - up to 400 gallons per day per room. Much of this is from washing bedding and towels after short stays, so travel slow and extend your time.

Go Electric

If you're renting a car for your travels, consider going electric. Drivers can find EV charging stations at a growing number of hotels, grocery stores, campgrounds and even some gas stations. Find station locations at chargehub.com.

Invasive plant and animal species are a problem across the Midwest, often hitching rides on motorboats or firewood. Remove vegetation from boats and clean them with hot water. Use local firewood at campsites.

Oklahoma has the highest proportion of Native people of any state. Learn about Indigenous history and culture at the **First Americans Museum** (p170) in Oklahoma City, the **Osage Nation Museum** (p169) in Pawhuska and the **Five Civilized Tribes Museum** (p170) in Muskogee.

BUY LOCAL

Locally grown and made products use fewer fossil fuels to transport, and buying them helps keep dollars in the communities where you're visiting. Farmers markets and cooperative grocery stores are great places to shop.

EAT MEAT-FREE MEALS

The Midwest loves its meat, but its production is a major contributor to greenhouse gas emissions, accelerating climate change. Order plant-based dishes – available even at barbecue restaurants! – to reduce your carbon footprint.

Travel by Train

Instead of flying or driving, take Amtrak to start your Midwest adventure in Chicago and then continue your explorations to Milwaukee, Kansas City, St Louis or Detroit, reachable in under seven hours from the Windy City.

Take Public Transit

Though most Midwest cities don't have comprehensive public transportation networks, travelers can get around the urban cores of many places by light rail, streetcar or bus. Fares are generally cheap – or in places like Kansas City, entirely free.

Cycle or Scooter to the Sights

Many cities have rentable scooters and bike-share schemes that make it easier than ever to get around. Most places have a good network of bicycle lanes, and some towns are connected to nature trails on former rail lines *(railstotrails.org)*.

Bring Your Own Bag

Some Midwest municipalities have started charging for using plastic bags – it's 10¢ in Chicago and a minimum of 5¢ in Minneapolis. Save your cents and help protect the environment by packing a reusable bag.

Respect Wildlife

Bison have been reintroduced to some national and state parks and wildlife preserves around the Midwest, but don't get too close to these enormous animals. The National Park Service recommends keeping a distance of at least 25yd.

Stargazing opportunities abound in the rural Midwest. Check DarkSky International *(darksky.org/locations/midwest-united-states)* for certified spots.

Seek out hotels with sustainability policies certified by a credible organization like LEED or EarthCheck.

Protecting the Prairie

Prairie once covered a third of North America but was decimated by plow-driven agriculture. Only a fraction remains today, and the Tallgrass Prairie National Preserve in Kansas is one of the best places to experience it.

RESOURCES

happycow.net
Vegetarian and vegan restaurants across the USA.

environmentamerica.org
A citizen-based environmental advocacy organization.

thedyrt.com
Top campsites in the Midwest and beyond.

FROM TOP: MICHAEL DECHEV/SHUTTERSTOCK, DERYABINKA/SHUTTERSTOCK

LGBTIQ+ Travelers

Attitudes vary from place to place in the Midwest, but in general, LGBTIQ+ travelers will feel more welcome in cities and college towns. Unfortunately, bigotry still exists. In rural and more conservative places, it's unwise to be openly out because violence and verbal abuse can sometimes occur. When in doubt, assume locals follow a 'don't ask, don't tell' policy.

Chicago's Gayborhood

Chicago is home to the nation's first official gayborhood, Northalsted (sometimes still called by its former name of Boystown), the go-to for finding LGBTIQ+ community. It's a short distance east of Wrigley Field – rainbow crosswalks stripe the intersections, and rainbow pylons rise from the sidewalks. To see the gayborhood at its most out and proud, visit at night. The neighborhood chills out during the day when it's mostly about shopping (weekdays) and brunch (weekends). Visit during August's Market Days for a queer-themed street festival.

WOMONTOWN, KANSAS CITY

In the 1980s and '90s, women fed up with being unable to get mortgages without a husband's or parent's signature bought 28 homes and 14 apartment buildings in midtown Kansas City to build a community run for and by LGBTIQ+ women. The neighborhood is almost all residential, so there's not much for travelers to actively see, but a free-to-watch PBS documentary details its fascinating history *(kansascitypbs.org/local-shows/womontown)*.

Midwest Pride

Most major and some smaller cities in the Midwest have Pride celebrations, which typically take place in June, bringing out parades and festivities in a rainbow of colors. Good cities to seek out include Minneapolis *(tcpride.org)*, which has a sizable queer scene, and Columbus, OH *(stonewallcolumbus.org)*.

LGBTIQ+ RESOURCES

Advocate *(advocate.com/travel)* News, LGBTIQ+ travel features and destination guides.
Damron *(damron.com)* Long-running, advertiser-driven gay travel guides and app.
LGBT National Help Center *(lgbthotline.org)* Counseling, information and referrals for people of all ages; special resources for youth.
Out Traveler *(outtraveler.com)* Free online magazine articles with travel tips, destination guides and resort reviews.

Stay Gay

The lodging website and app MisterB&B *(misterbandb.com)* lists gay-friendly hotels, apartments, private rooms and vacation homes for rent. Options abound across the country, and hosts are vetted to ensure all visitors are welcome.

SAUGATUCK, MICHIGAN

Saugatuck is one of the Gold Coast's most popular resort areas, known for its strong arts community, numerous B&Bs and LGBTIQ-friendly vibe. Douglas is its twin city a mile or so to the south, and they've pretty much sprawled into one. It's a touristy but funky place, with ice cream–licking families, yuppie boaters and martini-drinking gay couples sharing the waterfront.

 NEW AFRICA/SHUTTERSTOCK

Accessible Travel

If you have a physical disability, the Midwest can be an accommodating place, but you still need to plan your travels carefully. Larger cities and public buildings typically have good accessibility infrastructure in place, thanks largely to requirements put forth by the Americans with Disabilities Act (ADA). Natural areas can provide challenges.

Beach Accessibility

Half of Chicago's Lake Michigan beaches have mats on the sand to make access to the shoreline easier for wheelchairs, and some spots also rent out beach wheelchairs.

Airport

All US airports must comply with ADA regulations, which translate to accessible restrooms, step-free access to gates and airplanes, and wheelchair assistance (best requested through your airline in advance).

Accommodations

Hotels built after 1993 must meet specific accessibility requirements. Major chains usually have rooms adapted for accessibility needs, but book in advance and double-check they have what you require. House rentals and older properties might not be suitable.

ACCESSIBLE OUTDOORS

Many national parks and some state parks and recreation areas have wheelchair-accessible paved, graded dirt or boardwalk trails. Most national park websites have an accessibility page giving details on the park's accessible attractions. Start your search at nps.gov.

Park Access for All

The America the Beautiful Access Pass grants US citizens and permanent residents with disabilities free lifetime access to more than 2000 national parks and recreation sites.

Hidden Disabilities Sunflower Program

Not all disabilities are visible. Wearing a Hidden Disabilities Sunflower lanyard *(hdsunflower.com/us)* helps signal to staff at participating airports and train stations that you may need extra assistance – no explanation required.

AT THE MUSEUM

Many museums are boosting their accessibility features, including offering EnChroma glasses for color-blind visitors, noise-canceling headphones, hand fidgets, sign language interpreters and tours, and social narratives that show what a visit is like.

RESOURCES

AccessibleGO *(accessiblego.com)* Provides accessibility details and community reviews for hotels, flights and more.

Society for Accessible Travel & Hospitality *(sath.org)* Brings together organizations serving travelers with disabilities. It provides tons of helpful travel tips and access info.

TravelAbility *(travelability.net)* Accessibility resources listed by state.

Be My Eyes *(bemyeyes.com)* Excellent app that helps blind and visually impaired travelers navigate their environment through AI and live video.

Metro systems and city buses are typically wheelchair-friendly, and they are often equipped with wheelchair lifts and designated wheelchair spots. Amtrak passenger trains can accommodate wheelchairs with advance notice, but chair size and clearance requirements apply.

VINEYARD PERSPECTIVE/SHUTTERSTOCK

Gathering Place (p168), Tulsa

Nuts & Bolts

OPENING HOURS

The following is a general guideline. Shorter hours may apply during low seasons, or some venues close completely. Museums and tourist attractions are often closed on Mondays or Tuesdays (or both). After the COVID-19 pandemic, few restaurants, bars or stores are open 24/7, even in bigger cities.

Banks 8:30am to 5pm Monday to Friday; sometimes 9am to noon Saturday

Restaurants Breakfast 7am to 10am, lunch 11am to 2:30pm, dinner 5pm to 10pm

Bars 4pm to midnight or later, particularly in big cities

Shops 9am to 7pm Monday to Saturday; some open noon to 5pm Sunday

Wi-Fi

Many hotels, restaurants and cafes offer free wi-fi. Some cities and towns have free public wi-fi hotspots.

Bathrooms

Look for free public restrooms inside malls, public buildings, libraries, gas stations and some transportation hubs, as well as some parks.

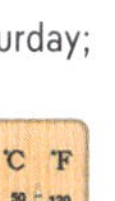

GOOD TO KNOW

Time zones
Mostly Central (GMT/UTC-6) and Eastern (GMT/UTC-5), with the western fringes in Mountain Standard Time (GMT/UTC-7)

Country calling code +1

Emergency number
911

Population
70.5 million

Electricity

Type A and B; 120V/60Hz

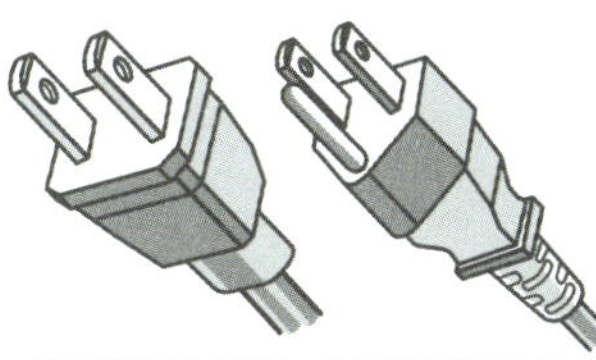

PUBLIC HOLIDAYS

On the following holidays, banks and post offices are closed, and transportation and museums might reduce their hours. Holidays falling on a weekend are usually observed the following Monday. Some states also have their own holidays, such as Truman Day (May 8) in Missouri.

New Year's Day January 1

Martin Luther King Jr Day Third Monday in January

Presidents' Day Third Monday in February

Memorial Day Last Monday in May

Juneteenth June 19

Independence Day July 4

Labor Day First Monday in September

Indigenous Peoples' Day (aka Columbus Day) Second Monday in October

Veterans Day November 11

Thanksgiving Fourth Thursday in November

Christmas Day December 25

Weights & Measures

The US uses the imperial system, except that bottled water and soft drinks are often sold by the liter. Temperatures are measured in Fahrenheit.

STORYBOOK

Our writers delve deep into different aspects of Midwest life

Cahokia Mounds State Historic Site (p73), Illinois

KENT RANEY/SHUTTERSTOCK

A HISTORY OF THE MIDWEST IN 15 PLACES

Caught between the coasts, the Midwest has long found itself at the crossroads of country-wide cultural changes. It has long been a land of travelers, from nomadic Plains tribes following bison herds to early American expeditioners charting the USA's largest land purchase and pioneers seeking a better life beyond the East Coast.

DOZENS OF NATIVE tribes called this land home before 15th-century colonizers set foot on a continent later called America, and the legacy of those with ancestral ties to the Great Lakes and the Great Plains lives on in many places. None of the Midwest states were part of the original 13 colonies, but European fur trappers were building trading posts along major rivers before the upstart colony declared independence, and some of these outposts later developed into major cities.

The concept of manifest destiny, the 19th-century imperialist idea that American colonizers had a god-given right to expand their territory from the east coast to the west, set the stage for prolonged conflict between Native people and newer arrivals. The question of slavery was also divisive – not just for the nation, but for the Midwest in particular, with the Missouri Compromise of 1820 allowing residents of that state to be slaveowners, while territories to the west were question marks that led to many bloody battles. In some ways, the region still bears the scars of these painful pieces of history, as the country at large continues to grapple with questions of immigration, civil rights and what it means to be an American today.

1. Tallgrass Prairie National Preserve

NORTH AMERICA'S LARGEST ECOSYSTEM

Long before amber waves of grain covered the Plains, it was prairie, a sea of grass that covered a third of the continent that stretched from Canada to Texas between the Rocky Mountains and the Mississippi River. Prairies see too much rain to be considered deserts, but they are too drought-stricken to support dense forests. The climate brings extreme temperatures, dropping far below freezing in winter and blasting the landscape with heat in summer. Before 1840, up to 60 million bison roamed the vast prairies, and the gentle giants, reintroduced in some areas, remain emblematic of the land.

For more on the Tallgrass Prairie National Preserve in Kansas, see page 160

2. Cahokia Mounds State Historic Site

A MAJOR PRE-COLUMBIAN CITY

Native people flourished along the Mississippi River from 800 to 1600 CE, and modern historians now refer to them collectively as the Mississippian culture. These communities were known for constructing huge earthwork mounds, which is why they are sometimes called Mound Builders, and Cahokia, in southern Illinois across the Mississippi from St Louis, contains 70 such surviving structures. Occupied from 800 to 1400 CE, Cahokia was the Mississippian culture's biggest and most influential city. With a population of up to 20,000 at its peak – as large as contemporary European cities – it was the biggest pre-Columbian settlement north of Mexico.

For more on Cahokia Mounds State Historic Site, see page 73

3. Lewis & Clark Interpretive Center

AMERICAN EXPANSION BEGINS

Fur-frenzied French colonizers claimed most of the land between the Mississippi and the Rocky Mountains for France. The territory passed to Spain in 1763, the French got it back in 1800 and then sold it to the USA in the 1803 Louisiana Purchase. President Thomas Jefferson sent his personal secretary, Meriwether Lewis, to chart his acquisition. Lewis, who had no training for exploration, convinced his friend William Clark, an experienced frontiersman and army veteran, to tag along. In 1804, their 40-member party left St Louis, MO. Guided by Shoshone tribeswoman Sacagawea, they trailblazed from St Louis to the Pacific Ocean and back.

For more on the Lewis & Clark Interpretive Center in Iowa, see page 194

4. First Americans Museum

ON THE TRAIL OF TEARS TO OKLAHOMA

Beginning in the 1830s, white farmers in the southeastern US wanted to expand into the ancestral lands of the Cherokee, Chickasaw, Choctaw, Muscogee and Seminole. The US Army forcibly removed these Native Americans from their homelands and sent them on forced marches hundreds of miles west, primarily to Indian Territory, the land that is today Oklahoma. Tens of thousands of Native Americans made the journey, later called the Trail of Tears. More than a third are thought to have died because of the brutal conditions. Today, Oklahoma is home to 39 tribal nations, and their rich ancestral heritage is celebrated in Oklahoma City's First Americans Museum.

For more on the First Americans Museum, see page 170

Gateway Arch National Park (p150)

PAUL BRADY PHOTOGRAPHY/SHUTTERSTOCK

5. Gateway Arch National Park

OPENING THE DOOR

The Gateway Arch is a symbol of both St Louis and westward expansion, despite having been erected in the 1960s. Built near the spot where Lewis and Clark set off on their expedition, this massive arch stands 630ft from the ground to its highest point and was conceptualized as a tribute to Thomas Jefferson's vision of a continental United States. While the four-minute tram ride to the top of the arch is a highlight, it's equally worth stopping by the museum under the Gateway Arch, where exhibits dive into topics in 19th-century American history, from the Lewis and Clark Expedition to the idea of manifest destiny.

For more on Gateway Arch National Park, see page 150

6. Chimney Rock National Historic Site

PIONEER TRAILS

An estimated 400,000 people trekked west across America between 1840 and 1860, lured by tales of gold, promises of religious freedom and visions of fertile farmland. One of the major routes was the Oregon Trail. Starting from Independence, MO, it spanned six states and sorely tested the travelers who embarked on this perilous journey. In the Nebraska Panhandle, bluff formations like Chimney Rock rise from the otherwise flat horizon, and this fragile 120ft spire in particular was an inspiring landmark for pioneers, mentioned in hundreds of journals. It marked the end of the first leg of the journey and the beginning of the tough push to the coast.

For more on Chimney Rock National Historic Site, see page 182

7. Lincoln Home National Historic Site

A HOUSE DIVIDED CANNOT STAND

In 1860, the Republican Party held its national political convention in Chicago and selected Abraham Lincoln, a lawyer from

Springfield, IL, as its presidential candidate. A month later, the Civil War erupted between the North and the South. The war's end on April 9, 1865, is marred by President Lincoln's assassination five days later. After his assassination, Lincoln's body was returned to Springfield, where it lies today. You can visit Lincoln's tomb, also the resting place of his wife, Mary, and three of their four sons. To see the only house Lincoln ever owned, head to the Lincoln Home National Historic Site in downtown Springfield.

For more on the Lincoln Home National Historic Site, see page 69

8. Deadwood

STRIKE IT RICH

Popular among fans of the HBO series of the same name, Deadwood, SD, feels a bit cheesy at first glance, with its casinos and monster truck rallies. However, if you give it a chance, you'll see that this National Historic Landmark is doing a fine job of preserving its history as a gold rush town. The gold rush in this area occurred because the US violated the 1868 Treaty of Fort Laramie with the Lakota, and its 1870s buildings are in great condition. History-themed tours cover everything from archaeology to Deadwood's Chinatown.

For more on Deadwood, see page 211

9. Homestead National Historical Park

HOME ON THE RANGE

The Homestead Act of 1862 changed the course of 'unsettled' territories of the western US significantly. It spurred American colonial expansion by taking public land (that had been Native land until the Indian Removal Act of 1830) and granting private citizens – including single women and formerly enslaved people – 160-acre plots to farm. The first of these plots is now Homestead National Historical Park in Nebraska, which tells the story of American homesteading and how it shaped the country. The park has a museum where you can learn about this era in history before heading to the nearby Palmer-Epard Cabin, an example of a typical homesteader dwelling.

For more on Homestead National Historical Park, see page 180

10. Brewing Heritage Trail

PROST!

It's estimated that seven million German-speaking immigrants arrived in the US from 1800 onward, and today, more Americans consider themselves to be of German ancestry than of any other group. Many of these arrivals settled in the upper Midwest, drawn to both employment opportunities in the burgeoning cities and the availability of farmland. Cincinnati still holds onto much of its German heritage, particularly in the historic neighborhood of Over-the-Rhine, where visitors can follow the Brewing Heritage Trail to drink in the city's beer-making history – Cincy was called the 'beer capital of the world' in the 1890s. The city also puts on the USA's largest Oktoberfest celebrations.

For more on the Brewing Heritage Trail, see p87

11. Frank Lloyd Wright Home & Studio

PRAIRIE SCHOOL

Prolific Wisconsin-born architect Frank Lloyd Wright endowed many places in the Midwest with a distinctive style: Prairie School, considered the first uniquely American form of architecture. Wright's buildings sought to reflect the landscape, emphasizing the horizontal over the vertical with long, low roof lines and rows of windows that seamlessly connect indoor spaces with the outdoors. To blend in with the landscape visually, natural materials such as brick, limestone and stucco were often used. Wright called this organic architecture, inspired by and aiming to exist harmoniously with nature. The first home Wright built, his own in Oak Park, IL, is a glimpse into the genius at work.

For more on the Frank Lloyd Wright Home & Studio, see p69

12. Ford Piquette Avenue Plant

THE US GOES MOBILE

The automobile age officially revved its engine when Henry Ford introduced the Model T at the Ford Piquette Avenue Plant in Detroit in 1908. Unlike its predecessors, which were playthings for the rich, Ford's invention was operationally foolproof and affordable, allowing middle-class Americans to trade in their horses for horsepower. An influx of drivers sparked a century-long roadside

Frank Lloyd Wright Home & Studio (p69), Illinois

revolution: the US government poured money into infrastructure, gas stations popped up like oil springs and motorists found freedom, reaching places trains never could. Detroit became Motor City, fueled by Ford's assembly-line empire. In the coming decades, train use declined, cars became king and the American landscape was redrawn in their image.

For more on the Ford Piquette Avenue Plant, see p99

13. Route 66

THE MOTHER ROAD

Stretching from Chicago to the California Coast, Route 66 served as a main road through the region for years. Established in 1926, it was the easiest way to get to California from the Midwest, and many Dust Bowl migrants traveled the road during the Great Depression, as chronicled in John Steinbeck's *The Grapes of Wrath*. Although Route 66 was officially decommissioned in 1985, many nostalgic drivers continue to retrace the route every year, often taking a slow approach and stopping along the way to see the many historic signs, roadside attractions and natural wonders that flank the so-called Mother Road.

For more on Route 66, see page 143

14. Brown v Board of Education National Historical Park

UNDOING 'SEPARATE BUT EQUAL'

From the 1890s until the 1950s, the USA's racist segregation policies followed the doctrine of 'separate but equal' after the Plessy v Ferguson Supreme Court case. The National Association for the Advancement of Colored People (NAACP) put forward five court cases that challenged this doctrine in public schools, which the Supreme Court consolidated into one, brought forward by a Topeka, KS, family: Brown v Board of Education. The Supreme Court's ruling was unanimous: 'The doctrine of "separate but equal" has no place. Separate educational facilities are inherently unequal.' This National Park Service–run site is inside the formerly segregated all-Black Monroe Elementary School.

For more on the Brown v Board of Education National Historical Park, see page 159

15. George Floyd Square

'I CAN'T BREATHE'

In May 2020, George Floyd, a Black man, was killed by Derek Chauvin, a white police officer, outside of a convenience store in Minneapolis. Chauvin knelt on Floyd's neck and back for nearly nine minutes, suffocating him. Floyd's dying words of 'I can't breathe' reignited worldwide protests against racial injustice and police brutality. The site where it happened is now known as George Floyd Square and has become a place for reflection and remembrance. People bring offerings to the ever-changing memorial that has taken over the intersection, and murals and raised-fist sculptures are on display for a block in each direction.

For more on George Floyd Square, see page 125

MEET THE MIDWESTERNERS

Even born-and-bred Midwesterners don't agree on exactly which states make up Middle America – Ohio? Oklahoma? – but shared stories still bind us. LAUREN KEITH introduces her people.

TO UNDERSTAND THE heart of the Heartland, Instagram is a good place to start, in particular the account called Midwest vs Everybody *(instagram.com/midwestvseverybody)*. If you're not from the region, the daily memes about gas stations, ranch dressing and watching tornadoes roll in from your garage might not make sense at first, but it's a good primer for what you'll encounter on your travels here.

While it's hard to generalize about such a diverse and expansive place, the hearty types who have settled the Midwest throughout history, from the dozens of Native tribes to later European colonizers and formerly enslaved people, are resilient. The people who attempted to inhabit the Great Plains after the Native Americans usually faced difficult lives of scarcity, uncertainty and isolation, and it literally drove many of them crazy. Others gave up and got out – failed homesteads dot the region. Only fiercely independent people could thrive in those conditions, and that I'll-make-it-on-my-own rugged individualism remains a core tenet of Midwestern culture.

'Midwest nice' is a common phrase used to describe the personalities of many people here, embodied by politeness, quiet restraint, and being helpful even when you might not agree or feel comfortable with the situation. We avoid confrontation and do our utmost to make visitors feel welcome, even if that means minimizing our own opinions to keep the peace. In a 2013 study published in the Journal of Personality and Social Psychology, researchers found that the three main regions of the US have different personality traits: East Coasters are temperamental and uninhibited, West Coasters are relaxed and creative, and Midwesterners are friendly and conventional. That was also associated with conservative social values and politics and lower levels of education. The demographers found that friendly and conventional types are more likely to live close to home near family and friends instead of moving away, even if that means foregoing educational or career opportunities.

Each of the Midwest states dogs on the others. Kansans' dislike of Missouri goes all the way back to before the Civil War, when pro-slavery 'border ruffians' crossed into Kansas Territory in the 1850s to ensure that the new state would allow slavery, usually by means of violence, including intimidation, harassment, burning towns to the ground and murder. But Midwesterners also band together to form a united front when made fun of by outsiders. We've all heard the jabs about being flyover states and about our landscapes being so flat that you can see your dog running away for three days.

Perhaps the TV character Ted Lasso, played by Kansas City–raised, Chicago-trained actor-comedian Jason Sudeikis, is the best version of ourselves: relentlessly optimistic, genuinely kind and curious but not judgmental.

Is Kansas Flatter Than a Pancake?

In 2003, scientists set out to answer this age-old, all-important question. Using topographic data from the United States Geological Survey and a pancake from the International House of Pancakes, they determined that Kansas is indeed flatter, describing it as 'damn flat'.

CLOCKWISE FROM TOP LEFT: WILLIAM PERUGINI/SHUTTERSTOCK, KARLA CASPARI/SHUTTERSTOCK, TERRANCE HT IP/SHUTTERSTOCK, IOFOTO/SHUTTERSTOCK

SPRECHEN SIE DEUTSCH?

From 1800 onward, about seven million German-speaking immigrants arrived in the United States. Some of them were my great-great-grandparents, who settled in tiny farming communities on the prairie north of Wichita, KS. Today, more Americans consider themselves to be of German ancestry than of any other group, but sadly, in many places and for many families, my own included, that history has faded significantly. Even my own grandfather spoke German at home and didn't learn English until he went to, ironically, kindergarten. My mom remembers her aunts speaking in German when they didn't want the kids to understand the conversation. The anti-German sentiment after the two world wars was the language's death knell in the US, and her generation did not learn it.

I decided to study German in school and even got a degree in it. While I can't fully resurrect my German heritage, when I drive through Kansas, I see it everywhere – it was my ancestors who brought the wheat.

STORM TRACKING IN TORNADO ALLEY

The United States records more tornadoes than any other country, and few places are hit harder than Tornado Alley. By Lauren Keith

FOUR DAYS INTO researching this guidebook, my phone started screeching with the dreaded all-caps alert: 'TORNADO WARNING in this area. Take shelter now.' I was driving on a two-lane highway in rural southern Missouri, surrounded by farmfields and the rolling hills of the Ozarks. My phone didn't have a strong enough signal to pull up the radar map, so I had no idea if I was driving straight into or away from the storm. Hail the size of ping-pong balls started pelting my car, strong enough that I was sure I wouldn't make it through without a busted windshield.

But as a Kansas native, this tornado warning was hardly my first rodeo.

What is a Tornado?

Tornadoes are Mother Nature's most violent expression. Developed as part of powerful thunderstorm systems, tornadoes are rotating columns of air that touch the ground, with wind speeds that can reach 300mph. The base of a tornado can be more than a mile wide, and its trail of destruction through neighborhoods and farmland can be 50 miles long. Tornadoes destroy much of what they encounter, but sometimes

Pictured clockwise from top left: Large hailstones; Tornado, Nebraska; Tornado-damaged high school in Greensburg, Kansas, in 2007; Storm chaser

CLOCKWISE FROM TOP LEFT: SUZANNE TUCKER/SHUTTERSTOCK; MIKE HOLLINGSHEAD/GETTY IMAGES; MICHAEL RAPHAEL, PUBLIC DOMAIN, VIA WIKIMEDIA COMMONS ©; CAPTURING ADVENTURE/SHUTTERSTOCK

they leave things eerily untouched: an entire house will be reduced to wooden splinters, but a living room bookcase will stand alone amid the wreckage with unmoved glass picture frames still on the shelf. Tornadoes develop quickly and can also dissipate quickly – most are on the ground for less than 15 minutes. Heavy rain and hail, sometimes as large as baseballs, are common companions, which can exacerbate the damage.

Tornadoes are notoriously unpredictable, but advisories come in two types, which Midwesterners often liken to a taco bar. A tornado watch means that you have all of the ingredients to make a taco. A tornado warning means that the tacos are ready to eat, and it's time to take action (by taking shelter, where hopefully there are tacos).

Why Does the US Have So Many Tornadoes?

Between 2020 and 2024, every state but Hawaii saw at least one tornado, according to the National Oceanic and Atmospheric Administration. Each year, the US records more than 1200 tornadoes across the country. The topography of the Midwest is the reason why so many tornadoes occur here: the middle of the country is flat, and pockets of air of differing temperatures – cool air from Canada and warm, moist air from the Gulf of Mexico – combine to create huge thunderstorms, some of which spawn tornadoes.

Tornado Alley doesn't have a strict geographical definition, but includes parts of Oklahoma, Kansas, South Dakota, Iowa and Nebraska in the Midwest, among other states. Texas records the highest number of tornadoes each year, but it's also the largest state in the continental US. If the number of tornadoes is taken per square mile, Florida and Kansas put up the highest numbers in the country. (Tornadoes can spawn from hurricanes, so they aren't uncommon along the southeastern US coast.)

Measuring Tornadoes & Their Aftermath

I grew up in Wichita, KS. Fortunately, I've never been directly caught in a tornado, but I have witnessed their destruction firsthand. In 1991, a tornado struck near McConnell Air Force Base – narrowly missing 10 B-1 bombers on the tarmac, two of which were equipped with nuclear warheads – before moving through a nearby suburb. In 2007, a tornado with a base 1.7 miles wide hit the tiny town of Greensburg, KS, nearly erasing it from the map. An estimated 95% of buildings were damaged, and half of the town's already small population moved away. When Greensburg decided to rebuild, it emphasized the 'green' in its name. It's now home to the most LEED-certified buildings per capita in the US and was the first US city to use all LED streetlights.

The intensity of tornadoes is measured using the Fujita scale (the Enhanced Fujita scale has been used in the US since 2007), based on wind speeds and damage to buildings. The 1991 tornado near Wichita grew to an F5, the highest classification with 'incredible' damage and 261mph to 318mph winds. The Greensburg tornado was the first to be classified as an EF5 on the new enhanced scale that had been implemented that year.

Storm-Chasing Tours

Most people run and hide from tornadoes, but storm-chasing companies actually lead travelers on tours across Middle America to witness these destructive wonders – from a safe distance. Since the release of the movie *Twisters* in 2024, demand for storm-chasing tours has skyrocketed. 'When we opened up the tours for 2025, they sold out in two months,' says Kim George, guest relations manager at Tempest Tours (*tempesttours.com*). 'My waiting list this year was more than 100 people who wanted to go on a single-day chase.'

George says Tempest Tours helped consult on *Twisters* and that a lot of the technical stuff is correct, but at the end of the day, it's Hollywood. 'We don't drive through people's fields, and we don't see a tornado every 10 minutes,' she says. 'Storm chasing is all about driving the long distances to get to your target.'

Tornadoes are seasonal, generally occurring between April and July. 'We know there are going to be storms during this season,' George says. On 'down days' on tour, travelers visit local attractions, but some tours in 2025 were out chasing daily.

What's the draw of witnessing such destruction and nature-made fury? 'It's never the same,' George says. 'You don't know what it's going to be until it comes. We have return guests who come year after year because every day is different.'

BELLA BENDER/SHUTTERSTOCK

INSIDE THE JOYFULLY BIZARRE WORLD OF MIDWEST STATE FAIR CULTURE

Welcome to the wild, weird, and wonderfully fried world of Midwest state fairs – where butter cows reign and calories (mostly) don't count. By Michael Mackie

WHILE SOME FOLKS dream of luxury and private islands, I've always been more of a deep-fried delusionist – envisioning a glorious life-size butter sculpture of Caitlin Clark and snacks on sticks as far as the eye can see. Forget champagne dreams. I'll take a red velvet funnel cake and a cholesterol spike, please.

That's what happens when you grow up less than 3 miles from the Iowa State Fair, which, like many a Midwest fairground, boasts a chaotic symphony of smells, sounds and sights. Held annually in Des Moines since 1886, the Iowa State Fair is one of the largest and most iconic in the country, drawing more than 1 million-ish people over 11 days each August. That's more than the population of six US states. (I'm looking at you, Wyoming and Vermont.)

By and large, most Midwest fairs are held in the dog days of summer, which creates a sort of corn-scented fever dream for fairgoers to enjoy. Throw in copious amounts of rockin' (and raucous) grandstand shows, midway carnival rides, and funnel cake stands on every corner, and you've created what I consider to be the world's best corn-fed commune, conveniently located under endlessly blue Midwestern skies.

The Briefest of Fair Histories: A Barn-Raised Backstory

Midwest fairs sprouted from agricultural roots, much like the crops that surround their respective states. Many date back to the mid-1800s and were originally launched as agricultural expos meant to showcase livestock, crops, and technological advances in farming. (Yes, there were technological advances in the 1800s, like the revolutionary corn picker that Edmund Quincy invented in 1850.)

What began as competitions over soybean yields and prized steers has evolved into full-blown free-for-alls featuring everything from Missouri State Fair's

death-defying BMX stunt shows to Indiana State Fair's llama-alpaca costume contests.

While each Midwest fair has its own rhythm, cadence, and abundance of frozen lemonades, they all have one thing in common. Each has blossomed into the zany hybrid of tradition and excess that it is today.

While Indiana, Missouri and Kansas hold their own in terms of style and substance, the Minnesota State Fair and Iowa State Fair often duke it out in terms of superior naming rights. *USA Today* once named the Minnesota State Fair the best in the nation. Not to be outdone, the Iowa State Fair has landed on the National Register of Historic Places and made the book *1000 Places to See Before You Die.*

Sibling rivalry, indeed.

Food: The Stranger, the More Gluttonous, the Better

Ask any attendee, state fairs are where diets go to die. It's a corn(dog)ucopia where everything is deep-fried and/or skewered and/or served with a side of caloric irony.

You want deep-fried butter? You got it. Bacon-wrapped grilled cheese on a stick? Absolutely. Funnel cake topped with pulled pork, cheese and garnished with Flamin' Hot Cheetos? Who am I to judge? If it can be impaled or battered, chances are it's been served up nuclear hot at the Iowa State Fair.

In recent years, fair vendors have outdone themselves with gut-bomb fare such as deep-fried Oreos and deep-fried Reese's PB Cups (because your arteries were on their last legs anyway), and alligator tacos (because the Wisconsin State Fair figures beef, pork, turkey and chicken aren't satisfying enough).

I don't want to brag (much), but my beloved Iowa State Fair reports that more than 70 different food items are served on sticks. It's the state's unofficial sixth food group.

The Sights & Sounds: Tractor Pulls, Contests Galore & Grandstand Glam

One can't yammer on about state fair culture without mentioning the bazillion other oddball attractions that make it great. (Bonus: many of 'em are free with admission.) Here's just a quirky sampler.

Tractor pulls This is where diesel power and dirt come together in odd harmonious balance. It's also where horsepower goes from metaphorical to very, very real. (Pro tip: bring earplugs.)

The cow chip throwing contest Yes, it's exactly what it sounds like. Also, if this isn't offered at your state fair, can you even call it a state fair? (Pro tip: bring hand sanitizer.)

Baby animal barns A mandatory rite of passage for every Midwest child? It's to pet a lamb while holding a corndog. (Pro tip: bring even more hand sanitizer.)

The Big Boar competition Past winners have tipped the scale at 1400+lb, because nothing says Iowa like celebrating massive pigs with even more humongous testicles. (Pro tip: they're so fat, they don't budge. Ever. Kinda how you'll feel after eating your weight in tiny cinnamon-sugar doughnuts.)

Mr Legs Contest I feel a kinship to this annual event as I've been a judge for the last decade. Categories range from most athletic to tannest, thinnest, palest, and longest (to name a few). Some categories are more obscurely à la mode – like when a Willie Nelson impersonator won the Most Willie Nelson–est leg award. (The crowd lost their ever-lovin' minds.)

Live music is another big draw – everyone from Johnny Cash to Katy Perry has played the state fair circuit at one point or another. Two noteworthy things: 1. My first concert was Dolly Parton at the Iowa State Fair in 1982; and 2. I was lucky enough to see The Chicks perform in a teeny-tiny, off-off-off-the-beaten-path side stage at the Iowa State Fair in 1996, exactly one year before the group's shooting star went supernova.

Also, if you were to peruse any line-up of concert headliners from any state fair, it would leave you scratching your head. Because concert organizers often try to appeal to a broad swath of fairgoers, it's often a quirky hodge-podge of acts. For me, nothing – and I mean nothing! – beats the eclectic 1988 Iowa State Fair rundown of Lisa Lisa, Alabama, the Smothers Brothers, The Beach Boys, the Oak Ridge Boys with Nitty Gritty Dirt Band, and Randy Travis and the Judds.

Fair Fashion: Where Cargo Shorts, Cowboy Boots & Caftans Come Together

The weather forecast at any Midwest summer fair is sweaty with a 100% chance of sweltering humidity. (The hottest day ever recorded at the Iowa State Fair was August 16, 1983, when the temperature reached 108°F.)

Thus, when it comes to fashion, there's no dress code, but there is an unironic, unapologetic look. Camouflage is considered neutral. Glitter is embraced, especially on toddlers and horse hooves.

Moreover, expect to see a steady parade of jorts (the oh-so timeless jean shorts, naturally), bedazzled visors (in order to repel and also radiate the blinding, blazing sun), shirts bearing catchy slogans like 'I went to the Missouri State Fair and all I got was diabetes', boots - cowboy, rubber, combat and occasionally Ugg (ugh), and sleeveless anything and everything, forever resplendent with tractor logos. Facts are facts, apparel with sleeves are constricting. How can anyone be expected to win a four-foot stuffed SpongeBob in a competitive game of ring toss with sleeves. Nope.

Mini corndogs

ASK ANY ATTENDEE, STATE FAIRS ARE WHERE DIETS GO TO DIE. IT'S A CORN(DOG)UCOPIA WHERE EVERYTHING IS DEEP-FRIED AND/OR SKEWERED AND/OR SERVED WITH A SIDE OF CALORIC IRONY.

Politics: Where Democracy Meets Deep-Fried Twinkies

Like clockwork, every four years, the state fair transforms into a campaign crucible - especially in Iowa, where the Iowa State Fair is less about rides and more about jockeying for position on the road to the White House.

Here, presidential hopefuls are required by law to shake up fresh lemonade like a part-time barista, kiss babies with stage-ready sincerity, and furtively try to operate a $500,000 combine. (You know, while pretending they know what a combine actually does.)

Central Iowans take this national media spotlight with a grain of salt corn. They also don't mess around. They forbid grandstanding in the actual grandstand. They ruthlessly size up candidates and will be the first to let you know who does (or doesn't) pass muster. (Sarah Palin's ex-hubs Todd got more love from the masses than she did in 2011. I saw it with my own eyes.)

Be advised, if you're a politico who can't handle the pressure of judging a pie contest in a tent in 95°F weather, you probably can't handle a global crisis.

Trust and believe, Midwest fairgrounds are where the American dream gets weird, wonderful, and can suffer from slight heatstroke. It's also a perfect equalizer — especially at the Iowa State Fair. There's a famous picture of Hilary Clinton waiting in line like everyone else to buy her pork chop (on a stick. Natch!). And who could forget the day presidential candidate Rick Santorum spent a good majority of his day walking by himself on countless fair concourses. The media horde was busy chasing after Bush. Also, Iowans don't suffer fools lightly.

Holding Court in the Livestock Pavilions

To this day, most fairs are still - at their core - deeply rooted in agriculture. Each and every barn is teeming with kids from

ZORYANCHIK/SHUTTERSTOCK

COTTON
CANDY
COTTON CANDY
DELICIOUS
CARMEL
CORN
MINNESOTA STATE FAIR
VISA

4-H and FFA (Future Farmers of America), proudly brushing their steers, bottle-feeding lambs or explaining the diet of their prize-winning rabbits. (Yes, it's a thing.)

Forget trophies. While accolades are nice, most competitors see it as a chance to showcase rural pride and generational knowledge. Winning a blue ribbon at the Iowa State Fair isn't just a triumph, rather it's the stuff of legend, with stories passed down like family recipes.

Speaking of recipes, the Iowa State Fair's food competition entries include more than 900 different categories, from best rhubarb pie to most original casserole. Somewhere in Central Iowa, there's a great aunt whose strawberry jam has won gold six years running, and she walks with the confidence of a rock star.

BY AND LARGE, MOST MIDWEST FAIRS ARE HELD IN THE DOG DAYS OF SUMMER, WHICH CREATES A SORT OF CORN-SCENTED FEVER DREAM FOR FAIRGOERS TO ENJOY.

And to anyone who sets foot in the hallowed halls of the Iowa State Fair Agriculture Building, be sure to make a pilgrimage and pay homage to the famous butter cow. She made her debut in 1911 and since then, she's become – dare I say – an udderly iconic fixture. (Sorry, not sorry.) Every year, 600lb of Iowa butter are sculpted into a life-size cow, refrigerated behind glass, and visited by more than a million spectators. If the Fair didn't already have a mascot, the butter cow would be a shoo-in. How revered is said bovine? Well, last year while she was appearing at the Grandstand, rocker Melissa Etheridge is said to have requested a picture with the butter cow. (I'm picturing a secret series of underground tunnels to shuttle the Grammy-winner back and forth so she wasn't mobbed by the masses.)

Why It Matters: Joy, Community & Controlled Chaos

At its heart, the Iowa State Fair – and state fair culture in general – is about collective community. It's where you run into your high school math teacher, your ex's cousin, and your second-grade best friend all within 30 minutes. If you go on the first Friday of the Fair – dubiously dubbed East Side Night – it won't even take that long. That particular evening is like old home week, just add beer.

It's truly become a bastion where urbanites and farmers stand shoulder to shoulder in line for a giant turkey leg. It's where nostalgia and novelty collide in one glorious, fried package.

In a world that's becoming grossly digital and curated, the fair harkens back to a time where analog ruled. It's refreshingly real. There's zero algorithm here – just grit, sugar, livestock and tradition.

And when the sun sets over the fairgrounds and the lights of the midway flicker on, you remember that joy doesn't have to be expensive or exclusive. Sometimes, it's just eating an obscene amount of cheese curds and riding on the Ferris wheel.

My suggestion? Come hungry. Leave sticky. And don't forget to wave at the butter cow.

Minnesota State Fair (p242)

KRISTIN CATO/ALAMY

Vineyard grapes, Wisconsin (p110)
RETIRED GUY PHOTOGRAPHY/SHUTTERSTOCK

MIDWEST, BOTTLED: THE CULTIVATION OF A UNIQUE IDENTITY

In the heart of the Midwest, winemakers are quietly redefining the region, one grape, one bottle, and one season at a time. By Katy Spratte Joyce

I VISITED DOOR County, Wisconsin expecting a quiet lakeside retreat and the usual orchard crops. Instead, I stumbled upon winemakers pushing boundaries, getting seriously creative, and rethinking what Midwestern viticulture and cold-hardy varietals can be. Channeling the region's longstanding sense of grit, the new generation of heartland growers and doers is proving that there's something truly special brewing here. It's not Napa, and it's not pretending to be. What's happening in the Midwest is an unexpected embrace of sense of place and rising to the challenging climate, full steam ahead.

Anchored Roots Aims High

I meet Eric Gale on a gray spring morning in Door County. Along the craggy shores of Lake Michigan, clapboard cottages and lighthouses stand against a steely sky. The air smells of thawing earth, a sign winter is finally loosening its grip. Gale, a Washington-trained viticulturalist, has returned home to the edge of the Wisconsin Ledge, where he's planting grape varieties unfamiliar to much of the wine world. He speaks passionately about his vision: a collaborative effort among Midwest winemakers to put the region on the map, his expertise and drive evident. For me, this conversation marks a shift, proof that the Midwest isn't just about corn and soybeans. It's becoming a place of viticultural ingenuity with a new agricultural identity. There's true grape innovation happening in the heartland.

'Fifty years ago Washington was barely a wine region, and today they're producing world-class wines garnering

attention all around the globe. We truly hope we can help to usher in the next generation of growth and quality in our own budding region,' explains Gale, co-owner and winemaker at Anchored Roots Vineyard and Winery in Egg Harbor, Wisconsin. It might not be Cabernet, Chardonnay and Riesling that grasp people's attention in the Wisconsin Ledge, but that might be the most exciting part about it. 'Wine itself is fun because a bottle of wine transports you to a new place and allows you to explore outside of your normal locale without leaving your dining table. The new frontier is here, and we want to help bring others into the know about this hidden gem and the wines that are being crafted right here in Door County,' he says.

Uncorking the Wisconsin Ledge AVA

The Wisconsin Ledge AVA (American Viticultural Area) is a relatively young grape-growing region, officially established in 2012. It spans the top of the Niagara Escarpment, a sweeping dolomitic limestone ridge that begins on the southeastern edge of Lake Winnebago and traces north along Lake Michigan, through Door County, and into Michigan's Upper Peninsula before arcing east to Niagara Falls. The AVA's foundation of gravelly, sandy glacial till over bedrock creates well-drained, relatively infertile soils, an asset in a Midwest landscape better known for fertile farmland. According to Gale, the escarpment's natural slope, combined with the moderating influence of Lake Michigan, helps shape the region's unique microclimate. Nowhere is this more apparent than on the Door Peninsula, where the warm waters of Green Bay provide additional protection. These conditions help limit spring and fall frosts and extend the ripening season, offering longer hang times for grapes, which is crucial for developing flavor and balance.

'The Ledge is still in the process of discovering its true identity,' says Gale. 'So far, crisp, aromatic white wines and rosés show incredible promise, and there are already excellent examples at many local wineries.' One initiative that highlights this potential is the Ledge Blanc project, a collaborative effort aiming to define a signature style for the region. Anchored Roots is a founding member, and the group recently received a USDA grant to help market what they hope will become the area's flagship wine. 'Traction for the project has been high,' Gale adds. 'We have a lot to be excited about.'

The future looks brighter, still. New cold-hardy varieties from the University of Minnesota and private breeders are thriving in the Wisconsin Ledge when treated with care in both vineyard and cellar. The resulting wines are 'crisp, clean, bright, fresh...plenty of fruit but also plenty of texture and minerality. These are wines that are worth getting excited about,' the winemaker effuses. So far the reception has been very positive. 'We are fighting an uphill battle as many wine industry folks have preconceived notions regarding what we can do with cold climate varieties, but this style of wine will change minds if they taste it,' Gale states. 'Currently our Ledge Blanc is our second-highest seller, so people are taking notice,' he adds.

Vineyard, Niagara Escarpment, Wisconsin (p110)

Little Grape on the Prairie

The current of winemaking creativity runs from the Great Lakes to the Great Plains, with Nebraska joining the fold and trying new things, too.

'Hybrid grapes exist in the Midwest not by accident but by design,' explains Sara Wiebold, Beverage Manager and Sommelier at Arbor Day Farm in Nebraska City. 'They were bred to withstand disease as well as the extreme cold and heat we experience.' These resilient crops closely resemble Midwestern fortitude. 'Hybrids persist, adapt, and steadily improve each season like the people that grow them,' she adds. 'They don't try to imitate their *Vitis vinifera* counterparts but show their own unique hardy attributes and varietal typicity,' Wiedbold says.

Winery, Nebraska (p174)

IT'S NOT NAPA, AND IT'S NOT PRETENDING TO BE. WHAT'S HAPPENING IN THE MIDWEST IS AN UNEXPECTED EMBRACE OF SENSE OF PLACE AND RISING TO THE CHALLENGING CLIMATE, FULL STEAM AHEAD.

Nebraska's wine industry is still young, with most winemakers and growers coming from small-town farming backgrounds, but that's beginning to change. A new wave of trained viticulturists and enologists is starting to take root in the region. 'It proves to me that our region is evolving, and that experienced professionals are beginning to recognize its potential,' she adds. At Arbor Day Farm, efforts are underway to reshape how hybrid grapes are grown and understood. Working with both an original vineyard site planted in the early 2000s and a newly established three-acre block in 2024, Wiebold has helped usher in a more intentional approach to viticulture. From site selection and cover cropping to trellising, pruning, harvest timing and winemaking techniques, the goal is clear: to highlight varietal typicity and raise overall wine quality.

'Statewide, there's a noticeable shift toward more refined vineyard and cellar practices. Winemakers are paying closer attention to metrics like brix and tannin structure, adjusting harvests accordingly to craft wines with greater precision and expression,' Wiebold explains. As the industry matures, there's a push to offer a wider stylistic range, from dry to sweet, showcasing what each grape can do. 'Hybrids are leading the charge. Marquette continues to impress with its firm tannins and spicy notes. Itasca delivers clean citrus and green apple flavors in a dry white style. Edelweiss performs well in both sweet and semi-dry expressions,' the sommelier states. In recent years, Midwestern wines have begun earning national attention, moving beyond novelty status. Nebraska's proximity to the Loess Hills District AVA, straddling the Missouri River between Iowa and Missouri, offers a promising benchmark. With continued exploration of what grows best and where, Nebraska is steadily carving out its own identity, and its own sense of terroir.

The Midwest is rewriting the American wine story, grape by grape, winemaker by winemaker. It doesn't look like the wine regions you know, and that's exactly the point. From the rocky slopes of the Wisconsin Ledge to the alluvial soils of Nebraska, winemakers are reimagining what American wine can be. What's happening here is original, homegrown, and just getting started.

FROM LEFT: BARBARA SMITS/SHUTTERSTOCK, GEORGE BURBA/SHUTTERSTOCK

INDEX

Map Pages **000**

H

I

J

Map Pages **000**

"Driving into the Boundary Waters on the Gunflint Trail (p133) is so pretty I didn't even care that the Moose Viewing Trail was moose-less."

"The first time I saw the trucks at the Hull Rust Mine Viewpoint (p133) my brain broke. How is it possible to drive a vehicle that enormous?"

FROM LEFT: NIKO HOUCK/SHUTTERSTOCK, JOHN BRUESKE/SHUTTERSTOCK

Mapping data sources:
© Lonely Planet
© OpenStreetMap http://openstreetmap.org/copyright

THIS BOOK

Destination Editor Melissa Yeager

Coordinating Editor Andrea Dobbin

Production Editor Ailbhe MacMahon

Image Editor Eoin T Loughney

Cartographer Anthony Phelan

Assisting Editors Robin Yule, Kate James, Holly Proctor, Lucy Jones, Kate Mathews, Charlotte Orr

Cover Researcher Giada de Agostinis

Thanks Alison Killilea, Saralinda Turner, Kellie Langdon, Rachel Imeson

Paper in this book is certified against the Forest Stewardship Council™ standards. FSC™ promotes environmentally responsible, socially beneficial and economically viable management of the world's forests.

Published by Lonely Planet Global Limited
CRN 554153
1st edition – Feb 2026
ISBN 978 1 83758 817 6

10 9 8 7 6 5 4 3
Printed in Malaysia